Seeking The Sakhu

Third World Press
Publishers since 1967

First Edition

10 09 08 07 06   10 9 8 7 6 5 4 3 2

Cover design by Lisa Moran
Inside text layout and design by Keir Thirus

Library of Congress Cataloging-in-Publication Data

Nobles, Wade W.
  Seeking the sakhu : foundational writings for an African psychology /
Wade W. Nobles (Nana Kwaku Berko I-Ifagbemi Sangodare).-- 1st ed.
      p. cm.
  Includes bibliographical references.
  ISBN-13: 978-0-88378-276-7 (pbk. : alk. paper)
  ISBN-10: 0-88378-276-6 (alk. paper)
1. African Americans--Psychology. 2. African Americans--Race identi-
ty. 3. Afrocentrism. 4. Blacks--Psychology. I. Title.
  E185.625.N63 2005
  155.8'496073--dc22

                                        2005029097

Seeking The Sakhu

FOUNDATIONAL WRITINGS
FOR an AFRICAN PSYCHOLOGY

Wade W. Nobles
(Nana Kwaku Berko I-Ifagbemi Sangodare)

THIRD WORLD PRESS
Chicago

To Vera Lynn
Whose enduring and powerful love
is the source
of my joy, beauty, faith and spirit.
She alone has inspired me
to be the best me I can be

To John, John and John

To All African people
who, in realizing that we are the living fulfillment
of our ancestors' rightful claim
to human potential and possibility,
will accept nothing less than full and complete
reparations of our spirit.

contents

BEING - SEARCHING FOR ORIGINS

BECOMING - PIERCING THE PARADIGM

contents

BELONGING - THOUGHTS ON APPLICATION

contents

BEGINNING - UNLOCKING THE SAKHU AND STEPPING INTO THE LIGHT

FOREWORD

Baffour Amankwatia II/Asa G. Hilliard III

Sakhu Sheti Dr. Wade Nobles, Nana Kwaku Berko, or simply Baba Wade, is much too young to summarize his life's work, which is much too vast to view in a single volume anyway. Yet it is important not to delay viewing a sample of it, especially in view of its revolutionary meaning for African people everywhere.

Dr. Nobles is a psychologist, in the best since of that word. However, he is much more than that, since his view of liberation, health, healing and development cannot be contained within Western traditional definitions of psychology, or even in any other definition of this single discipline, no matter how it may be defined. Human problems simply do not sort themselves neatly into the academic categories of the traditional European university curriculum, or paradigm. All reality is pan-disciplinary, at the very least; and conveniently defined "disciplines" are not self-sufficient for analysis and problem solving. For example, Baba Wade is as much a teacher, a cultural anthropologist, and more, as he is a psychologist. Also, he is a deft, critical and creative user of the common tools of the psychology discipline, even as he creates new tools to respond to a more refined look at the real world and to the needs of African People.

I discovered somewhere along the way in my own work, that time and time again, when I reached a point that required the deepest, clearest and most creative thought, thoughts that "connected the dots," and propelled thinking and actions far into the future, like many others, I called on Wade. Here are only a few examples. I called on him when I was asked to do a summative piece on psychological testing and African people. He wrote the opening essay and introduced and applied the term "cultural antinomy."[i] He situated the validity problem for mental measurement and its uses in scientific and cultural perspectives. I called upon him when we held the first annual conference for "The Infusion of African and African American Content in School Curriculum."[ii]As the lead keynote speaker whose paper is the lead chapter in the conference proceedings, he "connected the dots," while introducing the concept of the importance of "Intent" in curriculum as even more important than and integral to mere "content," and the application of both. When we held the national "Mbongi," a national convening of African scholars, a think-tank to examine "The Global Education and Socialization Agenda for African people," Baba Wade was the first invitee. As is his usual way, he made seminal contributions immediately by "connecting the dots."

Two final examples are the conferences of master educators that have been held in Atlanta, the Nsaka Sunsum [Touching the Spirit]. These conferences were inspired by and modeled after Baba Wade's innovative CACSEA's Nsaka Sunsum 5-day Professional Development Summer Institutes. The Nsaka Sunsum is a decade old series of conferences/demonstrations in Oakland-San Francisco Bay Area. These annual meetings are advanced far beyond any that I know of in teacher education anywhere. They featured only the greatest teachers and school leaders. By great, we mean only those who produce excellent student achievement in the common school curriculum and in African consciousness, which extends far beyond public schooling. These conferences are a bold challenge to the pessimists among educators who are not successful with low-income African students. IQ and cultural deprivation theories cannot stand the light of the successes presented in these conferences. In each of the Atlanta Nsaka Sunsum experiences Baba Wade has been the lead presenter, "connecting the dots," and advancing our ability to "Touch the Spirit of the African Child."

From these few of many possible examples, it should be clear that Baba Wade is a "conceptualizer," a researcher, a theoretician, a teacher, an organizer, an activist, a multidisciplinary scholar, and a powerful leader among his other talents. He is great at these things because he is first and foremost a strong family member, a father, husband, uncle, cousin, grandfather and African community member par excellence. He is great at these things because he is a Son of Africa. Baba Wade is a baobab tree for the global African community. It is after those things that he is a great psychologist, among many qualifications. I never use superlatives like "great" in a casual way.

It is common in the European world to refer simply to "psychology" as if the most common European version of it is a set of universal theories and practices that explain and respond to the human condition in general, regardless of ethnic diversity. Europeans who practice psychology, really European psychology, have virtually no cultural competency beyond their understanding of their own parochial culture if indeed they understand their own culture as simply one of many cultures. They have no cultural competency either in knowledge of other cultures, in knowledge of cultural principles, and especially in knowledge of the intersection of culture, psychology, and political economy. Anyone who sees European culture as normative for the world is deluded.

Black psychology as a movement, and, later as a discipline, began during the 1970s even though psychologists who were black had already made major contributions as correctives to the unilaterally declared validity of European psychology. As Robert Guthrie has shown in his book, *Even The Rat Was White,*[iii] the work of black psychologists goes back at least as far as Herman Canady. In fact it may be said that the heroic struggle of black psychologists to challenge the oppressive uses of psychology began with the very first Africans in the field. If we understand that Africans have responded to mental health challenges in traditional ways for thousands of years, then Black psychology is ancient.

In general, as Black psychology developed in the United States, it did not challenge the theoretical and philosophical basis of European psychology. It tended to try to hold European psychology accountable to its own rules, and it tended to demand that white supremacy abuses in European psychology be challenged and defeated. Much ink has been spilled by black psychologists writing about the fact that Black people are just as intelligent as whites, just as mentally healthy as whites, can learn just as well as whites, are missing from the samples of white researchers, are missing from the samples for test validation, are not full members of journal boards and the professional associations, do not get their priorities addressed by mainstream psychologists, and so forth. Inclusion and fairness were primary goals. We have done far less work questioning the rules of European psychology, or the philosophies, constructs and purposes that drive them. Baba Wade was present at the beginning of this thrust to challenge everything. His thinking was not at all limited to the inclusion and fairness agenda as his publications will show. He charged into the battle for truth and self-determination from the beginning.

African psychology began mainly around the early 1970s, with the heavy influence of psychologists at Stanford University, largely under the leadership of Dr. Syed Khatib and Dr. Philip McGee, where Dr. Nobles and others were students. African psychology differed from Black psychology, mainly, because it focused on the centrality of African culture and consciousness and the centrality of issues of African ethnic identity—not Negro, colored, at-risk, etc. Black psychology and African psychology are relatives since both developed largely under the umbrella of the Association of Black Psychologists. Both emerged and are still emerging from the linkages among those who see themselves as African and/or Black psychologists. This can be seen by examining anthologies of the works of both, edited by Dr. Reginald Jones in *Black Psychology*[iv] in Dr. Burlew et. al, in *African American Psychology*,[v] and Dr. Daudi Azibo in *African Psychology*,[vi] Important individual works by Dr. Kobi Kambon in *Misorientation*[vii] Dr. Wade Nobles in *African Psychology*,[viii] Dr. Tawede Grills in the article, *"African Psychology"*[ix] and Dr. Na'im Akbar in *Breaking the Chains of Psychological Slavery*.[x] From the beginning of the African Psychology Institutes at the annual meetings of the Association of Black Psychologists led by Dr. Darryl Rowe nearly a decade ago, and from the work of many other independent African psychologists, African psychology has blossomed. Foundational works by Azibo, Kambon, Grills, Akbar, Meyers, and others show this growth. Baba Wade has been at the center of these developments and is a monumental figure in it, as his many essays and books have shown.

African-American psychology is a kind of in-between position, and is hard to separate in chronology from African psychology. It tends to place greater emphasis on the national experiences of Africans in America, the United States, and it tends to argue for greater emphasis on the examination of the presumed American cultural part of the identity of African descendants in the United States. Black psychologists, including Africans, can be found who hold any of these positions, who affirm the views of European psychology. The positions of African psychologists are evolving with towering works of scholarship that cannot be ignored by any well-grounded psychologist. These include works such as those by Dr. Kobi K. Kambon, Dr. Amos Wilson, Dr. Daudi Azibo, Dr. Tawede Grills, Dr. Naim Akbar, and, especially, the life work of Dr. Reginald Jones, who has edited invaluable anthologies of the works of a wide variety of African psychologists. These are classical works for the ages, particularly, for the young African scholar/leaders who are yet to be born, but who will find the Sankofa power to heal our people.

Baba Wade has made so many great contributions to the field of psychology and social healing of African people that they cannot be enumerated adequately. One contribution in particular is in research methodology. In a work during the 1970s, *A Formulative and Empirical Study of Black Families*, done under the sponsorship of the Office of Child Development, Baba Wade followed an approach similar to Dr. Lorenzo Turner, the pioneering African linguist who documented the retention of African linguistic features in the language of Gullah Sea Islanders in Georgia. European linguists had argued, almost to the person, that nothing remained of the language of Africa in the speech of her descendants in America. Yet not one of these linguists had studied the culture of the Africans in Africa as preparation for examining the speech of Africans in Georgia. University of Chicago linguist Turner went to Africa and studied the language on the west coast. He returned to study the Gullah language, and only after he had prepared the way to do so by taking very sophisticated steps to establish rapport with the people of the Gullah community. Having done so, he discovered thousands of vocabulary items and other retentions that had been obscure to the unprepared alien researchers.

Baba Wade used similar understanding about the indispensable need to listen to those who are studied, in order to do his work in the San Francisco Bay Area. He knew that researchers did not and could not know everything. He and his assistants began by interviewing community members in order to become familiar with them by asking them what questions a researcher ought to ask about the community. Then they used the input from the community to craft the primary research questions and to refine their methodologies. Turner and Nobles' respect for the cultural reality of our African community resulted in the revelation of nuances that had been missed by alien researchers. Alien researchers work with blunt tools, standardized tests, standardized interrogation techniques and a form of English, they do not have the same questions or priorities that African psychologists have. This is another example of foundational academic work that is not in the mainstream. Baba Wade, predictably, is also in a leadership role on methodological matters.

Dr. Lewis King edited the volume, *African Philosophy: Assumptions and Paradigms for Research on Black Persons*[xi] that drew upon the thinking of great theorists, such as Dr. Vernon Dixon. Works such as these show that in any challenge to academic, professional or other thinking, especially when that thinking is part and parcel of the structure of domination growing out of the ideology of white supremacy, must first and foremost be challenged at the level of definitions, assumptions and paradigms. This will enable us to challenge the philosophies and theories. Indeed, this is the very essence of the work of African psychologists. The everyday practices and procedures of psychology are mere routines, which rarely get examined at their foundational level. Schmidt in his book, *Disciplined Minds*[xii] has described professionals and academics as victims of systematic structures and processes containment or "brainwashing." Thomas Kuhn in his book *The Structure of Scientific Revolutions*[xiii] anticipated Schmidt. New Zealand Maori scholar Dr. Linda Tuhiwa Smith's book, *Decolonizing Methodologies,*[xiv] has updated these arguments to add cultural essence as a critical factor in the critique of academic and professional structures of domination.

Baba Wade has always been there, not waiting for these scholars. Witness his seminal essay on "The So-Called Negro Self Concept." Yet, even now, European "self-concept" researchers appear to be either ignorant of or unmoved by such a valid challenge. This is due to the economic profiteering demands that depend upon standardization and mass-production in a pluralistic cultural reality. Responding to the reality of cultural diversity, requires deep study of diverse cultures, which is expensive. But, more importantly, it may not even be possible to validate this "transubstantiation." Another construct applied by Baba Wade;

it means using the cultural substance of one ethnic group to interpret the cultural substance of another which is inappropriate. As Baba Wade has shown, the construct of "self" does not carry the same cultural meaning from one ethnic group to the next. The construct conflict may be trivial to European psychologists, but such conflicts are matters of life and death to African people. Ethnic cleansing or cultural genocide is a final verdict in a culture war.

It is one thing to claim that African culture is a central factor in the lives of African people and, further, to claim the cultural unity of African people and to claim the family relationship of African people. It is quite another to document convincingly direct cultural connections, and to demonstrate those connections in real life. Some Africans may desire that there are connections, and may romanticize the idea that they exist. Many of us teach our children to memorize the Nguzo Saba, the Seven Principles, or the seven aspects of MAAT—Truth, Justice, Righteousness, Reciprocity, Harmony, Balance and Order—as a rote exercise without creating the conditions for internalizing these as internalized behavioral functions. We may speak of the need for solidarity as a people, without an appreciation of the fact that solidarity is an outcome of a shared world-view and values, leading to trust, which is the prerequisite to cooperation for our survival and development. We may have intellectual discussions of spirituality, which is supposed to be at the core of our being, without having the experience of being connected to spiritual reality.

However, Baba Wade has been among those who show that the connections are real, deep, and meaningful. Many scholars see Africans as black, poor, oppressed, culturally deprived, minority, and other pejorative and false labels. They see these labels as identities, not as mere adjectives that describe environmental conditions that deny the very existence of African people.

Baba Nobles has been involved deeply in both Africa and in the broad African diaspora for many years. He has traveled and worked in Ghana, Brazil, Mali, Egypt, Nigeria and the Caribbean, all over the United States, and in Europe. Among the many places that he and I have traveled together, Mali was very special. In the archives of the University of Sankore in Timbuktu, Baba Wade asked our colleagues a critical question. He asked how many of the thousands of manuscripts cover material that

is pre-Islamic or is non-Islamic. We learned as a result that nearly 5 percent were estimated to cover traditional cultural material. This is only one example of what still has to be done to
uncover the culture. Psychologists and others will find many
uses for the things that we find.

Baba Wade's work is crucial to our survival as a people.
Our existence as a global people can be nurtured as bridges are
being built. Sankofa is being achieved. Baba Wade created the
HAWK Federation Perfected Black Manhood and ASET Society
Perfected Black Womanhood Training and Development Process
as a rite of passage program which emerged from the "Cultural
Context Problem Solving and Program Development Process" of
the Institute for Advanced Study of Black Family Life and Culture.
These African-centered models of manhood and womanhood
development recognize that intervention strategies designed to
address behavioral dysfunctions, particularly low academic performance and disciplinary problems within the African-American
community, must be consistent with the best values in African
and African-American culture. He has inspired the rites of passage thinking and action for adults as well, especially for the
masses of us who missed what is normal for Africans. We have
the tools to rescue, reclaim, and reconstruct our birthright.

Baba Wade's life and work is a model for all African
scholars. All African scholars should begin with their own beginning, an in depth study of their own history and culture and especially of the history of their discipline within their own culture.
The physicist, mathematician, musician, artist, botanist etc., are
obligated to find out what part their own people played in antiquity in their field. All African scholars have the responsibility to
pose creative questions that reflect the knowledge of their own
traditions. All African scholars must determine how their work
can be used to enhance the position of their people, whatever else
they may do. All African scholars have the obligation to teach and
socialize young people and young scholars. All African scholars
have the responsibility to situate their work within the worldview and within the spiritual imperatives of their traditions. For
example, traditional African elder scholars shared in a world-view
that was centered in the profound spiritual principles of MAAT,
known variously by other names. African traditional master
scholars, known by such traditional names as Jegnoch, Dibia,

Jele and Jelimuso, Nganga, Zo, Seba or Sesh, have been characterized as follows. They are warriors who have been tested in struggle and battle. They produce an exceptionally high quality of work. At the price of their lives, they protect their people, land, and culture. They always speak truth. Baba Wade's work, some of which is collected in this volume, is in that tradition.

Seeking the Sakhu is a perfect title for this book, carrying the meaning that we must do more than merely dismantle the ideological, behavioral and physical structures of domination. We must repair that which has been in ruins. We must knit ourselves back together again. We must be whole. That means we must be African. In the final analysis the question before us is, "To be African or not to be." This compendium of some of Baba Wade's most important works shines the light, "illuminates" the many dark places, and provides a platform from which to do sankofa, to restore our spirits, to build solidarity, to frame our future.

I remember the 18 years that my family spent in the San Francisco Bay Area. I remember the family fellowship with Baba Wade and his equally powerful Queen Mama Vera and their children. Their back yard actually joined the yard of his brother's family who faced the next street, providing a seamless environment of two-way traffic to nurture family relationships, which expanded to include my family and other families. Later, as a graduation present, Baba Wade and Mama Vera sent each of their children to be a part of the "Holy Royal Family," my study tour to KMT (Egypt). I cite these two examples to show that the Nobles live their African beliefs in many ways. The great scholarship in psychology is only an addendum. All praises to Baba Wade, our shining African genius, who manifests the Sakhu. Our ancestors are pleased and Maat is satisfied.

PREFACE

ADISA AJAMU

Healing is work, not gambling. It is the work of inspiration, not manipulation. If we healers are to do the work
of helping to bring our people together again, we need to
know such work is the work of the community... The
work of healers is work for inspirers working long and
steadily, in a group that grows over the generations, till
there are inspirers, healers wherever our people are scattered, able to bring us together again.

—Ayi Kwei Armah, *The Healers*

There is nothing more difficult to take in hand, more
perilous to conduct, or more uncertain in its success than
to take the lead in the introduction of a new order of things.
Because the innovator has for enemies all those who have
done well under the old conditions, and lukewarm defenders in those who may do well under the new.

—Niccolo Machiavelli, *The Prince*

The imperative is to define what is right and do it.

—Barbara Jordan

I first came to know of Dr. Nobles, or Mwalimu (teacher
in Kiswahili) as I affectionately call him, while I was a teaching
assistant in Dr. Thomas Parham's (Anan) African psychology
course at U.C. Irvine. It was through his text *African Psychology:
Towards Its Reclamation and Reascension*, that I was informally

introduced to him and the idea of an African psychology for the first time. I remember the sapience and genius with which he was able to elucidate the idea of an African psychology and its concomitant philosophical foundations. It was as if his ideas seemed to resonate in my spirit, and in the reverberation of those ideas my mind was reawakened.

During the summer of 1992 at the Association of Black Psychologists National Convention, I had the good fortune of connecting with Dr. Nobles. In the ensuing three years that I apprenticed under him—before going off to graduate school—I came to appreciate him as a deep thinker of the highest order, a careful and rigorous scholar, a thoughtful teacher, a skilled practitioner and principled community activist. His clarity of thought, vision, integrity, and commitment to African peoples suggest a congruence between "Djhutian" thought and "Maatian" practice that is emblematic of the best African thinkers, and has become synonymous with the name Wade W. Nobles.

It's a wonderful experience as an apprentice to have the luxury of being able to appreciate both the mission and the man. When I sit down to write, I still feel his calm, instructive presence, palpably; his knowing voice booming the background, exhorting: "There is no substitute for excellence." To this day Mwalimu remains amongst the smallest cipher of thinkers I imagine when I reach for my stylus. The "illumination" that these writings provided me as I staggered and stumbled towards clarity proved invaluable in allowing me to move forward, largely unfettered.

To the unfamiliar reader, the very notion of an African psychology might pose a number of questions and quandaries. What is African psychology? How does it differ from European psychology? Why is African psychology important? They might posit that we are all human and that psychological norms and mores universal. This was the quandary in which I and many of my contemporaries found ourselves. After all much of what had been written in terms of the philosophical, theoretical and foundational constructs surrounding the emergence of African psychology had been written in the early seventies and early eighties while most of us were in either grade school or middle school. These writings were now buried in scholarly journals collecting dust. As a result, we simply were not aware that such theories and constructs existed, and we most certainly had not been introduced to the Nobles, Akbars, Myers, Hilliards, Wilsons or Kambons in many of our Western psychology classes. It later dawned on me, that as a student interested in the liberation of the African mind, that if I was not aware that this treasure trove of information was available, how much more so for the layperson? This book, *Seeking the Sakhu: Foundational Writing for an African Psychology*—along with the recently published, *Akbar Papers*—represents over three decades of some of the best thinking and doing around this gathering notion of an African psychology, by one of its foremost scholars and pre-eminent theorist. Students and scholars—from inside and outside the discipline of psychology—will find this to be an invaluable resource. It succeeds where the absence of critical discourse, debate and inquiry in African psychology has failed us. It allows the reader to see the strengths and weaknesses as the theories are developed over time. Moreover, the value of this collection of essays, in addition to being a critical source document for emerging thinkers, also allows the reader to witness the evolution of an important thinker. For example, the early seminal essay "African Philosophy: Foundation for a Black Psychology" (1972) was seminal precisely because it argued against the prevailing order of fragmentation and cultural discontinuity (natal alienation). While the penultimate essay, "To be African Or Not To Be" (1998), shows a mature scholar fully in command of his craft; all the knowledge and experience of thirty years distilled into one essay. The engagement with African deep thought, the comfortable intimacy with African spiritual systems, the ongoing dialogue with Nile Valley Civilizations, and deep and nuance commitment to praxis as the highest form of intellectual engagement.

For the students of African psychology this collection of articles represents some of the foundational theoretical constructs from which we can begin to launch our future foray into praxis and performance in African psychology. For "Black" psychologists trying to get beyond the circumscribed parameters of "conceptual incarceration," this endeavor represents one of the keys to unlocking the possibilities and potentialities for divergent types of discourse around the African mind. For those already engaged in the process of re-animating and liberating the African mind, this book personifies an important contribution to the arena of scholarly inquiry, discourse, discussion, and debate necessary for the understanding and illumination of the African spirit and the simultaneous resuscitation of the African world. The impatient reader slovenly looking for prefabricated answers in this anthology will not be rewarded; but for the astute reader who revels in the questions, the rewards will be immense and the opportunities it presents are immense.

In the 1960s, late in his career, and towards the end of his life, the imminent sociologist and arguably, one of the most influential thinkers of his time, E. Franklin Frazier upon surveying the current state of the Black Intelligentsia, lamented that "we have no philosophers or thinkers who command the respect of the intellectual community at large....I am talking about men who have reflected upon the fundamental problems which have always concerned philosophers such as the nature of human knowledge and the meaning or lack of meaning of human existence."

I believe the readers of this collection of essays will be satisfied that Dr. Nobles has responded vigorously to both Armah's prescient alarum to help develop a cadre of "inspirers working long and steadily, in a group that grows over the generations, till there are inspirers, healers wherever our people are scattered, who are able to bring us together again"; and to Dr. Frazier's challenge to reflect on the psychological meaning of human existence. I am equally certain that were Queen Hatshepsut with us today, she would say to Mwalimu and the Institute, what she said to the Lord of Heaven, "I offer you Maat because I know you live by it." These essays in the best of our traditions certainly do, as well.

Ankh, uja, sneb—All life, power, health.

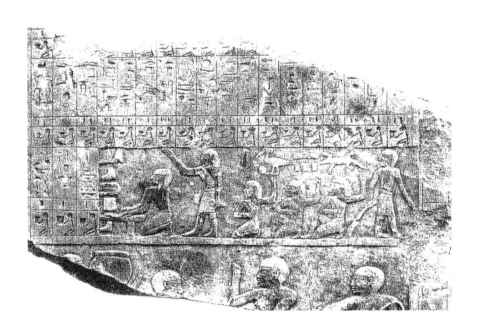

ACKNOWLEDGEMENTS

Almost two decades ago, a gifted and talented young intellectual named Adisa Ajamu who served as my research assistant and project collaborator suggested that I put together a collection of my writings so that younger psychologists and scholars would have a source document of the critical ideas associated with my work as one voice in the emerging field of Black Psychology. In part this collection is in answer to Adisa's request. In giving this collection of writings the title of *Seeking the Sakhu: Foundational Writings for an African Psychology*, I am attempting to frame my thirty years of engagement around the question of Black Psychology. In struggling with the parameters of thought, theory and therapy in Black Psychology, I have suggested (Nobles, 1986a; 1986b) that a complete and full understanding of African people should be governed by a deep, profound and penetrating search, study and mastery of the process of "illuminating" the human spirit or essence, ergo, the "Sakhu Sheti"(Nobles, 1997). As a framework, *Seeking the Sakhu* has been a search for a profound and penetrating understanding of the psychology of African people independent of non-African conceptualizations. Gerald Massey (1974) suggested that the word "Sakhu" meant understanding, the illuminator, the eye, the soul of being, that which inspires. Both Na'im Akbar (1985) and I (1986) suggested that "psyche" in the word "psychology" was probably derived from the Kemetic term, "Sakhu." In the desire to be accurate in the classification of my "Seeking the Sakhu," I asked Dr. Theophile Obenga, the foremost living Egyptologist in the world today, to translate the term "Seeking the Sakhu." Professor Obenga identified a relief from the private tomb at Sakkarah from the ninth or tenth Dynasty. In interpreting the relief, Professor Obenga pointed out that below the long tabulated list of funerary offerings there is a Sakhu scene. This scene depicts a Lector priest holding a text in his left hand and reciting the appropriate ritual. Directly behind the lector priest there are three kneeling lector priests who are chanting the "many Sakhu," the recitations designed to transform the deceased into a "glorious spirit," (i.e., akh, ahkju). Dr. Obenga noted that the language of ancient KMT would not say, "Seeking the Sakhu" as much as it would say "doing the ritual of the Sakhu." Hence, Dr. Obenga suggested that a good translation of "Seeking the Sakhu" would be 𓁹 𓊪 𓏏 𓅓 𓏤 𓏏 "iret her sakhu," "Performing the Sakhu."

My *Seeking the Sakhu* has been a continuous life long quest. In fact, I like to tell the story that my mother began working at the Boston State Hospital for the Mentally Ill in Mattapan, Massachusetts the year I was born and, in a pre-television age, she nurtured my brother and me with stories of "crazy" Black people, white doctors and the complexities and confusion she witnessed in the treatment and mistreatment of the mentally ill. So I think I started my Black Psychology training from birth. In many ways, I believe, I was bred to search for an understanding of the human condition of Black people. In actuality, each of us comes from heaven and enters into the world to follow a special path and to fulfill a particular purpose. My path has been seeking illumination and my purpose has been to participate in and encourage the reascension of African psychology.

The chapters in this volume are but personal footsteps on the path toward an African Psychology. At many points along this path, Dr. Na'im Akbar and I have found ourselves reaching the same places or noticing the same sign posts at almost the exact same time. We have marveled over the years about how often our thoughts and ideas vectored in a parallel trajectory. Na'im and I almost simultaneously identified the Kemetic term, Sakhu (illumination of the spirit) as the African antecedent to the Western term Psychology. We both were amazed that the ancient African dwellers of the Nile Valley were the first to contemplate the "knowing" of oneself and ushered in the dawning of human consciousness. With hindsight, my work over the last thirty years has been spent seeking the Sakhu along with a search for what Na'im calls the "place," African Psychology.

This volume is comprised of both previously published and unpublished essays and speeches. As such it reflects both the pedantic of scholarship and the colloquium of conversational speech. The inclusion of both styles in a single volume is intentional. It is important to be able to track the development of an intellectual orientation from a thought or idea in a speech to its fuller elaboration as part of an intellectual exposition or discourse. The intellectual journey reflected in this work represents the journey from ideas to thoughts to expositions to discourse to theory generation to research application to further ideas and conversation. It is the better part of the process of scholarship.

While the work captured in this volume began with my first publication, for me the path to African Psychology began formally as an undergraduate student at San Francisco State University. There I studied with Dr. Joseph White and Dr. Gerald West. It was Dr. White who gave me the opportunity to first teach a fledgling new course called "Black Psychology, (circa 1966-67). He guided and advised the Black student Psychology Club and suggested that I attend a professional psychologists' convention in San Francisco. It was at that APA convention that I first met Black Psychologists, the likes of Bob Williams, Anna Jackson, Charles Thomas, Bob Green, Henry Tomes, and others.

As a footnote to the history of the Association of Black Psychologists, this small band of Black people debated and argued throughout the night in a small room in a hotel in San Francisco. What was fueled by the anger of rejection and irrelevance of white Psychology and the radicalism of Black nationalist thought of the time passed through the initial call for the establishment of an APA Black caucus to the bold establishment of an independent, autonomous organization of Black psychologists, ABPsi. Hence, as a consequence of time, place, circumstance and destiny, I became, as a young student, in 1968 a "founding father" (errata: founding "baby father" of the Association of Black Psychologists.)

As a graduate student, my major professor, Cedric Clark (later to become Syed Khatib) suggested that I write a critique of a compilation of his work. At the time I honestly felt that I was not competent enough to comment on the work of a man whom I suspected to be possibly a genius and more probably a little insane—in the best sense of our use of that term. In a sense the papers in this volume represent the submission to critique the work of all those who, especially Syed, allowed me to capture a fragment or remnant of their best thinking.

I should mention that every intellectual is no more than a container and conduit of the best thinking of his or her time. Each is inspired and shaped by untold others and should never claim sole ownership of a thought or idea.   We never walk or think alone.   For me Na'im Akbar, D. Philliip McGee, and Syed Khatib have been lifelong fellow travelers.   Na'im has especially paralleled my steps in this intellectual sojourn.   Like him, I believe, African Psychology is a "place." By place we do not mean geography, ethnicity, or ideology. African Psychology reflects these things but so much more. It is a body of knowledge found in and continuously generated from that "place." It is our modern reconstructions of ancient African "truths" about a divinely governed universe and our ever-evolving human possibilities and potentials within it. I must also acknowledge fellow walkers like, William Cavil, Lawford Goddard, Patricia Canson, Yemi Elebuibon, Kobi Kambon, Marimba Ani, Leonard Jeffries, James Smalls, Henry B. Nobles, Adisa A. Ajamu, Derrick Wilson, Irving Brown. Frances Cress Welsing, Joyce King, Karen Winsor, Bobby Wright, Gerald Jackson, Bob Williams, Joseph White, Gerald West, Shirley Tarver, Molefi Asante, Warren Sloan, Maulana Karenga, Richard King, Pat Butler, Henry Obrafo Andrews, Chris Tinson, Nathan Hare, Terrence Eliot, Charlyn Harper Bolton, Oba T'Shaka, Reginald Jones, Maxine Chapman, Harold Braithwaite, Hannibal Afrik, Fred Logan, Miles Irving, Nsenga Warfield-Coppock, Edwin Nicols, Morris F. X. Jeff, Jr., Vernon Dixon, Lewis King, Edwin Cotton, Daudi Azibo, Ollie Glover, Thomas Parham, Solomon Davis, Paul Giles, Cheryl Tawede Grills, Harvette Gray, Jacob Carruthers, Adib Shakir, Malachi Andrews, Taasogle Daryl M. Rowe, Tony Browder, William Cross, Theophile Obenga, Pamela Y. George, Denise Makini Herd, Fred Phillips, Bill Jones, Sista Kefa, Leon Caldwell, Mengesha Wondowforo, Anna Jackson, Linda James Myers, Michael Suggs, Kariamu Welch-Asante, Jerome Schiele, Robert Guthrie, Joyce King, H.O. Maiga, William Hayes, Asa Hilliard, Fabunmi Webb-Msemaji, Thomas Hilliard, W. Curtis Banks, Carolyn Hodge, Amos Wilson, Horace Mitchell, Paul Logan, A. Wade Boykin, Kenneth Monteiro, Stan Sneed, Jerome Taylor, James Jones, Ernest Baston, Adiedo Spriggs, Lawrence Gary, Reginald Jones, Cecil C. Gray, Shiela Myers, Howard C. Stevenson and many many more who served simultaneously as my students, teachers, colleagues, critics and comrades. I especially want to acknowledge Vera, my wife, and Halima, my third daughter, whose critical eye, intellectual insights, editorial acumen and transcription skills guaranteed this document's quality in form and fact. In so acknowledging I equally recognize that the error, confusion and intellectual weakness found herein are totally mine. The value, insights, clarity and contribution, herein, are testament to the genius of a people.

I am calling these chapters "sketches" because I believe the full portrait of African Psychology is still in process and all the writings of contemporary Black psychologists are but fragments of ancient ideas made into sketches that will ultimately with time appear as a full grown masterpiece. Accordingly, the writings in this volume collectively represent one contribution, one experience and one attempt to concretize a body of thought leading to the conceptualization of the illumination of the human spirit, ergo African Psychology.

I have classified and sorted my work into four sections or considerations, which I thought to call "remnants" in light of my belief that our contemporary musings in African Psychology are mere remnants of an ancient African tapestry of deep thought. Each section could be thought of as a remnant because each represents a single yet interconnected focus that is only partially captured in what I know will become the reclamation of a larger tapestry of knowing. In fear that some may interpret my use of "remnant" as a fragment or fragmentation rather than interconnected pieces across time and space, I have organized this book to reflect what I believe to be the critical attributes or motifs of humanness: Being, Becoming, Belonging and Beginning. This last attribute, Beginning, was a welcomed suggestion from Adisa.

The chapters are in effect footprints of my personal thirty year walk along this collective path to uncover and rediscover the African truth about the human process of being, becoming and belonging. Each chapter is in a way only a sketch knitted together by an unrelenting desire to know and understand a people shaped by an unparalleled history of supreme achievement and incomprehensible tragedy. The sections are considerations knitted together by a common theme or thrust.

In looking back I can see in the first consideration, "Being: Searching for the Origins," I was concerned with "finding the origin" or intellectual grounding for a Black Psychology.

In the second consideration, "Becoming: Piercing the Paradigm," my work makes the shift from a Eurocentric framework to an African centered framework. In effect I was beginning to explore the possibilities of piercing the paradigm and ushering in new thought relative to the praxis of science and the construction of scientific paradigms in the service of African peoples' reality.

While the third consideration, "Belonging: Thoughts on Application," is a mixture of published and previously published work, it demonstrates the critical challenge of formulating new thought into applications relative to real world issues. Consideration three particularly reflects the importance of self conception, family processes and the problems of measurement in understanding Blackness.

Consideration four, "Beginning: Unlocking the Sakhu and Stepping into the Light," is a combination of unpublished and published works. The thinking represented in this section reflects the intellectual struggle; i.e., the comprehension and utilization of the key element in the construction of an authentic African Psychology; i.e., consciousness, that had paralleled these last thirty years. The ideas reflected here represent the bridge between the old and new thrusts in my work. It serves me as both a reminder that the task remains unfinished and that the contours of my continually evolving mental map must lead to the finding of a full and complete African/Black Psychology.

Ultimately, the under-girding issue driving my work has been to understand African consciousness and the parameters and implications an African conceptualization of this notion has for the notions of family life, self conception, mental illness, culture, healing, human development and transformation—Black Psychology.

What is reflected in the field today and, especially, what is captured in this volume are simply elegant footsteps and sketches—footsteps that reflect a time when the separation of mythology and religion had not occurred (see Akbar, 2002). I believe that the writings and applications found in Black Psychology today are but footsteps leading back to the future of humanity's primal perception of its own consciousness and sense of being. In piercing the paradigms of Western hegemony, Black Psychology has provided sketches of the limited human capacity possessed by African people once robbed of our own consciousness. We have sketches of African human beingness as human dysfunctioning; dysfunctioning that occurs as Na'im so eloquently notes, when a people's soul is stolen, they are "driven out of their minds." What we have are deconstructions of a mechanized and materialized psychology and the beginning attempt to reconstruct the "lost key to the divine spark that makes us human." What we have, or at least what my work reflects, are the limited sketches that reveal the possibility of a science of human beings whose resiliency and capacity to be restored to the celestial heights from which we emerged can be guaranteed.

I place myself in the tradition of an Nkrumah Pan Africanist, a Malcolm Black nationalist, a Garvey race man, and a Fanon revolutionary, all of whom valued and struggled to clarify the relevance and importance of being fully free and African for African people. As I look back over my thirty year walk, in many ways, my writings have been an attempt to seek the knowledge and insights that would allow for the construction of a science dedicated to "performing" the illumination of the glorious spirit of African people. As with the first half of my career, I dedicate and devote the remaining time of my life to the liberation of the African mind and the worldwide development of African people. I devote myself to the development of a science of the spirit wherein we can illuminate and understand the conditions and requisites for being, becoming, belonging and beginning humanity as African with all its unlimited and unbounded possibilities and potentials.

Seeking The Sakhu

BEING

searching for origins

Irosu Wori

II	I
I	I
I	II
II	II

Because of your wisdom, your compelling desire for good character and your internal strength. The thing needed to bring about the good condition in the world then are: wisdom that is fully adequate to govern the world; sacrifice; character; love of doing good for all people, especially those in need and those who seek assistance from us; and the eagerness and struggle to increase good in the world and let not any good at all be lost. People will continue to go to heaven; and they will go back and forth to earth after their transfiguration until everyone has achieved the good condition. Thus, when the children of Oduduwa gather together, those chosen to bring good into the world are called human beings or the chosen ones.

With three fundamental sketches this section, Being, seeks to both define and explain the meaning of African Psychology. The lead article "African Philosophy: Foundations for a Black Psychology" (1972) written while still a graduate student sets the tone and direction for my life's work.

The first sketch begins with clarifications and definitions of Black Psychology. Often seen as the "dark dimension" of psychology, Black Psychology takes its philosophies from positive aspects of African Philosophy. It is a collective philosophy, even among so-called dissimilar tribes, that is deeply rooted in the natural rhythm of nature, or a oneness with nature, and the preservation and continuation of self, or in many cases, the tribe or community.

The sketch then narrates the basic concepts of African Philosophy. Based on a sense of "collective consciousness," or ethos, this thinking was more of a way of life than a separation of one's life and religion. This belief system was their existence, not simply a part of it. Two fundamental philosophical beliefs are that the separated mind and body will unite and that there is a "non-linear" concept of time. Time, as expressed by traditional Africans, is divided into the sometimes overlapping periods of Sasa, the present, and Zamani, the past. The absence of a future period illustrates that the existence of man is in the here and now and past events, which also calls for the roles of death and immortality because they too are a part of this continual process of time.

Finally, the sketch ends with a discussion of kinship and communality. Reiterating the importance of community as a part of oneself, African Philosophy shows that such practices are well worth considering, especially when dealing with Black Psychology. It is here where the question of proof is discussed as it relates to the maintenance of the African orientation.

Written over thirty years ago this sketch served me as the tossing down of the gauntlet and the declaration of independent thought from white psychology and European hegemony. In this article the fundamental "sameness" between being African and being black was made. Emerging truly as a remnant of the collective thinking of the intellectual heritage of African people, "African Philosophy: Foundations for a Black Psychology," made explicit the unthinkable idea in psychology that black people in America are fundamentally and essentially African. It centered Africa for the first time in the discourse of Black peoples' psychology. Thus, this article guided and legitimized future attempts to challenge notions of Western epistemology, paradigms, and praxis.

Sketch 2 resonates the relationship between Ancient Egyptian Thought and Black Psychology. One acknowledgement that must be made is that the Ancient Egyptian Thought was embedded in symbolism, or the "intuitive vision" of the ancients. This method of understanding helped the ancients perceive the phenomena of nature symbolically, allowing for the understanding of the forces and laws governing the "material and spiritual" aspects of the universe.

One of the key considerations in this chapter is that the Ancient Egyptian Thought was centered on the essence of Being, or the soul. The physic nature of man was divided into seven parts that came together and formed the spiritual constitution of man. Based upon this, one must also acknowledge the human conduct that is central to Ancient Egyptian Thought and Black Psychology. Illustrating distinctions between behavior which is normal and that which is abnormal, cultural disposition and liberation become concrete and apparent, allowing for social change.

Sketch 3 illuminates the connection between history and human based sciences such as psychology and philosophy. African Psychology has its foundations in the following four historical events: Watergate, the 1973 war in the Middle East, Vietnam War, and the demise of the Civil Rights Movement. By showing these four events, it is evident how philosophy can play such a major role in creating and shaping change among social institutions. This leads to many questions of "Why?" which are discussed as being answered by philosophy and "How?" and "What?" which are said to be answered by "hard" science.

Truth and objectivity are introduced in this chapter. There is some discussion whether or not the two exist in and of themselves. But it poses the question, if there were truth and objectivity, under whose control does it lie? Causality is connected to the two in that they all seek to answer questions which prove relevant to African Psychology. The question of there being universal roles and rules for causality brings forth questions that remain to be answered, especially, when considering cultures that do not exist on a linear time frame.

African Philosophy
Foundations for Black Psychology

Black Americans derive their most fundamental self-definition from several cultural and philosophical premises which we share with most West African "tribes."[1] In exploring the character of these premises, which are basic conceptions of the nature of man and his relation to other men and his environment, we hope to establish a foundation upon which a Black psychology can be constructed. Thus, it will be contended that Black psychology is something more than the psychology of the so-called underprivileged peoples, more than the experience of living in ghettoes, and more than the genocidal atrocity of being forced into the dehumanizing condition of slavery. It is more than the "darker dimension" of general psychology. Its unique status is derived not from the negative aspects of being Black in white America, but rather from the positive features of basic African philosophy, which dictate the values, customs, attitudes, and behavior of Africans in Africa and the New World.

The notion of common experience or common ethos seems almost fictional if one accepts uncritically the research finding of many so-called Africanists who argue that the territory of the western region of Africa held and still does hold within its boundaries many different "tribes," each having its own language, religion, and customs. However, one must note the orientation of these many Africanists whose incidental whiteness colors much of what they have to say. One must, therefore, be conscious of the inherent social dialectic. That is to say, while most foreign students of Africa have maintained that the western "tribes" have little shared experience because each has a distinct language and religion and many unique customs, they have overlooked "the similarities of the forest for the differences between the trees." In this view, it is suggested that the overemphasis given tribal differences by white investigators is the anthropological or scientific version of the imperialist strategy of "divide and conquer." Hence, it is likely that many white ethnographers are predisposed by conscious or unconscious racist assumptions to focus upon superficial differences and, therefore, are blinded to underlying similarities in the experiential communality of African peoples. Fortunately, however, this anthropological analog of the "divide and conquer" strategy has been redressed by Black and even by a few white scholars.[2] These scholars maintain that "tribal" differences in Africa were minor compared to the binding quality of their communality. This author suggests that what supported this regional communality was a set of guiding beliefs—an ethos. Closer examination of the region indicates that this ethos determined two operational orders. The first is the notion that the people were part of the natural rhythm of nature; they were one with nature. The second order is the notion of the survival of one's people—that is, the "tribe." Hence, the African experience defines man's place or role in nature's scheme.

However, unlike a written constitution the ethos is more akin to a spiritual disposition and probably could best be described as collective consciousness. Although the ethos cannot be scientifically/empirically examined with current methodology, it is believed that one way to understand the essential and pervasive nature of the African/Black ethos is to explore and understand African philosophy.[3] It follows that insofar as the African/Black ethos is distinct from that of the prevailing white ethos upon which traditional psychology is founded, a Black psychology based upon the Black ethos must also be uniquely different from white psychology. It is this principle that allows African philosophy to take its place as the foundation for Black psychology.

Religion and Philosophy

John Mbiti[4] defines African philosophy as "the understanding, attitude of mind, logic, and perception behind the manner in which African peoples think, act, or speak in different situations of life." What is central to Brother Mbiti's definition is the "spiritual disposition," the "collective consciousness,"—in a word—the ethos. It should be made very explicit that ethos can be considered the operational definition of African philosophy. More specifically, this "collective consciousness" can be described as a vital attitude. That is to say, a kind of faith in a transcendental force and a sense of vital solidarity.

Examination of pre-slavery Africa suggests that there were hundreds of African peoples, or tribes, who some would suggest, each had its own philosophical system. More sophisticated scholarship indicates that West Africans, in general, shared one overriding philosophical system. It was through religion, however, that this philosophical system was expressed. In this sense religion and philosophy are the same phenomenon. Hence, to understand the essence of these peoples' existence, one must examine their religion, proverbs, oral traditions, ethics, and morals—keeping in mind that underlying the differences in detail is a general philosophical system which prevailed in Africa. Religion, however, is the more observable phenomenon and, as such, it permeated every aspect of the African's life. It was, in a very real sense, not something for the betterment of the individual, but rather something for the community of which the individual was an integral part. For the traditional African, to be human was to belong to the whole community.[5] Curiously enough, many African languages did not have a word for religion as such because religion was such an integral part of man's existence that it and he were inseparable. Religion accompanied the individual from conception to long after his physical death.

As most scholars of African religion will attest, one of the greatest difficulties in studying African religion and philosophy is that there are no sacred scriptures of that society. However, these beliefs and/or traditions were handed down from father to son for generation upon generation. As such, and in accordance with the prevailing oral tradition, the beliefs were corporate and the acts were communal. Traditional religion in Africa was not proselytized. The people were their religion. Thus, individuals could not "preach" their religion to "others."

As was noted above, religion was the observable phenomenon and, for the most part, tribes were seemingly different by observation. For instance, the Dogon conception of the universe is based, on the one hand, on the principle of vibrations of mat-

ter, and on the other hand, on a general movement of the universe as a whole.[6] For the Dogon proliferation of life was directed by a perpetual alternation of opposites: right-left, high-low,
odd-even, male-female,—all reflecting twin beings, living images
of the fundamental principle of twinness in creation, were each
equipped with two spiritual principles of opposites. Each of them
was a pair. This notion of man's unity with the universe is
reflected in the Dogon belief that "man is the seed of the universe."[7] Hence, the organization of the earth's system is reproduced in every individual.

Other tribes were not without their beliefs of man's existence and connection with the earth. The Fon of Dahomey
believed that at the beginning of the present world there were the
twins, Mawu-Lisa-Mawy, the female, and Lisa, the organization
of the world."[8] The Mende, also of West Africa, believed that
each parent gave to their offspring some aspect of the child's unified constitution. For instance, the Mende believed that the physical part of an individual is provided by the father through the
semen he puts into the mother. The child's spirit (Ngafa) is contributed by its mother. Contrary to the Mende, the Ashanti
believed that the human being is formed from the blood (Mogya)
of the mother and the spirit (Ntoro) of the father.[9] Both peoples
nevertheless believed that the initial separateness of the spirit and
the physical body and blood unite as one in making a new human
being. In this sense each tribe had its own religious system, and
for one to have propagated his religion would have involved
propagating the entire life of the people concerned. However, the
basic substance of each tribal life system was not different.

Traditional Africans made no distinction between the act
and the belief. "What people do is motivated by what they
believe, and what they believe springs from what they do and
experience."[10] Action and belief in traditional West African society were not separated. They belonged to a single whole.
Accordingly, traditional beliefs made no concrete distinction
between the spiritual and the physical. Note that the Mende perceived physical and spiritual components as uniting to make the
human.

The concept of life after death is found in all African societies. However, belief in the continuation of life after death did
not represent a hope for the future or possibly for a better life

when one died. For the African, once dead, there was neither Heaven to be hoped for, nor Hell to be feared. Again, this reflects the idea of vital force.

The whole of one's existence was an ontological religious phenomenon. The African was a deeply religious being, living in a religious universe.[11] For him to live was to be involved in, to be part of, a religious drama. As noted, traditional African religion was a religious ontology. As such, the ontology was characteristically very anthropocentric—everything was seen in terms of its relation to man.

Notion of Unity

The anthropocentric ontology was a complete unity, which nothing could break or destroy. Everything was functionally connected; to completely destroy one of the five categories would cause the destruction of the whole of existence, including the Creator. God was viewed as the originator and sustainer of man. The spirits explained man's destiny. Man was the center of the ontology. The animals, plants, and natural phenomena constituted the environment in which man lived. In addition to the five categories, there existed a force, a power, or energy which permeated the whole universe. In this kind of natural order (i.e., unity), God was the source and ultimate controller of the energy, but the spirits also had access to it. A few human beings—the Shaman (i.e., medicine men, priests, and rainmakers)—possessed the knowledge and ability to tap, manipulate, and use, to a limited degree, this powerful energy. For the Dogon the social order was projected in the individual. An indivisible cell that on the one hand is a microcosm of the whole, and on the other hand has a circumscribed function. Not only was a person the product of his institutions, he also was their motive power. Lacking, however, any special power in himself, he was the representative of the whole. The individual affected the cosmic order, which he also displayed.[12] As stated earlier, a prevailing belief (Dogon) was that the organization (unity) of the earth's system was reproduced in every individual. This notion of the unity of things was so ingrained that the Mende, for instance, had developed a sense of collective responsibility. Also ingrained in this notion of unity is a particular conception of time.

Concept of Time

African philosophy concerned itself with two dimensions of time—the past and the present; and this conception of time helped to explain the general life system of traditional Africans.[13] The direction of one's life system was from the present dimension backward to the past dimension. For the people, time itself was simply a composition of past events. Very little concern was given to time in and of itself. Time existed for Africans, but the concept was (is) very elastic. It encompassed events that had already occurred, those that are taking place, and those that would occur immediately.[14] What had no possibility of occurring immediately or had not taken place fell into the category of "no time."[15] Time was reckoned by phenomena. "Actual time" was what (events) was present or past and, because time essentially moved backward rather than forward, the traditional African set his mind not on future things but chiefly on what had taken place. Thus, the West African's understanding of things—that is, the individual, the tribe (community), and the five characters of the universe–was governed or dominated by these two dimensions (past and present) of time.

In order for the West African to make sense, or make real, time, it had to be experienced; and the way in which one experienced time was partly through the life of the individual and partly through the life of the tribe which went back many generations. Because time was reckoned by phenomena, "instead of numerical calendars, there were what one would call phenomenon calendars, in which the events or phenomena which constituted time were reckoned or considered in their relation with one another as they take place."[16] The Mandingo, for instance, had (have) a distinct "seasonal" calendar which reflected the changing of the seasons. Hence, the phenomenal changes of the environment constituted time. For most Africans, time was meaningful at the point of the event and not at the mathematical moment. Thus, in traditional life, any period of time was reckoned according to its significant events having been experienced.

Recognizing the associations and connotations that the English words past, present, and future have, Brother Mbiti uses two Swahili words (Sasa and Zamani) to represent present and past. Sasa has the sense of immediacy, nearness, nowness.[17] It is the period of immediate concern for the people because that is where or when they exist. For Africans, it is the period of personal recollections of events and phenomena. The Sasa period is not mathematically or numerically constant. Each member of the tribe has his own and, hence, the older the person, the longer his Sasa period. Each tribe (society, nation), therefore, also has its own Sasa period.

The Zamani period is not limited to what Europeans call the past. It overlaps and often encompasses the Sasa, making the two inseparable.

The Sasa feels or disappears into the Zamani. However, before events become incorporated into the Zamani, they have to be realized or actualized within the Sasa dimension. Thus, events (people) move backward from the Sasa dimension to the Zamani dimension. In a sense, Zamani is the graveyard of time.[18] Where the Sasa dimension binds together all created things, all is embraced within the Zamani.

Everything has its center of gravity in the Zamani period, with nothing ever ending. West African peoples expect human history to continue forever, because it too is part of the natural rhythm moving from Sasa to Zamani. The Mende apparently have a belief in rebirth or reincarnation. Children are sometimes named after a particular ancestor, especially when there is distinct resemblance. This behavior inevitably demonstrates that the Mende, like other West African peoples, have a notion that the life cycle is renewable. Human life is part of the rhythm of nature, and just as the days, months, seasons, and years have no end, there is a definite continuity in the rhythm of birth, puberty, initiation, marriage, procreation, old age, death, entry into the community of the departed (living dead), and entry into the company of the spirits. Life is an ontological rhythm, and abnormality or the unusual is what disrupts the ontological harmony.

Death and Immortality

In many African tribes, a person was not considered a full human being until he had gone through the whole rhythmic process of physical birth, naming ceremony, puberty, initiation rites (sometimes in the form of ceremonial rebirth), and finally marriage and procreation. Then, and only then, was one fully "born"—a complete person. Similarly, death initiated the systematic rhythmic process through which the person gradually was removed from the Sasa to the Zamani period. Hence, death and immortality have especial significance in West African traditions. After physical death, as long as a person was remembered and recognized (by name) by relatives and friends who knew him (i.e., remembered his personality, character, and words and incidents of his life), he would continue to exist in the Sasa period. When, however, the last person who knew him also died, then the former passed out of the horizon of the Sasa period and, in effect, became completely dead. He no longer had any claims to family ties. He entered the Zamani period; that is, he became a member in the company of spirits.

The departed person who was remembered (recognized) by name was what Brother Mbiti calls the living-dead. He was considered to be in a state of personal immortality. The Mende believed that a person survives after death and that his surviving personality goes to the land of the dead.[19] Those in personal immortality were treated symbolically like the living. The cycle of an individual ancestor, the Mende believed, lasted as long as the dead person was remembered in prayers and sacrifices.[20] Hence, they were respected, given food and drink in the form of libations, and listened to and obeyed.

Being remembered (recognized) and respected while in personal immortality was important for the traditional African, a fact which helps one to understand the religious significance and importance of marriage and procreation in West African societies. Procreation was the surest way to insure that one would not be cut off from personal immortality. In a kind of multiplicative fashion, polygamy reinforced one's insurance.

Inevitably, as stated earlier, there was a point when there were no longer any descendants alive who could recognize and give respect to the (living-dead) person. At that point, the process of dying was completed. However, he did not vanish out of existence. He then entered into the state of collective immortality. Now in the company of the spirits, he had at last entered the Zamani period. From this point on, the departed became nameless spirits who had no personal communication or ties with human families.

In terms of the ontology, entrance into the company of the spirits is man's final destiny. Paradoxically, death lies "in front" of the individual; it is a "future" event of sorts. But, when one dies, one enters the state of personal immortality and gradually "goes back" into the Zamani period. It should be emphasized that the African ontology was endless; such a view of man's destiny should not be construed to mean the end. Nothing ever ends.

Kinship: Collective Unity

Before concluding this brief and cursory review of African philosophy, a few words should be devoted to West African kinship, especially because kinship tied together the personal life system. Before they had carved up and colonized West Africa, Europeans had no idea where one tribe ended and another tribe began. The number of people that constituted, what might be considered a tribe, varied greatly. Depending upon the enumerator or ethnographer, many tribes were classified as unique and distinctly separate or simply as one.

Studies of African religious beliefs and practices demonstrate that among the many so-called distinct tribes there were more similarities (commonalities) than differences.[21] This author contends that all tribes shared basic beliefs—in the "survival of the tribe" and in the fact that the tribe was an integral and indispensable part of nature. Belief in tribal survival, was reflected in and sustained by a deep sense of kinship—probably one of the strongest cohesive devices in traditional life. Kinship controlled all relationships in the community.[22] It included animals, plants, and non-living objects. In effect, kinship bound together the entire life system of the tribe.

The kinship system stretched laterally (horizontally) in every direction as well as vertically. Hence, each member of the tribe was related not only to the tribal ancestors (both living-dead and spirits) but also to all those still unborn. In addition, each was a brother or sister, father or mother, grandmother or grandfather, cousin or brother-in-law, uncle or aunt, or some relation to everybody else. Africans still have many kinship terms which define the precise relationship binding any two people. Knowledge of one's tribal genealogy, vertical and horizontal, was extremely important. It imparted a sense of sacred obligation to extend the genealogical line. Through genealogies, persons (individuals) in the Sasa period were firmly linked to those who had entered the Zamani period.

This link manifested itself in the living as well. "In traditional life, the individual did not and could not exist alone."[23] The individual owed his very existence to other members of the "tribe." Not only those who conceived and nourished him but also those long dead and still unborn. The individual did not exist unless he was corporate or communal; he was simply an integral part of the collective unity. Africans believed that the community (tribe) made, created, or produced the individual; thus, the existence of the community was not imagined to be dependent on individual ingression.

Unlike Western philosophical systems, the African philosophical tradition does not place heavy emphasis on the "individual." Indeed one might say that in a sense it does not allow for individuals. It recognizes that "only in terms of other people does the individual become conscious of his own being."[24] Only through others does one learn his duties and responsibilities toward himself and others. Most initiation rites were designed to instill a sense of corporate responsibility and collective destiny. Thus, when one member of the tribe suffered, the entire tribe suffered; when one member of the tribe rejoiced, all of his kinsmen—living, dead, and still unborn—rejoiced with him. When one man got married, he was not alone, nor did his wife "belong" to him alone. Even the children were considered to be from unions which belonged to the collective body.

Whatever experiences or circumstances that happened to the individual, happened to the corporate body, the tribe, and whatever happened to the tribe, happened to the individual. A concept the Ashanti share with all other Akan peoples is that "the dead, the living, and those still to be born of the 'tribe' are all members of one family." A cardinal point in understanding the traditional African's view of himself, his self-concept is that he believes: "I am because we are; and because we are, therefore, I am."[25]

Experiential Communality : Cultural Configuration

Any basic cultural anthropology text will give one a gen-eral feeling about why and how man began to live in groups. However, what is not discussed in most texts is the interaction between man—in the group—and man's particular environment. The notion of particular environment is an important one for this presentation because it determines the common elements of the group's living experiences. For instance, primitive people living in the Sahara Desert respond differently to their environment than inhabitants of the frigid zones or polar regions.[26] And those living in the tropic regions of the Congo would respond still another way to the elements in their environment. A more point-ed example is provided by the differences between people living in post-industrial and pre-industrial environments. Plainly, it can be said that the uniqueness of one's environment determines the parameters of one's experience.

Experiential communality is defined here as the sharing of a particular experience by a group of people. Ultimately it helps to determine how the people will be, and concurrently, what ethos, or set of guiding beliefs, a people will follow. These guid-ing beliefs, in turn, dictate the creation and adoption of the val-ues and customs, which in the final analysis determine what social behavior a people will express in common—their cultural configuration. Thus experiential communality is important in determining society's fundamental principles—its beliefs about the nature of man and what kind of society man should create for himself.

The peoples of Africa have traditionally lived in units or clusters commonly referred to as "tribes." For centuries West Africa has characteristically consisted of rolling stretches of tall grassy plains with intermittent bush country and scattered tropi-cal rain forest.[27] Within this region, the traditional peoples (tribes) were closely related to each other, yet they still main-tained their distinctness. Each tribe had its own distinct lan-guage, which was related to the languages of all the other tribes in the region. African languages have been classified as being of the Sudanic family[28] and the Niger-Congo stock.[29] The closely related Bantu languages, the most well-known of the Niger-Congo group, were spoken mostly from the west coast to most of central

and southern Africa.[30] Clearly, just as there was a common geographical flavor to the region, so, too, did its inhabitants develop
and maintain common behaviors.[31]

The physical nature of the experiential communality is
important mainly in that the more unique or distinct it is, the higher the probability that the physical boundaries hinder the influx of
neighboring cultural elements. Likewise, it also allows for the
development and protective maintenance of indigenous cultural
elements. Just as important, however, is the interaction of communal man with his unique environment. The quintessence of
this phenomenon is that it results in a set of guiding beliefs, which
dictate the values and customs the people adopt. Ultimately, this
set (or sets) of values determines man's social behavior.

As noted earlier, close examination of the African ethos
suggests two operational orders: survival of the tribe and oneness
with nature. Being that this is the case, it is safe to say that this
ethos is probably the focal point of Black Psychology and the subject of which this research is based. Such research is devoted to
offering evidence pointing to the continuing of a functioning
African ethos.

African Reality and Psychological Assumptions

Black psychology is more than general psychology's
"darker" dimension. African (Black) psychology is rooted in the
nature of Black culture which is based on particular indigenous
(originally indigenous to Africa) philosophical assumptions. To
make Black psychology the dreaded darker dimension of general
psychology would amount to distorting African reality so that it
would fit Western psychological theories and/or assumptions.
For example, a study of the history of general psychology reveals
that the controversial mind-body problem stems from the set
early Greek myths known as the Orphic Mysteries. One myth
recounts how Dionysus was killed by the evil Titans and Zeus
saved Dionysus' heart and killed the Titans. Zeus then created
man from the "evil" Titan ashes and Dionysus' heart. Hence,
man has a dual nature: He is both evil and divine. However, the
assumptions arising from these early myths caused a problem.
There had to be an evaluation of what was "good" and what was

"bad." Assuming a dichotomy of the mind and the body, the early philosophers suggested that the body was the "bad" and the mind was the "good"—beliefs accepted unquestionably during the early period of general psychology's emergence as a "science." Not surprisingly, psychology chose the mind (good) as the domain of its inquiry.

The African concept of man is fundamentally different. Dogon, Mende, and Ashanti all assume man's dual nature but do not attempt to divide "mind" from "body" or refer to or imply an inherent good or evil in either aspect of the duality. The propositions of "the notion of unity," "one with nature," and "survival of the people" deny possibility of such an artificial and arbitrary dichotomy. What is seemingly dualistic is the concept of "twinness." However, as stated earlier, the twin components unite to make the unified man. For Africans, who believed that man, like the universe, is a complicated, integrated, unified whole, concerns such as the mind-body controversy would never arise and theoretical developments and/or analysis based solely on the explication of the "mind" or the "body" as separate entities would be useless.

Although the mind-body is a single example, it is believed sufficient to demonstrate how philosophical assumptions determined the scientific investigation of psychology. Certainly particular people cannot be meaningfully investigated and understood if their philosophical assumptions are not taken into account.

Toward Black Psychology

This brings us closer to Black psychology's evolution from African philosophy. The remaining question is how does one know or how can one "prove" that Africans living in the Western world, and in contemporary times, still have or maintain an African philosophical definition. Black psychology's development is contingent first upon analysis of the linkages between distinct experiential periods in the lives of Africans, and second upon the demonstration of the particular ways in which African philosophy, interacting with alien (particularly Euro-American) philosophies, has determined contemporary African (Black) people's perception of reality.

On the Question of Proof

History is an endeavor toward better understanding, and, consequently, a thing movement. To limit oneself to describing science as it is, will always be to betray it.[32]

For Black psychology—and the many other social science areas which attempt to "Blackenize" themselves in order to "explain" contemporary African peoples—the question of proof centers around more than determining whether a particular cultural element (e.g., an artifact) has been retained. The focus must be on the philosophical-psychological linkages between Africans and African-Americans (or Americanized Africans).

To determine whether—and to what extent—the African orientation has persisted, one must ask "How could it have been maintained?" "What mechanism or circumstances allowed it to be maintained?" An orientation stemming from a particular indigenous African philosophy could only be maintained when its cultural carriers were isolated (and/or insulated) from alien cultural interaction and if their behavioral expression of the orientation did not openly conflict with the cultural-behavioral elements of the "host" society. If the circumstances of the transplantation of New World Blacks met one or both of these conditions, then it is highly probable that the African orientation was retained. This writer maintains that a factor that often facilitated the retention of the African orientation was the particular region's physical features. And the slaves' accessibility to Western indoctrination was probably directly related to the degree of the retention of the African orientation. The rigidly enforced isolation of Blacks allowed New World Africans to retain their definition (orientation). Thus, the oppressive system of slavery indirectly encouraged the retention, rather than the destruction, of the African philosophical orientation.

Throughout the New World, large numbers of Africans lived, segregated in given areas. Lorenzo Turner[33] notes that "wherever Negroes were in the majority, African cultural elements had a better chance of surviving." In the United States, the policy of racial segregation must have often aided in keeping alive the African influence. It is proposed here that a comparative historical analysis of such areas as Brazil, Jamaica, Dutch Guinea, the rural South, and the northern ghetto would reveal a striking and direct correlation between (1) ecological and geographic factors and accessibility of interaction with Westerners and (2) maintenance of the African orientation. Not until the television "explosion" of the early 1950s did the African orientation come fully into contact with Western (Euro-American) styles of behavior and the American way of life.

Expressive behavior and cultural modalities are determined by philosophical definition. One can observe "Africanisms" throughout the New World because the orientation of which a people are allowed to develop or continue to utilize particular cultural elements was not interfered with. Thus, the statement "We are an African people" is valid because, for the most part, New World conditions did not permit the enculturation of the African orientation.

Considerations for Black Psychology

The experiential communality of African peoples can be subdivided into periods. For Africans living in the Western world, particularly in North America, the breakdown used here is (1) the African experience (prior to 1600), (2) the slavery experience (1600 to 1865), and (3) contemporary Black America (1865 to present).

However, rather than treat a few specific behavioral transitions, the discussion will focus on several major philosophical positions and correlative behavioral modalities. The first is survival of the people. From this philosophical position an extended definition of self evolved. That is to say, the self was by philosophical definition the "we" instead of the "I." Tribal membership became the most important identity. One's identity was thus rooted in being an Ashanti, or an Ibo rather than the person, Lodagaa Nyakyusi, who just happened to be an Igbera. Thrust into an alien culture, the "we" notion seemingly came under severe attack. Many scholars note, for example, the prevalent practice during slavery (second distinct experiential communality period) of purposely separating members of the same tribe in order to break down the collective reinforcement of a common definition.

However, additional information suggests that in North America the system of slavery was extremely unstructured in its beginning. Nevertheless, the system eventually came to define itself in terms of Black people. During this same period, the notion of tribe or peoplehood, which is crucial to the "we" notion underwent a particular modification. Clearly, Africans recognized and respected the distinctions of the tribe and understanding that one was an Igbira, or an Ibo, suggested many things. However, the philosophical position within each tribe was the set of guiding beliefs, which prescribed the survival of the tribe as a first order. As the system of American slavery began to define slavery in terms of Africans, tribe was more broadly defined in the minds of the Africans. Hence, one sees Africans no longer giving the Ibo, or Igbira, distinction its former level of importance but rather adopting broader categories. Thus, as slavery was moving closer and closer to its final definition, the slaves themselves were moving closer to the generic terms of African or Black as the final definition of tribe. Thus, the notion of survival of the tribe was not changed or modified during the slavery experience. In fact, one could suggest that the slavery experience allowed the underlying communality of West Africa to surface and define itself as African. Hence, in slavery, the cardinal point, "I am because we are; and because we are, therefore, I am," was not destroyed, but rather strengthened. In contemporary times, one can note the prevalence of benevolent societies and the role of the Negro church as expressing clear concern for the survival of the tribe.

The second philosophical position that has survived the effects of different experiential periods is the idea of man being an integral part of the "natural rhythm of nature," or, one with nature. Clearly, this can be seen within the African experience in terms of the anthropocentric ontology. The expression of this natural rhythm in the initiation rites gave definition to many of the periods within a person's Sasa dimension. This notion of rhythm also was expressed in the "talking drums."

In traditional African society, the living setting was the community itself and the emphasis was placed on living in that community, not in a particular household. Even in contemporary times, the "community" seems to manifest this same perception. One could propose that seeing oneself as an integral part of a community is the contemporary definition of man being an integral part of the natural rhythm of nature.

The oral tradition has clearly been transmitted throughout the three experiential periods. As indicated earlier, beliefs and traditions were handed down from father to son for generations upon generations. This tradition gave tremendous importance to the mind or the memory. Remembering phenomenal events in one's Sasa period was very important, if not crucial. The slavery tradition seemingly allowed this tradition to continue. That is, because oral communication was the only acceptable system—laws prohibited slaves from being taught to read and write—slavery unknowingly permitted the cultural transmission of the African traditional emphasis of oration and its consequent effects on the mind or memory to remain pretty much in tact. Brother Dr. Joseph White[34] suggests that playing the "dozens" as part of the oral tradition is a game used by Black youngsters to teach themselves to keep cool, think fast under pressure, and not say what is really on their minds. Verbal rituals like rapping and playing the dozens could also be viewed as initiation rites or possibly instances where the "power" of the word is used to make the "individual" psychologically feel better. For example, the Avogan and the Lobi Singi[35] are ritualized orations and dance ceremonies where the offended is afforded release of suppressed emotions by ridiculing another. Similarly, the Dogon have a very interesting practice in which certain relations are characterized by exchanges of, often, obscene insults and gestures.[36] Often the language, or name, typifies a special event in the child's life. Hence, because a person acquired names as he associated with different special experiences, one person may have many names. One need only examine the names of Black people to reveal historical tenacity in this orientation—for example, Bojangles, Brown Bomber, Stepin Fetchit, Wilt-the-Stilt, Muddy Waters, Iceberg Slim.

With certain modifications, tribalisms have been transmitted in the form of Africanisms throughout the New World experiential periods. Cooperative effort (tribalism) was expressed in the slavery experience. The "Knights of Wise" symbolized that notion along with the notion of the survival of the tribe. Funerals in contemporary Black America are very symbolic of the custom of reaffirming the bonds of kinship. Distinct motor habits also have been maintained up to the present. For example, photographic analysis of a particular dance in the Ashanti Kwaside rite illustrates a perfect example of the "Charleston." Morality was taught in traditional times via the use of animal tales. Parables were widely prevalent during slavery—the most notable being the "Brer Fox, Brer Rabbit Tales." In contemporary times, one simply notes the use of animal names to denote certain qualities. In the Black communities (villages) throughout this country, women and men are referred to as "foxes," "cows," "bears," "buzzards," "dogs," and so forth. The style of talking (dramatic pauses, intonation, and the like), are all reminiscent of a people in tune with the natural rhythm of nature—in tune with the oneness of nature.

The concept of time clearly is illustrative. The attitude that time is phenomenal rather than mathematical can be demonstrated to persist throughout the suggested experiential periods. The notion of CPT (colored people's time) has been translated to mean thirty minutes to an hour later than the scheduled meeting time. However, in the minds of Africans (Blacks), time is flexible and the event begins when one gets there. This author thus suggests that a more appropriate enunciation of CPT is "communal potential time," thereby emphasizing the communal aspect of time.

Black psychology must concern itself with the question of "rhythm." It must discuss, at some great length, "the oral tradition." It must unfold the mysteries of the spiritual energy now known as "soul." It must explain the notion of "extended self" and the "natural" orientation of African peoples to insure the "survival of the tribe." Briefly, it must examine the elements and dimensions of the experiential communalities of African peoples.

It is my contention, therefore, that Black Psychology must concern itself with the mechanism by which our African definition has been maintained and what value its maintenance has offered Black people. Hence, the task of Black psychology is to offer an understanding of the behavioral definition of African philosophy and to document what, if any, modifications it has undergone during particular experiential periods.

[1972]

Ancient Egyptian Thought and The Development of African Psychology

An understanding of the relationship between Ancient Egyptian Thought and African/Black Psychology requires first and foremost the recognition that the Ancient African World was a world of symbolism and that much of what is meaningful in African psychology today has gone unrecognized and misunderstood because of our inability to understand the role of symbolism in the African mind-both ancient and modern. Typically for most of us today, symbols and symbolism represent the abbreviated designations which "stand-for" something. Symbolism amounts to a kind of metaphoric device. However, symbolism in the context of this discussion must be thought of as the set of rules and methods for analytically interpreting Ancient African Thought. Through the use of symbols and symbolism the ancients' intuitive vision approached the world of knowing with an attitude which perceived all the phenomena of nature as symbolic writing, capable of revealing the forces and laws governing the material and spiritual aspects of their universe. In ancient times such usage was in fact the means for transmitting a precise and exact rational, if not suprarational, knowledge which emerged from the intuitive vision. This Schwaller de Lubicz[1] contends was the major aspect of ancient science. Unlike the "stand-for" connotation of the symbolic that is utilized today, the symbolic of ancient African times, and I would say the contemporary African as well, was a symbolism that went beyond the "representational-sequential-analytical" mode to the "transformation-synchronistic-analogic" mode.

Unlike reading where signs stand for the object, the object and the symbol or sign become identical in African Thought. In Ancient Africa, for example, the symbol of an animal was worshipped as an act of consecration to the vital functions which the animal incarnated. The symbol of the animal was identical to the law of nature embodied by the animal. Through the use of symbols one can understand in this regard, that so-called primitive animal worship was not in reality the worship of animals, but a method used to identify and clarify the essential function or law of nature embodied in the particular animal. Perceptually, the symbol and the symbolic should be viewed as material representations of immaterial qualities and functions. It is the objectification of things subjective in us and subliminal in nature.[2] Hence, the method of interpreting Ancient African Thought requires us to experience the symbol and the symbolic.

In this regard it has been suggested[3] that in being grounded in the symbolic method, Ancient Egypt educated the neurological structures of the brain so as to be able to maintain an active conscious connection between the bilateral lobes of the cerebral cortex and the impulses and subliminal information received from the more ancient and deeper brain centers. In so doing, the more ancient aspects of our nature were integrated into the activity of human reasoning and thought.

Parenthetically, support for this conception of symbolism and mental functioning is found in modern medical research regarding the anatomical evolution of the brain. Macleans[4] proposes that the triune anatomical division of the brain into hindbrain, midbrain and cerebral cortex parallels distinct functions, which developed during successive evolutionary phases. Each new division of the brain grew as a peripheral structure enveloping and encasing the prior brain component. Each division of the brain, though interconnected, can therefore be distinguished neuro-anatomically (each contains different distributions of the neurochemicals dopamine and choli nesterase). Each, according to Macleans, also has its own special intelligence, subjectivity, sense of time and space, memory and motor function. Macleans believes that even today the midbrain and hindbrain, lying beneath the cerebral cortex, still perform as they did in our most remote ancestors.

Ancient Egyptian Thought

As stated above, the symbolic attitude or mentality of the ancients cultivated the intellect to the extent or degree that humans were accustomed to perceiving all the phenomena of nature as a symbolic script capable of revealing the forces and laws governing the universe.

It is the opinion of this author that the activity of ancient human reasoning and thought is only understood via an understanding of the symbolic method (transformation-synchronistic-analogic modality) and that it is the inability of effective symbolism which communicates the appreciation and comprehension of Ancient African Thought.

Thought which emerges from the use of symbol and the symbolic can be called "speculative" or "imaginative"; with the caution that "speculative" as it is used here should not be tainted with meaning similar to fantasy. Speculative thought is more akin to intuitive, if not visionary, modes of apprehension. Speculative thought attempts to explain, order and, above all else, unify experience for the "knower."

Reality for the ancients was always conceived as the synthesis of the visible and the invisible, the material and immaterial, the cognitive and emotive, the inner and the outer. Accordingly, the phenomenal world was known through speculative thought as the representative of the subliminal.

Problems in the Study

In addition to the difficulties associated with attempting to understand one thought system with methods relevant to another thought system, the study of Ancient Egyptian Thought is also marred by the proliferation of information about ancient African Life from the perspective of white vested interest. This latter point is understood if one understands that the political control of knowledge is a necessary condition for white supremacy; and in this regard, as Diop[5] has pointed out, the common denominator characterizing the study of Ancient Egypt by White Egyptologists has been their seemingly desperate pathological necessity and unrelenting attempt to refute ancient Africa's Blackness. Consequently, information regarding ancient Africa has been destroyed, distorted, falsified, suppressed and intentionally made unclear.

Hence, given that the remaining discussion is obviously influenced by these two levels of concern, the analysis offered here is more an initial beginning step than a definitive conclusion. In order to overcome the dangerous limitations and misinterpretations associated with this dilemma, one must attempt to seek out and utilize the techniques of thinking practiced by the ancients. The ancient technique of thinking depended upon a fuller and richer integration of mind, body and spirit. Hence, we are proposing that we utilize this technique while simultaneously attempting to uncover the very system which one is utilizing in order to discover the thinking system.

The solution to this problem in part will be achieved when, as Jacob Carruthers[6] points out, the methodological problems are solved (evolutionary theory, spatial perceptions, linguistic and historiographical context, chronological perspective and identification) and the ideological accuracy associated with reformulating an African World view from Ancient Egyptian data is adopted. In regards to Ancient Egyptian Thought this author accepts as irrefutable the data that demonstrate that the oldest records of human culture were found in Africa and that the people who created and invented the cultural foundations for and developments of religion, science, art, mathematics, medicine and education were Black.

In relation to Ancient Egyptian Thought one must recognize that of the thirty dynasties representing Egyptian civilization, it was during the indigenous Black dynasties (I, XII, XVIII, and XXV) that the greatest creativity and achievements were accomplished. In fact, as noted by Clark,[7] by the end of the sixth dynasty or what is referred to as the old kingdom, the pattern of African civilization and African thought was complete. Clark goes on to maintain that there was no fundamental change in the philosophy of Ancient Africa as represented by the Egyptian experience until the conversion to Christianity in the fourth and fifth Century A.D.

In recognition of the maxim that "ideas are the substance of behavior," the accomplishments of Black dynastic Egypt provide us with a wellspring of insight and direction for understanding the thought of Ancient Africa and the subsequent development of psychology. Even though this analysis will concentrate on Dynasties I through IV, XVIII and XXV, it should be noted that Dynastic Egypt didn't simply materialize out of nothing. In fact one must recognize as did Chancellor Williams[8] that the thinking reflected in early dynastic Egypt was essentially the formalization of pre-dynastic Egyptian Thought.

In extending this analysis, at another time, it would be important to also understand the ideas which were the substance of the behavior of Mentuhotep II of the eleventh dynasty who undertook to settle the White-Asian problem by reversing the policy of integration and expelling Whites from lower Egypt. Additionally, it would be important to understand why a revival of learning, science, art and the crafts occurred along with or only with the expulsion of the Whites. What ideas characterized this period of Black rule? What ideas or thoughts served as the substance of the behavior of Pharaoh Kamose?

As a reflection of the thought and experience of a people the analytical value of myth is that it serves as a measure and/or reflection of the human possibilities, probabilities and potentialities of a people. Myth should therefore be taken seriously because it reveals a significant if unverifiable truth. When taken as concrete and analyzed symbolically, it can provide us with an important tool for understanding Ancient African Thought as well as contemporary African and African American Conduct.   In the Memphite theology, the ancient Africans spoke the language of myth and it is here that we shall turn to obtain an understanding of Ancient African Thought.

The inscription called the "Memphite Theology" was taken from a stone bearing the name of an Egyptian pharaoh who ruled about 700 B.C. The text itself is the documentation of African thought which comes from the earliest periods of Egyptian recorded history when the first dynasties made their capital at Memphis in the city of the god, Ptah. The actual ideas found in the Memphite theological text is that it brings together Ancient African ideas about creation into a broad philosophical system about the nature of the universe. The text itself is also in part a theological argument regarding the primacy of the god Ptah and the centrality of Memphis in the theocratic state.[9]

Overall the Memphite text takes the earlier African ideas about creation—Atum coming into being out of the primeval waters, and then bringing forth the Ennead of Gods into existence and places or subsumes them into a symbolic system which reveals the divine laws of nature.

In the Memphite theology, for instance "The primate of the gods, Ptah, conceived in his heart, everything that exists and by his utterance created them all." The god, Ptah, is first to emerge from the primeval waters of "Nun" as a primeval hill. Next the god, Atum emerges from the waters and sits upon Ptah. In the primeval waters there remain four pairs of male and female gods: (1) Nun and Naunet (primeval water and counter heaven; (2) High and Haauhet (the boundless and its complement or opposite); (3) Kuk and Kauket (darkness and its complement or opposite); and (4) Amum and Amaunet (the hidden and its complement or opposite). It should be noted that according to the Memphite theology, while the sun god, Atum, sits upon Ptah, the primeval hill, he accomplishes the work of creation.[10]

It is important to recognize that the creation story for the Black ancients was not simply a record of a series of events in time. The creation story was a "speculation" about the principle of life and the order of the universe. From this perspective one can see that the theology of Memphis perceived God as a spirit and the fundamental or founding principle of the world's organization as ideas.[11]

When one examines this mythology as mythic symbolism, a very clear system of ideas and a specific pattern of thought emerges. In this theology all the characters or actors in the primeval drama are aspects of Ptah, the supreme power. Ptah is not only the creator of the gods, but also the provider of their particular power. Symbolically, the Ennead of Gods is an attribute of Divine Being and Law. In re-noting that the imagery and thought reflected in the myth are inseparable from the laws of nature embodied in the drama, this myth provides us with an objectification of the subliminal.

In analyzing the myth as symbolism and speculative thought, one is able to see that overall, the myth of the ancients accomplished two things. First, it outlined the steps whereby the universe was arranged or created; and, second, it provided a series of symbols to describe the origin and development of human consciousness. In this first regard, the Coffin text (IV, 342) for example, suggests that God, while still motionless in the primeval waters, "thought" out the ideas of all the creatures in the universe before creation began. Wallis Budge[12] notes that in *The Book of Knowing the Evolutions of Ra*, the god Neb-er-tcher records the following story of creation and the birth of the gods: The text states:

> I AM HE WHO EVOLVED HIMSELF UNDER THE FORM OF THE GOD KHEPERA. I, THE EVOLVER OF THE EVOLUTIONS AND DEVELOPMENTS WHICH CAME FORTH FROM MY MOUTH. NO HEAVEN EXISTED, AND NO EARTH, AND NO TERRESTRIAL ANIMALS OR REPTILES HAD COME INTO BEING. I FORMED THEM OUT OF THE INERT MASS OF WATERY MATTER I FOUND NO PLACE WHEREON TO STAND..., I WAS ALONE, AND THE GODS SHU AND TEFNUT HAD NOT GONE FORTH FROM ME; THERE EXISTED NONE OTHER WHO WORKED WITH ME. I LAID THE FOUNDATIONS OF ALL THINGS BY MY WILL, AND ALL THINGS EVOLVED THEMSELVES THEREFROM. I UNITED MYSELF TO MY SHADOW, AND SET FORTH SHU AND TEFNUT OUT OF MYSELF; THUS FROM BEING ONE GOD I BECAME THREE, AND SHU AND TEFNUT GAVE BIRTH TO NUT AND SEB, AND NUT GAVE BIRTH TO OSIRIS, HORUS. KHENT-AN-MAA, SUT, ISIS AND NEPHTHYS, AT ONE BIRTH, ONE AFTER THE OTHER, AND THEIR CHILDREN MULTIPLY UPON THIS EARTH.

In Ancient African cosmogony the "primeval waters" and the Divine mind are fundamental to all creation. In the Memphite theology God is both a spirit and fundamental principle of the world's organization.

The essence of God is revealed as thought and command. The symbols or signs of heart and tongue become the material representation of the immaterial qualities or attributes of will (thought) and intent (command). The essence of Ptah is therefore will and intent. One text states:

> IN THE FORM OF ATUM THERE CAME INTO BEING HEART AND THERE CAME INTO BEING TONGUE. BUT THE SUPREME GOD IS PTAH, WHO HAS ENDOWED ALL THE GODS AND THEIR KA'S THROUGH THAT HEART WHICH APPEARED IN THE FORM OF HORUS AND THROUGH THAT TONGUE WHICH APPEARED IN THE FORM OF THOTH, BOTH OF WHICH WERE FORMS OF PTAH.

The heart is the organ which conceives thought and the tongue is the organ which creates the conceived thought as a phenomenal actuality. As an attempt to explain order and unify experience, in other words to serve as speculative thought, the Memphite theology essentially states that the natural attributes of the Divine mind were will and intent or divine intelligence. In chapter 85 of *The Book of the Dead*, the creator is heard to say:
I CAME INTO BEING OF MYSELF IN THE MIDST OF THE PRIMEVAL WATERS . . .

During another period Atum is conceived as the aboriginal deity. Atum, which meant self-created everything and nothing, the all-inclusive and the emptiness, was considered a demiurge possessing creative powers.[13]   Atum was not only God but all things to come. In ancient text, Atum is seen creating from him/herself all else. In the pyramid text, for example, (see Utterance 527) the text states:
ATUM WAS CREATIVE IN THAT HE PROCEEDED TO MASTURBATE WITH HIMSELF...; HE PUT HIS PENIS IN HIS HAND THAT HE MIGHT OBTAIN THE PLEASURE OF EMISSION THEREBY AND THERE WAS BORN BROTHER AND SISTER - THAT IS SHU AND TEFNUT.

In another myth, Shu and Tefnut come into being by being spat forth from the creator's mouth. Utterance 600 of the pyramid text states:
YOU SPAT FORTH AS SHU, YOU EXPECTORATED AS TEFNUT, YOU PUT YOUR ARMS AROUND THEM IN AN ACT OF KA-GIVING SO THAT YOUR KA MIGHT BE IN THEM.

In noting the symbolism in the creation story as well as the role of speculative thought, one is able to understand why in Ancient African mythology there is no story or drama of the separate creation of man. Conceptually or more accurately, the intuitive vision of the Ancients saw no firm and final dividing line between gods and men. To the ancients all the elements of the universe were "consubstantial." That is to say the nature of all things was of the same spirit or Ka. The Divine willed first itself to be and then manifested itself as complementary male-female gods who in having the attributes, the Ka, of the Divine manifested themselves as man and woman. Hence, all things are endowed with the spirit of God; i.e., the Ka of God.

In remembering that mythology is symbolic writing designed to reveal the natural law and forces governing the universe, and that Ancient Thought was speculative thought, one can speculate that what is being revealed here is an account of creation as physical and spiritual generation. In terms of symbolic thought the masturbation version accounts for or explains creation in terms of physical self-generation; whereas the spitting version symbolically expresses creation as the entry of the breath of life or divine word.

It shall be noted that these two versions are not alternative explanations but complementary text. The masturbation motif stresses the physical reproductive aspect of life behind which lies the spiritual essence of life. Hence the generation of Shu and Tefnut are described in terms of both masturbation/physical and spitting/spiritual. The early Coffin text in fact clarifies this point. It states:

THIS WAS THE MANNER OF YOUR ENGENDERING: YOU CONCEIVED WITH YOUR MOUTH AND YOU GAVE BIRTH FROM YOUR HAND IN THE PLEASURE OF EMISSION.

The underlying law being revealed here is: (1) that Being, as represented by the creation story, is simultaneously "spiritual" and "physical"; and (2) that the reality or creation is the consequence of both the idea and the act. Human reality results therefore from both thinking and doing.

If one looks closely at ancient African Thought particularly as revealed in mythology, the underlying law which governs the universe becomes rather evident. For instance, the Jackal in Ancient African Thought was the symbol of judgment. However, as symbol it represents "digestion" which in turn should be viewed as the precise act of innate discrimination and analysis. The process of eating is an act of ingestion and digestion wherein we separate out the elements capable of transformation and digestion wherein we separate out the elements that are transmutable into energy and future evolution from the elements that are not transmutable into waste. Digestion is a "destructive-productive" process of transformation. The Jackal, which symbolically represents the incarnation of this, thereby, represents the recognition of "Gorm" in the universe being capable of breaking down into its constituent elements which in turn serves as the base for continued evolution (the process of transformation). In brief, death of the old gives life to the new. Other "underlying laws" revealed in the symbolism of Ancient Egyptian Thought are growth, assimilation, coagulation, decomposition and of course transformation.

A summary reading of mythology reveals that Ancient Egyptian Thought can be characterized as possessing: (1) "ideas of thought" which represent the human capacity to have "will" and to invent or create; (2) "ideas of command" which represent the human capacity to have "intent" and to produce that which it wills; and (3) "ideas of ascension" which represent the human capacity to change.   These ideas combined, Will, Intent, Ascension and Transformation, comprise the features of Ancient African Thought. However, their comprehension in ancient text or mythology is only revealed through the process of symbolic analysis and speculative thought.

Before attempting to apply the sets of ideas found in Ancient Egyptian Thought to the emergence of Black psychology, one must discuss the ancient notion of soul or spirit in Egyptian metaphysics. Psychology technically means the study of the soul or spirit. Thus, Black psychology must be the study of the soul belonging to a particular group of people whose class membership is rooted in the historical and cultural experience of African people and who are euphemistically called Black.

Soul in Egyptian Metaphysics

Ancient Egyptian Thought was fundamentally concerned with the "essential" or "essence" of being, which, when codified, became the "ontological principle of consubstantiation". This principle is in fact the primary principle underlying the universal laws of nature. The African proverb, "whatever is in the first place is spirit" is an abstract codification of this principle as reflected in a more contemporary African experience. The principle of consubstantiality states that the elements of the universe are of one substance. With the essence of being of the same substance, the Ancient African Law of Transformation and the later practice of substitution makes sense and shares some of the personality of that other. One can only have a conception of growth which results from the Jackal function if the essence of all things is the same. Similarly, one can only accept the substitution of one thing for another if the important aspects of the nature of each are the same. The essence of all things is spirit. Hence, it is very important that we understand the conceptualization of the spirit or soul in Egyptian Thought.

Division of the Psychic Nature

The psychic or spiritual constitution in Ancient Egyptian Thought was believed to be comprised of seven parts or divisions. The "Ka," the principle body, was the first division of the psychic nature. Like all the others it had a formal structure capable of ultimate disintegration and would return to the elements from which it came unless it was Osirified or mummified.

The "Ba," soul of breath, was the second division of the psychic nature. It represented the transmission of the breath of life. The Ancients believed that there was only one power which was symbolically represented as "the breath"; and, that this power or breath was transmitted from the ancestors to the descendants. The Ancients believed that this power or energy has always existed and will always exist. The Ba was the invisible source like electricity of all visible functions. The Ba was in effect, the vital principle which represented the essence of all things.

The third division of the psychic nature, called the "Khaba," was in fact a luminous intangible covering of the vital principle, Ba. In the Egyptian language Khaba means to veil or to cover. The Ancients believed that the phenomena which it produced are human emotion and motion. It was further thought to be responsible for sustaining the sensory perceptions and the phenomena of color, total harmony and the circulation of blood. It was also responsible for delusions and was sometimes called the sin body of the Ancients. Finally, because it was the abode of the psyche pattern by which the body was afflicted, it was believed to play a significant part in disease.

Known as the seat of "intelligence" and "mental perception," the "Akhu" was named for this fourth division of the psychic nature. It was in the area of Akhu, the Ancients believed, that the whole mystery of the human mind was to be comprehended. The mind was in fact, an entity in and of itself and only during physical life was the human mind the instrument of the human spirit. The concerns of the mind were primarily the survival of its own thinking processes. The Akhu was characterized by attributes like judgment, analysis, and mental reflection, all of which could be trained and disciplined so as to be dedicated to the service of the higher being.

The sebor ancestral soul was the fifth division of the psychic nature. It does not manifest itself in humans until puberty or adolescence. The evidence of the presence of the "Seb," as it was also called, was the power of the human being to generate his own kind. The Seb is in effect the self-creative power of Being.

The sixth division of the psychic nature, called "Putah," represented the "first intellectual father." The Putah was associated with the mental maturity of the individual. The coming of Putah marked the union of the brain with the mind. It was the Putah which established the fact of the person and from the moment of its manifestation or attainment it was believed that intellect (will and intent) alone governed conduct.

The final division of the soul was the "Atmu." It was considered the divine or the eternal soul. In some texts it is identified with the seventh creation, the god Atmu who inspired the breath of life everlasting. In ritual this division of the soul is represented as parenthood which symbolically stood for the presence of full creative powers and perpetual continuation.

Although Atmu represented the presence of such fullness, enwrapping and serving as the essence of all the divisions of the soul was the Ka of God. In some texts the Ka is thought of as the sum of the above mentioned seven. However, this is only true if the sum is considered greater than the total of its parts. The Ka was the divine spirit which endowed all things and which survived past the physical life of the individual. The Ka, it was thought, had magical powers and could cause the dead to live again in the thoughts of the survivors and could even enter into a mummified being, animate it internally and cause it to have a continued inner life or existence. The Ka was the intangible likeness of the living. It appeared in the dream state and some believed actually traveled independently of the body during those times.

Implications for the Emergent African Psychology and Black Human Conduct

Admittedly this research is diminished by the lack of a full discussion of the changes occurring in the intellectual history of human kind resulting from European and/or Western dominance. For instance "the Mesopotamian shift" which resulted in a very different psychological mood wherein man came to distrust the cosmic order, is of paramount importance for a fuller appreciation of the intellectual history of human being.

Similarly, the Greek mutations are most informative. For example, the Greek so-called derivation of Atum from "alpha" the negative prefix meaning not, and "temnein" the present infinitive active of "temno" to cut, resulted in a meaning of Atum as "that which can not be cut". This was a distortion of the Ancient African meaning of "Atum"—the "all and the not yet being." The shift in thinking and emphasis resulting from the exchange of Egypt with Mesopotamia and the distortion occurring along side or simultaneously with the ascension of Judeo-Christian Greco-Roman world dominance requires major analytical treatment.[14] In fact, an analysis of the Mesopotamian shift and the Judeo-Greco-Roman distortion will be necessary if we are to truly understand what is wrong with Western Psychology.

Nevertheless, the implications that Ancient African Thought has for the development of Black psychology are clear and concise. These implications are found in the definition of Beingness and Becoming.

Speculative thought would therefore suggest in this regard that human nature is in fact a symbolic presentation of divine Ka. Hence, to be human is to possess "will" and "intent" (Divine Intelligence) and to have the capacity to develop and change. Humans have "intent" and are innately endowed with the capacity to ascend or grow to the higher condition. Implied in the capacity to grow is the law of transformation. The implications of what the Ancient African ideas of transformation have for human psychology is the recognition that humans have the capacity to change.

Beingness would therefore be comprised of having the capacity of will and intent and the ability to command and produce that which it wills. By definition, Becoming, in turn, would be by definition the innate capacity to develop and change. Given Ancient African thought, both Beingness and Becoming would be based on the principle of Ka or universal spirit. The fundamental basis of all things as a state of being or the process of becoming is spirit or energy.

African Psychology and Black Human Conduct

Hence, Black human conduct is or should be the behavioral representation of African Thought. Ideas are the substance of behavior. Given the Ancient African ideas discussed above, one can see not only a predictable and consistent value system, principle of identity and cultural common sense, one can also speculate as to the appropriate human conduct and social order emerging from the African philosophy and culture. For example, human purpose, the distortion of which is the root of almost all human mal-functioning short of biological or chemical based maladies, and the "meaningfulness" of one's action, is revealed in the awareness of one's intent and will. Similarly, a sense of self as collective (pars pro toto) extended the comprehension and respect of the sameness of self and others; the interdependence and synthesis of human beings, all emerge from and are dependent upon the African ontological principle of consubstantiation.

African-American Mentality

Almost as if motivated by the ancestral spirit several Black Psychologists began to develop conceptualizations of Black mental health that recognized natural functioning was the result of being centered in and consistent with one-self. In an earlier article, this author[15] noted for instance, that the natural consciousness of Black people is forced to relate to a reality defined by the cultural prerequisites of whites. It was argued that such a situation was tantamount to Black people living in an insane environment. It is insane for Black people, where national consciousness understands the interdependence and harmonious aspects of the universe, to mold their behavior and thinking in a fashion consistent with a reality which is based on independence/selfishness and conflict/competition in the universe.

The cause of this insanity is in fact a disruption in the natural, harmonious relationship between the spiritual, material, conceptual, affective and cognitive aspects of Black psycho-social and geophysical reality. One consequence of this disruption is a perceptual and emotional distortion. Hence, insane Blacks deny their self and kind. Consequently, a Black who kills another Black doesn't realize his act is suicide and not homicide. Another consequence of this disruption is cognitive and political confusion. Here we find insane Black people deifying white people and dehumanizing Black people. Conceptually, whites are viewed by such Blacks as omnipotent which suggests that, if anything has to get done, it is they who must do it. Here we find Black people also denying our communality and epitomizing our individuality. Politically therefore, Black people should unite, affirm and protect their own. The Black dope pusher, pimp and killer are only symptomatic of Black people living in white insanity. And, as long as Black people respond to and accept without question white reality we will never be able to see, think, feel and act in a fashion that affirms and protects our being.

Consistent with the above-mentioned Ancient African ideas, Akbar[16] identified mental health as the affirmative identification and commitment to our natural African identity. In utilizing one's own natural identity as the core being, he went on to conceptualize a system of mental disorders (anti-self, alien-self, etc.), which demonstrated that African-American insanity is the result of engaging in behavior that denies one's African identity and survival imperatives. The key to understanding abnormal and/or aberrant functioning is found in ancient thought; i.e., know thy Ka. In knowing one's nature, having will and intent and the capacity to produce that which one wills, one is less likely to allow societal conditions to become internalized and in so doing become the agent of psychological maladaptation and mental dysfunctioning.

Features of Normal and Abnormal Functioning

Unlike the mathematical illusion of normality found in the west, normality which would be consistent with African Thought is a normality which is equivalent to one's nature. Human development is normally a natural and an orderly process. It in fact parallels and in many instances mirrors the growth and development of everything endowed with a "Ka," all living things. It is believed what living things have in common in terms of the developmental process, is: (1) a sense of "Self," which gives it some understanding of its own integrity; (2) Motion, which implies its changing nature; (3) Order, which defines the natural connections and separations of its integrity; (4) Form, which outlines its integrity and marks the point of distinction; and (5) Direction, which identifies its purpose and mission. These five characteristics can be thought of as developmental needs or conditions not stages in the human process. Human development, therefore is characterized by: (1) the condition of self wherein humans have a need to understand and define that which represents their own essence (integrity); (2) the condition of motion wherein humans have a need to be active, to grow or change; (3) the condition of order wherein humans have a need for balance between synthesis (connection), and contradiction (antagonism); (4) the condition of form wherein humans have a need to outline or define the essence or integrity of being human; and (5) the condition of direction wherein humans have a need to define their purpose which is always a response to affirm one's humanity.

Thus, to be normal is to be consistent with the dictates of one's Ka. This normality is to possess thought and command and to have the ability to produce that which one wills. Attitudinal and behavioral normality, or naturally functioning, is represented by: (1) a sense of self which is collective or extended; (2) an attitude wherein one understands and respects the sameness in oneself and others; (3) a clear sense of one's spiritual connection to the universe; (4) the sense of mutual responsibility; and (5) a conscious understanding that human abnormality and/or deviancy is any act which is in opposition to oneself and kind, or that which is in opposition to the Ka of God.

As noted above, Akbar's notions of mental disorders are predicated on the notion of opposition or alienation from one's self.

Abnormal functioning, he contends can be the results of: (1) an alien-self disorder wherein the person's thought and actions are characterized by an active "rejection" of themselves and of their natural and/or ethnic dispositions; (2) an anti-self disorder wherein the person's thoughts and actions are characterized by an overwhelming identification with the dominant/oppressive alien social group and the adoption of an active hostility to one's group of origin; (3) a self-destructive disorder wherein the person's thoughts and actions are characterized by engaging in practices which are personally and/or culturally self-destructive i.e., alcoholism and drug addiction, homosexuality, etc.; and (4) organic disorders which are behavioral dysfunctions which result from major physiological and/or biochemical dysfunctions or poisoning.

African-American Thought Patterns: Implications For Contemporary Black Social Life

The development of African/Black psychology has, from the discipline's inception in modern times, been enriched by the recognition of the need to grapple with an understanding of the fundamental nature of what it is to be human.[17] Black Psychology's leading theoreticians[18] have embraced a line of reasoning which views the behavior of African-Americans as having as its antecedents Ancient African Thought and philosophy. In this tradition Matthews[19] has specifically noted that the African mode of thought has explanatory importance for understanding how African-Americans come to know and respond to their reality.

In what, to some, is considered one of the "classics" in African/Black psychology, *Voodoo or I.Q.: An Introduction* to *African Psychology*, Cedric X[20] has effectively argued that since African psychology is based on an African conceptual or paradigmatic framework for "knowing" the world, the discipline of African psychology must first explicate and understand Ancient Human Thought.

Implications for Social Thought, Action and Definition

Given the Ancient African Thought discussed above, one can simply note that ontologically, the African belief system understood that the nature of all things in the universe was the Ka of God.[21] Therefore, it is logical when one believes that all things, including man, were endowed with the same supreme Force, the Ka of God, one would also believe that all things are "essentially" one or the same. For Africans our most comprehensive ideas about order would be based on the ontological identification of "being in the universe" as being characterized by a cosmological "participation in the Supreme Force." Parenthetically, it is understandable that if ontologically the African believes that the nature of all things is Force, then the African would, accordingly, view the variety of cosmic beings as quantitative alterations of the same Supreme Energy.[22]

What characterized African peoples' understanding of the universe was, consequently, a simultaneous respect for the concrete detail in the multiplicity of forms and the rejection of the possibility of an absence or vacuum of forms. In this case, the African conception of the world and the phenomena within it amounts to a set of synthesis and contradictions linked to the particular classification of beings as differential quantifications of force. Combined, these "connectual" and "antagonistic" participatory sets form the whole of universal relations. Accordingly, relationships in the universe are determined by elements belonging to the same metaphysical plane, "participating by resemblance" or by elements belonging to different metaphysical planes, "participating by difference."[23] The dynamic quality of the total universe is, however, thought to be the conciliation of these various "participatory sets." In fact, the conciliation of, on the one hand, the unity of the cosmos and, on the other, the diverseness of beings within the cosmos make for the special features of the traditional African worldview, e.g., dynamism, interdependence, variety, optimism, etc.

Psychologically or in terms of social life, individual consciousness becomes such that the family or peoplehood constituted the reference point wherein one's existence was perceived as being interconnected to the existence of all else. The individual was an integral part of the collective unity, i.e., the family. In recognition of this kind of awareness, others[24] have noted that the traditional African view of "self" is contingent upon the existence of and interconnectedness with others (The Oneness of Being).

Existence therefore is at the level of the family or peoplehood. That is, the existence of family or peoplehood is more important than individual existence. As an aside, we can note that in terms of the notion of "genetic proximity," wherein simply stated, the "begetter is always more powerful" than the offspring, the family entity constitutes more power or force than the individual entity. Accordingly, family or people existence is "paramount" to individual existence and to paraphrase Satre, the family essence or essence of peoplehood precedes the individual essence. The family, including the living, the dead, and those yet-to-be-born,[25] is the center, the focal point wherein the essence of the community is kept alive. The family or peoplehood is the center of existence, it is the center of the universe. Our peoplehood then becomes the source of our definition.

Just as African Thought should and does influence our definition of who we are, it should also, as it does, influence how we respond to our concrete conditions.

Behavioral Response and Dispositional Features

Given the Ancient African Thought and its modern day replications, one would be remiss in not pointing out that there is a recognizable and identifiable African-American style of responding to and manipulating our reality, which has its roots in our African Beingness. Psychologically the techniques associated with our cultural disposition are "Improvisation," "Transcendence," and "Transformation." These techniques are all governed by the human possibilities defined by our indigenous African-American cultural substance and mythic consciousness.

Although these three techniques are associated collectively with our cultural disposition, they all have distinct qualities of their own. The technique of improvisation is a process of spontaneously creating, inventing or arranging a known experience, situation, or event such that the known experience is extended into the unknown and thereby results in a new experience. Secondly, the technique of transcendence is the quality, state or ability to exceed, go beyond or rise above the limits of an experience, condition or situation. And, finally, the technique of transformation is the predisposition to recognize that the condition, quality or nature of an experience or element has the potential to change into a different experience or element.

The relationship between the social and psychological development of our people and the social structures and institutions, government, education, health, etc., theoretically designed to affirm our people's being, is ultimately a question of transformation. We would contend that where the social structures and/or institutions are cultural transplants and do not emerge from and reflect the cultural definition of our people, the social structures will serve only to change, probably dehumanize, and oppress our people. It is further suggested that the emergence of counter ideologies and popular liberation movements in Black ruled communities and countries are evidence of our people's rejection of the cultural transplants reflected in the adoption of foreign institutions. It is not enough to have Africans operate and control institutions emerging from and reflective of the cultural reality of foreigners.

Conclusion

As an active response to reclaim mastery of one's own "productive forces," liberation struggles implicitly require the capacity to also control the nature, definition, and meaning of these "productive forces." At its simplest level, total struggle requires that one wages both a physical and a psychological war against oppression and the oppressor. If culture is the ultimate expression and definition of a people's capacity to create progress and/or determine history, then critical thought or science, which is the reconstruction of that culture, must be one of the mechanisms for expressing and defining the people's capacity to create progress.

It is in the reclamation of culture and Ancient Thought and in the creative reconstruction of them as psychology that one seizes control over the interpretation of reality and, consequently, connects struggle with our human development. As the expression of all that constitutes the every day way of life of a people, culture defines and gives meaning to everything experienced by the living. Accordingly, culture defines and gives meaning to the notion of human development. Science as its reconstruction simply further refines the definition and meaning of that human development. If social life for people who are oppressed is a social life motivated by liberation, and, if liberation struggles are struggles to reclaim the right of culture (the eight of a vast indigenous structure of languages, behavior, customs knowledge, symbols, ideas, and values which influence the general design for living and patterns for interpreting reality), then liberation struggles must develop and utilize a system of critical thought emerging from our own Ancient indigenous thought.

As a reconstruction of the systematic and cumulative ideas, beliefs and knowledge of our people, the role of psychology in liberation struggles must be to provide an analysis and understanding of our Beingness and Becoming. This will further filter, organize and transform our natural "sensations" into particular mental impressions and behavioral dispositions and/or responses that affirm our Being and resist our oppression. This should be the essence of our social life. Liberation should be the fundamental reason or value in understanding Ancient Egyptian thought for contemporary African peoples.

[1986]

Historical Foundations of African Psychology and Their Philosophical Consequences

The historical foundations of African Psychology have their origins in four recent societal events: (1) Watergate, and all that this term implies with regard to Governmental misconduct; (2) the October 1973 war in the Middle East; (3) the demise of the Civil Rights Movement of the 1960s; and (4) the Vietnam War.

Before discussing these events in any detail, it is perhaps necessary to explain the reason for the consideration of such social events in the context of an academic or scientific discipline such as Psychology.

Our primary reason for such a consideration stems from an appreciation of the role which philosophy plays in the development of scientific and academic disciplines. As shall be discussed in more detail subsequently, this role is one which both expands and restricts the range of inquiry permitted by the particular discipline.

More importantly for present purposes, the role of philosophy in shaping social institutions including, but not restricted to, educational institutions, cannot be fully appreciated without a simultaneous concern with the historical context which is given by the identification of major social events and their consequences on the thoughts and behavior of people.

In a very real sense, the sequence of events referred to has resulted in a conceptual change of the social universe which is similar to the change accompanying Copernicus' recognition of a new physical order of the universe 500 years ago. The analogy between the two events may be made even more strongly; whereas, in Copernicus' time the world was viewed as "earth-centered," and it was revolutionary to think of it as a solar system.

Equally true, in a European dominated world, it is revolutionary to think of the world as being "Asian or African-centered." The importance of conceiving the world as European-based versus African-based is easily appreciated if we remember that most of our standards of "normality" of human behavior are shaped by the adoption of one perspective or another.

However, it is the general principle which is of primary concern in this article—the fact that different perspectives do exist, and that these perspectives affect the observations and conclusions not only of lay people, but of psychologists as well.

The importance of such differences in perspectives, as they relate to academic fields such as Psychology, is the primary concern of that branch of academic inquiry termed "the Philosophy of Science." The study of this subject not only acquaints one with the effect of different perspectives on scientific inquiry but also, to the extent that it pays attention to the history of science, informs us as to what created these perspectives in the first place. There is a close, intimate relationship between the "Philosophy of Science" and the "History of Science," as academic disciplines. Whether history shapes philosophy more than philosophy shapes history is yet an issue of controversy—at least to the extent that the two subject areas can be differentiated at all —but there is no controversy surrounding the fact that both affect the practice of science.

Psychology is one of those sciences affected even though it is not a "science" in the same sense as are physics and chemistry. In fact, it is precisely because Psychology is a "soft," "human-related," science, that the effects of history and philosophy are so important. Why this should be so can be appreciated if we note that the problems with which Psychology is usually concerned typically involve answers to "Why" types of questions. For example, a common question in psychology is why a person behaves the way he or she does. Strictly speaking, such a question is outside the limits of "science" since "science" does not involve itself with the answers to "Why" type questions. Or, perhaps more precisely stated, scientific causality is not the same thing as psychological causality. Questions concerning "What? and "How?" are considered the proper domain of Science; whereas questions of "Why?" are considered the proper domain of philosophy.

The relevance of this is clear from the title of this sketch. What kind of "causality" exists with respect to Voodoo? Or, more generally, "What kind of causality is recognized by non-European philosophical perspectives?" What is the implication of such causality for the development of an African Psychology?

The present sketch is designed to offer some preliminary answers to these and related questions. It is important, first of all, as was mentioned earlier, to acknowledge the historical context in which an increase of interest in "Black" and "African" Psychology has emerged. An acknowledgement of such will thus enable us to speculate on some of the philosophical concomitants of these historical events. We can then describe some of the implications these philosophical aspects have for the creation and maintenance of an African Psychology.

The Historical Context of African Psychology I: Watergate

The significance of "Watergate" for African Psychology, and all other academic pursuits, is that it has revealed the weakness of the authority structure in America. While the particular authority structure in Watergate was political or governmental, the ramifications of the entire affair have affected authority structures in science, medicine, and law. There is an increased prevalence of "malpractice" suits in science. The number of student revolts can be also interpreted as an assault upon the authority structure of academia. The number of "Black Studies" Departments urged and/or created in recent years is also an indication of the extent to which traditional acceptance of academic authority has declined.

It is important to note that education has its own authority structure, as does politics and other human societal activities. By definition, such authority structures are generally immune to attack or serious question, let alone blatant disrespect. However, the years immediately prior to and concomitant with Watergate have seen systematic and widespread attacks on authority structures and figures of all kinds.

These phenomena have had certain philosophical consequences as well. It is perhaps apparent that problems of epistemology, the validity of knowledge, have an intricate connection with problems of authority, irrespective of specific field. This is, of course, because the authorities are presumed to have "expertise" in terms of the knowledge connected with their particular field. When such people are attacked, either personally or indirectly by implication, there is a simultaneous attack on their knowledge base as well. Such people are no longer thought as "infallible" or capable of doing or knowing anything that is false.

These epistemological issues concerning the validity of knowledge form a major part of the work of philosophers of science and are relevant to the study of African Psychology. In essence, the question is whether an African Psychology can or should adopt the same epistemological bases as do other branches of scientific inquiry. This question is different from the question concerning causality, referred to earlier. The questions are related, of course, but they are analytically distinct. For example, the question of epistemology might involve consideration of the role that "wisdom of the ancestors" has in supporting the veracity of given proposition. That African Psychology considers the unrecorded testimony of deceased ancestors as a valid source of authority for information concerning the psychological state of Black people is perhaps one of its unique attributes. It is typically the case that people rely on printed European or European-trained authorities for the assessment of most psychological principles. This tendency has, however, been altered as a result of the Watergate affair; people are no longer reluctant to question authority, and this reluctance has provided a favorable climate for the serious consideration of alternative sources and, by extension, alternative ways of thinking and perceiving. The discipline of African Psychology has been a beneficiary of such intellectual skepticism.

The Historical Context of African Psychology II:
The Middle Eastern War

A further blow to the authority structure of the European world came as a result of Israel's defeat in the 1973 Middle Eastern War. It is perhaps obvious that an authority structure, and the knowledge base upon which it is constructed, can be no stronger than the political integrity of the country involved. When a nation wages war, it risks not only the lives of its soldiers, but also it risks the vulnerability of its ideological support system. This ideological system contains basic philosophical premises, many of which concern epistemological preferences. To the extent that the Jewish ideological system permeates the intellectual atmosphere of the United States—to that extent the intellectual climate within which African Psychology operates has been altered as a result of the Middle Eastern War. The specific areas in which this effect has occurred is perhaps better left to another article. In this context, all that is necessary is to remind ourselves that much of the discipline of traditional Psychology owes its origins to certain characteristics of Jewish ideological thought. This is not to say that people like Freud have nothing to contribute to the understanding of African people, but that such contributions are perhaps seen in a different perspective now that the ideological supremacy surrounding them has been severely shaken. This shaking has facilitated the emergence of African Psychology as an alternative philosophical and ideological system for the understanding of the psychology of African and other non-European people.

The Historical Context of African Psychology III: The Vietnam War

What was said with regard to the Middle Eastern War in reference to Israel may also be said with regard to the Vietnam War in reference to the United States. Whatever else one might want to say about the war, it is fairly obvious that one of the victims of it has been the credibility of the authorities responsible for the waging of the war. Again this lessening of confidence in the authority structure has affected non-governmental areas of life as well and academia in particular. That many academic people participated in the conduct of the war simply hastened the spread of a loss of confidence in the intellectual and academic authority structure.

It should be apparent that our concern here is not with an assessment of whether or not the war in Vietnam was "lost," or, if so, by whom. The only concern is to make explicit some of the costs involved in waging that war. The chief cost is a widespread loss of confidence in the authority structure. This has affected non-governmental areas of life as well, academia in particular. That many academic people participated in the conduct of the war simply hastened the spread of a loss of confidence in the intellectual and academic authority structure.

In any case, the field of African Psychology has again been the beneficiary of the general loss of confidence in the authority structure since the philosophical bases of African Psychology were not consistent with this authority structure and, in some cases, antagonistic to it. In their search for alternative ways of conceptualizing man and the psychology of man, many people found the principles of African Psychology useful.

The Historical Context of African Psychology IV: The Demise of the Civil Rights Movement

The final historical event which has had a beneficial effect on the emergence and acceptance of African Psychology is the demise of a series of activities generically referred to as the "Civil Rights Movement." It is perhaps not immediately obvious that African Psychology has been a beneficiary of this decline in civil rights activity. However, it can be noted that virtually all "Black-oriented" academic programs came about after the end of civil rights action. Indeed, one might argue that the precise purpose of some of the civil rights action was to establish the kind of "Black Studies" programs which would be predicated on its failure to exist as a stable movement. In other words, the "Movement" was to become institutionalized if it was to succeed at all; and this institutionalization would be achieved at its demise.

There is another area, however, in which the demise of the Civil Rights Movement contributed to the development of African Psychology. This area concerns the philosophy of the movement, insofar as that philosophy was based on the idea that Black people in America were more American than they were African. Such a philosophy was, of course, necessary for the Civil Rights Movement to accomplish many of its goals with respect to the integration of Black people into American public facilities. The philosophy did overlook, however, the existence of large numbers of Black people who were not particularly interested in integration with Whites and who, if asked, would have identified themselves as Africans rather than Americans.

It would seem from the label that African Psychology would also adopt this particular identification stance. However, African Psychology is concerned not so much with a specific answer to the question of Black identity but, rather, with focusing attention on the question itself: Is the Black person in America basically African or basically American? While this question has always been fundamental to a proper understanding of the psychology of Black people, it was not until the demise of the Civil Rights Movement that it became sharply in focus.

While four historical events (Watergate, Middle East, Vietnam, and the Civil Rights Movement) are in many ways unique, they are common insofar as they have affected the growth and development of African Psychology. Their commonality of effect stems from the challenge which they each, in their own way, offered to the authority structure or "Establishment." This challenge, as we have seen, brought with it certain articulated and unarticulated philosophical attacks on the ideology which has governed the relationship between Whites and Non-whites, not only in America but throughout the world. As a result of such attacks, it is now clear that Whites or Europeans are no longer the standard by which the psychology of people is judged. However, saying that one standard no longer exists is not the same thing as saying that an alternative does exist. The development of such an alternative, even if the need for such is painstakingly obvious, does not occur automatically or without struggle. The fact that the struggle being waged by Blacks is, in fact, an ideological or philosophical one—and perhaps has always been so—is not something which is generally recognized and accepted. Even less generally recognized is that such philosophical activities are directly related to the study of a particular area of science such as psychology. The remainder of this paper will attempt to delineate more explicitly some of the philosophical issues involved, and the manner in which African Psychology, as an academic discipline, attempts to grapple with them.

The Issue of Valid Knowledge or "Truth"

On what basis should a person accept the truth of a given statement or proposition? Does it depend on the credentials of the person making the statement? If so, what sort of credentials are necessary for what degree of acceptance? Are there cultural differences with respect to the acceptance of any given statement? If so, which culture can be said to have the "Truth?"

These are not easy questions to answer, and African Psychology does not pretend to offer final and definitive answers. We have suggested, however, that historical events often raise such questions and shape our responses to them. This is particularly the case when we are dealing with "authorities" as the primary source of valid knowledge. In the first instance these authorities are people, who have become identified with particular books or the principles and laws contained in such books.

It should be noted in this context that writing, as we know it, dates back only to some 500 years or so. Does this mean, then, that prior to that time no knowledge existed, or that whatever knowledge did exist was not valid? It is doubtful whether many would maintain such a proposition. Yet the implication is there if one restricts sources of valid knowledge to the appearance of the printed word. This issue is particularly important for students since much of contemporary education requires that one "cites authorities"—the written record. The educational process of requiring students to perform such citation accomplishes two objectives: (1) it reminds, or perhaps "teaches," the student that his or her own knowledge is by definition faulty; and (2) it reinforces whatever authority system exists with respect to the particular subject matter being studied.

We should be clear to state that we are not saying that reliance on external authorities is always improper or destined to lead one in an erroneous direction; indeed, civilization itself would not be possible if it were not for the existence of established authority for the determination of valid knowledge. What we are saying, however, is that "Established Authority" is not always right, as the events of recent years have revealed.

Philosophers and philosophers of science often distinguish between two different sources of knowledge or "epistemologies." These include, on one hand, external sources and, on the other, internal sources. The former include all of those authorities which reside "outside of self"; e.g., books, other people, etc. The latter include the Self as the ultimate authority of Truth and Falsity.

The discipline of science has adopted the former, external, mode of acquiring valid knowledge and has adopted the procedure of experimentation and observation as the requisite knowledge tools. To the extent that Psychology has defined itself as a "science," it too has adopted such tools. It is clear, however, that the adoption of such tools for the study of living, conscious people is a procedure far different from that involved in the examination of inanimate objects.

This does not mean that one cannot gain knowledge from the observation and perhaps experimentation on other people; such knowledge, however, will be only as valid as it accords with the meaning given to such behavior by the actor himself. This issue of meaning is one which has historically plagued efforts to acquire knowledge about living people through traditional scientific psychological methods. The problem stems from the same sort of considerations discussed earlier with respect to questions. The objects of science are typically described only with respect to their positions in space and time, and an accounting of their mass. Since such objects do not "think," it is unnecessary to incorporate into an explanatory scheme any dimension concerning the "meaning" of an object's behavior. Such is not the case with respect to the behavior of people.

Many philosophers, because of these and other difficulties in determining the validity of external sources of knowledge, favor internal sources. The problem here is that there is no way to verify the information acquired since it is by definition personal. It is clear that this only becomes a "problem" if such verification is necessary or desirable. An example of such internal sources of knowledge is given by the concept of "revelation." Is the person who claims to have had knowledge "revealed" to him or her any less of an authority than one who claims to have read the knowledge from a book or some other external authority?

The Issue of "Objectivity"

Is there such a thing as an "Objective" or unbiased, observation? This question has also commanded the attention of philosophers and philosophers of science.

The problem involves whether or not man can be considered separated from his objects of observation. Early 19th Century there seemed to be little doubt that he could. However, as the science of Physics developed in the latter part of the nineteenth and early twentieth century, it became clear that there was no sharp distinction between the scientist as an observer, and the minute molecules he was attempting to observe. In fact, the smaller the molecules observed, the more likely it was that the scientist himself was participating in the behavior of the molecules. Such a state of affairs led to the development of the "Heisenberg Principle," the relevance of which to the study of man's behavior is becoming increasingly obvious.

The purpose here is not to examine in detail the scientific and philosophical intricacies of the Heisenberg "Uncertainty" principle; it is merely to demonstrate that many physicists have abandoned the notion of "Objectivity" that is prevalent in much of contemporary Psychology. This is particularly anomalous since Psychology often purports to adopt Physics as a model for theoretical development.

The point for us to consider is that "objectivity" as traditionally defined, is impossible. This is particularly so in the study of human behavior, where the observer's own value system determines what behavior will be examined, and what questions will be asked concerning that behavior. It should be noted in this connection that the questions a person asks often are answers to the questions not asked. For example, to ask a man, "When did you stop beating your wife?" carries with it an implicit affirmative answer to the unasked question, "Did you ever beat your wife?" An analogous situation exists with respect to the question: "Are Black people less intelligent than white people because of their environment or because of their genes?" The question, thus phrased, answers negatively the unasked question as to whether Blacks are equal to or superior to whites in intelligence.

While "objectivity" in the sense of "unbiased" is thus impossible to achieve in Psychology, it is possible for psychologists to reach an agreement as to what constitutes a given state of affairs. Such an agreement is based, normally, on a consensus of the opinion of those who are actively involved in the pursuit of some particular area of psychological inquiry. The question is not whether a given proposition is "true" or not, but whether certain people agree that it is true. Quite often, particularly in the physical sciences, it is a matter of convenience whether A is true or B is true. For example, it is sometimes convenient to view the nature of light as a particle; at other times, for other purposes, it is more convenient to view light as a wave. It is the purpose of the scientist to determine which is to be the case in any given situation.

We may note, in this context, that a similar situation might exist with respect to the question as to whether Black people are "African" or "American." The answer, in the final analysis, might depend on whose convenience is served by one response as opposed to the other. A truly "objective" answer to this question, and many other important questions in Psychology, is simply impossible.

The Issue of Causality

If a person imputes his illness to the fact that he failed to visit his mother-in-law the preceding week, is he considered an unintelligent person? What causes illness, or, more generally, what is a cause?

It is not our intent in this article to answer this question, but only to show its relevance to an African Psychology. The question cannot be considered independently of the issues discussed above with regard to "objectivity" and "truth."

Within the philosophical dictates of Western civilization, a "cause" must be distinguishable from its "effect." But does this not involve a separation between Event X and Event Y? Are such events any more distinguishable than is an observer from his objects of observation which, we found earlier, was to a large extent arbitrary? Moreover, for Event X to be a "cause" of Event Y, it is said that Event X must "come before" Event Y. Does this temporal sequence always exist; i.e., how important is it that the "effect" comes after the "cause?" Do all cultures adopt a linear time frame so as to make such an inference of causality "true?"

It is in the context of the answers to these questions that the title of this article might become more meaningful. We have not dealt extensively with these particular characteristics of African culture or people which one might typically expect in an article concerning "African Psychology." However, it should not be concluded from this omission that such characteristics are irrelevant; it is merely that, in our opinion, they are subordinate to a consideration of some of the more philosophical issues involved. By way of conclusion, it might be useful to speculate on some of the specific characteristics of African people which will serve to elucidate the issues discussed.

One of the first of these to note is the character of the African conception of self as extended in time and space. This conception has certain implications for Africans both as observers or scientists and as subjects or objects of observation. It may also set the parameters of "convenience" with respect to the determination of "truth."

The African conception of time is another area in which future research is important. African music, in particular, is reflective of a temporal consciousness which is different from the European, as are the related activities of song and dance.

Also important are the substantive content areas concerning the relevance of the skin-color producing substance melanin, particularly as this substance affects the operation of the central nervous system and, by implication, a person's basic intelligence.

Finally, the entire area of African philosophy, as this is manifested on a daily basis—in ceremonies, rituals, family, religion, etc.—deserves systematic examination in light of the New World Order in which we currently find ourselves.

It is clear that such an examination will require the creation of new and distinctive methodologies; this, however, should be viewed as a welcome challenge to those concerned with the development of an African Psychology.

[1978]

BECOMING

PIERCING THE PARADIGM

Oturupon Meji

II	II
II	II
I	I
II	II

Then, he took his situation under consideration and went to a babalawo for advice. He was advised that it was because of his Ancestral rites which he had neglected that he was in such confusion. He was told to go to the graves of his ancestors and to pay homage and ask guidance. After he had done so, he started to enjoy his life.

Section II, Becoming, moves a step further in the explanation of science and culture and their relationship to the self. Beginning with what many believe to be the classic treatise in Black psychology, *Voodoo or I.Q: An Introduction to African Psychology*, the question, "Who let the dogs out?" was heard loud and clear. Co-authored by Syed Khatib, D. Phillip McGee, Na'im Akbar, and myself this fragment captured our ongoing collaboration, conversations, and considerations concerning the need to think differently about the psychology of black people. It also represents the value and power of collective scholarship. *Voodoo or I.Q* signaled the onset of our African psychology project. It not only served as a preview into the work of its four authors, but also it generated and guided the theory, research, and practice of the second and third generations of black psychologists and remains the benchmark reference for the field of African psychology.

58 Becoming: Piercing the Paradigm

Syed Khatib's grasp of the sociology of knowledge, the philosophy of science, and the politicization of the episteme was forecast in this article. The ability to critique the limitations of white psychology definitions, theories, and formulations was grounded here and further legitimized in the assignment of black scholars the task of discerning the difference between "black studies" and the "study of black people."

In foretelling the interest in psychobiology and its birth child the genome project, D. Phillip McGee's contribution to this classic spoke of the critical aspects of blackness; i.e., melanin in understanding the biological basis of African consciousness. In studying and teaching about melanin Phil helped to clarify the distinction yet connection between epidermal melanin and neuromelanin, the bio-spiritual markers of human consciousness. First introduced in this article McGee posited that black behavior was due to more than just skin color and that a full appreciation of the psychology of the people would require a new conception of the blending of the physical and the spiritual.

The work of Na'im Akbar who is a trained clinical psychologist in the field of personality development and dysfunctioning was set in this article as well. Clarifying the centrality of self-knowledge as a critical factor in establishing a healthy personality, Akbar's contribution reshaped the field of black personality and called forth the need to understand the "African self" if one is to truly comprehend the self-knowledge critical to black personality.

My interests in the areas of African American family dynamics, the psychological aspects of mythology, black child development and parenting systems of human transformation and development, identity formation, and human consciousness have all been guided by the initial framework established in this article. Throughout my career, I have had the desire to understand and identify the correct position and parameters for illuminating (understanding) the spirit (psychology) of African people. It has been within the content of condition and the context of culture that I have tried to clarify the meaning of being human for African people. *Voodoo or I.Q.: An Introduction to African Psychology* was later reprinted in a pamphlet series by the Institute of Positive Education (1976) and appeared in the collection of papers entitled *Reflections on Black Psychology*, edited by Smith, Burlew, Mosley, and Whitney (1979). In retrospect

Voodoo or I.Q: An Introduction to African Psychology has served me and hopefully others in axiomatically recognizing the need and value of recognizing the fundamental "Africanity" of African people. It has directed me in my work to be obedient to the emerging clarification of an authentically African hermeneutic and epistemology.

Sketch 5 focuses on culture and its definition as a scientific construct representing language, behavior, knowledge, symbols, and values of a people. The chapter continues by pointing to the understanding that human development is a result of the knowledge of one's history, which is to be gained by rejection of ideological oppression via transformation.

Sketch 6 carefully traces the origins of man's ability to be subjective and how Westerners' idea of self-evolved, making special note of the importance of the central nervous system. It is said that the self evolved subjectively in three modes: phylogenesis, ontogenesis, and autogenesis. The chapter ends with the two biosemiotic laws of "will" and "thought," which further explain the idea of African oneness and European individualism. Sketch 7 connects this section to those chapters to come by addressing the issues of both science and the struggle for liberation. One must be aware that science has been an effective tool in expressing the domination and racism of the oppressor. Being that science is a reconstruction of a people's set of systematic ideas and beliefs, or "common sense," it is necessary to reclaim culture and reconstruct science in order to control the interpretations of reality, so as to bridge the gaps and gain liberation.

African Science and Black Research: The Consciousness of Self

We suggest that it is probably through an understanding or self-realization particular to the Europeans that will allow us to see the clear reflections of Western consciousness in Western science. Likewise, we contend that it will probably be through our understanding of the particular phylogenetic process of self-realization for African peoples that we will derive a basis for establishing African science and its requisite methodologies.

The Meta-Epistemological Dilemma

Axiomatically, we recognize that there exists a fundamental core of dissimilarity between Africans and Europeans. We, Blacks, are African people by virtue of our genetic and cultural ancestral heritage. African-Americans are African peoples who have been separated from their natural environment and have been incarcerated in European-American conceptions of reality. This conceptual incarceration creates the severe need to explore and explicate those differences relevant to African and European conceptions of reality. It also provides us with a kind of meta-epistemological dilemma. The recognition of this conceptual incarceration also points to the appropriateness of discovering and heightening the psychological similarities amongst African peoples.

The conceptual incarceration of African peoples inhibits the Black intellectual. We recognize, for instance, that the Black intellectual is limited in what he can know about himself by what he does know about himself, even though he probably does not know what he knows. The knowledge of self is critical to the liberation of the African conception of reality. Yet, we are trained, educated, and indoctrinated into believing and accepting the Western conception of reality, which by its nature is an abbreviated or attenuated understanding of the total reality. Hence, the meta-epistemological dilemma the Black intellectual finds himself in is one in which he seeks an awareness of reality or knowledge, yet the parameters of the definition of what constitutes knowledge is defined according to the Western conceptions of reality which is, in itself, distorted. At this point, consequently, our task is to develop our intrinsic African apperception, to become conscious of our own consciousness, which is fundamentally different from being aware of accepted reality. It is, therefore, necessary that Africans define and crystallize our knowledge of self and kind, our apperceptive mass.

Basic to our awakening or becoming conscious of our own consciousness is a clear recognition of the process of self-realization. If we return to the question of the nature of the particular phylogenetic processes of self-realization for Africans vs. European peoples, then the issue which must be discussed is a proposed differential phylogenetic process.

A Theory of Differential Self-Realization

Consciousness, Self-Realization, and Knowledge

The genesis of man's subjectivity or consciousness occurs in three modes: phylogenesis, ontogenesis, and autogenesis. Phylogenetically, man's consciousness arises in the evolution of the species. Ontogenetically, it reveals itself in the development from ovum into completed organism or the development of the "body person." Third, it takes shape as a form of autogenesis of existential acts.

In terms of the phylogenesis of life, we know that the capacity of life appears in the genes. Genes are macromolecules within the chromosomes which bear the information specifying the structure of the species type—including the melanocytic capacity. Parenthetically, we suggested at the outset that it is the presence of melanic genes which we think may be the key to suggest differential phylogenetic process of self-realization.

The highest known communication system for most known vertebrates is their central nervous system. Man, however, is believed to differ from the vertebrates in that a further or even higher communication system is super imposed over the central nervous system. This higher system of communication has been called the "logical act of consciousness." Until recently, this higher system was not believed to be established by nature in the form of a physical endowment. Consequently, most research and theory dealing with the development of consciousness has been autogenetic studies, which are based on determining the effects of existential experiences on the establishment and/or development of consciousness of the species.

Some research has suggested that insight and thought will emerge together with developing speech and once emerged, they work to transform perception, emotions, and behavior in specific ways. This suggests that the state of channeling the hormonal and chemical excitations in the central nervous system is inhibited and/or released with the emergence of thought and will in conjunction with language. The central nervous system, therefore, functions to organize information in novel and particular ways. We recognize, however, that the channeling of hormonal and chemical excitations in the central nervous system can be cast in particular molds of varying excitation configurations. Consequently, an understanding of the phylogenesis of consciousness is predicated upon a clear understanding of the relationship between genetic definition and the differential hormonal and chemical excitation patterns in the central nervous system. Thus, we must return to a discussion of the melanocytic capacity of the species.

Professor D. Philip McGee[1] has pointed out that there is a direct biological relationship between the chemical melanin and the central nervous system. McGee notes, for instance, that the melanocyte, which is a specialized pigment cell, and the nerve cell, which is the basis for the central nervous system, both develop from the neural crest of the human embryo. That is, both melanocyte and the nerve cell start out as the same thing and in the process of cellular specialization make one aspect the nerve cell and the other aspect becomes the melanocyte cell.

We know that man's central nervous system performs a critical information processing role which is essential for optimal neurological and metabolic functioning. We believe that through particular ways of channeling hormonal and chemical excitations, the central nervous system organizes information in novel and particular ways. The data found in neuro-physiological, neuro-chemical, and neuro-hormonal research suggest that there is a positive correlation between specific levels of sensory activity and states of pigmentation. Relationships have also been found to exist between melanin and the cerebellum, between it and the reticular formation and the red nucleus. Unfortunately, the precise nature of these relationships have yet to be defined. Nevertheless, one is compelled to believe that the predominance of melanin is more than an added ingredient, which refines the central nervous system and produces a highly sensitive sensory motor network. A rethinking of the relationship between melanin and the central nervous system suggests that melanin and its structural development parallels the development of the nerve cell into the central nervous system.

The rethinking of this author suggests that the relationship between the melanocyte cell and the nerve cell, both developing from the neural crest, is the basis for a complementary sensory system network, which has a dichotomous feature. That is, through cellular specialization one component of the sensory network evolves from and through the melanocyte cell and the other component evolves from the nerve cell. The result of this dichotomic complementary development is that the human sensory network has two aspects. The aspect developing from the nerve cell is what we all recognize to be the central nervous system. The unmentioned aspect which develops from the melanocyte cell should be called the essential melanic system. The rationale for this classification should be evident later in the discussion.

A reading of biosemiotic laws points out, however, that self-realization or inner self consciousness and the recognition of alien essences (conscious of other) are conflicting intentions. To overcome this conflicting contrast, the next evolutionary step in the phylogenesis of life was achieved. This step is represented by what the geneticist calls "the diploidy of chromosomes." Here, couples of equal and different primal units combined in what is called symbiosis. It is suggested that via this diploid cellular association one of the primal units could attend to self-realization and the other could attend to fusion with alien essences. This new inner polarization is necessary in order for the subjectivity of the organism to communicate with other alien entities while simultaneously realizing its own self.

If we examine the relationship between melanin and the central nervous system, one could suggest that the neural crest of the human embryo is at the stage of phylogenesis where self-realization is a unity. The cellular specialization, which results in a distinct nerve cell and melanocyte cell can parallel the process of diploid cellular association.

In terms of consciousness is it not possible that the diploid cellular association was such that the neural crest through cellular specialization divides wherein the nerve cell and, subsequently, the central nervous system attend to fusion or communication with other alien essences? The purpose of this fusion or communication is to make the entity conscious of others. The melanocyte cell, we suggest, develops into the essential melanic system and attends to self-realization—the purpose of which is to make the entity conscious of its own essence.

In recognizing that a small percent of the species does not have the ability to naturally produce significant amounts of melanin, we suggest that, for them, the minority, the process of symbiosis would not in all likelihood be a proposition of equal units combining together. Likewise, if cellular association for the neural crest involves the melanocyte and the nerve cells, then the proposition of symbiosis for those without an essential ingredient would be a variation of the combining of equal units. If it is, in fact, true that the phylogenetic process of self-realization is related to the establishment of consciousness, then we could suggest and understand that the consciousness of the melanocytic people and the non-melanocytic people would subsequently differ.

If this is proven to be true, it would also help in the understanding that those of the species with less developed essential melanic systems would emphasize in their consciousness an orientation or dependency for outward validation. Likewise, one could expect that those of the species who have a truly balanced sensory system would emphasize in their consciousness a synthesis or union or complementarity between one's essence and external things. Parenthetically, we note with interest that in the areas of the world where the largest number of high-melanic possessing peoples are found, so-called para-normal powers, psy-chokinesis and precognition, generally referred to as voodoo or witchcraft, are also found.

Science and the Self

The above discussion suggests that a discussion of science and the development of consciousness are paramount. As noted earlier, however, the discussion of the development of conscious-ness has been primarily autogenetic. Consequently, the logical act of consciousness and the development of science are traditionally viewed as being determined by existential experiences. Though limited, this kind of analysis does have some explicative import. For instance, in terms of the effects of existential experience we can note that those men who found their survival at issue with the natural elements of Northern Europe, and those who found theirs at issue with the elements of Africa and Asia experienced two totally different situations. A closer examination of this geograph-ical fact is rather revealing. The man who came to be known as the European was nurtured in what most ecologists describe as a very hostile environment. Not only were the natural elements harsh and bitter (a fact evidenced by his movement into the caves), but survival itself depended on their personal hostility. A scarcity of food and other of life's materials gave way to only the most competitive and strong. Thus, the European found himself competing for not only resources but life itself. The issue became one of man against nature—including other men.

On the other hand, those men who found their survival at issue with Africa, those who came to be known as Africans, were nurtured by an environment, that with the exception of beast of prey offered warmth as well as an overabundance of food and life's material. As a consequence, it was not necessary to be as competitive as their European counterparts. That is, the African did not find himself at issue with other men over a scarcity of resources. The environment itself gave cooperative efforts to the most rewards and the African felt or thought of himself as being in accordance with nature and in commune with his fellow man. Thus, the issue became one of man with nature.

These experiential distinctions have more real explicative import when added to the above-suggested discussion of the evolution of consciousness (self) in man.

The Extended Self and African Science

In review, the issues of philosophy and the philosophy of science can note that the general characteristics of European and Euro-American philosophy are different from the characteristics of African and African-American philosophy. For instance, the European worldview is tempered with the general guiding principle of individual survival and mastery of nature. These have affected the nature of European values and customs, including what is considered science. If one examines the typical values and customs representative of the European community, the over-emphasis on competition, individual existence, "rights," independence, separateness, uniqueness, and difference is striking. The subsequent psycho-behavioral modalities characterizing the European community, likewise, are reflective of its philosophical worldview.

A study of the African worldview suggests, in comparison, that it is tempered with the general guiding principle of the survival of the collective body, tribe, and harmony with nature. These, in turn, are reflected in a value for and cultural expressions of the sense of cooperation, interdependence, collective responsibility, commonality, similarity, and sameness. The subsequent psycho-behavioral modalities characterizing the African community are also reflective of its philosophical worldview.

Even though it is predictable that when "African data" is processed by the guiding principles of European and Euro-American orientations, results and conclusions distort the integrity of the original nature of the data, the total effect of these different worldviews on the nature of science has yet to be understood.

Science and the Self

At this point, let us suggest that a peoples' philosophy or guiding principles may not be an autogenetic process. In fact, we can now suggest that a peoples' philosophical orientation may well be the consequence of the phylogenetic process of self realization and, subsequently, science or the nature of science is rooted in man's ontogenetic evolution of the sensory system.

With its emphasis on the mechanical explanations, determinism and reductionism, the nature of science in the Western world speaks to, or reflects itself in, conceptions of reality which parallel the conception of self; i.e., independence, individualism, uniqueness, separateness. We contend that the nature of the sensory system itself determines how one conceives of the self as well as the universe around oneself. We further contend that if the nature of the sensory system is as hypothesized, then the differential process of self-realization would express itself in differential orientations to the world. For example, if there is this complementary sensory system network, and, if the process of self-realization is dependent upon the development of consciousness, then one could expect different types of consciousnesses and sciences as a result of the nature of the sensory system.

It should be understood that for those people whose sensory system is attenuated, lacking in its complete complementary nature, the process of understanding oneself and the universe would be outward, while those people with complete sensory systems, having both the essential melanic system component and the central nervous system component, would be both inward and outward. Those with only the central nervous system would become conscious of self through outward validation, likewise, science for them would follow the same path as self-realization.

Similarly, those people with the central nervous system and the essential melanic system would become conscious of self through being aware of alien essences, outward validation, and awareness of its own essence, inward validation. The nature of science in the latter would naturally be different. The nature of self for the melanic producing peoples with full complementary sensory systems would be interdependent based on the complementarity of sensory receptors and, therefore, extended. We note as an example, the common feeling among African peoples is that one's self is part of the self of other African peoples. That is, that one's self-definition is dependent upon the corporate definition of one's people. In effect, the collective definition transcends the individual definition of self, and the individual conception of self extends to include one's self and kind. The transcendent relationship (between self and kind) has been called the extended-self.

If one were to epitomize African science, it would best be described by the philosophy of rhythm or harmony. Based on this conceptualization one can further understand why the behavioral modalities which are characteristic of African lifestyles throughout the Diaspora are based on; (1) the particular phylogenesis of self-realization; and (2) the autogenesis of the several philosophical assumptions and conception of reality. Combined, these two invariably reflect the sense of ontological harmony, synthesis, and rhythm. Related to this is an African philosophical orientation, which emphasizes the notion of interdependence. This notion conceives of man and all the other elements of the universe as being part of a unified and integrated whole. As stated before, the African philosophical tradition determines the two fundamental operational orders or guiding beliefs that man is part of the natural rhythm of nature, or one with nature, and the conception of the universe as a vitalistic pneumaticism. This latter conception means a belief in the sense of vital solidarity, or survival of the tribe. Descriptively, it refers to a kind of vital attitude about one's existence or what Westerners term a sense of common fate.

In accordance with these two aspects, the phylogenesis of self-realization and the autogenesis of an existential worldview, the African is aware of experience as an intense complementary rhythmic connection between the person and reality. We contend this is because of the presence of the complementary sensory system.

The dominant aspect of African science and Black research, therefore, must reflect in its assumptions, questions, and methodology the polyvalent principle of the oneness of being.

The Question of Research

The question of research in the Black community, however, presents a special or additional set of problems for the Black researcher. We are, at the same time, part of the Black community and the inheritors of a procedure, research methodology, which characteristically has exploited and misused that community. We must recognize that we are the users of a procedure, which is predicated upon the assumption of separateness and independence, even after the thinking of Heisenberg has enjoyed some popularity. We are part of the community and at the same time forced to be mentally outside of it.

Subsequently, we are initially seen as a continuation of a long line of activity, which has never really benefited the Black community. It is, naturally so, because we have not dared to ask or think the so-called unanswerable. As long as the Black researcher asks the same questions and theorizes the same theories as his White counterpart, the Black researcher will continue to be part and parcel of a system which perpetuates the misunderstanding of Black reality and consequently, contributes to our degradation. We will continue to practice science as it is, rather than contribute to the development of science as it is becoming.

In recognition of the epistemological dilemma of Black intellectual activity, we must immediately see the necessity of developing an intellectual tradition, which particularly respects our people and is compelled to reflect in its questions, methodologies and procedures the essence of being Black. We must liberate ourselves from this conceptual incarceration, which inhibits our ability to think. We must go beyond rejection and begin to conceive of ourselves and reconstruct our reality in response to our own essence.

[1976]

Understanding Human Transformation: The Praxis of Science and Culture

The issue of science and culture and their role in the area of human development requires one to explicate the meaning of the essential phenomena, science, culture, and human transformation, as well as the emergent definition of their interaction. Part and parcel of the discussion relevant to the topic of this discussion will be to (1) explicate meaning, and (2) identify emergent definitions of human processes. The overriding supposition of this writing is the recognition that human development can only be understood in the context of how a particular people come to know their reality. Accordingly, human transformation can only be understood in the context of a people's particular culture and history. The relevance or authenticity of human transformation for African peoples can only be understood in the context of African culture and history. That is to say, the understanding of human transformation for African peoples necessitates first an understanding of how Africans come to know their reality.

The Role of Culture

The role of culture in the understanding of human reality has in part been misunderstood and confused by the relegation of culture to a concept only representing the stylistic peculiarity of a people. Culture rightfully should be viewed as a scientific construct representing the vast structure of language, behavior, customs, knowledge, symbols, ideas and values which provide a people with a general design for living and patterns for interpreting reality. The factors of culture which influence the general design and patterns for interpreting reality are those which speak to: (1) the structure and origin of the universe, (2) the nature of

being or existence, and (3) the particular character which gov-
erns/defines universal relationships. The way in which a people
address these cosmological, ontological and axiological factors of
culture combine to determine for them a general design for living
and patterns for interpreting reality. What emerges from a people's intrinsic culture definition are issues of ideology, ethos, and
worldview. A people's worldview contains their most comprehensive ideas about order. It naturally reflects their cosmological, axiological and ontological position. A people's ethos emerges from
these same cultural factors as a set of guiding principles, which
reflect their style and sentiment. The ethos of a people represents
their character, tone, quality or mode of being. In this trilogy ideology emerges as the closest concept representing an instrument
for determining how a people should see their reality. It determines in part what is considered good, valuable and appropriate;
and, conversely, what is bad, dangerous and inappropriate in a
people's social milieu. Ideology is the map which clarifies and
gives perspective to problematic aspects of a people's social reality. In so doing, it provides the matrix for creating the collective
conscious of a people. Like the ethos and worldview, it too should
reflect the cultural factors of a people.

Obviously, the relationship between these emergent
aspects of culture are cybernetic. The ethos of a people, for
instance, is made intellectually understandable when the emergent guiding principles are shown to represent an "appropriate"
response, as determined by ideology, to the actuality of their
experience as revealed by their world-view. It is in the process of
each acting with and upon the other that the style or nature of a
people becomes crystallized or concrete.

What is most often understood as culture is in actuality
the manifestations or expressions of culture. They are the aspects
like behavior, ideas, values, language, etc., which mark a people's
sentiment or style. The manifestations of culture are or should be
viewed as the overt expressions of the cultural aspects and factors of a people. Culture is a process that gives a people a general design for living and patterns for interpreting reality and
implies change. In fact, change is an "intrinsic" aspect of the
human constant, culture. It is in the interaction between the
emergent aspects of culture, namely, ideology, ethos, worldview,
and the concrete experiences, the history, of a people that the
construct "culture" continues to change and in changing, the

emergent aspects likewise change. Hence, the construct plays a critical role in understanding human reality and the subsequent issue of human transformation.

It is its interaction with experience that culture takes on the added role of helping to define, select, and create the general design for living and patterns for interpreting reality.

The examination of culture[1] and its relationship to the "meaning" of a people's reality occurs by examining first its factors, cosmology, ontology, and axiology; second, its emergent aspects, ideology, ethos, and worldview; and, third, its manifestations, customs, behavior, language, symbols, ideas, values, etc.

Historically, the meaning of a people's reality and indirectly, their culture, was examined via philosophical inquiry and speculation about the nature of things and the principles, which guide human behavior. Parenthetically, as a consequence of the Greek distortion and its subsequent imprint on modern, particularly Western, man's thinking, most people view the speculation about the nature of things and the principles guiding human behavior as natural and moral philosophy, respectively. Philosophy, in this regard, was viewed as a critical expression of culture. It represented, as Dewey noted, the interpretation of a people's past for the purpose of solving specific problems presently confronting their cultural way of life. It also represented the critical thought of a society. However, with the ascendance of empiricism and experimentation over speculative modes of inquiry, philosophy, as a critical thought, has come under criticism for indulging in and representing only speculation about the human condition. Accordingly, in modern times, philosophy has been replaced by science. Science has become the critical thought of a society. Thus, our attention must next turn to the issue of science.

The Issue of Science

Traditionally, in the Western world science has been defined as a process which seeks to discover and to formulate in general terms, the conditions under which events of various sorts occur. The explanation of such events is defined by statements explicating the determining conditions. The task of science is, therefore, to establish general laws, which serve as instruments for systematic explanation and, in turn, provide the basis for dependable prediction.

Science, as explanation and prediction, accordingly, does not develop in abstract space. The ideas, interests, theories and definition of science exist in a human world; and, human experiences are influenced, if not governed, by culture. It is extremely important, therefore, to recognize that the conduct of science is, subsequently, a process of questioning and analyzing the perceptions, sensations, feelings, and actions, which comprise the experiences and interest of scientists who are cultural animals. The four imperatives of Western science—universalism, communism, disinterestedness, and organized skepticism—must be recognized as the guiding principles which underlie the creative invention of a particular group of cultural animals. Science, as a critical thought, like philosophy, reflects and represents the manifestations—ideas, values, etc., aspects—ideology, ethos, and worldview, and factors—cosmology, ontology and axiology, of a particular culture. The definition of science, as a human activity, is therefore not universal. In fact universalism as an imperative of science emerges from a particular cultural perspective and therefore, is not universal. Since what we know as science represents and reflects someone's culture, it is important to explicate the relationship between culture and science.

It is important to note here that consistent with a previous work,[2] the thinking governing this discussion is guided by the position that African peoples in Africa and throughout the world are bound by a common history, most recently, that of colonialism, slavery and racial oppression, and a commonality of culture. It is important then that we grapple with this supposition of common history and commonality of culture. Boxill[3] has suggested that "to speak of the common history of a group is to attempt to explain some present aspect or character of its members, by reference to a long, or very long line of common ancestry."

A group, therefore, he argues, will be said: "...to have a common history if either its members have a common culture or share a similar sentiment and spirit, and if these likenesses are explained by the fact that each individual is descended from the members of an earlier group distinguished by a common experience and condition."

I would immediately argue that this reference to condition as distinct from experience could and does include the biological definition of a people. Hence, common history is in part dependent upon a common biological condition.

Since the notion of common history depends on experience and condition, it is enough to find one generation of a people with the feeling and perception of having a common culture (spirit) and destiny for it to be appropriate to speak of their descendants as having a common history.

A common history is, therefore, a phenomena characterized by a shared sentiment and spirit which is traceable to or connected by a common experience and/or condition. The obviously critical dimensions of this notion of common history is the underlying theme of culture and the concepts of condition and experience. Clearly stated, the commonality of culture is a condition wherein a people simply share a similar general design for living and patterns for interpreting reality. Different peoples could have a commonality of culture if the factors, aspects and manifestations of their cultures are found to be similar or congruent.

Hence, the generic term, African peoples, has utility because it represents a label for a people who are characterized by a shared sentiment and spirit which is traceable to a common experience and/or condition and who have a similar general design for living and patterns for interpreting reality. The concept of African peoples used in this manner does not deny the specialness of the distinct contemporary experiences of different groups of African peoples; i.e., Africans from Africa, the Antilles and the Americas. In fact, it allows, if not mandates one, to examine how the particular or special histories of various African peoples have influenced our human development.

The relationship between culture and the concrete experience of a people has never been adequately understood. This failure is due in part to a misunderstanding of the human significance and meaning of culture. Most analyses of the relationship have viewed the culture part as represented by values or customs or belief systems of a people and the experience part representing their behavior or history. Understanding was consequently guided by questions of whether culture determines experience or does experience determine culture.

Because this epistemological dilemma may be more a quandary created by Cartesian duality, I will not debate the correctness or error of either statement. What is important to address in this discussion is: (1) the recognition of the connection between science as critical thought and culture, particularly its ideological aspect; and (2) the relationship between a people's critical thought, culture, and human transformation.

The connection between science and the ideological aspect of culture is obvious even if it is seldom made explicit. Ideology is essentially an instrument, which, provides a critique of reality and thereby influences the nature of its awareness (consciousness). As such, and as noted above, ideology defines and guides appropriate behavior or action, and serves to refine and raise the level of practice.[4] Since science is a system of inquiry guided by theory and/or models of reality, it is nothing more than a set of ideas representing reality. It is, in fact, no more than a formal reconstruction of a people's reality.

Since ideology serves to influence a people's awareness of their reality, science—particularly social science, must incorporate in its reconstruction, the prevailing ideological position of its creators. It is extremely important to recognize that the ideas of science and the interest of science, and even the definition of science, is bound in the time and historical condition of the society in which its developers live. The science of which we grapple with today is, without question, influenced by the way in which its developers came to historically understand reality. Therefore, there is no science which is not in part a "social" science.

Since science is a reconstruction of reality, and ideology is an instrument which influences the awareness of reality, science can only reconstruct the awareness which ideology provides. When the social reality is defined by racism and oppression or colonialism and slavery, or in a society where the prevailing ideology is racist, there can be no science that is not oppressive and racist. Science in the West is a reconstruction of racism. One need only note that just as science served this society in the creation and use of technical and industrial power, it also has served it in the creation and use of theories and ideas designed to control the use of power by its oppressed.

Of African thinkers, the artist, more so than the scientist, has seen the connection between culture and oppression. For instance, Paul Robeson throughout most of his career saw culture as an instrument in a people's liberation and, conversely, the suppression or denial of culture as an instrument of their enslavement.

Amilcar Cabral[5] noted that oppression or domination of a people is only secured when the cultural life of a people is destroyed, paralyzed, or at least neutralized. Parenthetically, it may be the case that the different forms of oppression experienced by African peoples is determined by the emphasis placed on destroying, paralyzing or neutralizing the culture of the people under domination.

Cabral goes on to note that the ideal situation for foreign domination is either to liquidate practically all the dominated people or to harmonize the oppressor's economic and political domination of the people without damaging the culture of the dominated. The dilemma of culture is one wherein culture naturally resists its own oppression and the act of oppression requires the elimination of that which naturally resists it. Cabral correctly recognized that in order to escape this "dilemma of culture," the oppressor has to continually create scientific theories which have translated into a permanent state of siege of African peoples. Science, or more correctly, Western science, particularly social science, like the economic and political institutions, is an instrument designed to reflect the culture of the oppressor and to allow for the most efficient domination and oppression of African peoples.

In recognizing the relationship between consciousness, culture and science, our current thinking suggests that culture is the basis of consciousness; and a people's consciousness reveals itself in the science and paradigms created by that culture to assess and evaluate itself. Hence, culture becomes the necessary and sufficient condition for understanding the natural human processes of a people, as well as their liberation from domination.

In effect, as a reconstruction of culture, science and its paradigms are essentially methods for reflecting man's sensation of his own experiential reality; i.e., consciousness. In sensing one's own experiential reality both internal—subjective, and external—objective, consciousness becomes equivalent to awareness.

It is important to realize that when one uses the sciences and paradigms of another culture, one adopts their consciousness and implicit meaning of reality. In so doing, one also limits the natural capacity of the indigenous culture to act or react in relation to nature and the material and spiritual conditions defined by it. Hence, through the consciousness of Western science, the oppressor has limited the capacity of the oppressed to, in Cabral's terms, "create progress" and determine the process of their own history.

As noted above, it is our contention that culture is the thing which naturally resists its own oppression. Culture is, therefore, the mechanism for continuing the history of a people. The oppression of a people is an act designed to remove them from history. That is, to remove them from the "process of history" itself.[6] Hence, oppression only becomes complete when the oppressed become infected with or internalizes the ideological premise, or cultural meaning of their oppressor.

When African peoples, under the guise of being trained in the science, internalized social science and its varied theories, we simultaneously become culturally transformed, and in so doing, participate in eliminating the natural resistance of our own culture to its oppression. Implicit in Western social science is not only a way of thinking, but also the What, How, When, Where, and Why of thinking. Consequently, it is not surprising that we frequently find African thinkers in the name of science, adopting and applying the pathological, deviancy and/or other social-political theories stemming from the ideological definition of the oppressor.

It is only through an accurate understanding of a people's cultural factors—cosmology, ontology and axiology, aspects—ideology, ethos, and worldview, and manifestations—behavior, customs, ideas, etc., that the social scientist is able to accurately represent and interpret the outcomes of their particular human processes. Consistent with Fanon's use of authenticity, the process of science is only authentic when it (the process) reflects, represents and is consistent with the cultural factors, aspects, and manifestations of a people's reality. In brief, science and its associate theories are authentic when they manifest an understanding and appreciation of a people's culture and history and, as Fanon would argue, attempts to either criticize or justify them.

Without understanding the culture of a people, especially the ideological aspect of their culture, science cannot accurately reconstruct their reality. Because it is unable to know how the cultural ideology of one people influences their awareness of reality, science, which develops from another people's cultural base, will always fail to accurately establish general laws which serve as instruments for systematic explanation and provide the basis for dependable prediction. Since science now serves the function of critical thought for a society, its accuracy is extremely consequential to the development of that society. Serious errors have been made concerning the reality of African life as a consequence of: (1) the misinterpretation and de-legitimization of our culture; and (2) the use of knowledge created from a science inconsistent with our culture. The error toward culture we have defined as conceptual incarceration and the error toward knowing as transubstantiation.

Transubstantiation[7] is a process wherein the substance of one culture is transformed into the substance of another culture. The process amounts to a kind of elemental transformation. When the social scientist or researcher does not respect the integrity of a people's cultural perspective particularly its ideological base, he/she is prone to fall victim to what we have defined as the transubstantive error, an error wherein one defines or interprets the behavior and/or medium of one culture with meanings appropriate to and consistent with another culture. For instance, if the cultural substance, or the belief system of one culture as seen and defined by the people of that culture is translated or transformed into the cultural substance or belief system of another culture, then an act of transubstantiation has occurred. To the extent that a people's understanding of their world is misinterpreted in the translation of their belief system one has a "transubstantive error."

The potential for committing the transubstantive error is decreased as one increases the understanding of the cultural substance of a particular people as seen and defined by that particular group of people.

Because the error toward culture denies the basic and general essence by which a people come to know reality, for Africans to participate in the denial of our own culture is an act of participating in one's own dehumanization. We dehumanize ourselves when we (1) placidly adopt another people's science that is inconsistent with our culture; and (2) fail to initiate and develop a science that authentically represents and expresses the reality of African peoples. This we view as conceptual incarceration.

This state of conceptual incarceration inhibits the African thinker from asking the right questions and developing an authentic theory. We are limited in what we can know about African social reality by what we think we know about the dynamics of social reality in general an understanding which is guided by the ideological premise of another people's science. This epistemological dilemma for African social scientists is that we find ourselves seeking an awareness and understanding of our own reality, yet the parameters of the definition of what constitutes knowledge about reality (the ideological base of science) is defined according to non-Black conceptions.

The issue of human transformation, the question of knowing and the role of science as reconstructed reality are obviously complicated by: (1) the implicit ideological aspect embedded in the prevailing definition of science and its associate theories; and (2) the continual and simultaneous changing of African culture. Because cultural change always involves an ideological shift, the emergence of counter ideology warrants some discussion.

Because ideology is an indispensable ingredient in the cultural perspective of a people, it is never absent. It may not always take the form of an organized objective expression, but it is always present. Since ideology serves to influence a people's awareness of their reality, it serves as the nexus between a people's consciousness and condition. Some would even argue that ideology emerges and takes form, becomes objective, in response to a people's consciousness and condition. Such thinking recognizes that ideology emerges in response to that which it influences awareness of, consciousness and experience. In referring to the work of Shils, Karenga[8] notes that ideology develops, or more correctly, a counter ideology develops because there is an objective need for it. In a way, the very conditions that oppress a people create the necessary social consciousness which will resist that oppression. As Karenga points out, "an ideology arises because there are strongly felt needs which are not satisfied by the prevailing outlook, nor give explanation of important experiences....and legitimization of the value and dignity of the persons who feel these needs." It is important to add to this view that ideology, as a tool for explaining experiences, does not simply develop solely as a pure reaction to the conditions being experienced. In the case of the dehumanization of a people, the counter ideology will develop as a consequence of both their cultural consciousness prior to their oppression and the conditions which define that oppression. Hence, the counter ideology is a product of the current concrete conditions and the people's historical culture.

When we adopt theories of science and apply them to our condition, we accept the knowledge produced by these theories and never question whether the information and ideas so produced are, indeed, authentic. We simply conclude that the information, ideas and systems are valid because they emerged from the scientific process. A process which now serves as the instrument for constantly questioning the tacit assumptions and unarticulated prescriptions of previous ideas and interpretations of our behavior, as well as scrutinizing the norms, solutions, and self-image of which past interpretations have endorsed and/or fostered. It is also a process that has, unfortunately, become sacred.

In addressing the way a people define the nature of being, and the structure of reality and the particular character of universal relations (aspects of culture), as well as their customs, ideas, beliefs, behavior, language, etc., (manifestations of culture) culture influences the meaning of reality. It should, therefore, be obvious that a denial or misunderstanding of culture will lead to the development of inauthentic systems and institutions, which will, in turn, cause the misunderstanding of the process of human transformation.

To insure the proper transformation of society, one must reject the ideological oppression as expressed in scientific colonialism and domination. One must reclaim the right of culture, or more specifically, reclaim mastery of one's own productive forces. The act of reclamation requires both an armed struggle or physical defense of one's capacity to act or react in relation to nature and the scientific or ideological struggle, or the act of creating reality, ideas and information.

The reclamation of culture requires the development of an indigenous process of understanding which is consistent with the culture and cultural substance of one's people. It requires the amplification and specification of our shared, symbolic, systematic, and cumulative ideas, beliefs, and knowledge. It requires the reconstruction of our own cultural sensations without compromising the empirical truth of our people's concrete historical condition.

It is in the reclamation of culture and in the creative reconstruction of it as science, that one seizes control over the interpretation of reality; and consequently, connects struggle with human development and transformation. As the expression of all that constitutes the everyday way of life of a people, culture defines and gives meaning to everything experienced by the living. Accordingly, culture defines and gives meaning to the notion of human development and transformation; and science, as its reconstruction, simply further refines the definition and meaning of that human development. Naturally, the dangers addressed above, science as a tool of expression, can only be avoided when the science of a people is consistent with, and directly evolves from the culture of those people. Only in so doing will the definitions and meanings be representative of the people.

Development and Transformation

The issue of human transformation in African reality is in part necessitated by the historical disruption of our normal developmental process. Accordingly, human transformation cannot be completely addressed without giving some attention to that disruption. Essentially, it is argued that at least six historical events have participated in the disruption of the African Essence. These events, though not experienced simultaneously in time, have been experienced in a parallel fashion by both Africans on the continent of Africa and Africans in the New World. It is the experience of these events, which were brought about by contact with and domination by foreigners, that led to the disruption of the African essence. The six events which we view for continental Africans as critical are: (1) religious proselytization; (2) colonialism; (3) de-colonialization: (4) neo-colonialism; (5) industrialization; and (6) nationalism. The six parallel events impacting on Africans in the New World are (1) religious proselytization (conversion), (2) New World slavery, (3) emancipation, (4) reconstruction, (5) urbanization, and (6) Black nationalism.

Humans express their human essence through several domains or activities; i.e., perceptual, physical, cognitive, emotional and behavioral. These events disturbed the essence of a people and when the essence is disrupted or disturbed, similar disruption is seen in their consciousness. For instance, when the essence of a people is distorted, one can witness a change in their perceptions of reality. Parenthetically, this is, of course, also witnessed by the ideological shift discussed above. Similarly, how they come to understand or know is also distorted. Transformation, therefore, requires in part, the re-established aspect of a cultural essence to create and/or invest new responses to a condition and/or a totally new condition.

If this discussion is correct, it is obvious that the disruption and human transformation of African people are characterized by very similar issues and concerns although our exact, concrete contemporary condition may differ. Hence, it is imperative that we exchange and share our creative insights and invention in response to our common task of transformation.

Understanding Human Transformation

Given the discussion above, it should be obvious that discussion of human transformation must be guided by critical thought that reflects the ideological aspect of one's culture. Integral to the discussion of human transformation is an implicit notion of human development. This notion is, of course, guided by one's cultural assumptions about how humans should develop and what elements or conditions are appropriate to that development, as well as what evidence is acceptable when that development in itself is occurring. The obvious indispensable ingredient in the implicit definition of human development is one's ideology. The should, appropriate, and acceptable aspects of human development are all guided by cultural ideology.

Subjectivity and Symbolic Mediation

It has been suggested that man's subjectivity was determined by the phylogenetic evolution of his internal sign system. Remember, it was stated that the central nervous system is in fact a communication system. Recognizing this, it is further suggested or theorized that through the use of biosemiotic laws one can understand the connection between the structure and function of this system.[9]

The genesis of man's subjectivity occurs in three modes: phylogenesis, ontogenesis, and autogenesis. Phylogenetically, man's subjectivity arises in the evolution of the species or race. Ontogenetically, it reveals itself in the development from ovum to completed organism or the development of the body person. Thirdly, at every moment of (waking) life it takes shape as a form of autogenesis of existential acts.[10]

Following Rothschild's symbolic mediation, I will first briefly carry the analysis through the phases of the evolution of life and then transfer the genesis of thought to an analysis of self. Phylogenetically, the capacity of life appears in the genes. Genes are macromolecules within the chromosomes, which bear the information specifying the structure of the species type.[11] Biologists, geneticists, and evolutionists hold that these units existed and multiplied as autonomous structures in the primal atmosphere of earth.[12]

From the point of view of biosemiotic law in the primal atmosphere an intention of self-realization of motion, the cultural aspect of ideology would apply this need to its societal institutions and would develop institutions which believe that people should have an active part in determining their condition and, therefore, would encourage and reinforce growth. And, if one focused on the manifestations of culture, for example behavior, then the condition of direction would translate to systems which reinforce behavior that represented and reinforced an affirmation of the people.

The relationship between the social and psychological development of our people and the social structures and institutions is ultimately the question of transformation although theoretically it is designed to affirm the people's being. We would contend that where the social structures and/or institutions are cultural transplants and do not emerge from, and reflect the cultural definition of the people, they will serve only to change and probably dehumanize and oppress the people. I would suggest that the emergence of counter ideologies and popular liberation movements in Black ruled communities/countries is evidence of a people's rejection of the cultural transplant reflected in the adoption of foreign institutions. It is not enough to have Africans operate and control institutions emerging from the cultural reality of foreigners. We can learn from the experience of African-Americans and the observations of Somali life in this regard.

The Case of African-Americans:
Transformation of a Community

In comparing the condition of African-Americans/Blacks with other Americans/whites, it becomes very clear that the struggles of Blacks for equality and freedom of opportunity have not been won. The ability to determine one's destiny, or to use Cabral's term, to "create progress," as reflected by access to opportunity (education and employment) and the quality of life (health and safety) for Blacks, still remains significantly below that of white Americans. In 1954, four percentage points separated the jobless figures for young Blacks and whites. In 1978, twenty-two percentage points separated the jobless figures for whites and Blacks. This disparity was aggravated by the fact that the median income for working Blacks was 41 % less than whites. It is obvious that the conditions in America were getting worse for Blacks and better for whites.

In response to this historical and continued condition of racism and oppression, the call for community control and determination of one's own destiny were strategies to change the conditions of the African-American reality. They were essentially a call for the transformation of our community. However, when we look at the African-American control of American institutions that impact on our lives no significant change in our general condition has occurred. In terms of government alone in 1977 twenty-three Blacks sat in the Georgia State Legislature. There were a total of seventeen in California, Michigan and Washington. Yet the concrete condition of African-Americans had not changed. Institutions protect and defend cultural ideals of a society. Hence, the transformation of a society will not occur as a consequence of changing the agents who operate its institutions. Societies transform when the institutions within them change, and institutions change when the cultural base, in particular ideology, upon which they are founded change

The social structures and/or institutions will adequately foster the human development of a people when, and only when, they emerge from, and are defined by, the culture and conditions of the people with whom they interact. The issue of transformation will, therefore, be assisted by the creation, modification, and/or invention of social systems which foster the developmental process defined by the people's culture and condition.

Conclusion

It is believed that the transformation of a country such as Somalia, or the transformation of a community such as the Black communities in America, should be guided by its people's cultural factors, aspects, and manifestations. The role of authentic science in this transformation must be that of providing critical thought. Critical thought becomes essential in the process of transformation because it provides the mechanism for constantly testing the tacit assumptions and behavioral consequence of theory. Authentic science as critical thought articulates the unarticulated prescriptions of previous interpretations and current solutions. The authentic science of a people should scrutinize the human norms, which past interpretation and current solutions endorse. It should ultimately crystallize the self-image and developmental process representing a people. Authentic science should, as Fanon believed culture did, reflect, represent, and help create the whole body of efforts made by a people in the sphere of thought to describe, justify, and praise the actions through which that people have created and maintained itself in existence.

[1978]

Voodoo or I.Q.: An Introduction to African Psychology

Definition and Rationale

African Psychology is the recognition and practice of a body of knowledge which is fundamentally different in origin, content, and direction than that recognized and practiced by Euro-American psychologists. The differences between African Psychology and Euro-American Psychology reflect the differences between Black people and White people or, in terms of basic culture, between Africans and Europeans.

It is one of those many anomalies of the Euro-American (white or Western) scientific tradition that, while differences between Blacks and Whites are recognized enough to warrant a systematic study and the formulation of unique public policies concerning for each, these same differences are not recognized enough to preclude measurements with common instruments and to warrant the formulation of distinct disciplinary orientations devoted toward their explanation. This anomaly is due, in part, to the peculiar nature of social and psychological inquiry. Unlike the physical sciences, the behavioral sciences have yet to agree on uniform standards by which behavior can be appropriately judged. Also unlike the physical sciences, the behavioral sciences employ concepts which are derived not from universally agreed-upon criteria, but from the peculiar cultural experience of the scientists themselves.

These are issues with which the better Euro-American behavioral scientists are quite aware; they are thus often embarrassed by the attempts of some of their colleagues, e.g., Jensen, to liken concepts such as "intelligence" to physical concepts such as "electricity"—with the argument that, since nobody knows what such phenomena "really are," it is quite appropriate to adopt "operational definitions" which serve utilitarian ends if not "truth."

The embarrassment of these better-trained scientists has not yet been articulated in a form which would effectively counter the actions taken, under the name of science, by their less well-endowed colleagues. Part of the reason for this might be attributed to the fact that while the better-trained scientists might find serious fault with the logic and methods of their better known colleagues, they are in basic agreement with some of the utilitarian ends sought. It is this "common agreement concerning ends" which, in sensitive areas such as racial intelligence, has permitted legitimate scientific and philosophical issues to be translated as issues concerning "freedom of speech" or "civil rights."

Responsible white scientists are, for example, quite familiar with Thomas Kuhn's reminder that every revolution carries with it a concomitant revolution in the scientific enterprise. And many of these scientists would probably recognize that we are now living in the midst of a social revolution characterized by a substantial change in race relations, not only in America but throughout the world.

Such changes in social relationships are invariably accompanied by changes in the mental or conceptual sphere, a point which Marx and Mannheim pointed out long before Kuhn presented it to his scientific colleagues. These changes in the conceptual sphere call into question some of the basic assumptions under which scientists, like all other participants in a given culture, operate.

Some changes are not easily absorbed into the scientific world, a fact which even those only nominally familiar with the history of scientific revolutions are cognizant.

In deference to the probability that most readers are ignorant of scientific history, we can note that just as most 14th century scientists found it difficult to cease viewing the earth as the center of the physical universe, many of today's behavioral scientists find it difficult to cease viewing the Caucasian race or European culture as the center of the social universe. It is for this reason that Euro-American psychology adopts, as the conceptual and behavioral standard, the characteristics of a minority (less than 10%) of the world's population. Indeed, if history is to be a judge, it would be a most remarkable occurrence if the participants in Euro-American hegemony would recognize and accept conceptual changes that would undermine their privileged positions vis-à-vis others. This is particularly true for those participants whose very occupations are intimately involved with the maintenance of an established conceptual universe; i.e. educators, scientists, and politicians.

This conceptual universe was once bounded by the issues of "integration vs. segregation." These conceptual parameters guided most of the scientific thinking and research in the area of race relations; moreover, public policies were adopted within this frame of reference. This frame of reference or what Kuhn refers to as a "paradigm" has been all but shattered for most Blacks; indeed, it is questionable whether in fact this ever was the way most Blacks viewed the world, particularly, if Black scholars as distinct from Black spokesmen accurately reflected the thinking of the majority of Black people. The writings of the novelist-essayist James Baldwin are particularly relevant in this connection. Baldwin, over a decade ago, asked a question which struck a deep, responsive chord in the minds of many Blacks but was almost completely baffling to most Whites. His question was: "Who wants to integrate into a burning house?" This question, it should be emphasized, was asked long before the release of the Pentagon papers, the crimes of Watergate and its cover-up, the cnergy crises and all other phenomena which, today, make the question perhaps less baffling to whites. There is an important lesson that can be learned from this example, that is, that Black people see things about white people which white people do not see about themselves. A cynic might observe that this is because whites spend more time looking at Blacks than they do looking at themselves—an observation which is perhaps less comforting to the scientific community because it is perhaps more relevant to it.

It is because of this difference in perception that the conceptual universes and their resultant paradigms differ for white people and Black people. This difference eventually manifests itself in the kinds of questions people ask in the area of racial relations. While many whites question whether integration or segregation is best for America, many Blacks question whether America is best for Black people. The conceptual paradigm governing the former question is bounded by an "integration vs. segregation" dichotomy whereas the conceptual paradigm governing the latter is bounded by a "liberation vs. control" dichotomy. The differences between the two paradigms is important for any peaceful settlement of the racial issue. The Euro-American "integration vs. segregation" paradigm carries an important common dimension, viz., control by whites whereas the "liberation vs. control" addresses itself directly to what many Blacks believe is the critical issue: self-control or other-control. The failure of Euro-American psychology to recognize and or appreciate this alternative paradigm is what leads many thinking Black students to dismiss much contemporary research as "irrelevant."

White scientists, if they are truly interested in science as distinct from politics should not assume that just because George Gallup has not asked Blacks whether or not they want to integrate in white society that, therefore, they do; nor should these scientists assume that just because some Black politicians and social scientists promote schemes such as "compensatory education" or "affirmative action" that, therefore, the majority of Black people believe themselves to be in need of compensation and affirmation. These programs and policies reflect political decisions based on social expediency. They do not necessarily reflect Black public opinion nor, for that matter, sound scientific thinking.

In brief African Psychology recognizes, perhaps more so than Euro-American psychology, that the way in which a question is asked predetermines the range of possible answers. If the question is asked in terms of "integration vs. segregation," the answer perforce excludes "separation." If the question is asked in terms of "Which is more important in determining Black intellectual inferiority, genes or environment?" the answer perforce excludes the possibility that Blacks are not intellectually inferior. If the question is asked "Are Blacks equal in intelligence to whites?" the answer perforce excludes the possibility that Blacks are superior in intelligence to whites.

Because of this recognition that scientific questions are, at the same time, often political and social answers, African Psychology is quite sensitive to problems concerning the history and philosophy of science itself. It thus views itself as not only different from Euro-American psychology, but as superior to it in the same way that philosophy is superior to science in that the latter is valid only if certain assumptions of the former are accepted.

The Content Emphases of African Psychology

So much, then, for the "Why?" of African psychology; let us turn our attention to the "What?" bearing in mind that its content differences are a result of its conceptual or paradigm differences.

Before proceeding with this discussion of content, we should first acknowledge in deference to alternative paradigms the essential radical nature of African Psychology. It is radical not so much in the political sense, but in a scientific and philosophical sense; i.e., it is "radical" because it addresses itself first and foremost to the roots of human thought. For, we believe, only when such roots are exposed and examined critically can a solid foundation be constructed for the subsequent investigation of specific psychological phenomena.

Consistent with this content of "root" questions, the issues which African Psychology attempt to understand are many.

1. Which is the Original Race, the Caucasian or the African?

Many Euro-American psychologists, no doubt, would consider this question a theological one at best and irrelevant at worse. Such apparent unconcern with questions of origin is rather peculiar, given the great current concern with the role of genetic factors in human behavior. Clearly, if one is to be consistent with any genetic thesis, one must surely give at least nominal attention to the nature of the first human gene pool for it is from this original gene pool that all contemporary genes were derived. If, then, we are to be concerned about the genetic transmission of human intelligence, we must admit only one of two possibilities: either the white race is evolutionary prior to the Black, in which case whatever intelligence (or lack thereof) Blacks have has been inherited from whites; or the Black race is evolutionary prior to white, in which case the reverse would be true. We should perhaps note, again in deference to alternative paradigms, that either position would effectively nullify the conclusions of some modern-day genetic intelligence theorists.

In this connection many Euro-American and Euro-American-trained psychologists tend to minimize the significance of this issue of origins. Some adopt a neo-Darwinian perspective and assert that there has been an evolutionary improvement in the species, so that the Caucasian race represents the highest end of the evolutionary scale. This perspective equates technological superiority with intellectual and moral superiority.

The Honorable Elijah Muhammad, the Messenger of Allah, was the first to raise and answer this question of racial origins. African Psychology works on the assumption that the African race evolved prior to the Caucasian race; therefore, the African race is the original source of whatever genetic factors account for contemporary white and Black behavior in the world. African Psychology thus attributes the decline of Black civilizations not to genetic weaknesses but to a spiritual decay which was left in its wake; however, a high testimonial to its original intellectual supremacy in the form of stone monuments spread across Africa; monuments which reflect a mastery of mathematics, geometry, physics, and all other sciences known to man. The construction of the African pyramids has, to this day, baffled Western scientists to such an extent that the most recent explanation is that they were built, not by the Africans themselves, but by alien space creatures!

While African Psychology accepts as a "given" that the original race was African and not European, it does attempt to validate this hypothesis on grounds other than assumption or authority. Why these other sources of validation are necessary for African Psychology and not Euro-American psychology says more about the dynamics of racism in the Western world than it does about anything else. So ingrained is this racism in America's educational institutions that many geography books, even today, separate Egypt from Africa in order to foster the idea that the Egyptian civilization was built by non-Africans. Hollywood has played a major role in insuring the perception of Africans as uncivilized.

Because of the way in which the mass media and educational institutions have attempted to present the world as white, African Psychology recognizes its need to validate some of its own assumptions to the extent it is possible to validate assumptions with empirical research. This validation is done not so much to convince whites, a task which we have recognized as virtually impossible, as to convince Blacks, particularly those Blacks who receive their education in white institutions. Indeed, this particular educational constituency is very important in the eyes of African Psychology, for it is precisely this group of people who often come to be recognized by established white institutions as "leaders" of other Black people. Such people become "spokesmen" even though (or perhaps because) they lack the most essential educational ingredient of all: knowledge of self. The importance of this element of knowledge is discussed in later paragraphs.

The point we wish to make in this context is that however much we might deplore it, it is still a fact that many Black people in American will continue to be educated by whites and, this being the case, it is only natural for such people to develop a conception of self as inferior to whites. This negative self-conception extends itself to other Blacks and, as a result, such people are more likely to be influenced by what whites have to say about them than by what their own people have to say. Indeed, such a tendency is frequently associated with "success" and "intelligence" in American society.

Because of this, African Psychology recognizes the necessity of supporting its assumptions by referring to research published within the Euro-American tradition. Thus, in support of our assumption that the original race was African, not European, we call attention to the research of Professor Louis Leakey, a British anthropologist. Shortly after Leakey's death a few years ago, his son, Dr. Richard Leakey, made an archeological finding which completely revolutionized scientific thinking concerning the origin of man. He found remnants of early man in East Africa dating back some three million years.

While Black Muslim scholars know that this date is wrong in an absolute sense (the origins of man date back much, much farther than this), Leakey's finding is correct. It clearly establishes the biological priority of the African relative to the European. Moreover, we know from the science of biology that it is biologically impossible for whites to produce offspring of color, whereas it is quite possible for Blacks to produce white offspring. Thus, as far as African Psychology is concerned, there is no question as to the fact that the original race was African.

2.What is the Mystery of Melanin?

If, then, the first man on earth was dark as opposed to light, then one of the substantive content questions African Psychology must concern itself with is the role of the skin-color producing substance called melanin.

Although the word "melanin" comes from the Greek word, "melanos," meaning "Black," in biological science it is used to designate a pigment whose natural color in human ranges from pale yellow over reddish brown to almost Black.

Melanin is synthesized and dispersed by specialized cells which are called melanocytes. Melanocytes synthesize melanin through a series of bio-chemical reactions beginning with the consumption of the amino acid, phenylalanine. Each subsequent biochemical reaction in the chain is controlled by a specific enzyme. If all the essential enzymes are present, the pigment melanin is produced in considerable quantity. When this occurs, an individual has skin which is dark in color, hair which is Black, and eyes which are brown. If any of the enzymes are relatively inactive, the pigment production is correspondingly curtailed and the individual manifests a pale skin color, hair which is light or blond, and eyes which are blue. The occurrence defines a state of depigmentation; i.e., the genetic inability to produce sufficient amounts of melanin. It is worth noting, however, that all human organisms produce some degree of melanin; variation occurs with regard to the specific level of melanin activity which takes place within the cytoplasm of the melanocyte.

Melanin and The Central Nervous System

A major portion of the empirical research conducted in African Psychology involves a systematic examination of the relationship between melanocytes and the nerve cells of the central nervous system. We know, for example, that both are embryologically derived from a single neuroblast in the neural crest of the developing human fetus. This fact leads us to systematically investigate the patterns of neural interdependence that neurons of the brain, neurons of the spinal cord, and melanocytes manifest on human metabolic processes and nervous system functioning.

We know that man's central nervous system performs a critical information-processing role which is essential for optimal neurological and metabolic functioning. Damage to the central nervous system can potentially impair the nervous activity which is essential to human sensitivity and consciousness.

Our research has discerned a high, positive correlation between specific levels of sensory acuity and states of pigmentation. An examination of neuro-physiological, neuro-chemical, and neuro-humoral data reveals this correlation quite clearly. Relationships have been found to exist between melanin and the cerebellum; between melanin and the red nucleus; and between melanin and the reticular formation. Our research has not yet been able to define the precise nature of these relationships, but we are led to believe in concurrence with Professor Welsing of Howard University that melanin refines the central nervous system and, in so doing, produces a highly sensitized sensory-motor network.

It is interesting to note in this context that Parkinson's disease, a hereditary disease of the central nervous system, is associated with loss of melanin-pigment by the cells of the substantia nigra. It is for this reason that it is a disease which is largely confined to Whites. Lesions to the substantia nigra, literally translated from Latin, "Black substance," produce the complex motor syndrome (Paralysis agitans and akinsesia) commonly seen in Parkinson's disease. The substantia nigra is located in the midbrain (mesencephalon) near the cerebellum; it forms part of the cerebral peduncles near the red nucleus. Research has suggested the substantia nigra has a critical relationship with the reticular formation in the sense that it provides "starter" impulses which facilitate phasic muscular contractions. The muscular contractions are important for postural adjustment and the rapid and exact movement of specific muscle groups.

Other evidence of the importance of melanin in preventing central nervous system disorders is found in research concerning the hereditary disease known as phenylketonuria or PKU. This disease, again more common among Whites than Blacks, is characterized by purposeless movements such as pill-rolling movements of the hand and irregular tic-like motions.

The occurrence of PKU is caused by the absence or ineffective performance of an enzyme called phenylalanase. This enzyme, when present in humans, catalyzes the amino acid phenylalanine and forms one of the raw materials out of which melanin is formed. When phenylalanase is absent, the phenylalanine is converted instead to phenylpyruvic acid, which is excreted in the urine. This mis-conversion process also results in certain mental defects which are associated with the PKU disease (hereditary idiocy).

We are convinced that the absence of melanin is directly associated with the mal-functioning of the central nervous system. However, we are also convinced that the presence of melanin is directly associated with the proper functioning of the central nervous system. It must be admitted, however, that the bio-chemical processes involved in this latter relationship are quite complex and poorly understood. It is always easier to explain what is "wrong" than what is "right" since science tends to focus on deviations from normality as opposed to normality itself.

In any case, we can attempt to explain this "normal" functioning by noting that, under normal conditions, the amino acid tyrosine is formed from the enzymatic action of phenylalanase on phenylalanine. The enzyme tyrosinase then catalyzes tyrosine to produce dopamine. Dopamine is oxidized into norepinephrine and norepinephrine is converted into epinephrine. Finally, epinephrine or adrenaline is converted into melanin.

Norepinephrine and epinephrine are under the control of the autonomic nervous system. The adrenal medulla secretes these in response to conditions of emotion or changes in the discharge of neurons in the automatic nervous system. Part of the autonomic nervous system, the sympathetic, accelerates the activity of all essential vital organs through the secretion of norepinephrine. From these facts, we conclude that there is a positive correlation between the intensity of emotional arousal and the urinary excretion of epinephrine and norepineprine.

Implicit in this conclusion is the belief that emotional arousal is a positive trait; this might be strange to most Euro-Americans, inasmuch as emotional arousal tends to have a negative connotation in the Western psychological tradition. In fact, this difference of attitudes is one of the basic features differentiating African Psychology from Euro-American psychology. We believe, in short, that non-whites are indeed "more emotional" than whites and, not only is this positive in its own right, it is directly related to that phenomenon we call "intelligence." In fact, the "mystery" of melanin, as we see it, relates directly to the fact that while we have a fairly good idea of the bio-chemical properties of melanin and how these are related to nervous system functioning, we do not yet know the specifics of this in relationship to human intelligence. We do, however, have our hunches, and these are articulated in more detail below.

3. What is the Nature of Black Intelligence?

From our research into melanin, we are led to believe that it is the concept of sensitivity which is of fundamental importance to human intelligence. A related concept, consciousness, is also considered important in our consideration of human intelligence.

Consideration of these two concepts, sensitivity and consciousness, underscores the fact that African Psychology adopts a different philosophical base than contemporary Euro-American Psychology. Our ontological position asserts that there is more to the world than meets our material eyes, which are always limited by the present state of technology. In this sense, we agree with those modern physicists who recognize a non-material or spiritual reality underlying all observed material phenomena. Whether one prefers to call this non-material reality "energy", "spirit", "mana" or any other term is of little significance, what is important is the recognition that it does exist. We believe that any psychology worthy of its name must incorporate this reality into its philosophical premises, if not content domain. African Psychology, of course, does both and, for this reason, the concepts of sensitivity and consciousness are of paramount importance. The word "consciousness" means "with knowledge" and to the extent that intelligence is related to knowledge, the concepts are fundamentally related.

The type of knowledge with which African Psychology is concerned is not that type commonly associated with traditional psychology. It is more closely associated with an Eastern esoteric tradition which recognizes self-knowledge as the ultimate source of all knowledge. Thus, our epistemological position also differs from Western, Euro-American psychology. That is, our position recognizes the supremacy of internal knowledge, as opposed to external knowledge. While there are a few Western trained scholars who agree with us in this regard notably Michael Polanyi, the dominant thrust of Western Psychology has been the acceptance of an epistemological position which accepts external sources as the only sources of valid knowledge. This position is incorporated in the very foundations of positivist, empirical psychology.

This, of course, does not mean that African Psychology dismisses empirical research: indeed, our research into the melanin issue stands in sharp contradiction to such a stance. What it does mean, however, is that external, empirical types of knowledge represent only one source and, insofar as the discipline of psychology is concerned, a relatively insignificant one. It is insignificant in the sense that it does not contribute to the acquisition of self-knowledge and that, we feel, is most important.

In accord with Eastern esoteric tradition African Psychology recognizes the total field of self-knowledge as consisting of 360 degrees. Complete knowledge of self expresses all 360 degrees and is frequently referred to as "wisdom." There are in all societies and at all times various institutions which have been established to guide students in their search for self-knowledge. These are not, of course, "schools" in the sense that most Americans recognize them; i.e., they are not publicly supported, nor do they provide training in the various disciplines which are characteristic of established universities. Most of these institutions (lodges, temples, orders, etc.) are designed to "raise the level of consciousness" of their students to 32 degrees or more. The pursuit of such degrees may occupy a person's entire lifetime, but the type of knowledge acquired is considered well worth the effort.

It is important to recognize that "intelligence," as measured by "degrees of consciousness" or self-knowledge, is completely independent of success in public schools or occupational ranking. Thus, it is not surprising to find a highly "intelligent" person having less than a high school diploma and perhaps working at a very low-status occupation. This is not surprising to those familiar with Eastern intellectual traditions because it is recognized that money, status, and prestige are usually associated with intelligence in this country and have little to do with intelligence, as conceived outside of the Western world. The correlates one should look for in regard to intelligence are not the material ones, but the spiritual ones: happiness, peace of mind, good health, longevity, humor, etc.

There is one aspect of the Euro-American psychological tradition which relates to the Eastern and African conception of intelligence. This aspect involves a field of psychological inquiry which has only recently been granted scientific legitimacy. Generically, this field is known as parapsychology.

Because of the peculiar position of Black people in America, genetically Eastern and socially Western, it is the area of parapsychology which we find the most useful in bridging the East-West gap and, at the same time, providing an additional empirical orientation in African psychological research.

The field of parapsychology is related to the African conception of intelligence in the following sense: As self-knowledge approaches 360 degrees, the individual becomes better equipped to manifest those mental abilities associated with parapsychology. These abilities can be classified in two general categories: "mind over matter" or psychokinesis, and "mind-reading" or precognition.

African Psychology, if called upon to provide an operational definition of "intelligence" or "consciousness," would cite as representative the manifestation of these psychic abilities. Of course Eastern psychological traditions have long recognized these abilities, but only recently have they begun to be accepted in the West. Interestingly enough, this acceptance has been more at the hands of physicists and other "hard scientists" than it has of psychologists.

To the extent that consciousness and sensitivity are related to the presence of melanin, and these, in turn, to the development of psychic abilities, African Psychology expects that intelligence is directly related to the presence of melanin. It is this hypothesis which is currently being investigated in our laboratories, both in America and in other parts of the world.

It might be useful for us to mention some of the reasons which led us to the formulation of this hypothesis relating melanin to psychic abilities. The most significant of these is derived from anthropological research in sub-Saharan Africa where the largest number of high-melanin possessing people are found. This research has documented, for over a century, the para-normal powers possessed by a large number of Africans. These powers have been frequently referred to as vodoo and/or witchcraft; but, stripped of such largely pejorative labeling, the

observed phenomena represents nothing more than the manifestation of psychokinesis and precognition. Not all Africans possess this ability, of course; one might suspect that they are distributed in a Gausian fashion, as are other human traits, but the evidence certainly seems overwhelming that such abilities are more
characteristic of African people than they are of other people on
earth. While one might suggest that geographical, cultural, or
religious factors account for this, our own position suggests that
the dominant factor is genetic and related to the presence of
melanin. Thus, one of the major content areas of African
Psychology concerns this relationship between melanin and psychic ability, the latter conceived to be the essential material manifestation of human intelligence.

4.What is the Nature of Black Self and Black Personality?

Because self-knowledge is considered an important element of consciousness and intelligence, African Psychology
defines it as an important content area, the nature of the self.
Like many other areas related to African peoples and Black
behavior, the research in this area of self-conception is characterized by several important subjective tendencies. First of all, the
research about African/Black people has been and is being produced largely by non-Black peoples. Second, the orientation of
most of this research has been and is to support the pre-con-
ceived notion that African people are deviant from and hence
abnormal to white people. The third tendency, related to the second, is the adoption of a priori assumptions characteristic of
Euro-American philosophy as opposed to African philosophy. The
fourth and final tendency is the almost total absence of Africa and
Africanity in the theories and research on the so-called Negroes'
self-concept.
These tendencies have led us to conclude that if one
accepts Euro-American assumptions about African reality, the
questions and answers about Black people are going to be in a
predetermined manner in response to Euro-American reality.
However valuable such an exercise might be, it is not our intent
to explain why or how Euro-American researchers have created a
pseudo-reality of negative "Negro" self-concept. Our intention is,

rather, to suggest some reasons for considering an alternative framework or perspective in understanding African/Black peoples' conception of themselves.

African Self-Concept: The Extended Self

Having implied throughout this discussion that African Psychology is rooted in the nature of a Black culture which is fundamentally African as opposed to European, we contend that a dominant aspect of the Black mentality reflects the polyvalent principle of the "Oneness of Being." If one were to epitomize African Psychology, it would be best described as the philosophy of rhythm or harmony.

The behavioral modalities which are characteristic of African lifestyles throughout the "Diaspora" are based on several philosophical assumptions and a conception of "reality" which, when analyzed, reflects a sense of ontological harmony or rhythm. Related to this is an African philosophical orientation which emphasizes the notion of interdependence. This notion conceives of man and all the other elements of the universe as being part of a unified and integrated whole. The African philosophical tradition, in turn, determines two fundamental operational orders or guiding beliefs. The first belief is that man is part of the natural rhythm of nature or one with nature. The second is a conception of the universe as a "vitalistic pneumaticism." This latter conception means a belief in the sense of "vital solidarity," or survival of the tribe. Descriptively, it refers to a kind of vital attitude about one's existence or what Westerners term a sense of "common fate."

In accordance with these two notions the African thinks of experience as an intense complementary rhythmic connection or synthesis between the person and reality.

How this relates to African self-conception is as important as it is difficult to express in the English language. First, we must recognize that the philosophical orientation determines both what is "real" and how one defines or validates its reality. In terms of self-conception, the African philosophical tradition, unlike western philosophical systems, does not place emphasis on the "individual" or "individuality." In fact, one could say that in a sense, it does not allow for "individuals." It recognizes that only in terms of one's people does the "individual" become conscious of one's own being. It is, in fact, only through others that one learns his duties and responsibilities toward himself and the collective self or tribe. Historically, initiation rites were designed to instill this sense of corporate responsibility and collective destiny.

When we examine closely the African philosophical tradition, we recognize that from this tradition an extended definition of self evolved. That is to say, the African self-concept is, by philosophical definition, the "We" instead of the "I."

Africans believe that whatever happens to the "individual" self, the "I," also happens to the corporate body, the "We," and vice-versa. The cardinal point, therefore, in understanding the traditional African conception of self, is the belief that "I am because we are; and because we are, therefore, I am." This belief underscores the extent to which the African feels himself to be part of all other African peoples. Descriptively, this relationship of interdependence can be termed the "extended-self."

This notion of the "We" as opposed to the "I" may become clearer through an ontological analysis of the self. It is generally accepted in the Euro-American psychological tradition that the establishment of self is accomplished by recognizing in others qualities or characteristics similar to one's self and/or denying qualities and characteristics similar to one's self. The "self," therefore, occurs as the consequence of either of two processes—opposition and/or apposition. The way in which African peoples are extended into themselves, however, is not completely explained by this kind of distinction. What one must distinguish between are the "levels of reality": the material, the lower level, and the spiritual the higher level.

The "oneness of being" is predicated on Man being an integrated and indispensable part of the universe. Being in the world also means to participate in its social time. Hence, to be is to be what you are because of your historical past as well as what you anticipate to be in your historical future. In recognizing the historical grounding of one's being, one has also to accept the collective and social sense of one's history. The collective "self" is not contained only in his physical presence in finite time. The twin notions of interdependence and oneness of being allow for a conception of self which transcends, through the historical consciousness of one's people, the finiteness of both Newtonian space and time.

Self-awareness is not therefore limited to just the "cognitive" awareness of one's uniqueness, individuality, and historical finiteness as in the Euro-American tradition. It is the awareness of self as an awareness of one's historical consciousness and the sense of "we" being one.

If "we," however, portrays the properties of self as only collectively intersubjective or as only individually unique, we distort the totality of the notion. African self refers both to the grounding of the being which transcends empirical or physical entities and to the discrete entities that are capable of being located in space and having recognizable and measurable properties. The self is not only a permanently determined physical entity. That is, it is not reducible, or merely equivalent, to the biological organism. It is important, however, to make this "property" distinction clear for analytical purposes.

The most compelling property, of course, is the ontological grounding of the self in the collective and social sense of history. It is in this sense that the self is portrayed as a "transcendence into extendation"—that is, the conception of self transcends and extends into the collective consciousness of one's people. However, self-conception is also related to the physically recognizable properties of the discrete entities. And this is a critical point for the consideration of "Black American" self-concept.

The physical situation in which Africans—particularly in the Americas—find themselves involves the domination and imposition of a fundamental European system of "reality" on an African people. This situation naturally causes confusion because it denies the most compelling property of the African conception of self. It is this situation which has produced the entity referred to as the "Negro"—a concept referring to the African person who attempts to or is forced to deny the philosophical basis of his Africanity, even though he cannot negate the recognizable properties or physiological facts of it. To be a "Negro" therefore, is to be in a state of confusion. The infliction of the Euro-American philosophical tradition, as it relates to self-conception (individuality, separateness, etc.) for African peoples causes many to falsely believe that their natural temperament, tendencies, and characteristic spirit were and are "wrong." Such conclusions have been created and sustained by the Euro-American psychological tradition. The results of such beliefs naturally lead to negative conceptions of self and attitudes of self-hatred. This, in turn, has implications for certain other maladies affecting the Black personality, a content area of which we turn our attention below.

5. What is the Nature of the Black Personality?

Traditional (Euro-American) theories of personality functioning all adopt, as a norm, those behaviors which are derived from the European lifestyle. The above discussions of intelligence and melanin have already suggested some of the basic normative differences between the Black and white personalities. If these differences exist, and the social milieu systematically rewards those behaviors which are in accord with the society's norms, it is not surprising that a child may respond negatively to his natural tendencies when they are not in accord with the existing social order. A repeated association of one's natural tendencies with painful or negative stimulation leads to a conditioned inhibition of those tendencies in himself and a rejection of similar tendencies in others. This results in a psychologically unhealthy form of conditioning which most whites and many white-educated Blacks confuse with "success." The most extreme examples are those attempts at physical alteration in which Blacks have tried to alter their appearance by bleaching creams, hair straighteners, etc., to bring their physical appearance into accord with the social norm of physical attractiveness. Some popular race-intelligence theoreticians have equated such imitative behavior of the holders of power as evidence of the inherent superiority of the white race. Interestingly enough, these same theoreticians do not concern themselves with such "anomalies" as white efforts to produce melanin via sun tanning.

The more subtle yet more insidious form of this conditioned self-rejection is its psychological manifestation, well-documented in the voluminous research on Black self-concept. Low self-esteem is almost a sine qua non of living in an environment of oppression. A major problem with such research, of course, is that it focuses attention on the results of oppression rather than its causes. Attention is also focused more on the effects of low self-esteem rather than the origins of low self-esteem.

Perhaps more important than just differences in orientation, African Psychology differs radically from Euro-American psychology in the assumptions concerning the basic nature of man. In this regard, we unashamedly align ourselves with the majority of the world's population in our rejection of Cartesian duality and our acceptance of man as a spiritual being. Even though Western observers have rather historically described these assumptions as primitive, heathenistic, superstitious, or pagan, the point remains that, without exception, Black behavior is most clearly understood by Black people as extensions of a spiritual core. An assumption of a spiritual core implies the existence of an irreducible element in man which has a divine origin, an eternal fate and a moral function.

With such differences in basic assumptions about the nature of man, one will necessarily find wide disparities in the organization of societies and the behaviors which are considered normative for those people. If one follows the history of Black people from West African societies as a recent referent through the American slavery experience and neo-slavery experience, one finds, as a thread of continuity, the religious nature of the Black man. The European's intrusion into African society was permitted without resistance largely because the African assumed that he lived in a religious world and that strangers were to be accepted as creatures of a similar divine origin and with high moral intent. The faultiness of this assumption is evidenced by the next four hundred years of the Black man's history following this intrusion. However, even this condition (of slavery) was made meaningful as a religious experience for Blacks. The adaptation of Christianity to the Black religious experience maintained and cultivated the idea of a divine plan at work. The problem continued to be one which assumed the universality of that divinity which, as viewed retrospectively, too frequently permitted a passive adaptation to an alien way of life.

The alien (Euro-American) way of life assumed man to be first and foremost a material being in search of physical gratification. Normative behavior is thus viewed in terms of the maximal gratification of one's material ambitions variously referred to as achievement motivation, territorial dominance, political power,

etc. The exploitation of people and resources is considered of little consequence, inasmuch as the core of it all is believed to be
dispensable material. One can readily perceive the incompatibili-
ty of the victim, assuming that even his exploitation is of a spiritual quality with the oppressor viewing the spiritual as material.

The emphasis on the spiritual core summarizes the African
psychological perspective on Black personality. All descriptions of
the normal functioning Black personality are thus viewed in the
context of this core. For example, the recent upsurge in Black
homicides, drug usage, mental disorders, and the virtual disintegration of the Black society within the American context can be
systematically correlated with the deterioration of the religious
function in Black personality. The increased adoption by Blacks
of alien assumptions of materialism has resulted in a concomitant
adoption of European lifestyles. Such an adopted life style is dysfunctional when it is superficial and contrary to the natural Black
lifestyle. This adoption is viewed as superficial because, even
though the Black man succeeds in emulating the White lifestyle,
it frequently results in neurosis or other forms of implicit self-
rejection. The spiritual tendencies of African people are antithetical to the material tendencies of Europeans and acceptance of the
one almost invariably requires rejection of the other.

The Black personality which has ostensibly adjusted to
Western society is characterized by what Euro-American psychologists would call a "schizoid" adjustment. This means that he
lives in two worlds which diametrically differ on many key dimensions. He works to foster an image which will make him acceptable to the material world of the European, e.g., high achievement
motivation, emphasis on cognition to the exclusion of affective
experience and individualism. On the other hand, he will attempt
to maintain at least tenuous ties to his opposite Black origins. The
growing failure of such schizoid adjustment is seen in the increase
of suicide rates among middle class Blacks as well as the growing
incidence of depression and general malcontentedness.

African Psychology, in short, does not assume that the
similar behaviors of the White majority and Black middle-class
have the same origins. Because of this, we recognize that a
renewal of the spiritual core of the Black man is the most effective therapy for his adjustment disorders. This perhaps begins to

explain the very high level of success achieved by the followers of the Honorable Elijah Muhammad in resolving those problems of Black people where traditionally-trained psychologists have been utter failures. This has been particularly true of drug addiction and other so-called "incorrigible" conditions.

Finally, after four hundred years, we can begin to understand that the solutions to the problems of the Black man are different from the solutions to the problems of the people of European descent. People of African origin cannot be made citizens of the world by acting in accord with the European model of behavior, despite material inducements to do so. The price is too high, and the ultimate rewards too low.

Conclusion

The five content areas discussed above do not, of course, exhaust the list of various subjects with which African Psychology is concerned. The five which have been discussed do, however, represent the foundations of our inquiry into the psychological nature of the Black man.

We should perhaps mention, in this context, that we are under few illusions concerning the difficulty of the intellectual work ahead of us. Nor do we have any illusions concerning the extent some will go in the attempt to hinder our progress. Indeed, some of us have already been refused academic jobs or fired from them because of our determined efforts to forge a psychology which validates the experience of Black people. If American history is any kind of accurate reflector of what is held in store for us, we should perhaps consider ourselves fortunate that we are not killed or imprisoned for our work—so bitter is White resistance to independent Black thinking.

Despite expected obstacles from both whites and Blacks we are assured of final success. This is because our work does not represent a reaction against anything so much as it does a response to certain things. It is a response to the call of incarcerated Black men who seek answers to the why's and wherefore's of their miserable condition; it is a response to Black women who fall victim to the politics of population control carried forth in the name of North America. It is a response to these and many other calls emanating from the mouths of Black people. It is, in short, a response to something which few Whites understand—a response to a divine call. Being thus, it is at once divinely inspired, divinely guided, and, hopefully, divinely expressed.

[1976]

BELONGING

THOUGHTS ON APPLICATION

Osa Gunda

I   II

I   I

I   I

II   I

All goodness became a grouping together in harmony. The grouping together of the strands of hair covered the head. The grouping together of hairs on the chin became an object of atten- tion. The grouping together of trees became a forest. The grouping together of the eruwa grasses became a savannah. The grouping together of the beehives hold up the roof of the house. And the grouping together of the ita ants led to their covering the earth. Alasuwada, Great Being who creates all beings in groups, humbly we ask you to grant us things gathered in groups, so that they bring together all things good for us.

Section III, Belonging, speaks to the difficult issue of application. How are the new constructions used to guide research and theory development? The writing in this section speaks to the critical issues of self-conception, family dynamics, the effect of societal forces on mental health, substance abuse and alienation, language acquisition, international development, and questions of mental measurement. In effect, the application of the newly formulated theories and frameworks in Black Psychology was and is almost equivalent to designing a jet plane while flying it across the country. Application like theory devel- opment is an on-going process. What is reflected here are prelim- inary attempts.

Starting with an early attempt to formulate differential evolutionary formulation of self, the sketches in this section, turn to a more hands-on approach to dealing with the issue of African/Black Psychology. Sketch 7 and 8 discuss the difference in worldviews of the African and European but add something which has yet to fully develop, the idea of "scientific colonialism." Scientific colonialism is explored as a tool of psychological domination and oppression. In so doing, the psychological literature on Black self-concept has distorted the African sense of self concept and in its place added a self concept of degradation and negativity. Because the power to define the meaning of Black self-concept has been usurped, the full and accurate conception of Black self-concept is never realized. As counter to the Western definition of self, a re-conceptualization of Black self-concept as the "extended self" is offered and explored. Expressing the importance of a strong African centered worldview, Sketch 9 calls for the examination of the Black family, not based on a European worldview or philosophical orientation, but rather by the nature and ecological factors of the Black family. Dispelling the myth of Black mental health, Sketch 10 recognizes that mental illness is based on the way one responds to reality. The discussion directs the reader to realize the crucial distinction between worldviews because it is here where Black mental health is being misdiagnosed. In so doing it is suggested that what is perceived as Black mental illness should actually be considered white insanity. Sketch 11 identifies the preservation of key principles that can maintain the African centered family in spite of racism. Sketch 12 is concerned mainly with societal forces, public policy and building Black family strengths. Sketch 13 addresses the fact that science should be used to understand, not control, through the use of facts. In this regard it explores the question of mental measurement. It notes and builds on the idea that one's conceptual universe determines human capacities and guides development. Hence, when the conceptual process is misguided, the measurement of outcomes will be misguided as well. In raising the question of cultural antimony, the discussion highlights the concern with psychometrics as a racist science with capitalist interests. Sketch 14 grimly points to the horrendous statistics of alcohol and drug use in America and offers some suggestions of its causes. It does, however, manage to offer guidance for the reconceptualization of the teenager. By eliminating the idea of the teenage "character flaw," it is clear to see how alcohol and drugs are consumed in search of human meaning as attempts of closing the "gap" of alienation, especially, in a society with a philosophical heritage of loneliness and disconnectedness. Sketch 15 explores the ways in which language and culture are connected and allow for the understanding of both oppression and liberation. It is suggested that the elimination of polarities in language, i.e., good/bad, correct/incorrect, must occur. It is also suggested that international development can only truly happen when the developmental process is in line with the people's indigenous language and culture.

The Autogenic Evolution of Self: African and European

Many writers have given as their introductory remarks to the genesis of the development of self, an account of the historical treatment of the subject. In so doing, the results invariably have read like brief treatises reflecting the thoughts of such thinkers as Descartes, Hume, Locke, Mills, Herbart, Kant, and Hegel. This was, or at least it was thought, necessary due to the enormous philosophical inheritance psychology and particularly self or ego-psychology received as a consequence of its birth period. However, if one takes a more global view of man, then one must conclude that these men made particular common assumptions about self. It was or is this commonality in their weltanschauung which has led me to attempt to offer, first of all, some reason for their commonality, and, second, to suggest that they collectively do not account for man's conception of himself in a global sense.

The one thing that is common about all Western thinkers concerning self is that they view the "phenomenon" as individuated and independent unto itself. That is, the self of any one person is independent and individuated from the selves of other persons. It is true that this may have been the consequence of the rise of Behaviorism and the enthronement of Logical Positivism, but no matter who won the historical philosophical battle, the common assumption was and is that the self is individuated and independent.

Now, if I were to attempt to establish the reason for this as being the fact that all these thinkers were socialized in the Western world, most readers would object to this by stating the many different experiences each of the abovementioned must have had. Thus, the refutation would be one based on the differential complexity of France, Germany, England, and early

America. This is, in fact, a valid criticism at one dimension or level. However, I propose to suggest that the commonality within each of these men is not found necessarily or exclusively in their Western world socialization, but more fundamentally in the autogenetic evolution of their kind.

In order to offer evidence for this assertion and in the same research allow for another conception of self, I will continue the remainder of this argument from the stand point of the evolution of self in man. It is hoped that my conclusion will suffice to draw both aspects of this treatise together.

Evolution of Self in Man

The meaning that one has for being one within oneself and his universe, or what is felt as an inner-feeling of oneness with oneself is the result of an interpretive process which evolved in the course of hundreds of millions of years.[1] This inner something, which we call the "self" or "real me," is the result of an evolutionary production which in the end, at least up to this point, left man believing in the consistency of his own internal organized system. The consistency or make-up of man's internal system is not, however, organized the same for all people. This will become clearer later.

Nevertheless, in order to understand what makes man believe in and understand all the dimensions of his human inwardness, it is necessary to analyze the evolutionary process of his internal system; i.e., his biogenetic structure. It is believed that the most useful method for our analysis is the Symbol Theory of Psychophysical Relations. This theory suggests that the personality of a human being is found in the meaning of his words and actions and his habits and gestures.[2] This meaning is experienced, Rothschild believes, as being identical with bodily bearer. Thus, the unity of the symbol and the meaning are the keys to human understanding. Accordingly, just as human thought is linked with language, the emergence of self or psyche in man is associated with sign systems in the function of a symbolic medium. The central nervous system can be viewed as a communication system that transforms organic sensory excitation and signals received through hormonal and chemical substances into a code of its own excitation. The central nervous system allows the organism to decode these excitations. It is through this latter process that the organism discloses to itself the significance of its own experiences and situations. That is to say, by encoding and decoding the organic sensory excitation signals, it yields the phenomena of mental life; i.e., images, emotions, perceptions, etc.

This internal sign system, like all systems, has a structure which aids in our remaining analysis. The hierarchical nature of this structure for contemporary man has language ranked highest in the internal sign system, and from there the structure flows to its lowest communication process level which is the somatic periphery of the sense organs—namely, the peripheral nerves and muscles.

In the course of evolution Rothschild argues that each level in the communication hierarchy was superimposed on each proceeding layer. Hence, the evolution of man can be thought of as the evolution of man's own subjectivity. And the whole process can best be understood if one lets the "evolution of subjectivity" exemplify the evolutionary analysis of internal sign systems.

Darwin, as well as his followers, has led us to believe that protozoa, invertebrates, vertebrates, and, finally, man can be seen as continual in the evolutionary process. Rothschild has suggested, however, that each of these evolutionary developments can be also discussed via symbolic laws with four developmental stages of subjectivity. As such, in each stage, a new sign system is superimposed on the already established one and thus makes the unfolding of a new and higher level possible. Thus, man using the information stored and forever re-actualized within the phylogenetically ordered system finally achieved his own depth and range of understanding.[3] Of all the wonders of the world and marvels of the universe, this fact, man's creation of his own creation, alone is the most astonishing and the most confusing.

Though exposed or revealed by these evolutionary laws, the evolution of subjectivity takes man outside these same laws. That is, once established, man's subjectivity causes and responds to a totally different reality; i.e., the reality of consciousness. This, however, in a way is another discussion topic. The task immediately at hand is man's subjectivity. What is it? What is its nature?

Subjectivity and Symbolic Mediation

The only answer to these questions, if one can be given at all, is one which can be determined indirectly. It has been suggested that man's subjectivity was determined by the phylogenetic evolution of his internal sign system. Remember, it was stated that the central nervous system is in fact a communication system. Recognizing this, it is further suggested or theorized that through the use of biosemiotic laws one can understand the connection between the structure and function of this system[4].

The genesis of man's subjectivity occurs in three modes: phylogenesis, ontogenesis, and autogenesis. Phylogenetically, man's subjectivity arises in the evolution of the species or race. Ontogenetically, it reveals itself in the development from ovum to completed organism or the development of the body person. Thirdly, at every moment of waking life, it takes shape as a form of autogenesis of existential acts.[5]

Following Rothschild's symbolic mediation, I will first briefly carry the analysis through the phases of the evolution of life and then transfer the genesis of thought to an analysis of self. Phylogenetically, the capacity of life appears in the genes. Genes are macromolecules within the chromosomes, which bear the information specifying the structure of the species type.[6] Biologists, geneticists, and evolutionists hold that these units existed and multiplied as autonomous structures in the primal atmosphere of earth.[7] From the point of view of biosemiotic law, in the primal atmosphere an intention of "self-realization," which by self-reduplication achieved fulfillment, found expression. Such communication of one's own essence to other matter, presupposes the capacity to preserve one's elementary organismic unity against all agents of change. Similarly, the first biosemiotic law expresses the intention to safeguard the structure that conveys its own essence, the self as a coherent unity.[8] Biologically, what this means is that only if the established structure (being the bearer of its own essence) has the capacity to defend against agents of change, is self-realization possible. Genetically, Mendel (1822-1881), Darwin (1809-1882), and others have shown that disturbances of the established chromosomal arrangement causes mutants. Accordingly, disturbances of the established arrangements of genes; e.g., changes in the composition of the gene

pool) may lead to mutations that are changes of essential character. Returning to the case of the phylogenesis of life, what the
mutation process in fact accomplished was the distortion if not
the destruction of the organism as a self-asserting unity; i.e., self-
realization or self-reduplicating process. Now these mutations or
the primal life form's inability to defend against the agents of
change, elicited from the organism a component of activity which
transformed the organism from an inner self-asserting/self-redu-
plicating entity to one of reproductive intercourse.

The second biosemiotic law is inner polarization. Again,
historically the genesis of life was such that it became impossible
for cells or genes or virus to live independently during this known
period of earth's history. This period of cellular mutation is reg-
istered by the fact that as utilizable sources of energy and life
building material were no longer available when elaborate
processes like photosynthesis and respiration took over and
served as energy providers for the newly acquired complex ana-
bolic processes. Rothschild suggests that this increased the danger of destruction for the structure carrying the essential sense of
the organism. Self-realization now necessitated fusion or intercourse with alien elements, and, thus, required the understanding of other forms (essences) in order to deal with them, to han-
dle them, and to use or defend against them. Self-reproduction of
the organism now required communication with alien elements
in order to recognize its character.   .

However, self-realization and recognition of the alien
essence are conflicting intentions. As such, they together produce
a static situation at best and the next evolutionary step required
in overcoming this conflicting contrast. This was in fact accomplished and is represented by what geneticists call the "diploidy
of chromosomes."[9] Thus, couples of equal or nearly equal primal
units combined in symbiosis. Hence, via this diploid cellular
association, one of the primal units could attend to self-realization and the other to communication or fusion with the alien
essence. This inner polarization is necessary in order for the subjectivity of the organism to communicate with other objects of the
world while simultaneously realizing its own self. This relationship dominates the arrangements of all communication systems
whether cells or computers or man.

The biosemiotic law is very important, particularly as it applies to man, representing the up-to-now end-point of phylogenesis. This is the law of dominance. It suggests that by stages new communication systems appear by successively overlapping the proceeding one. That is, by dominating the previous one. However, before discussing why this law is particularly important in man, allow me to go back and attempt to discuss via these semiotic laws the evolution of self and how, if in any way, the analysis of these laws may differ for different peoples.

What we have in fact said thus far is that during the evolutionary history of life forms, cells, for example, went through three related modes: (1) the development of the species type — Phylogenesis; (2) the development of specific kinds within the species-type—Ontogenesis; and (3) the effect of the existential experience on the species-types—Autogenesis.

Autogenesis

It was specifically shown that the interaction between cells and the primal atmosphere led to changes in form. These mutations from the establishment of any one species-type are what we call phylogenesis. Taking any one stage or period in the phylogenetic history and examining the species kind, we call ontogenesis. Finally, the examination of the species kind and the effect its experiences have rendered unto it is what we call autogenesis.

The examination of the differential evolution of self in this sense must be called autogenesis. It is hoped that by looking at the autogenesis of self from the standpoint of the semiotic laws, we will better develop an answer to the question of which was first alluded. This will be the task of the remainder of this chapter.

The highest communication system for the known vertebrates is their central nervous system. Man, however, differs from the other vertebrates in that a further or higher communication system became superimposed over his central nervous system. Unfortunately, this higher system is not established by nature in the form of a physical structure. Rothschild calls this higher system of communication the "logical act of consciousness."[10]

Through it he suggests that "thought" and "will" emerge together with developing speech. Once merged, thought, will, and
speech work to transform perceptions, emotions, and behavior in
specific ways. Consequently, the central nervous system of
human beings functions to organize information in a novel and
particular way. That is to say, the style of channeling the hormonal and chemical excitations in the central nervous system is inhibited and/or released with the emergence of thought and will.
These channeled excitations are cast in new molds of excitation
configurations. This simple but very important fact is the fundamental distinction between man and animal. It is this primary
independence from a code based solely on the central nervous
system which Rothschild believes makes the intersubjectivity of
man possible. This conclusion can be drawn because he believes
that the form of functioning for this "higher" code is identical for
all persons and thereby endows the world of human spirit with
its objective character.[11]

Biosemiotic Laws and the Evolution of Self

The first biosemiotic law states that there is an "intention
to safeguard the structure that conveys the own essence." In
order to survive as an entity of nature, man had to preserve his
elementary organismic unity against all agents of change. These
being defined as the natural elements and other animal forms.
The second biosemiotic law is the everlasting "life force"[12] which
made the concern for self-realization almost separate from one's
personal capacity to "defend" against agents of change. The
African conception of self was one of oneness with nature and his
kith and kinship.
Subsequently, the natural law of inner polarization must
have taken the form of identifying and understanding other
aspects of the universe (note the early African concern and interest in astrology and alchemy). For the African it would therefore
seem that self-realization occurred simultaneously with the
fusion of "alien" essences in the universe. This, in its highest
sense, is descriptive of the African notion of "one with nature."
The subjectivity of the African must have therefore logically

viewed the self in commonality with other men and nature. This is not only reflected in the African consciousness but phenomenologically and pragmatically in the African lifestyle; e.g., kinship systems, naming ceremonies, etc.

One is almost tempted to say that it is unfortunate that African peoples never gave the notion of self conceptual and rational consideration but in quickly realizing that our reason and logic is bound by our sense of or consciousness of the universe and not the Euro-centric parameters of man's mind, then, one resolves the disappointment in the reflection that the African notion of self will only be found or realized when we become fully conscious of our Africanity.

The European, on the other hand, found the agents of change to be not only the natural environment but his fellow kind as well. Thus, he had to preserve the organism (himself) against nature and other men. Thus, self-realization (biosemiotic law of unity) was dependent upon the European's capacity to defend against all agents of change—other men being defined as agents of change. Since other men were potential change agents, the European's conception of self must have necessitated a feeling or notion of separateness from kind or individuation. This in fact must have heightened the inner polarization (second biosemiotic law). A larger portion of energy must have been given to the polar element concerned with identifying, handling, understanding, and defending against other forms (essences) including men. That is to say, less of the "conscious units" were reserved for attending to the realization of self and most was spent communicating; i.e., the process of fusion. As a result, the subjectivity of the European could only logically view the self as its relation to (against) other organisms.

Evidence of the omnipotence of the European's autogenesis is seen in their thoughts about their consciousness. Even it is viewed as individuated and independent.[13] It is no wonder that European thinkers, particularly the earlier mentioned ones, made at least one common assumption about self. Their system of reason and logic, shaped by their naturally formed conscious, could not determine otherwise. The organization reflected in their perceived consistency of their own internal sign system was heavily influenced by a polarity which gives emphasis to setting oneself apart from, or separateness from, or uniqueness to, or being against all other men and things.

One could suggest that the autogenetic evolution of self for the European race necessitated individuation and independence. It is no surprise then that the thought and theories of European writers and thinkers express this same character. It is their nature. A fact that is determined by the laws of nature.

[1974]

Extended Self: Rethinking the So-Called Negro Self-Concept

"For the oppressed to be really free, he must go beyond revolt, by another path he must begin other ways, conceive of himself and reconstruct himself independently of the Master."[1]

It is indeed no accident that in this society the subjects of social and psychological studies are in some capacity the powerless. It is, in fact, the powerful who study the powerless. Social scientists of all disciplines have traditionally occupied positions of economic, political and psychological superiority over the people they select to study. In a very real sense, the position of the social scientist is similar to that of the colonial master and his subject people.

In this regard, Lewis[2] has noted the relationship between colonialism and anthropology; and like Galtuny[3], she has recognized the parallels between the exploitation by social scientists in terms of data and the creation of information and the political and economical exploitation by colonists in terms of natural resources and wealth. Both Galtuny and Lewis note that to exploit data taken from a country or community for processing into manufactured goods such as books and articles, is no different than exporting raw materials and wealth from a colony for the purpose of "processing" into manufactured goods.

Galtuny continues by saying that in the academic arena this process is no less than "scientific colonialism," whereby the "center of gravity for the acquisition of knowledge about a nation is located outside the nation itself." We note, in this analogy, that just as the colonial power felt it had the right to claim and use for its benefit any product of commercial value in the colonies, so too the major aspect of scientific colonialism is the "idea" of unlimited right of access to data and the creation of information.

Comparative Colonialisms

No where has social science been more guilty of scientific colonialism than in the disciplines of psychology and anthropology. Psychology especially has contributed most clearly to the domination and continued oppression of peoples of color. It has become the single most powerful tool of oppression and its single most effective technique has been to place itself, its conceptions, and formulations as the standard by which all peoples of the world are to be understood.

Following the scientific colonialism model further, one can see where psychologists and social scientists in general, like other colonialists, have historically reaped huge economic and political benefits in the form of better jobs, ease of publication, recognition and fame. Similar to many anthropologists who return from the "bush," the psychologists who return from our communities to create information on the lives and people of the ghetto, often have found a prestigious institution of learning as a consequence of their trek into the unknown.

Western psychology as a tool of oppression and domination is probably best seen in this country in the scientific investigation of Negro intelligence and self-conception. The remainder of this chapter will, however, address itself to only the scientific investigation of the so-called Negro self-concept.

The Negro Self-Concept And Scientific Colonialism

Clearly, the assessment of the Negro self-concept literature and its creators, in terms of (1) data being exported from the community to foreign shores for processing into manufactured goods (books and articles), (2) the center of gravity for the acquisition of knowledge about Negro self-concept being located outside of so-called Negroes themselves, (3) the unlimited right of access to data and the creation of information, and (4) the profitable enterprise of studying and creating information about the lives and people of the ghetto, qualifies this literature as a prime example, almost by definition, of scientific colonialism.

However, of the aspects, which define this literature as a scientific colonialism, the understanding of how raw material was processed is far more critical than the actual technique of raiding Black communities to capture the raw material. The process is critical solely because it is here that the scientist's own assumptions, guiding principles, and ways of thinking and perceiving the world, are forged with the raw material to produce the created information.

In terms of the so-called Negro self-concept, the process by which information was created naturally reflected the thinking, perceptions, assumptions, and guiding principles of the investigators who conducted the studies. The process is most clearly seen in the major philosophical and theoretical approaches of the study of Negro self-concept.

We contend that the process factor, philosophical/theoretical assumptions, etc., is directly related to the nature of the findings characteristic of the literature—finished product. The way in which information concerning self-conception, particularly the so-called Negro self-concept, was processed is indeed revealing given in the above-mentioned relationship. The process factor for the study of Negro self-conception, like the self-concept literature in general, is characterized by four major philosophical-based approaches.[4]

It is this relationship (the relationship between philosophy and scientific evidence or results) that Black psychologists particularly must be aware of, or more directly, need to recognize in what manner the literature created by non-African investigators represents a valid picture of Black reality. The key to this understanding is, of course, in the fact that the kinds of questions asked predetermine the type of answers possible.[5] It is, however, the scientist's philosophy that determines the kinds of questions he will ask.

There is not only a clear and particular relationship between the kinds of questions you ask and the kinds of answers you will get, but there is also an even stronger relationship between one's guiding beliefs or philosophy and the kinds of questions one will ask. Thus, one can see that once there is acceptance of the a priori assumptions and subsequent questions concerning a particular issue, one has at the same time predetermined the realm in which your answers may fall.

Answers are consistent with the questions asked. It is consistent, therefore, that if one asks a question, for instance, why are so-called Negroes inferior to whites? the question itself will predetermine the realm of the answer. That is, the answer can only relate to the already accepted assumption, in this example, the inferiority of Black people.

We contend, however, that the above-mentioned characteristics of the so-called Negro self-concept literature, combined with the philosophy-questions-answers relationship, requires one to conclude that if you believe the Euro-American a priori assumptions and ask questions consistent with it, then one must also accept the answers characteristic of the research. That is, having accepted Euro-American assumptions about Black/African reality, one's questions and answers about Black/African people will be a predetermined matter in response to the Euro-American reality.

The relationship between the philosophical and theoretical assumptions affecting the findings relationship is particularly critical for understanding Western scholarship as it relates to African peoples. We contend that through the recognition of this relational aspect one can best illustrate: (1) the fundamental relationship between the scientist's guiding principles (philosophy) and his scientific investigations (results); and (2) the point at which the scientist's guiding principles invalidate his analysis of a particular area or subject.

We note that the general characteristics of Euro-American philosophy or guiding principles are different from those of African philosophy. Consequently, when African data is processed by the guiding principles of Euro-Americans, the finished results distort the integrity of the original nature of the data. For instance, the European worldview is tempered with the general guiding principles of: (1) survival of the fittest; and (2) "control over nature." These, in turn, naturally affect the nature of European values and customs. The emphasis on competition, individual rights, and the position of independence and separateness are clearly linked to the above-mentioned guiding principles. Likewise, the overemphasis on individuality, uniqueness, and difference in European based psycho-behavioral modalities is traceable to the values and customs characteristic of that community and the guiding principles reflected in it.

On the other hand, if one examines the African world-view and compares it with the European, one can readily note the differences and their implications for understanding Black self-conception. Rather than survival of the fittest and control over nature, the African worldview is tempered with the general guiding principles of: (1) survival of the tribe, and (2) one with nature. In contrast with the European worldview, the values and customs consistent with the African worldview are characteristically reflective of the sense of cooperation, interdependence, and collective responsibility. Similarly, the emphasis in African psycho-behavioral modalities is not on individuality and difference. The modalities consistent with the African worldview, we note, emphasize commonality, groupness, and similarity.

Comparative Worldview Schematic

The effects of these two different worldviews on the under-standing of Black self-concept are critical. The nature of the pro-cessing of data regarding Black people and our self-conceptions was in fact, filtered through the European worldview and to the extent that Black people are an African people, the process has sig-nificantly distorted the validity of Black self-conception.

We have contended that African psychology is rooted in the nature of Black culture, which is based on particular forms of African philosophical principles.[6] Consequently, the understand-ing of the psychology of Black people, more appropriately classified as Americanized Africans, must be African-based. Similarly, if we are to rid the literature of its scientific, colonial tone, the proper understanding of Black self-concept must be based on African assumptions and must incorporate African-based analyses and conceptualizations. In this regard, we can clearly see the impor-tance of understanding the African self-concept and its psycholog-ical basis for Black self-concept.

African Self-Concept: The Extended Self

When we examine the African philosophical tradition, par-ticularly the ethos orders of survival of the people and one with nature, we logically recognize that from this philosophical position an extended definition of self evolved. That is to say, the African self-concept was by philosophical definition the "we" instead of the "I." Hence, in terms of self-conception, the African philosophical tradition, unlike Western philosophical systems, does not place heavy emphasis on the individual or individuality. It recognizes, rather, that only in terms of one's people does the individual become conscious of one's own being.[7] It is, in fact, only through others that one learns his duties and responsibilities toward himself and the collective self (tribe or people).

In terms of the African ethos, then the first order or guiding belief (one with nature) suggests that African peoples believe themselves to be part of the natural rhythm of nature. The second order or guiding principle (survival of the tribe) suggests that African peoples believe in the cosmological and onto-logical importance of life which says that people are paramount and perma-nent. In accordance with the notions of one with nature and survival of the tribe, the African consequently thinks of experience as an intense complemen-tary rhythmic connection or synthesis between the person and reality.

The cardinal point, therefore, in understanding the tradition-al African conception of self, is the belief that "I am because We are, and because We are, therefore I am."[8]   Descriptively, we have defined this relationship (the interdependence of African peoples) as the "extended-self."[9]

In recognizing that in terms of self-conception, the relation-ship of interdependence and oneness of being translates to an extended definition, we note again that the African feels himself as part of all other African peoples or his tribe. One's self-definition is dependent upon the corporate definition of one's people. In effect, the people definition transcends the individual definition of self, and the individual conception of self extends to include one's self and kind. This transcendent relationship between self and kind is the extended-self.

The notion of the we instead of the I may become clearer through the following ontological analysis of the self. It is generally safe to say that the establishment of self is accomplished by (1) rec-ognizing qualities or characteristics similar to one's own, and/or (2) denying qualities and/or characteristics similar to one's own and/or other people. The self, therefore, can be considered the conse-quences of either of two processes-opposition and/or apposition. The way, however, in which African peoples are extended into themselves is not clear in this kind of simplistic distinction. What one must distinguish between is the levels and relativity of reality.

The meaning that one has for being one within himself and his universe, oneness of being, or what is felt as an inner feeling of oneness with oneself is the result of an interpretive process which evolved over the course of hundreds of millions of years. This inner something, which is called the self, is, in fact, the result of an evo-lutionary production, which in the end left man believing in the consistency of his own internalized organized system. The evolu-tion and consistency of the internalized systems of varying groups of people is not, however, always the same.

The philosophical notion of the oneness of being, for instance, is predicated on man being an integrated and indispensa-ble part of the universe. For the African, the oneness of being sug-gests that man participates in social space and elastic time as deter-mined by the character of the universe. Hence, it is true that one's being is possible because of one's historical past as well as antici-pated historical future. In an existential manner, therefore, having recognized the historical grounding of one's being, one also accepts the collective and social history of one's people. African people, in turn, realize that one's self is not contained only in one's physical being and finite time. The notion of interdependence and oneness of being allows for a conception of self, which transcends, through the historical consciousness of one's people, the finiteness of the physical body, finite space, and absolute time.

Self-awareness or self-conception is not, therefore, limited as in the Euro-American tradition, just to the cognitive awareness of one's uniqueness, individuality and historical finiteness. It is, in the African tradition, awareness of self as the awareness of one's historical consciousness (collective spirituality) and the subsequent sense of we or being one. It is in this sense that the self is portrayed as a TRANSCENDANCE INTO "EXTENDATION." That is, the conception of self transcends and extends into the collective consciousness of one's people.

Black Self-Concept

At this point in history, one cannot, however, talk about the African self-concept without talking about the effect of African peoples being dominated, oppressed, and subjugated by European peoples. In noting that the juxtaposition of Africans and Europeans affected the traditions of both the Europeans and the Africans, we do not believe that the negative contact with Europeans resulted in the total destruction of things African. We do believe, however, that each system was different and that even now, after a relatively long period of contact, the systems of consciousness (self knowledge) are still different. For example, the European philosophical tradition bases the notion of self on the concept of independence.[10] Consequently, the Euro-Americans' self-concept is believed to be developed through the process of establishing uniqueness and separateness, "I am (my) self to others." To discover oneself, therefore, in this tradition is to establish one's individuality.

In accordance with the African philosophical tradition, the analysis is different. Here, we find, as alluded to earlier, very little importance or significance given to individuality. When one takes into account the notion of interdependence and the oneness of being, then one can rightfully see that a single person's conception of self and/or his self identity is rooted in being whatever his people's definition is or was. Tribal or people membership, the we, in accordance with the extended definition of self, becomes the most fundamental and critical identity. One's conception of self is thus rooted in being an Ashanti or Ibo or Black or African.

Clearly, the physical situation in which Africans, particularly in the Americas, find themselves involves the domination and imposition of a fundamentally European system of reality on a non-European people. This situation has naturally caused psychological confusion because by nature of European reality, it denied the most compelling property (cosmological grounding of self in the collective, social and spiritual sense of history) of the African conception of self.

Parenthetically, it is suggested that this situation produces the pseudo-entity referred to as the Negro. The concept Negro refers to the African person who attempts to deny or is forced to or convinced to deny the philosophical basis of his Africanity, even though he cannot negate the recognizable properties (psychological facts) of his Africanity.[11] This denial, it is believed, is due to the person being caught in the contradiction between the two philosophical systems, i.e., the African/Black and the Euro-American/white. To be a Negro, therefore, is to be in a natural state of philosophical confusion.[12]

The infliction of the Euro-American philosophical tradition, as it relates to self-conception (individuality, separateness) for African peoples, causes many of us to falsely believe that our natural temperamental tendencies and characteristic spirits were and are wrong and/or uncivilized. This confusion is fundamentally based on the fact that the Euro-American tradition denies the African his historical roots or the grounding of self into the collective and social definition of one's peoples, and that the so-called Negro is taught that the Euro-American culture is: (1) the right, the only civilized culture; and (2) that he will or can be assimilated into it under prescribed conditions.

Hence, the Black self-concept is reflective of a situation[13] described well over seventy years ago. It is, in fact, "two warring idols in one dark body, one Negro and one American." It is clearly the African in us that has never been acknowledged and until this aspect is shared, the self-concept of the Black man will never be fully and accurately understood.
[1976]

SKETCH 9

African Root and American Fruit: The Black Family

One of the most important things for any scholar interested in the Black family to recognize is that the Black Family, its definition, character, and form, does not begin with the American experience of slavery.

We begin our discussion with this point to highlight the importance of our understanding the significance of our total history. That is, explicitly we recognize that the Black family as a unit has a historical continuation that did not begin with the American experience; it extends backward far into the ancestral periods existing prior to the intrusion of Europe and its culture on the continent of Africa. The Black family is therefore, best understood as a unit or system deriving its most fundamental character from its African heritage.

However, before discussing specifically the dynamics inculcated in that heritage, let us note briefly that in understanding the family unit to be a system we in turn recognize that the unit itself becomes an organization of units or sub-elements which are united in some particular form characterized by, among other things, a regular pattern of interactions and interdependencies.[1] It is one's culture that defines the inter- and intra-relationships belonging to the system as well as the social behavior, moral values, and functional and/or structural characteristics of the system.

Many commentators on the family unit have suggested that generally speaking there are two types of family structures in America: the patriarch, or male-headed family, and the matriarch, or female-headed family. This characterization, as noted by Andrew Billingsley,[2] is invariably, juxtaposed to the assertion that of the two types of families the male-headed family is superior. The validity of this particular assertion will not however be

debated in this writing in as much as we hope to offer a definition of the Black family that dismisses the notion and concern for
sexually related dominance in the Black family system.

It is Dr. Billingsley's position, however, that three general
categories of families, each with several specific sub-types, can be
identified. He suggests for instance, that the family unit can be
identified as: (1) nuclear or primary, (2) extended, and (3) aug-
mented. Each of these types, Dr. Billingsley notes, can be found
with several sub-variations, e.g., incipient extended vs. simple
extended vs. attenuated extended,

Even though Billingsley's typology is a workable description of what he at the time contended to be the Black Family system, its limitation is in Dr. Billingsley acknowledging but contributing little significance to the total historical definition.

Philosophical Heritage of Black Families

It is suggested that what determines the peculiar form
Black families take and the peculiar relational patterns expressed
by Black families is the sense of Africanity, or being in tune with
the African cosmological sense of the universe. By this we simply
mean that the basic African philosophical orientation or worldview still permeates and gives direction or definition to the Black
family unit. Once this basic or fundamental orientation is understood, several general features of the African/Black family unit
and its life system can be shown viable in contemporary Black
family systems.

Essentially we suggest that the African cultural heritage
was not severed by the Middle Passage or the severity of New
World slavery and that the continuance of this heritage defines
the fundamental or most basic structure and function of the
Black family.

African cosmological sense as represented by African philosophy is defined as "the understanding, attitude of mind, logic
and perception behind the manner in which African peoples
think, act, or speak in different situations of life."[3] It has been
suggested elsewhere[4] that this definition of African philosophy
and cosmology implies an ethos common to African people.
Again, this we assert to be true in spite of the offerings of many

so-called Africanists who argue that the territory of the western region of Africa held within its boundaries many different tribes, and, therefore, no single or common ethos could be derived from the area. Most of these "students" of Africa and African peoples have maintained that the tribes in the western region had little sharing of experiences because each had distinct religions, customs, and languages. Therefore, no common ethos could possibly come from the area. However, this overemphasis given to tribal differences can, mainly by white or non-African investigators, be considered as the anthropological analog of the divide and conquer strategy. We suggest that a significant number of these ethnographers were and are predisposed to conscious and unconscious racist assumptions, which, in turn, focused their attention to noting superficial differences while selectively misperceiving the underlying similarities in the experiential communality of African peoples.

In redressing this misperception of the African reality, several contemporary thinkers[5] maintain that tribal differences in Africa were minor compared to the binding quality of their commonality. What supported this regional commonality, we suggest, was a set of common guiding beliefs or, if you will, an African ethos. It is further suggested that this ethos or set of guiding principles determined or defined two operational orders. The first order concerns the notion that African people were part of the natural rhythm of nature. In effect the people were one with nature. The second order is the notion of the survival of one's people. That is, the survival of the tribe.

This author contends that African peoples share in these basic beliefs: the survival of the tribe and the tribe being in an integral and indispensable unity with nature. It is further suggested that this ethos is coupled with several philosophical principles, unity, cooperative effort, and mutual responsibility, influence every aspect of Black social reality.

Both the ethos and philosophical principles are reflected in and reinforced by a deep sense of family or kinship. Kinship, in fact, controlled all the relations in traditional communities[6] and was probably one of the strongest cohesive devices in traditional as well as contemporary African life.

Structural Character of the Black Family

The traditional family system structurally stretched later-ally in every direction as well as vertically in both directions, taking into account every member of the community. Hence, a person was related to the tribal ancestors, those persons yet-to-be-born, and every living person in the tribe. As stated before, each person was a brother or sister, father or mother, grandmother or grandfather, aunt or uncle, cousin or some relation to everybody else. The mere knowledge of one's tribal or family genealogy was thought to impart a sense of sacred obligation to extend and continue the genealogical line.[7] In brief, the individual owed his very existence to not only those who conceived and nourished him but to all the members of the tribe.

It is, we believe, this common ethos, which makes a group share with others who have been tagged as different by many scholars. It is because of this shared belief system that African people like the Ashanti share with all peoples of Africa. This is the belief that "the dead, the living and those still to-be-born of the tribe are all members of one family." Thus, one could suggest that by definition the African/Black family is simply a group of persons related by marriage and/or ancestry.

The point to underscore here is that this definition is still applicable to contemporary African/Black families and that it makes the family not bound to household facilities. That is, the critical distinction in this definition is that the family goes beyond the household. It transcends household boundaries to include every member of the community who is by marriage or ancestry related. The family, as defined, is constituted by the several households, which make up the particular community.[8] In this sense, the Billingsley breakdown discussed earlier is more applicable to households than to families. The point, however, to be made by this discussion is that the African worldview defined the structural character of the family and that this character has been the fundamental basis for Black families up to and including present Black family units. This can best be demonstrated by briefly discussing what, if any, significant changes the historical definition of Black families have undergone in response to particular situations and circumstances.

Experiential Communality Periods

Experiential communality is defined as the sharing of a particular experience by a group of people. In light of the above-mentioned set of guiding beliefs (the ethos), we contend that the Black family has existed through three distinct experiential periods. The breakdown most nearly reflecting the actual historical distinctions consists of: (a) the African experience (prior to 1600), (b) the New World slavery experience (1600-1865), and (c) contemporary Black America (1865-present).

The Black family definition in pre-European Africa included every member of the tribe. The experience of New World slavery, we contend, did not significantly disrupt the traditional family definition. We note, as do other commentators on the Black family, that during slavery the prevalent practice of purposely separating members of the same tribe in order to breakdown the collective reinforcement of a common definition did in fact occur. Many scholars[9] contend that this practice also destroyed the sense of family amongst the new world slaves. However, several sources suggest that in North America the system of slavery was extremely unstructured in its beginning and only slowly came to define itself in terms of Black people. We further note that in accordance with the traditional philosophical orientation, the kinship or family system bound the life and existence of each individual. In this sense, traditional Africans believed that kinship system was more important than the individual identity. By philosophical definition the African "I" was really a "we."

Thus, being thrust into bondage in an alien culture, one's identity was rooted in being a Fulani, or Ibo, or Igbera. What reinforced this sense of family or tribal membership was the African ethos; and, accordingly within each tribe, the set of guiding beliefs, which prescribed the survival of the tribe as first order was present.

The consequence of the European forced separation of tribal membership was nothing more than a reorganization of tribal affiliation. That is, as the system of American slavery moved closer and closer to its final definition of slavery, meaning Africans or Black people in bondage, the slaves themselves were moving closer to African or Black as the definition of tribe. So, the traditional ethos principle of "survival of the tribe" was not destroyed and the structural definition based on that principle was also not destroyed. This sense of tribe was reinforced throughout slavery and beyond. The typical collective responsibility and cooperative work —African philosophical principles — outlined in slave narratives and folktales also support the New World maintenance of the African Worldview. The prevalence of benevolent societies[10] and the definition of the Negro church express further support for a clear concern throughout slavery for the survival of the tribe.

With the introduction of technological society, all families underwent severe challenges to their structural definition. However, the African family being additionally burdened with the effects of Euro-American racism and ignorance underwent a more extreme version of this challenge.

We should note the similarity in the forces of change affecting African peoples, whether in America or on the continent during this technological period. Primarily, that the relationship between Africans and the sense of being "one with nature" was disturbed. The relationship between man and the land was weakened. That is to say, on the one hand, Africans were removed from their land—a situation we have called the slave trade; and, on the other hand, the land was taken away from the African — a situation we have called colonialism. In both cases, the relation between man and the land was altered. Secondly, the major challenge to contemporary African families was the strange admixture or confusion of Christianity with western culture, politics, science, technology, and education. The effect of these was, not only a re-tribalization, but also a kind of change best described as a de-tribalization.

In traditional life, even during slavery, the sense of tribe or family was the nucleus of both individual and corporate existence. The sudden detachment from the land and the admixture of Christianity and Western culture produced situations where corporate existence was minimally reinforced. The results of such a change were to produce or create individuals cut off from or independent of the collective morality, customs and tradition. In contemporary times the dominant culture reinforces members of Black families for living as individuals.

Technological society introduced something known as a money economy, which in turn defined time as a commodity to be bought and sold. This concept (the money economy) heightened the importance of the individual. Consequently, the individualism of contemporary life demanded its own code of ethics. In traditional life, the individual was defined by the family. However, as a result of technological society and the subsequent money economy, individualism with its "do-your-own-thing" philosophy allowed personal identity to be locked up in a reality of its own making. In modern times members of Black families were and are explicitly reinforced for living as individuals.

Though we recognize that there is a direct relation between the structural makeup of a system and its functional capacity, we contend that the structural damage to the Black family is very recent, reaching its most intense form with the television explosion of the 1950s. The process of shifting, which ultimately will affect the functional character of the family unit, has not completed itself. That is, even though the historical definition of the Black family is undergoing a change which is similar to the unit transformation occurring in all post-technological societies, the shift has not been completed and, more importantly, if allowed to complete itself, will its effects be similar for Black people as it is for non-Black peoples? For instance, not only will the consequence of this shift be the disintegration of the structural and functional character of the Black family, but also it will be the elimination of the protective buffer that the family affords its members against a hostile and racist society which by its very nature particularly dehumanizes Black people.

Functional Aspects of Black Family Life

The purpose of the family unit is to fulfill certain tasks, responsibilities, and/or basic needs of its members. In meeting these needs, the family unit demonstrates its value as a system.

Pragmatic and Psychological Functions of the Family Unit

Generally speaking, one can divide the functional character of the family unit into two areas: (1) the pragmatic functions, and (2) the psychological functions. Pragmatically, the family insures the provision of food, shelter, clothing and protection.

Psychologically, the family unit offers a sense of belonging. It is via the psychological functions of the family unit that its members become conscious of their own being and purpose. Through the psychological capacity of the family, one learns his duties and responsibilities to himself and toward other people.

The family unit has the capacity to: (1) sustain its members economically, and (2) enhance the emotional relationships within as well as without the unit. It is not only important to recognize that these two functions, pragmatic and psychological, are interrelated but also that the functional capacity of the family unit is dependent upon the structural character of the family. This is more clearly demonstrated when we historically trace the functional aspects of the Black family unit.

Historically, just as the traditional philosophical orientation defined the family structurally, so too did traditional philosophical principles define it functionally. For instance, the notion of unity as a philosophical principle relates directly to the anthropocentric ontology characteristic of traditional conceptions of the universe. When we examine the family unit functionally we, in fact, can note this general feature of unity. The notion of unity coupled with the principle of the survival of the tribe determines a particular, if not unique, approach to the pragmatic functions of Black families. First of all, they suggest that whatever is necessary to maintain and insure the survival of the unit is proper and acceptable; and concurrently, anything antagonistic to its survival is not acceptable or proper.

In terms of the household leadership, for instance, it made little difference whether it was male-headed or female-headed. The important element was not matriarchy or patriarchy but the maintenance and survival of the family unit. In fact, in some instances traditional families were matriarchs while in other cases they were patriarchs.[11] In all instances the most important characteristic was that the family membership was to insure its survival.

In light of the fact that the underlying principle of the whole family scheme was that of a "sense of peoplehood" based on equality in tribal membership,[12] Black family units are more appropriately classified as "tribalarchies." This is not to say that members in the family or tribe did not have roles; each did. However, each one had the responsibility to fulfill the role of another when necessary. Males shared equally in the rearing of children—women shared equally in the defense of the family. Men, women, and children shared in the provision of food, shelter and clothing. The unity within the family disallowed any element which endangered its capacity to survive. A system where the family totally dissolves or radically disintegrates because one member is lost (the father or mother dies or abandons the unit) would be antithetical to the traditional principle, which defined the African Family.

It is our feeling that the same philosophical principles and guiding beliefs which give the Black family its definition; i.e., notion of unity, collective responsibility, survival of the tribe, and one with nature, also guided it through the horrors of American slavery. An abundance of information points to the pragmatic quality of family life during slavery. On being thrust into such a situation, we feel, the pragmatic functions were, in fact, heightened.

The popularized tales of slavery, however, refer mainly to the rivalry between so-called "house niggahs" and "field niggahs" and the internalization of selfish and individualistic survival tendencies. On the contrary, many tales refer to the cooperation and collective responsibility demonstrated by slaves of all categories.[13] The most notable example of these is the slave rebellions—particularly Nat Turner's. Not only did he and seventy or so other Black people assert their humanity in the clearest terms possible, but also the refugees were sheltered, fed, clothed and protected for well over two months by other slaves—by the family, if you will.

Many scholars refer to, or worse, assume to be factual, the notion that slavery destroyed the Black family unit. On the contrary, when one closely examines the records,[14] we find numerous accounts of newly freed slaves returning to buy their husbands, wives, and children or some relative's freedom. In response to this practice, many White legislators began to pass laws disallowing newly freed slaves the right to residency in their former counties. There was but one obvious way for a people who believed in the survival of the family unit to respond.

In contemporary times, we can note the racist practices of dominant society, especially as they are reflected in the operations of welfare and other social service agencies, to see plainly

that institutional racism results in a system which is detrimental
to the structural character of the Black family unit. Functionally,
the unit compensates for this. For example, in terms of welfare
many agencies deny aid if a male is present in the household. In
response, Black men have in some cases actually left the household and in others only mocked desertion. In most cases, however, the desire was to insure the provision of aid to the family.
Structurally, the family appears to be disintegrating by Euro-
American standards, but functionally the membership is striving
for its pragmatic survival and maintenance. Note: Social-psycho-
logically, the sense of belonging provides one with a special sense
of both ancestral and future oriented identification with one's
group or people. Again, the survival of the tribe or family was
and is most important.

The psychological function of the Black family unit can
best be demonstrated by illustrating, for instance, the way in
which self-identity and/or self-conception are handled. Most
scholars recognize that the establishment of self is accomplished
by comparing or contrasting one's image with other people.[15]
That is to say, the self is established as the consequence of one of
two processes-apposition and/or opposition. In opposition, the
sense of self is established by defining one's self as separate from
others. In apposition, the sense of self is established by defining
one's self as the same as other.[16]

Whatever the case, it is the family unit which socializes
members of society to one or the other approaches to the establishment of self-conception. In the typical Euro-American family
unit, self-conception is characteristically created by establishing a
feeling in the person that I am myself by virtue of setting myself
off and away from others, by opposing myself to others. In families functioning in accordance with the African worldview, a
totally different emphasis on self-identity is found.[17] Here the orientation is to conceive of the self as coming into being as a consequence of the group's being. In African/Black families, self-
conception is created by instilling in its members the principle: "I
am because we are, and because we are therefore, I am."[18] In so
doing, the Black family unit psychologically sets its members to
perceive no real distinction between personal self and other members of the family. They are in a sense, one and the same. One's
being is the group's or family's being. One's self is the "self of

one's people." One's being is the "we" instead of the "I". One's self identity is, therefore, always a people identity or what could be called an extended identity or extended self.[19] Rather than tracing this particular psychological function through the above-mentioned experiential periods, we feel that here the historical consistency can be equally demonstrated by discussing briefly some of the noted problems apparently expressed by Black families in the United States.

It is our feeling that many of the reported and/or otherwise documented problems are in fact the result of the African family being assimilated, civilized and oppressed by the Euro-American definition of the family. Secondly, we feel, that in order to understand the needs of Black families, it is incumbent upon Black scholars and/or health services professionals to understand the dynamics of this interaction; the African worldview clashing with the Euro-American worldview. It is only through such understanding that we can best offer the kinds of assistance to strengthen and liberate Black families. Therefore, Black scholarship and health care must, like African literature, be committed. We cannot afford scholarship and service, which are expressions of "art for art's sake."

In brief, the training, theories, and practices of Black scholars and health professionals must be intimately identified with African/Black people. They must reflect through explana tion, application, and documentation our aspirations, failures, hopes, frustration, history, culture and soul.

African Root and American Fruit: Suggestions for Research, Training, and Service

In this chapter, we have tried to demonstrate briefly the simple fact that as a system the Black family is similar to a plant. More importantly, we want to show that like a plant, the Black family in America has been transplanted and that the root of this plant is without question African. As a consequence of the transplantation, the fruit of the plant reflects the ecological nourishment offered by the new host culture or environment.

In terms of the scientific environment, Euro-American culture has almost consistently defined the experience of and

within the Black families as deviant, abnormal, and/or destructive.[20] Most, if not all, of the research coming out of this community makes the deviancy analysis somewhat believable because
Euro-American scholars believed that the culture-less Blacks had
no other option but to mimic White family systems. This deviancy is, therefore, a kind of artifact created by comparing African
families to Euro-American families with a Euro-American yard-
stick. For instance, it is frequently reported that so-called dominant Black families are detrimental to the normal growth and
development of Black children. The occurrence of father-absent
families is another area given to erroneous analysis. And, in a
strange way, particular child-rearing practices have been interpreted negatively as well.

In terms of scholarship and/or health services, the re-
examination of these typical problem areas should be guided by
two important considerations. The first is that Black families
should be understood, analyzed and evaluated by criteria com-
patible to its most fundamental definition. Second, the analysis
must take into account the ecological factors impinging on the
Black family unit, in this society the main ecological factor is
racism. What we should be aware of ecologically, therefore, is the
fact that via the racist, dominant communications channels; e.g.,
schools, welfare programs, hospitals, movies, and television,
Black people are bombarded more intensely—polluted, if you
will—with the Euro-American definition of what constitutes the
family. As a result, Black people are more likely to internalize the
Euro-American family definition as our own particularly since the
1950s. When this occurs, Black people begin to make the same
assertions that white scholars make. Even more is the possibility
that in accepting and making the same assertions, Black people
will begin to view our fundamental unit, the family, as destructive to our personal development rather than rightfully viewing
and understanding that the Euro-American system within which
the Black family unit is embedded is the destructive element.

We believe the role or potential role of Black scholars and
health professionals must be to understand that fundamentally
most, if not all, of the psychological, sociological and educational theories and systems concerning the Black family were developed with European and/or American social reality in mind.

Hence, the task for us is to undertake whatever research and study necessary to develop sound viable psychological, sociological and educational theories and systems based on our most fundamental definition—we are African people.

[1976]

Black People In White Insanity: An Issue For Black Community Mental Health

On February 5, 1963, the President of the United States, John F. Kennedy, delivered to the 88th Congress a special message on mental health and mental retardation, which proposed a new national mental health program.[1] In this message the President asserted that mental illness and mental retardation are this country's most critical health problem. Kennedy further suggested that the time had come for us to identify some clear objectives as well as a bold new approach to the issue of mental health. First he stated, "we must seek out the causes of mental illness and mental retardation and eradicate them." Second, he said, "we must strengthen the underlying resources of knowledge and above all of skilled manpower which are necessary to mount and sustain our attack on mental disability for many years to come." And third, he stressed, "we must strengthen and improve the programs and facilities serving the mentally ill."

Specific to this third goal, the President asked the Congress for a national mental health program, which would assist the nation in the establishment of a new emphasis and approach on the cure of the mentally ill. Central to the President's new mental health program was a concept of comprehensive community mental health centers.

The distinguishing features of the president's message were seemingly clear. First, the new approach would have an emphasis on community rather than institutional care. And second, and in contrast to the heretofore existing mental health centers, the new approach would emphasize comprehensiveness. In this light, Professor Bloom[2] has suggested that the term "community mental health" should refer to all activities undertaken in the community in the name of mental health. Hence, the focus is on the total community or a defined population rather than on individual patients or single individuals.

Much has been done to establish, maintain and facilitate comprehensive community mental health centers and in most instances, some semblance of respect and adherence to the intent of the new approach has been maintained; i.e., rational planning is a forerunner to center construction and staffing continuity of care, sufficiency of quality and quality of services, etc. However, the materialization of community mental health centers does not necessarily guarantee the accomplishment of the first two objectives in Kennedy's trilogy, namely, the search for the causes of mental illness and the strengthening of the resources of knowledge and skilled manpower necessary to sustain the attack on mental disability. For the most part, community mental health centers have shouldered the awesome task of providing mental health care or services to all people of a particular community.

However, one of the greater challenges to the community mental health center movement was to seek out the causes of mental illness. This is especially true on the question of Black mental health. It is hoped that the reader will not fall victim to the trap of wanting to debate the reality of Black mental health. Clearly, one must be able to see that the socio-cultural reality, particularly in the United States, of Black and white people are different in many significant and fundamental ways, and to the extent that the time and space coordinates of one's mental disposition to the socio-cultural indices of one's existence are different, then one can rightfully label or categorize the mental disposition of Black people as such.

In meeting the challenge, therefore, Black mental health professionals must, in addition to providing services, seek out the causes of Black mental illness. Such a task is extremely complex. In fact unless the Black mental health professional is willing to recognize and call to question their own way of thinking and conceiving of mental health issues, the task may be impossible.

Recently, Alfred Memmi[3] suggested that for the oppressed to be really free, he must begin in other ways to conceive of himself and reconstruct himself independently of the master. Implicit in such a reconstruction is for us to recognize that the continued "master-slave" relation, which has historically characterized white-Black relationships in this country is, in part, the results of and maintained by the social sciences. In a very real way Western social sciences have replaced the chains of our previous bondage. Instead of physical slavery, Black people are victims of mental enslavement, which is predicated upon and maintained by Western social science and scholarship. We must, accordingly, be willing to recognize that we mistakenly conceive of ourselves, our people and our realities in relation to white people and their reality.

Western Social Science, Psychology and Mental Health

Western social science should be viewed as the creation and reflection of European-Western man and his particular self-defined practice of Western social science was predetermined by the particular way in which its developers, Western man, understood and were conscious of their own awareness of reality. That is, Western social science was modeled after and reflects the Euro-American's conscious understanding of his own consciousness. In general, Black people and Black professionals are trained, educated and indoctrinated into believing and accepting Western conceptions of reality and their implicit definitions of psychology and mental health. Hence, the dilemma in which the Black mental health professional finds himself in is one of his own reality or knowledge. Yet the parameters defining what constitutes mental health have been defined according to the Western Euro-American conception of mental health quite arbitrarily. This conceptual incarceration of the African-American inhibits the search for the causes of Black mental illness. It seems to me, therefore, that our immediate task is to become conscious of our own consciousness, which is fundamentally different from merely being aware of the accepted Euro-American reality.

In searching for the causes of Black mental illness, it is first necessary to liberate oneself from this state of mental bondage. This, it is suggested, can only be achieved at the point where we develop and become aware of our intrinsic "African Apperceptions."

Contrasting Worldview and Mental Health

In their article, "Critical Elements of Black Mental Health",[4] Drs. McGee and X (Clark) have stated that "in comparison to White people, Black people live in an 'altered style of consciousness' and because of this, the models of mental health and functioning which are applicable to Whites are inapplicable to Blacks." The models of mental health and conversely mental illness are based, as noted above, on a particular worldview. We contend that because each culture has its own vision of man; its own implicit worldview or philosophy of man. Each culture will also have its own way of conceiving and defining mental health and functioning. Drs. McGee and X are quick to point out that there is a natural state of mental health and functioning for Black people and that it is not unusual for those white people who are not in the state of Black consciousness to perceive those who are, as mentally ill.

The definition of mental health and/or illness is a function of what reality or state of consciousness a people of a particular psycho-social time and geophysical space reality respond to. In this regard, we contend that an understanding of a people's worldview is extremely important because it is via the explication of it and its intrinsic implications that one clarifies the appropriateness of the mental health model. For example, the major model of mental health in this country can be derived directly from a European worldview. We can safely say that there are very distinct differences in the two worldviews. One of which is more communal, that being the African, and the other being more individualized, that of the European.

The differences in worldviews are similarly related to the differences in perceptions of mental health. Consequently, it would follow that the definitions of mental health and functioning would differ. For reasons that are not yet fully understood, the European man's ecological and evolutionary development took form wherein a set of guiding principles, (or ethos) which related to the question of self-preservation and survival, became paramount over other possibilities.

The European worldview is clearly distinct from that of the African and it is through these beliefs that meaning and understanding are achieved, thereby, demonstrating that there will be clear and distinct differences in the diagnosis of what is mental illness. For instance, in the ontological (nature of existence) understanding of and relationship to the universe, the European ethos defines two operational orders: (1) survival of the fittest and (2) control over nature. In turn, these ethical orders reflected themselves in the values and customs characteristic of European cultures. More importantly, however, they influenced if not determined, the consciousness of European peoples: a consciousness, which is predicated upon the recognition of difference and the sense of self-separateness or individuality. We suggest that the extreme concern with uniqueness, difference and individuality are directly related to the way in which European peoples perceive and understand the universe; i.e., their conscious awareness of their consciousness. Accordingly, the way in which mental health and mental illness are defined is likewise related to their particular worldview. It is not surprising, therefore, that the so-called healthy person in a European society is self-sufficient; perceives nature as something to be controlled; is highly competitive; has a respect for the individual rights of others; a clear sense of his own uniqueness; and is independent.

The African worldview suggests a different set of psycho-behavioral modalities characteristic of mental health and functioning. Traditional African belief systems[5] understand everything in the universe to be endowed with the "Supreme Force."[6] Accordingly, the nature of existence or being, the ontological conception of the universe, was believed to be Force or Spirit or Power.[7] Because all things were endowed with the same Supreme Force or Power, it was logical to believe that all things are interconnected or interdependent or one. This kind of philosophical orientation or worldview implies a certain set of guiding principles, which are also related to the question of self-preservation. The paramount set of operational orders determined by the African ethos, however, suggested the importance of: (1) survival of the tribe; and (2) oneness with nature. In recognition that a philosophical orientation derived, regulated, and determined all the relations within traditional communities,[8] we can note that this ethos reflected itself in the values and customs characteristic of most traditional African communities, and more importantly, it influenced and determined the consciousness of African peoples. One interpretation of this analysis suggests that the African consciousness would be predicated on the awareness or recognition of the sense of collective self, or communality. We suggest that a mentally healthy person in the African-based, Black, worldview would be a person who is cooperative; who understands and respects the "sameness" of himself and other persons; who has a clear sense of his spiritual connection to and is in harmony with the natural universe; and who has a high sense of personal responsibility for the well-being of himself and others. In brief, the mentally healthy person is one who perceives the interdependence of man and nature. It is a person whose presence does not disrupt the natural law and harmony of the universe. One could suggest then that a mentally healthy Black person is one who has a real sense of their Africanity.

Given the clear disparity between the logical definitions of mental health stemming from the European and African traditions, the Black and white mental health professional should be compelled to reassess their models of mental health and functioning for racially and culturally different peoples. If we are serious about seeking out the causes of Black mental illness, then such an understanding is more than necessary—it is critical. We, the victims of racism, cannot be afraid to raise the unasked question of racial mental health or racial insanity. A response to such a question cannot be made in the confines of the length of any single book, let alone an article and this author would not even attempt to do so. However, I would like to share some preliminary thoughts on the question in terms of Black people in the United States.

The Challenge of Black Mental Health

Without question the greatest challenge to community mental health centers in Black communities is to seek out the causes of Black mental dysfunction or illness. It is equally true for me that the natural consciousness of Black people is forced to equate to a reality defined by white consciousness. Contemporary Black people in the United States live in a psycho-social reality consistent to and supportive of white mental function. Such a situation is tantamount to Black people living in white insanity.

It is insane for Black people whose natural consciousness understands the interdependence and harmonious aspects of the universe to mold their behavior and thinking in a fashion consistent with a reality that is based on independence, conflict and competition in the universe. The cause of this insanity, I believe, is a disruption in the natural, harmonious relationship between the spiritual, material, conceptual, affective and cognitive aspects of Black psycho-social and geophysical reality. One consequence of this disruption is a perceptual and emotional distortion. Hence, insane Blacks deny their self and kind. Consequently, a Black who kills another Black does not realize his act is suicide and not homicide. Another consequence of this disruption is cognitive and political confusion.

Here we find insane Black people deifying white people and dehumanizing Black people. As expressed earlier whites are viewed by Blacks as omnipotent and this belief suggests, in effect, that if anything has to get done, it is they who must do it. Here we find Black people also denying our communality and epitomizing our individuality. Politically, Black people should unite, affirm and protect their own.

The black dope pusher, pimp and killer are only symptomatic of Black people living in white insanity. As long as Black people respond to and accept white reality without question, we will never be able to see, think, feel and act in a fashion that affirms and protects our being.

The implication of this is clear. The Black mental health professional must accept the challenge to seek out the causes of Black mental illness and define Black mental health. In daring to make a prediction, I will conclude by saying if we accept the challenge, the search for a cure for Black mental illness will lead us to the position of requiring the eradication and metamorphosis of the fundamental premises upon which white American society is based.

[1976]

Alienation, Human Transformation and Adolescent Drug Use: Toward a Reconceptualization of the Problem

Alcoholism is ranked fourth among this nation's health problems and is outranked only by mental illness, heart disease and cancer.[1] There are an estimated 70 to 80 million Americans that drink, and at least one out of every eight Americans who drinks is an out-and-out alcoholic. According to the National Institute of Alcohol Abuse and Alcoholism, 7% of the total adult population in the United States has an alcohol problem, and 19% of young Americans between the ages of fourteen and seventeen are believed to have drinking problems. Given that it is currently estimated that at least three additional persons (spouse, children, parents, employer, etc) are affected by every single individual's drug and alcohol related problem, the above-mentioned figures are even more alarming. If one accepts that 9 to 10 million adults have an alcohol problem, then alcoholism and drug-related problems directly and indirectly affect about 30 to 40 million adults, or roughly one out of every five American adults.

The abuse of legal and/or illegal drugs other than alcohol is also a serious problem in the United States. The illegal use of prescription drugs combined with illegal drugs has become rampant. It is estimated by the National Institute of Drug Abuse that almost five million Americans use cocaine and another five hundred thousand use heroin for non-medical reasons. It is also estimated that approximately 18% of young Americans between the ages eighteen to twenty-five use stimulants, sedatives, and/or tranquilizers for non-medical purposes. The overwhelming prevalence of alcoholism and drug abuse in our society has, in part, led some researchers to suspect that the key factors associated with alcoholism may be biological in origin. Some believe there may be, for instance, inborn enzyme dysfunction, an atypical ADH,[2] or there may be chromosomal abnormalities.[3]

In seeking to ascertain the etiology of alcoholism, Davis and Walsh[4] suggested that a spontaneous molecular reorganization may result from the condensation of acetaldehyde with nor-epinephrine, epinephrine, or serotonin to form tetrahydrosio-quinoline or tetrahydropapaverine. The molecular structure of tetrahydroisoquinoline, for instance, is similar to that of a number of plant alkaloids that have high addictive potency. If spontaneous molecular reorganization is true, then one could see an immediate relationship between it and low alcohol tolerance and/or abstinence capability. Though ripe with intriguing possibilities, especially for high melanin concentrated groups, the etiology of alcoholism is extremely complex. It is so complex that Williams[5] concluded in probably the most comprehensive treatment of Black alcoholism from a medical vantage point that, in regard to its etiology, no single factor can adequately explain the condition.

Nevertheless, many and varied theories have been offered for the possible cause of alcoholism and drug abuse. In the field of psychology, for instance, Freud believed that alcoholism/drug abuse was the result of strong oral influences in childhood, while Menninger offered his theory of the self-destructive drive as a prime component of alcoholism/drug abuse. On the other hand, Alfred Adler suggested that alcohol and drug addiction was due to powerful feelings of insecurity and the desire to escape responsibility. Beyond the psychological explanations, various other theories, ranging from genetics through learning theory and physiological analysis to socio-historical-environmental hypotheses, have been put forth. Predictably, the issue of alcoholism and drug abuse has been examined from several different vantage points and various methodological approaches.

Conventional Conceptualizations of the Problem

Upon reviewing the adolescent alcoholism literature, for instance, one finds studies which posit a hereditary link to adolescent alcoholism;[6] studies which explore the physiological and psychological bases of adolescent alcoholism;[7] studies which attempt to identify the relationship between social/ environmental factors and adolescent alcoholism[8] as well as a series of multivariate studies which attempt to identify the relative weight of different factors associated with adolescent alcoholism.[9]

While the literature is rich and provocative, like most socio-behavioral science research literature, the adolescent alcoholism and drug use literature is replete with contradictory findings and methodological inconsistencies. Though an important task, to critique the methodological techniques reflected in the literature is not the purpose of this discussion. The intent of this chapter is to move the analysis of adolescent alcoholism and drug usage to the point of reconceptualization.

Teen-Age character Flaw

It is of interest to note that, in general, the adolescent alcoholism and drug abuse literature reflects an implicit assumption about the teenager. That implicit assumption is that the adolescent alcoholic or drug addict has a personal character flaw due either to his or her genetic make-up, socio-historical background, or individual psychological constructs. The logic of the character flaw in adolescent alcoholics/addicts is typically found in studies which theorize about: (1) personal inadequacies; (2) dependency-conflicts; or (3) the question of self control (internal/external) in teenagers. Burk[10] for instance, in observing the problem-solving, coping, and behavioral patterns of alcoholic parents, found that certain children develop characteristics which make them vulnerable to alcoholism in adult life.

In an earlier study, Glatt[11] demonstrated that young alcoholics could be distinguished from normal alcohol users by their early use of alcohol, the purpose of alcohol usage and a pattern of drinking alone. In relationship to "the dependency-conflicts continuum" and "personal inadequacies approach," Braucht[12] found that adolescent problem drinkers have parents who drink heavily, belong to peer groups in which drinking is encouraged and, generally, exhibit relatively high aggressive, impulsive and anxiety filled behavior. Additionally, adolescent alcoholics are characterized by low self-esteem, depression and loose affiliations with groups having alcohol consumption prohibitions; e.g., religious abstinence groups.

In an attempt to examine the etiology of alcoholism in adolescents, Lisansky-Gomberg[13] reported that the potential problem drinker appears to be a male child who has difficulty and/or inadequate control over his aggressive impulses. In general, these alcoholic-prone males overplay their assertiveness, independence, and other masculine-oriented behaviors and then use denial as an ego defense. In further support of the personal inadequacy assumption, the work of Jones[14] indicates that the problem drinker is characterized by several traits which result in the alcoholic being socially maladaptive and socially incompetent. In regards to self-control, many studies[15] found that alcoholics are consistently more internally oriented and characterized more by lower self-esteem than the non-alcoholics. Segal[16] found that internal orientation was associated with non-alcoholics while external orientation was associated with the alcoholic. In a study to identify the psychological factors associated with drug and alcohol usage, Eisenthal[17] found that indirect social pressure from one's peer group had the strongest relationship to personal alcohol and drug use. The obvious implication of the above-mentioned perspective is that individuals are thought to be substance abusers or at risk of substance abuse because of membership in a vulnerable group or because they possess flaws in their personal character.

Toward a Reconceptualization

In the late sixties, however, the seeds for an alternative perspective were planted. During this period of fundamental challenge and critique of American values led by Black Nationalist and Civil Rights movements, it was suggested that alcoholism and the drinking problems of Black Americans, for example, were the results of societal adaptations. In a very important yet unheralded study, Vitols[18] predicted that Black Americans would assume the pattern of white alcoholic behavior as the Black American further assimilates into white American culture and society. The implications of this work are, of course, that the cultural underpinnings of a particular group may have important consequences for our understanding of adolescent alcoholism and drug usage.

This implication was further strengthened in the mid seventies by Bacon's[19] cross-cultural examination of the "dependency conflict hypothesis." In reanalyzing data from fifty-three different societies, Bacon found that drunkenness correlated with pressure toward achievement in childhood and diffusion of nurturance. It is widely recognized that these two characteristic pressures vary across different socio-cultural communities. Adolescent alcoholism and drug abuse may, therefore, be better conceptualized as a symptom related to the value base or, in some instances, to a larger crisis in society.

Adolescent alcoholism may be symptomatic of the crisis of societal alienation permeating this country. The issue of alienation, however, is not new. The concept of alienation in most instances has been used as a synonym for a personal mental disorder, which distorts the individual's recognition wherein, in turn, familiar situations or persons appear unfamiliar and/or strange. This traditional use of alienation is, in effect, another way of positing a personal character flaw.

However, the "coefficient of alienation" is the measure of the degree in which two variables are unrelated. As so defined, the coefficient of alienation is not equivalent to a personal or individual character flaw. Interestingly enough, Marcuse's[20] discussion of language and meaning comes closest to explicating this notion of alienation. Marcuse notes that in the space between words, meaning enters when systematic, fixed metaphors conflict, and when the gap between signifier and signified, God and man, or man and man is open to reveal being. What Marcuse is suggesting is that when fixed variables, metaphors, conflict, the gap between the variables impact on the subjective sense of being and result in a self-conscious sense of alienation. Accordingly, the degree to which one variable, the meaning of human being, is unrelated to other variables, the experience of human beings, is a measure of the degree of alienation in the society. Clearly, in this formulation, the degree to which one's meaning of self differs from the experience of self is a measure of alienation. The coefficient of alienation is associated with the fundamental meaning of what it is to be a human being and the degree to which a people's experience is defined by that meaning.

The Bases of Societal Alienation or Explicating the Gap

The question and understanding of human meaning for any society requires a trek through the murky tidewaters of ancestral beliefs and the contemporary philosophical outreaches of the society's value system. The length of this discussion, however, prohibits such a daring exploration. Few scholars nevertheless deny or even require extensive verification that the value system(s) found in the United States of America have their philosophical roots in ancient Greco-Roman and Judeo-Christian thought. It is in this philosophical heritage that the meaning of what it is to be a human being is found. Similarly, it is in the retention of the Greco-Roman and Judeo-Christian thought that the roots of modern man's alienation is prescribed. In fact, an analysis of the Greek myths or tragedies known as the Orphic Mysteries, reveals the seeds of the coefficient of alienation and the resultant larger societal character flaw.

In one of the ancient Greek creation mythologies Zeus creates man from the evil ashes of the Titans and the pure heart of his son Dionysius. Human nature is thus dual. It is both good and evil. More fundamental to this discussion is that this tale reveals a conceptualization of God wherein the Supreme possesses the dual notions of impotence and omnipotence as well as an unpredictable, uncontrollable, vengeful and punishing nature.[21] The Roman, Judeo and Christian responses and/or modifications of this basic theme have done little to salvage the resultant conceptualization of man as imperfect and an object of contempt and victimization by superior threatening others, namely, the Supreme. Hence, Western man's consciousness is influenced by a perception of man as both subject to and victim of his or her circumstance.

The Greco-Roman/Judeo-Christian roots to modern man's conceptual universe not only provides us with insights about the meaning of what it is to be a human being, but also it provides us with an understanding of the character of human interactions which reveal themselves upon closer examination as a societal character flaw. Human interactions in the West are filtered through a philosophical heritage, which posits a separate unconnected, threatening, and dangerous "other." The process of becoming and/or the issues of human growth and development are likewise filtered through a value base wherein growth, the development of or expansion toward a higher stage or greater complexity, implicitly "means" development toward or emulation of a higher stage (the supreme), which in itself, according to mythology, is stress-provoking and contradictory. That is to say, the conceptual universe resulting from the Greco-Roman/Judeo-Christian philosophical system defines the Supreme Being and man's relation to the Supreme in contradictory terms; e.g., omnipotent and impotent, vengeful and forgiving, accepting and rejecting, etc. As a result of this conceptualization of reality Western man's awareness of his own beingness was significantly influenced by the presence of an all-powerful threatening "other."

The implication of this philosophical heritage is that Western man's awareness of self is guided by principles, which primarily reflect the issue of self-preservation. Individual survival or extreme individualism thus became paramount over all other human possibilities. In response to the presence of a dangerous, all-powerful, threatening "other," the psycho-behavioral spin-off of this heritage is that Western man's consciousness is shaped by the necessity to perceive his own sense of separateness and individuality as all important. The resultant meaning of a human being is that a human is an object, which is self-sufficient, aggressively independent and perceives other beings and nature as something to be controlled and dominated.

Essentially, Western man's perception of his or her own beingness as a unique self-sufficient, independent, competitive and domineering Being is the result of or symptomatic of the gap between, as Marcuse notes and Greek mythology reveals, God and man. The meaning found in the Western gap is that God is dangerous and man is an object of contempt with no essential connection to the other, including the Supreme. In this regard one can suggest that the extent to which a society's meaning of human being reflects separateness or unrelatedness one will find a gap between the signifier and the signified in that society.

The emphasis on separateness, individuality, unrelatedness and independence in a society can be viewed as evidence of a conflict between fixed elements (concepts, ideas, beings etc.) in that society and accordingly, also serve as predictors of self-conscious societal alienation. A society with a value base congruent with the abovementioned emphasis would, it is suggested, be characterized by a gap between the meaning of human being, the signifier, and the experience of human beings, the signified. The gap between the meaning of one's being and the meaning of one's experience thus represents the inconsistency, incongruity or alienation of self-hood. In societies so defined, one will also find a deeper, more fundamental sense of alienation. Alienation in this sense is embedded in the very value base of the society and consequently is far more difficult to evaluate.

The gap is the consequence of the value base of the society and as such is inescapable without fundamental transformation of the value base of the society. The coefficient of alienation is viewed as a crisis of societal meaningness, and when applied to the problem of teenage alcoholism and drug abuse, it forces us to re-conceptualize the character, definition and etiology of the phenomenon. It essentially requires that the problem be raised from the level of personal character flaw to the level of human meaningness as reinforced by the nature of our societal character flaw.

Transformation

Reconceptualizing the problem of alcoholism and drug abuse as symptomatic of the pathological nature of the value base of American society almost defines the problem as insoluble. Clearly, in a society whose value base reinforces a consciousness which is predicated upon the recognition of difference and the sense of self-separateness or individuality, the presence of pathological psycho-behavioral modalities, drug and substance abuse, is not simply an individual malady even though, as implied by the discussion of alienation, it is related to the individual internalization of individualism, independence, etc. Adolescent alcoholism and drug abuse is a predictable response by young people in search of meaningfulness, which is the fundamental crisis of adolescents, in a society whose philosophical heritage reinforces loneliness, separateness, and irrelevancy.

The recognition of a relationship between teenage alcoholism/drug abuse and societal alienation should not be construed to mean that teenagers engage in pathological substance abuse as an attempt to close the gap or combat their sense of alienation and frustration. Teenage alcoholism is a symptom, not a remedy.

It is suggested that adolescent alcoholism and drug abuse are symptoms of the gap between signifier and signified. Accordingly, it is believed that the remediation of drug and substance abuse in America will require a radical transformation of Western man. It will require a conscious attempt to reunite the signifier with the signified, the experience with the experienced, and ultimately to close the gap between man and God.

In fact this author believes that to the extent that the white Western society can emulate and/or develop a society based on non-Western values, African and/or Eastern, it will be able to close the gap. The works of several scholars[22] support the recognition that the African worldview suggests a different set of psycho-behavioral modalities characteristic of mental health and human functioning. These authors note for instance, that traditional African belief systems understood everything in the universe to be endowed with the same Supreme force. Because all things were endowed with the same Supreme force or power, it was logical to believe that all things are inter-connected or inter-dependent or one with the Supreme and consequently man could not posit a gap between self and the supreme. As such, to perceive no relationship between the meaning of human being, the signifier, and the learned helplessness, which is posited as a conditional factor of adolescent alcoholism, would be hard to establish. Hence, the basis of or reason for alcoholism and drug abuse would be eliminated.

Essentially, this reconceptualization of the problem implies that the solution to the problem of adolescent and for that matter adult alcoholism and drug abuse will require the Africanization of America.

[1984]

Building African-American Family Strengths with an Afrocentric Foundation

The task of building African-American family strengths requires a plan or model that will serve to guide African-American reconstruction while protecting its integrity as uniquely African and American. As such, the reconstruction model should help to: (1) clarify the real world position and purpose of African-American families in the context of a fundamentally hostile, non-supportive and racist/oppressive environment; (2) reveal the specific and varying conditions which affect and influence African-American family life and development; and (3) prescribe and excite solutions or remedies to the downward spiral of the African-American family's material and spiritual condition. In effect, the model should serve as an instrument of family praxis. By praxis is simply meant that which one does to self-consciously shape human experience and its historical conditions. In effect praxis is the set of thoughts, feelings and activities a people perform in response to the advancement of their own image and interest. In regards to family, praxis is, therefore, the combined systematic processes which develop and stimulate the knowledge, skill, ability, attitude and character necessary for the members of a family to undertake socially-defined, goal-oriented and culturally-meaningful activities designed to develop competent, confident and conscious human beings whose human creativity is reflected in his/her personal conduct, social conscience, and moral character.

The Question of Culture and Family Dynamics

Obviously, the key to both African-American family praxis and the Afrocentric foundation for a reconstruction model is culture. Technically, culture is the vast structure of behaviors, ideas, attitudes, values, habits, beliefs, customs, language, rituals, ceremonies and practices peculiar to a particular group of people and which provides them with a general design for living and patterns for interpreting reality. The system of culture teaches the people to recognize phenomena and to respect certain logical relations amongst phenomena. Culture gives meaning to reality. As such, culture has the power to compel behavior and the capacity to reinforce ideas and beliefs about human functioning, including issues of intra- and inter-family dynamics.

As such, culture is the invisible medium in which all human functioning occurs. It is, in fact, important to note that nothing human happens outside of culture. It shapes and gives meaning to our total environment. To think of culture as the medium in the petri dish is an appropriate analogy. It is the substance in which human development occurs. Culture is like the electricity that illuminates the light bulb. We can only know or understand the electricity by what it does. Accordingly, if we are going to develop or reconstruct the African-American family, then it should be clear that we need to understand the electricity that is going to guide its functioning, processes and praxis.

In regard to family dynamics, culture is the electricity which energizes, guides and gives meaning to what is family. As such, culture is not simply one of the many different behaviors or customs that a family expresses. It is not the unique and/or exotic patterns of music and dance. As the electricity or energizer and definer of family process and praxis, culture provides people with a moral demand system. In this regard, culture inscribes and provides certain self-evident truths (culturally implicit affirmations), features and/or ideas that have the power to compel behavior and to reinforce human conduct. As the electricity or energizer and definer of family process and praxis, culture also provides people with a symbolic system. As the determiner and provider of the symbolism of a people's conceptual universe, culture provides a natural legitimacy to certain traditions and ideas which allow for the relevance and acceptability of certain phenomena and the omission of others.

Parenthetically, it is important to note the connection between a people's cultural traditions and their psychological self-worth and self-esteem. In regards to the psychology of a people, the principle of "Identity" reveals and determines the form in which a people's human energy is structured. Identity is recognized as the component or aspect of oneself that best approximates who and how you are. By providing the symbolism of one's conceptual universe and the dynamic affirmations of one's operational process, culture clearly influences the form in which a people's human energy is structured. Accordingly, for any particular group of people, when their cultural symbols lose their legitimacy, and, thereby, their power to compel thought and action, they lose at the same time the power to determine how their human energy is structured. Then psychological disruption will occur in that people.

One of the purposes or functions of culture is to give people the capacity to act and to re-act in relation to their material/spiritual condition and their own self-vested interest as defined by the conceptual universe. In this regard Fanon, Sarason as well as others have made the point that the destruction of a people's indigenous culture is the necessary requisite to the effective colonialization and political domination of the people. Hence, to dominate or oppress a people requires that one usurp a people's cultural integrity and the best way to usurp a people's culture is to have their tool of development and transformation, i.e., the family to be cultureless or acculturated to an alien cultural form.

African-American Family Life Conditions: Destroyed and Betrayed

History clearly documents that, in order to enslave African people, the European and Arab communities/cultures had to accomplish two things. As an act of cultural and political oppression/exploitation these two communities attempted to: (1) destroy the African sense of familyhood/peoplehood; and (2) emasculate or deconstruct the sense and meaning of African manhood.

In African society the purpose of family was to affirm life. Accordingly, in African societies the role of the man and the

woman was to protect and to provide for children who symbolically represented the continuation of the life of the tribe. By dominating and/or destroying the African's sense of self and peoplehood, systems and/or agents of oppression attempted to eliminate the African community's ability to (1) defend itself, (2)
determine the pattern for its own vested development, (3) secure
its own basic survival, (4) continually and create that which is
good for itself.

The result of this historical seizure has been that when
one examines the contemporary African-American family, one is
likely to not see greatness and vitality but dishonor and degradation. Almost everywhere in the world, African families suffer
from (dis)ease, (dis)harmony and (dis)unity, all of which can be
directly linked to the cultural (dis)alignment caused by direct
racism, oppression and exploitation. How else can one explain
that at a time when the wider society is popularizing the idea of
African-American progress, recent census data indicate that the
relative position of the African-American population is becoming
worse and that the image of progress is more real than the reality of actual progress.

In terms of income distribution, for instance, the income
disparity between African-American and white families has
widened since 1970 and throughout the nation is becoming
close to the pattern that had prevailed in the South in the early
1960s. The ratio of the median African-American family income
to the white family median fell from 0.61 in 1970 to 0.56 in
1981. Economically, therefore, the African-American family has
only 56 cents on the average for every dollar the white family
has to spend.

In terms of employment, unemployment affects the
African-American family to a greater extent than the white family. Unemployment in the African-American population increased
by a whopping 140% between 1972 and 1982. In 1982 the unemployment rate for African-Americans was 19% almost doubled
that for white population. The data further indicates that African-
Americans tend to remain unemployed longer and are discouraged from the labor force at higher rates than whites. Among
African-American teenagers, unemployment is as high as 42%.
The implication of this analysis is that a significant proportion of
African-American youths will grow into adulthood without hav-

ing the experience of working at the time when most employers are giving more weight to prior job experience over education qualifications in the selection process. The consequence of this is that African-Americans see and experience the negative consequences of unemployment far more often and in more different forms than whites.

Employed African-American families are similarly affected in our positions in the occupational structure. The data on the occupational distribution of the African-American population indicate that in spite of some shifts in the pattern of employment in the 1960s, the African-American population is still considerably disadvantaged. For example, African-American growth in the professional field was concentrated among counselors, technicians and health technologists. Within managerial and administrative occupations African-Americans were typically managers of small-scale organizations and/or high-risk, unstable ventures.

In addition, the relative gains made in skilled and semi-skilled occupations (blue-collar jobs) are being eroded by the structural changes taking place in the economy. For example, within the manufacturing sector a whole class of semi-skilled workers is being displaced by technological and scientific advances as the American economy attempts to re-tool its technology in an effort to increase productivity and maintain a competitive edge in the world market. The kinds of industrial dislocations associated with the basic manufacturing industries (steel, automobile, rubber) in which African-Americans made the greatest advances in the past decade have dealt a serious blow to the economic position of the African-American population. In spite of some occupational upgrading, African-American workers, however, are still found disproportionately in lower-skilled, lower-paying, service-oriented occupations, which are characterized by high turnover rates, greater incidence of unemployment and limited opportunities for mobility.

The actual structure and composition of the African-American family has also been undergoing tremendous and predictable changes during the last twenty-five years. Whereas in 1960 husband-wife families accounted for 74% of all African-American families, unfortunately by 1983 this proportion had declined to 55%. Just under half of all African-American families are single parent families composed usually of a woman and her children. The consequence of this is that only 42% of all African-American children under eighteen years of age are living with both parents. The ability of these single parent units to provide adequate care and sustenance for their children will be severely taxed due to the changing economy and the pattern of employment.

The single most important aspect of the contemporary conditions affecting African-American families may very well be the urban experience. As a people, in just over one hundred years we have become transplanted out of a rural-based agricultural population into an urban-based industrial population. Within the urban areas the majority of the African-American population is concentrated in central cities where limited employment opportunities, environmental pollutants, adverse morbidity conditions, poor recreational facilities and poor health experiences negatively impact on the life chances and quality of life of the African—American family.

The generally poor ecological conditions of the urban experience directly affect the health status and psychological well-being of the African-American population. Within the urban environment the African-American population lives in neighborhoods with crowded and poorly structured living quarters depleted of community services and resources and lacking viable business infrastructures. These neighborhoods also experience an inordinate share of environmental pollutants with constant exposure to high levels of automobile emissions, lack of open space, and high noise levels.

The consequence of these conditions has been an increase in deaths in the African-American community due to degenerative diseases such as heart disease, strokes and cancer. In the last twenty-five years the cancer incidence rate in African-Americans increased 27% while the mortality rates due to cancer increased by 34%. Resulting from this change the figures show that three out of every four African-American families will have a cancer victim and the figures go on to show that one out of six African-Americans die of cancer each year. In general, African-Americans on the average can expect to live five years less than whites. The implication of the health status of America is such that African-Americans enter the world in a state of disadvantage based upon the poor environmental conditions, inadequate prenatal care, etc.

This disadvantage carries through life in terms of higher infant mortality rates, lower rates of immunization, higher death rates and lower life expectancy.

The Deconstruction of African Manhood

This data is made even more alarming when we focus on the status of African-American men. Such a focus is indeed warranted and critical when one recognizes that there can be no African-American family in the absence of a cultural base and that there can be no viable African-American family in the absence of equally functioning and participating men and women. The data is clear that the African-American man faces a precarious future. On almost every indicator of socio-economic well-being the African-American male lags far behind almost every other sector and ethnic group in the country.

One of the most noticed conditions where the African-American male is behind is seen when calculating life expectancy rates. The African-American male has a lower life expectancy rate than any other sex and ethnic group. Indeed, within the past two years the African-American male life expectancy rate has actually declined. In 1983, the African-American male mortality rate (1,020 per 100,000) was almost double that for white males (698 per 100,000) and African-American females (590 per 100,000) and three times that for white females (393 per 100,000). The incidence of drug-related disease (cirrhosis of the liver) for African-American males under 35 years is 12 times higher than with any other comparable group. In 1983, the death rate for cirrhosis of the liver for African-American males was 23 per 100,000, almost double that of White males of 13 per 100,000, double that of African-American females of 11 per 100,000 and four times that of White females of 6 per 100,000. The death rate for heart diseases for African-American males was 308 per 100,000, the highest rate for all sex and ethnic groups.

The African-American male has a 1 in 21 chance of being murdered in his lifetime (by age 65) compared to a 1 in 104 chance for the African-American female, a 1 in 131 chance for the White male and a 1 in 369 chance for the White female. Homicide is the leading cause of death among African-American males 15-

24 and one out of every three deaths (38.5%) of African-American males 20-24 was due to homicide. The African-American male homicide rate of 54 per 100,000 males was seven times that for White males, five times that for African-American females and eighteen times that for White females. Although African-American males comprise only 6% of the total population of America. they account for 34% of all the murder victims.

Although the African-American population represents 12% of the total population, it accounts for 46% of the prison population. Of the African-American prison population, African-American males account for 89%; 54% of the African-American males in prison were below 29 years of age. In addition to this data, incarceration data indicates a new level of drug-related behavior in the African-American community.

In terms of the opportunities for participation in the mainstream economic activities the data indicates that African-American males are increasingly becoming a marginal group. Labor force participation rates for African-American males fell from 83% in 1960 to 75% in 1983. At the same time the unemployment ratio for African-American males has remained constantly double that of White males and currently stands at 14.9%. Unemployment among African-American male adolescents was 49.6% in 1983. The implication of these data is that large portions of the African-American male population are not participating in the formal economic structure of American society.

Educational data indicate that African-American youth, in general, are scoring consistently below the national average across all grade levels and subjects and, consequently, are not being prepared for college entry. In addition, the data shows that African-American male students drop-out, or are pushed-out of the school system at higher rates than other sex and ethnic groups.

Drugs, youth gangs, violence, victimization and crime are increasingly becoming part of the everyday experiences of African-American males. There can be little doubt that drug use and abuse have reached epidemic proportions within the African-American community. The primary drugs in the African-American community have traditionally been marijuana and heroin, with cocaine being seen as the drug of the rich and powerful. However, within recent years there has been a dramatic shift in the drug of choice in the community. While the incidence of marijuana and heroin use appears to have stabilized, cocaine use has skyrocketed with the emergence of crack. In Oakland, California, for example, it is estimated that 90% of the drug trafficking is in cocaine. The emergence of this drug has brought the more expensive and addictive cocaine into the reach of the poorer sectors of the community. Crack is cheap, easy to hide and use. It is evident that crack is deadly, potent and highly addictive. In this regard, data from the latest National Survey of Drug Use (1987) reported that one out of every twenty-five high school seniors (4.1%) reported having tried crack in the past year. Usage rates were substantially higher among the non-college bound (5.2%) than the college bound (2.8%); and in the larger cities (5.9%) higher than the smaller cities and non-urban areas (3.5% each).

The increase in drug-related activities is reflected in a corresponding increase in arrests for drug offenses. There was a 19% increase in arrests for drug offenses in 1984, compared to 1983. The alarming trend in this statistic is that there was an 11% increase in arrests for heroin and cocaine sales and a 7% decline in marijuana sales. These data reflect a shift in the pattern of drug activities to the more addictive drugs of heroin and cocaine.

The context of drug use in the African-American community is especially problematic, in that most children learn about drugs and are offered drugs the first time by social peers and sometimes even relatives. The consequence of this is that children are exposed at early ages to the presence of drugs; they are capable of identifying the behavioral modalities associated with drug use; and these children become quickly acclimated to a drug-infested environment.

One must not forget diseases that afflict members of the community as well although there is a definite presence of drugs in African-American communities. AIDS is the newest and most frightening danger to emerge from the presence of drugs in the African-American community. However, until recently, in the African-American community, AIDS had been considered a disease affecting white homosexual and bisexual men and some African-American intravenous drug users. At present, African-Americans, mostly males, represent 25% of AIDS cases, but they are only 12% of the national population. Among children the situation is even worse. Currently 59% of children with AIDS are African-American. Almost all of these children have been infect-

ed in utero; 89% of diagnosed children have at least one intravenous drug-using parent.

Due to the prevailing pattern of drug use in the African-
American community, the sharing of needles, common among
heroin users, represents the primary mode of transmission of the
virus in the African-American community. Similarly, the increase
in teenage prostitution associated with crack houses is placing a
large proportion of young women at risk of contracting the virus
through sexual intercourse with multiple partners. There is little
doubt that the incidence of drug use and sexual misconduct have
placed the African-American population at great risk of contracting this deadly virus. Without a doubt the primary effect of substance abuse and sexual misconduct in the African-American
community is one of death, devastation and destruction as lives
are lost, careers are destroyed, families are torn apart, and the
future resources of the community are depleted.

Given the concrete conditions experienced by the
African-American population, it is evident that African-
American families are worse off than whites in every area of
American life; and, if allowed to remain unchanged, we shall
become the first permanent racial caste in American history. In
spite of these facts, the popular press and the former governmental social engineers claim that the African-American problem has been solved. However, even though there has been this
transparent attempt to reinforce the lie that conditions have
improved for African-American people, economic exploitation,
racial oppression and political domination and disenfranchisement remain a critical part of the overall African-American
experience. African-Americans continue to enter and leave this
world in a state of disadvantage.

The Afrocentric Foundation for Building
African-American Family Strengths

The condition and status of African and African-American
families have not always been as depicted above. In fact, according to anthropological, archaeological and paleontological
records, it is clearly evident that Africans invented and were the
first people to develop codes of conduct that directed social life

and family purpose. According to Kemetic Sacred Lore, for instance, there were initially Ten Divine Creative Principles, which through the fusion of spirit into matter (Alchemical Initiation), resulted in the full manifestation of God as the fully developed and perfected human soul. Hence, the life cycle was a cycle of constant transformation and development. The role of the family, accordingly, was to guide and direct the transformation of human beings from lesser material beings to higher spiritual beings. In Kemetic thought, the three basic attributes of the "Life Process" which the family system had to direct and guide were desire, thought and action. The developmental cycle was thought to reflect a process wherein *Desire* was followed by *Thought*, which, in turn was followed by *Action*, which then gave rise to further *Desire*. This was considered the "Spiral" or "Wheel of Life." In terms of these basic attributes of life, "Alchemical Initiation" was the term given to the perfecting of each cycle until all desire became pure love, all thought became clear understanding, and all actions became acts of sacrifice or service for the benefit of the whole.

The three stages of "Alchemical Initiation" required to reach "perfected man" were symbolized by: (1) The God Tehuti —signified Perfect Love;   (2) The Goddess MAAT—signified Perfect Understanding or Cosmic Consciousness; and (3) The God Heru Pa Khret signified Perfect Sacrifice or service. These African philosophical ideas, in turn, suggested that all human beings were organically related to everything in the universe and the family represented the primary arena of universal functioning. Hence, knowledge and being were derived from participation with and experience in the universe. Beingness, including social or family being, was measured by the concept of balance. Everything had its complementary aspect and natural position of balance.

Family relatedness was, therefore, the praxis point of humanity. Accordingly, the mode of African family was that of participation, equilibrium, relatedness and harmony. African (Kemetic) familyhood was ultimately revealed in the symbolism of MAAT and the spirituality of the Africanity. The principles underlying the symbolism of MAAT were believed to be the proper quality of all Being and Becoming. Hence, family functioning and society itself were driven by the Seven Ancient Cardinal

Virtues of MAAT: Truth, Justice, Righteousness, Harmony, Balance, Propriety, and Order. What the cardinal virtues of MAAT revealed was that familyhood should be based upon the belief that: (1) a just and proper relationship characterizes everything including the relationships of the husband and wife; parents and children; rulers and the ruled; the teachers and the taught; the living and the dead, etc.; and (2) that something is true, not only because it is susceptible to testing and validation, but also because its Beingness is recognized as being in its true and proper place in a divinely ruled universe.

These perceptions and the philosophical concepts, which underlie them can be represented by the notion of Afrocentricity. Afrocentricity is, in fact, the intellectual and philosophical foundation upon which African people create the political, scientific and moral criteria for authenticating the reality of African family processes. Afrocentricity is a quality of thought and practice which is rooted in the cultural image and interest of African people. It, therefore, refers to the life experiences, history and traditions of African people as the center of one's analyses and functioning. Accordingly, as the core and fundamental quality of African Beingness and Becoming, Afrocentricity reaffirms the right of African people to: (1) exist as a people; (2) contribute to the forward flowing process of human civilization and culture; and (3) to share with as well as shape the world in response to our energy and spirit.

The African–American family, therefore, becomes a term used to characterize a group of people who are biologically and spiritually bonded or connected, and whose members' relations to each other and the outside world are governed by a particular set of cultural beliefs, historical experiences and behavioral practices. The African-American family is embedded in a Euro-American cultural milieu but clearly derives its primary characteristics and definition from its African nature. In terms of cultural beliefs and behavioral practices the so-called African-American family should be thought of as an Americanized African family, or more correctly, an African-American family.

In building African-American family strengths, the ultimate test will be our ability to reclaim an Afrocentric: (1) purpose of family; (2) socialization processes; (3) organizational functioning; and (4) inter- and intra-personal relationships.

In terms of the organizational purpose of the African-American family, the family's reason for being should be considered child-centeredness. By this is meant that the purpose of the African-American family focused on, if not required, the presence of children. The family unit exists for the growth and development of children, rather than for the self-actualization of the adult members of the unit. Relative to the centrality of children in African-American family life, it should be pointed out that childrearing or socialization is the most important aspect of African-American reality. The values and beliefs associated with our childrearing practices ultimately become the ideas our children have about who they are and what they can become. In this sense socialization influences the actual awareness of reality. That is, the childrearing practices adopted and the value stressed reflect the intrinsic cultural value system as it is mediated by the concrete historical conditions in which a people are located.

The most significant feature of the African-American socialization process is the indoctrination of the young with a strong sense of morality and humaneness. Generally, childrearing practices in African-American families are characterized by an atmosphere of family orientation and unconditional love which places a special emphasis on strong family ties, respect for elders, and sees the child as possessing a natural goodness. Within such families, children are socialized to assume significant responsibilities and express mature social behavior at a young age. Self-reliance or responsible behavior is inculcated at early ages in African-American children as a reflection of their cultural worldview, which suggests that all things are interconnected and thus everyone has a part to play in the welfare and survival of the whole. Cognitively, the household responsibilities assumed by African-American children reinforce their own sense of self-esteem and provide them with some appropriate practical skills to negotiate the adult world and the wider social system.

The social organization—that is, the organized pattern of relations within the organization—of African-American families should reveal a close networking of relationships within and between families not necessarily related by blood. This principle of inclusivity is functional in as much as these social relatives or para-kin are almost indistinguishable from biological and/or legal relatives. The special aspect of the family networking is worth highlighting as the elastic nature of the family. Structurally, the African-American family is a living organism that stretches and diminishes in response to external conditions that impact on it. Thus, at any one time in its cycle of contraction and expansion, the family will take a different form. There is no one particular type or kind of African-American family.

When we consider interpersonal relations, that is the typical relations within the organization of African-American families, we should see that the African-American family will be comprised of several individual households with family definition and the lines of authority and support often transcending any one individual household unit which comprises the family. Interpersonal relations are characterized by a principle of interfamilial consensual adoption wherein children are allowed to stay with extended kin for relatively long periods of time and become members of the immediate household. Interpersonal relations are also characterized by a principle of multiple parentage wherein several individuals perform the parenting function. In this context older siblings perform significant childrearing functions in the African-American family.

Role relations, that is to say, the proper and customary functions of members of the organization, within the African-American family are flexible and interchangeable. Role definition is expressed in sex-related terms. There is a distinction between what it means to be a man and what it means to be a woman in the society. However, in terms of the performance of the roles, there was no distinction based on sex. Males and females perform the same functions within the family in efforts to maintain the functioning and cohesion of the whole.

Although there were no distinct sex roles within the African-American family, the elderly hold a special position. They represent the keepers of the family's heritage and the repository of the family's history and accordingly have been given respect for their insights and guidance in matters of the family. Storytelling was used as a means of transmitting a particular culture that is, language, values, rhythm, beliefs and established traditions, to the young in African-American families. The Institute's research indicates that the elderly are most often the storytellers in the family, thereby serving the critical function of instilling in a sense of history and family to the young via stories.

Parenthetically, we must note that the live storytelling which older African-Americans experienced as children has been almost replaced by television for the current generation of African-American children.

The task of building African-American family strengths with an Afrocentric foundation must, in effect, represent the reclamation of parenting techniques, which reflect and respect the notions discussed above. The indigenous cultural system of African and African-American communities can serve as a natural inoculation against inappropriate and dysfunctional family life by parenting through Afrocentric principles. African-American parenting should be governed, therefore, by a strong sense of appropriateness and excellence which emerged from a belief in the interconnectedness and oneness of the African-American family. In order to make a difference in our families we must seek traditional practices that can strengthen the family unit. There are seven traditional African-American parenting techniques which do, in fact, reflect the Ancient African notions of "Alchemical Initiation" to perfection and the traditional sense of Afrocentricity.

The first parenting principle is "unconditional love." What the ancients would call the transformative life cycle of "desire to pure love." In regards to unconditional love, African-American parents should be demonstrative in showing love and establishing bonding. In so doing, we will be able to use and develop in our children the conscious recognition that the family spirit is ever-present and the family bond is unbreakable. Afrocentric parenting from the principle of unconditional love results in the performance of the parental responsibilities of discipline, guidance and correction being done as acts of interdependence and love and not domination and control.

The second parenting principle is "reciprocity." What the ancients would call the transformative life cycle of "action to perfect sacrifice." In regards to reciprocity, African-American parenting techniques should help our children to understand that individually they are interconnected and interdependent with each other and what happens to one, happens to all. Afrocentric parenting from the principle of reciprocity will result in African-American parents helping their children to understand that they can determine what happens to them by what they choose to do.

The third parenting principle is "restraint." What the ancients called the transformative life cycle of "action to perfect sacrifice." African-American parenting techniques should encourage our children to appreciate self-control and value personal restraint. The consequence of this is that our children recognize that their individual rights are always balanced against the requirements of the group. Afrocentric parenting from the principle of restraint will result in African-American parents developing and using family rituals and practices, which reinforce personal restraint and reward sacrifice for the good of the family.

The fourth parenting principle is "responsibility". What the ancients would call the transformative life cycle of "desire to perfect love." This principle should reinforce the sense of belonging and family relationships as well as reward the children for being responsible for each other. In part, this is done by encouraging children to use formal salutations and familial entitlements. Consistent with the technique of responsibility, African-American parents should develop family rituals and practices, which encourage collective effort and mutual responsibility amongst their children.

The fifth parenting principle is "adaptability." What the ancients would call the transformative life cycle of "thought to clear understanding," This principle should help our children to understand that they have no limitations and are capable of performing any task. As such, African-American parenting techniques should routinely create time for our children to engage in reflection, imagination, and creativity. We should allow our children time and the opportunity to be spontaneous. Consistent with the technique of adaptability, African-American parents should develop family rituals and practices which will help their sons and daughters to recognize the importance of the biological and meta-physical differences between men and women while simultaneously encouraging their children to reject any sex-linked and/or artificially imposed limitations.

The sixth parenting principle is "inclusivity." What the ancients would call the transformative life cycle of "desire to perfect love." In regards to inclusivity, African-American parenting techniques are based on the recognition that our children are highly affective and sensitive to all the cues, which include as well as exclude them from psychologically belonging to the family. Consistent with the technique of inclusivity, African-American parents should develop family rituals and practices which, reinforce their children's importance to and membership in the family.

Finally, the seventh parenting principle is "respect." What the ancients would call the transformative life cycle of "action to perfect sacrifice." In regards to respect, African-American parenting techniques encourage in our children a willingness to acknowledge and respect the accomplishments and achievements of each other. As African-American parents, we need to take every opportunity to openly reward behaviors in our children, which take into account and show appreciation for the feelings of others. African-American parents have developed family rituals and practices, which reinforce in our children a code of conduct which instills self-respect and honors the status and wisdom of the elders in our family.

In summary, the ability of African-American parents to develop competent and confident African-American children, while at the same time, withstanding the debilitating and dehumanizing effects of racism and oppression, is directly related to the ability of African-American parents to reclaim our cultural tradition and to re-establish our own unique and appropriate codes of family conduct and parenting practices. It is this task of withstanding and maintaining against racism and oppression that brings most thinking African-American practitioners to ultimately recognize that the survival of the African-American family subsequently depends upon our collective ability to change the basic assumptions and value orientations governing relationships in this society. In effect a proper reading of the concrete conditions effecting African-American life and family viability requires a fundamental reordering of the American philosophical, political and economic systems.

[1988]

Public Policy and the African-American Family

The debate over whether the African-American family is an organization inherently laden with problems and inadequacies has raged literally from the beginning of the twentieth century.[1] Scholarly debate about the reasons for the intrinsic weakness of the African-American family has paralleled and mirrored the wider society's negative and pejorative image of African-American people. The fact of the matter is that the school of thought, which posited an exclusively pathological or negative African-American family system, resulted from racist and ideological contamination of scientific analysis. The family qua family is an institution, and all family systems have a particular functional integrity and are influenced by their interactions with wider societal systems. The African-American family is no exception to this empirical generalization. A sound understanding of the African-American family as an institution, with strengths and weaknesses resulting from both its functional integrity and its structural relationship with external societal forces, as well as the way these conditions are affected by public policy, necessitates the unraveling of several commingling issues. As an institution, the African-American family is situated in a society characterized by the twin forces of social and political exploitation and racial and cultural dehumanization.

The ongoing debate regarding the proper role of government and public policy in relation to society in general, and the African-American family in particular, must always be qualified by the historical experiences of African-Americans. This issue of the proper role of government has most often been couched in terms of the extent to which the public sector and the private sector ought to allocate society's resources and ensure the acquisition of basic necessities. In effect, the question becomes to what extent should command mechanisms, the authority of the government, rather than market mechanisms, the laws of commerce, be utilized to allocate societal resources and security.[2] This debate seems reasonable, and although in the United States there is a historical bias in favor of market/private sector allocation, command/public sector mechanisms have been utilized to direct and redistribute resources and services. In relation to African-Americans, however, the debate over public versus private sector resources is somewhat specious.

Two facts must be recognized if one is to observe clearly and distinctly the pervasive and insidious nature of the phenomena that negatively affect African-American families. One must first recognize that discrimination is an act designed to separate people for the purpose of allowing one group to receive preferential treatment and advantage; and second, that in a system characterized by racism and oppression, almost every element or process managed by the racist system is designed primarily to continue and secure the status of all the advantaged people by guaranteeing preference in all arenas. Consequently, the conceptual and empirical connection between sociopolitical exploitation and racial/cultural dehumanization makes the distinction between the public and private imperceptible.

The history of the public and private sector treatment of African-Americans and its consequences for the African-American family mirror the same image. The private sector, which has and should serve the arena for bettering one's life chances and conditions, has never allowed African-American people the opportunity to benefit from full and open participation. The structure of discrimination, which is the foremost tool of the twin forces of exploitation and dehumanization, has served virtually to prevent African-American advancement. Discrimination in education and employment has restricted and continues to restrict, if not eliminate, the paths to development and security for African-American people. At the turn of the century, for example, the United States was becoming an urban, industrial-based society; by participating in the private sector, some people were able to gain economic independence and to guarantee that their children would move up the socioeconomic ladder. But at the same time African-American people, regardless of education, were generally considered to be inferior, and relegated to low-status, poorly-paid occupations in the private sector.

In fact, the structure of racial discrimination was such that northern white industrialists looked to Europe for the labor needed to build the burgeoning urban-industrial economy, rather than recruiting African-American freedmen from the labor-intensive South.[3] From industrial/corporate ownership to union/labor membership, racism and prejudice in the private sector have for the most part, formed for African-American people an impenetrable barrier to permanent personal advancement and long term family security.

Norman Bell and Ezra Vogel[4] have posited that the family contributes its loyalty to the government in exchange for leadership and governance, which will provide for direct and indirect benefits to the family. The underlying assumption here is that governmental intervention will serve the family. There is little doubt that African-American people have been loyal to the United States, but, although citizens, they have derived few reciprocal benefits for their loyalty.[5] The public sector has the power to change positively the conditions affecting African-American family life. However, as Andrew Billingsley observes, when the public sector is contaminated by the philosophies of domination and control, the mechanisms it utilizes are by definition incapable of intervening positively on behalf of the disenfranchised and exploited African-American people. To the contrary, the power of the public sector serves as an additional negative force in shaping the conditions under which African-American people live.[6] Almost from the very moment that Africans were captured and enslaved in the United States, the public sector has pursued and established policies which have partially contributed to or guaranteed the victimization of the African-American family.[7]

During the period of American slavery the public sector legally defined the African as less than human. Subsequent laws and practices, e.g., enslaved Africans could make no binding contracts or have legal redress, established the precedent for and ensured the exploitation of the African-American family. Public sector acts of commission and omission, e.g., the slave commodity exchange was more valued than African-American family bonds, resulted in the government doing nothing to ensure stable African-American family life. In fact, the national government was committed to the institution of slavery and the dehumanization of the African. The public sector in the United States in effect defaulted on its responsibility to protect the integrity of the African-American family. More recent public sector initiatives ranging from AFDC to Social Security to the policies of "benign neglect" and the "workfare" must be viewed in this historical context. In fact, to look at public sector initiatives ahistorically results in confusion and distortions regarding what they can or should do. Historical events and experiences place both public and private initiatives in context. The contextual framework of ideas, beliefs, attitudes and forces which shapes and determines human events is very important. The idea of context, for example, helps to explain the difference in outcomes between one running on an asphalt track and one running in two feet of water. Just as asphalt and water are contextual variables influencing both time and distance in running, the ideas held about African-American people and beliefs about reasonable use of command mechanisms influence and shape the development of public policy. Ideas and beliefs constitute an intellectual—and contextual—atmosphere which reflects the society's conceptual universe. This same context or intellectual atmosphere also influences the scientific examination and understanding of African-American family dynamics.

One must examine the issue of the African-American family and public policy in terms of both African-American family's functional integrity and its structural relationship to the set of ideas and beliefs constituting America's political context. For example, many scholars reject the idea of the African-American family, arguing that the phenomenon known as the African-American family is not monolithic; African-American families do not march in lockstep and do not exhibit the same features, structures or practices. The same scholars then argue that there is no such thing as the African- American family; rather there are many different types of African-American families. Although not accepting the myopic, monolithic stereotype of the African-American family, this author does not reject the appropriateness and applicability of the idea of the African-American family as an institution, especially in regard to its relevance to public policy.

The appropriateness of the concept of the African-American family as opposed to the African-American families relates directly to how one defines the constellation of beings, ideas, values, beliefs, attitudes and practices, which represent a family system. When one works with and studies African-American families thoroughly over an extended period of time, one cannot help but recognize that many different family forms and structures exist in African-American communities. However, scientific investigation of the African-American family also teaches one that in conjunction with the diversity of forms and structures, much similarity can be found among the different types of African-American families.

As social systems, families are products of society. Thus, the recognizable "specialness" of a particular kind of family emerges as function of the family's culture and its relationship with the larger society. Hence, the communality or special sameness found among African-American families is the result of their common historical experiences, and the relationship between the group, the roots of which rest in sociopolitical exploitation and racial/cultural dehumanization, and its common cultural ancestry, the base of which is African. Technically, therefore, the term African-American family has utility because the phenomenon so named has definable parameters, which allow it to be located in time and space, recognized by the senses, and distinguished from other like phenomena. In effect, African-American family is a term used to classify the social and human organization of a group of people of African descent who are biologically and spiritually bonded, and whose relation to each other and the outside world are governed by a particular set of cultural beliefs, historical experiences and behavioral practices.

Institutions share a key attribute with organisms; as both weaken, their abilities to resist the ill effects of their environments diminish correspondingly. The African-American family is no different; the ill effects of American society, in the form of sociopolitical exploitation and racial/cultural dehumanization, constantly bombard African-American families, both directly and indirectly. Yet, the societal problems experienced by the African-American family and its members are often viewed as personal character flaws or indicators of racial inferiority. It is important, however, to note that the perception and definition of African-American family problems are influenced by the same societal values and forces. African-American family problems are not isolated, individualized and personal problems experienced by racially inferior people. The problems have their moorings in societal causations. Teenage pregnancy, for example, emanates not only from teenage sexuality and immaturity, but also from a larger array of societal influences. Substance abuse is not just a problem of individual character flaws, but it is also a societal problem. Interpersonal violence is not only the failure of individual problem solving and coping strategies. The feminization of poverty is clearly a problem of the devaluation of women in this society. Educational failure is grounded in the inability of schools to teach the young. The criminalization of African-American youth ultimately results from this society providing only limited options for their development, thus narrowing if not eliminating their choices for adult productivity. And finally, the clearest example of societal problems masking themselves as family problems is economic dependency. Economic dependency and unacceptable levels of African-American unemployment are without question the results of a society whose core value system is corroded and unjust. Hence, economic dependency is also a societal problem.

The problems experienced by the African-American family result from its structural relationship with American society, leading to a weakening of the family's functional integrity. This weakening is best revealed in the area of culture. The de-legitimization/defamation of African culture, in fact, has been the principal instrument in the negative transformation of the African-American family institution. From its very origin American society articulated the racist and unsubstantiated opinion that African people were innately inferior. Purportedly, Africans and those of African descent had no culture worthy of respect, or, at best, had a deviant culture deserving of ridicule and rejection.

Unfortunately, and probably as a consequence of our socialization to judge a culture by its material artifacts and affluence, many African-American people have come to believe in the lie that African-American culture either is nonexistent or deviant. But culture is more than its material representations. Culture is a process, which gives people a general design for living and patterns for interpreting reality. As such, culture emerges as a dynamic human system of features, factors, and functions with sets of guiding principles, assumptions, codes, conventions, beliefs and rules which permit and determine how members of a group relate to each other and develop their creative potential. Accordingly, nothing human happens outside of the realm of culture. Most cross cultural psychologists now recognize that when the symbols, rituals, and rites of a culture lose their legitimacy and power to compel thought and action, disruption occurs within the cultural orientation and reflects itself as a pathology in the psychology of the people belonging to that culture.

Given that American society has often, via public policy and private action, attacked and denigrated African culture, and given that culture serves as the social cement for familial and societal functioning, the question becomes how the government can direct and redistribute resources and services in such a way so that the functional integrity of the African-American family system can be maintained and enhanced. In order to make this determination, one must fully understand and appreciate the concrete reality of African-American family life as well as the antecedent and consequential conditions in relation to that reality.

The African-American family has been subject of study and investigation for over one hundred years, and for almost the total duration of that period; scientists, scholars and commentators have put forth the opinion that there is something intrinsically wrong with it. Nathan and Julia Hare[8] and Benjamin Bowser[9] call attention to the problem of African family analyses, pointing to the confusion surrounding the importance of culture and class, as well as to the influences of internal versus external factors. In spite of the difficulty in assessing accurately the African American family, there are data to support the observation that African American families across this nation are experiencing an ever-increasing weakness in their ability to function as viable human organizations. The emerging weaknesses in the African-American family are clear; decreasing self-reliance; the perpetuation of intergenerational dependency (the so-called welfare syndrome); increasing alienation and violence among the young; social isolation of the elderly; and most important, a loss of spiritual values, or at least an exchange of spiritual values for materialist ones. These factors are all both causes and symptoms of the erosion of African-American family integrity.

In 1987, the estimated 29.6 million African-American people living in the United States represented 12.2% of an estimated total population of 242.8 million, or approximately one in every eight persons in the society. This number comprised 7.1 million African-American families. Structurally, the African-American family has undergone distressing and predictable change since the mid-twentieth century. In 1960, two-parent families nationally accounted for 80% of all African-American families. Almost three decades later in 1987, this state of affairs had been reversed, and single-parent families constituted 58.5% of all African-American (55.3% were headed by women and 3.2% were headed by men), while 41.5% were traditional two-parent families.[10] Approximately three-fifths of all African-American families reside in New York, California, Louisiana, Michigan and Ohio. In 1985, these ten states, in addition to Alabama, Maryland, New Jersey, Pennsylvania, South Carolina and Virginia, each had an African-American population in excess of one million.[11]

At a time when the wider society is popularizing the idea of African-American progress, census data indicate that the relative position of the African-American population is becoming worse and that the image of progress is more real than the reality of progress. For example, across the nation the ratio of the median African-American family income to the white family median fell from 0.61 in 1970 to 0.58 in 1980 and 0.56 in 1987.[12] In 1987, the African-American family had only fifty-six cents for every dollar the white family had to obtain the necessities of life.

Moreover, unemployment continues to be a more common experience of African-Americans than their white counterparts. It is well known that since the Korean War, the unemployment rate of African-Americans has remained roughly 2 to 2.5 times greater than that of whites, regardless of whether the economy was expanding or contracting. In 1972, for example, the white unemployment rate was 5.1%, but for African-Americans it was 10.4%. In 1982 at the height of the 1981-1983 recession, they were 8.6% and 18.9%, respectively, and in 1987 the figures were 5.3% for whites and 13.0% for African-Americans.[13] Also, national data indicate that African-Americans remain unemployed longer than whites, and tend to become discouraged from seeking to join the work force at higher rates. The longevity of the condition suggests that for many African-American families, the basic lifestyle is one of unemployment and economic dependence. In 1983, 48.5% or nearly one out of every two African-American teenagers was unemployed, a figure that had decreased

to a still unacceptable 34.7% in 1987.[14] Sensitive to the historical context mentioned earlier, one can project that a significant
proportion of African-American youth, the next generation of parents, will grow into adulthood and most likely parenthood without having had the experience of working and the feeling of self-
reliance. It is known that unemployment during adolescence follows the African-American throughout his/her life cycle, making
it more difficult to gain employment as an adult. One result of this
is that the African-American family feels and experiences the negative consequences of unemployment far more often and in more
different forms than the white family.

Turning to personal security and safety, it is known that
African-Americans experience violent crimes, both as victims and
offenders, at an overall rate higher than that of any other
racial/ethnic group. Nationally, African-American people represent approximately two-fifths of the total arrests for violent
crimes; i.e., murder, rape, robbery, etc. Of the murder victims in
1980, 95% were killed by someone in their own social network.
In terms of victimization, African-American families are more
likely to suffer from residential burglary than other groups, and
overall, crime tends to be intra-racial, with most of the crimes
committed by African-Americans against other African-
Americans. Given African-American youths' involvement with
the criminal justice system at an increasingly younger age, it
appears that the criminalization is becoming a major pattern of
socialization for African-American youth, especially males, across
the country.

The implication this has for the African-American family
is almost beyond imagination, but lamentably not beyond reality.
Crime, poverty, unemployment and violence are becoming synonymous with the urban experience, which is the single most
important aspect of the contemporary conditions affecting
African-American families. Until the mid-twentieth century, most
African-American families were from rural southern areas. For
some time now, though, the migratory pattern has been from the
rural south into the urban central city, where limited employment
opportunities, environmental pollutants, adverse mobility and
decrepit housing, poor recreational facilities and unhealthy living
conditions all affect negatively the life chances and quality of life
of the African-American family.

Education, which is so essential to the well-being of the African-American family, must be mentioned here, if only briefly. At a time when success demands a college education or technical training, the failure of the African-American youngsters to go on to college is all too troublesome. In 1987, the American Council on Education reported:

> Since 1976, Black high school graduates have been enrolling in college at a substantially lower rate. College enrollment rates for Blacks increased from 29.2% of high school graduates in 1971 to 33.5% in 1976.... however, between 1976 and 1985 the percentage dropped to 26.1%.... this decline is particularly alarming since during this same period the number and rate of Blacks graduating from high school increased significantly. In 1976 just over two-thirds, or 67.5%, of the 3.3 million 18-24 year old Blacks graduated from high school. In 1985, those figures had increased to 75.6% and 3.7 million, respectively.[15]

Concerning health, it is known that the generally poorer and environmentally inferior conditions of the inner city urban experience directly affect the health status and psychological well-being of African-American families. Within the urban environment, most African-Americans live in neighborhoods with crowded living quarters of poor quality, depleted of community services and resources, and lacking viable business infrastructures. African-American people, as urban dwellers, also encounter an inordinate and inestimable amount of environmental hazards, with constant exposure to high levels of automobile emissions, a lack of open space and high noise levels. These conditions may be associated with a higher death rate in the African-American community from heart diseases, strokes and cancers. Since the mid-1960s, the cancer incident rate in African-Americans has increased by 34%. The consequence of this is that three out of every four African-American families will have a cancer victim, and that one out of six African-American deaths is attributable to cancer each year.

Teenage pregnancy and parenting, though not exclusively health issues, must also be mentioned. The problem of teenage pregnancy is severe and appears to strike at the very basis of African-American family's ability to provide education and training to its young members. In 1981, 562,000 or 16% of all births in the United States were to teenagers; 27% of those teenage births, or 152,000, were to African-American teenagers. One out of every four African-American births was to a teenager. In addition, the majority of these births was to unmarried women. This suggests that African-American women begin the process of childbearing at very young ages. Over the long term, early childbearing results in undesirable life conditions for the teenage parent. It is also generally acknowledged that infants born to teenage parents are an at-risk population in terms of both social and emotional development, as well as physical abuse and neglect. Hence, lower levels of education, arrested career development, greater dependency on public assistance and a host of other vexations are becoming the norm for these children.

It is extremely important, however, that in addressing the teenage pregnancy and parenting problem, we are conscious of the fact that it is not simply the girl's problem. There is a male side to the equation that must be addressed as well. Sensitive and sound adult interaction with teenage males as well as females is critical to the prevention of teenage pregnancy, which is a social and cultural phenomenon, and not simply one of gender.

Nationally, drug-related behavior and drug trafficking have become the newest and most dangerous problem confronting African-American families. Few understand the full implications of the drug culture and drug lifestyles, which are emerging as the standard and model of African-American community life. Also, the tie between drugs and crime is obvious. Recent research on the mental health impact of drugs and drug trafficking on African-American children and families in Oakland[16] suggests that the emerging drug culture may be responsible for the ultimate destruction of the African American family.

Lawford L. Goddard, a sociologist and demographer associated with the Institute for the Advanced Study of Black Family Life and Culture and the Drew King Medical School at UCLA, subscribes to the observation that were the past and present socioeconomic trends to continue, we would witness the establishment of a permanent African-American underclass in the United States. He believes that basic demographic changes have affected the structure of the African-American population. In 1980, the African-American population of 26.7 million people comprised 11.8% of the nation's population. Of this group, 45% of the males and 34% of the females were under twenty years old. There were ninety males for every one hundred females. The African-American population is a relatively young one with a median age of 23.6 years for males and 26.2 years for females. This population is projected to increase to 33 million by 1995 and 35 million by the year 2000.[17] This population will, of course, age somewhat. It is projected that by 2000, 35% of the males and 31% of the females will be less than twenty years of age. In spite of this aging, the African-American population will continue to be young relative to the national population.

The most significant demographic change in the African-American population has been the change in the sex ratio. It has declined steadily throughout the twentieth century although it was projected to be ninety-one males for every one hundred females at the onset of the twenty-first century. The decline in the sex ratio has been the consequence of three fundamental processes affecting African-American males.[18] First, there was a significant loss of African-American males in the Korean and Vietnam Wars, resulting in noteworthy shortages of African-American males in the middle age group, thirty-five to forty-nine years old. Second, African-American males have been incarcerated disproportionately in relation to their white counterparts. Prison data indicated that African Americans accounted for 46.5% of the federal and state prison population in 1980 and 45.9% in 1985. Moreover, of the 227, 137 African Americans incarcerated in these prisons in 1985, only 10,793 or 4.75% were females.[19] African-Americans are also more likely to receive longer prison terms than white counterparts for the same crimes, which is consistent with a long-established historical pattern. Finally, the African-American sex ratio is affected by violence. African-American males are more likely to be victims of violent crime than any other group in the society. In 1980, the African-American male homicide rate of 66.6 per 100,000 was nearly five times the rate of 13.5 for African-American females, six times the rate of 10.9 for white males, and twenty times the rate of 3.2 for white females. In 1986, the figures were 55.0, 12.1, 8.6 and 3.0 respectively.[20] In the age group of twenty-to-twenty-four years, homicide is the leading cause of death among African-American males. Among African American male teenagers, violence—suicide, accidents, homicide—is the leading cause of death.

These social processes affect the African-American male population in that age range, twenty-to-forty years old, that is most significant in the process of family formation. This basic demographic change affected the composition of the African-American population to such an extent that the single-parent household has become a common form of family structure. If demographic shifts such as the sex ratio continue, the single-parent household is likely to be the major form of African-American family organization in the twenty first century.

The structure and composition of the African-American family has changed to such an extent that the proportion of the families maintained by a woman with no husband present has more than doubled since the 1960s. African-American female-headed families increased from 22% of families in 1960 to 45% of families in 1983. Along with this increase in female-headed African-American families has been a relative decline in the proportion of childless African-American families, which fell from 44% in 1960 to 40% in 1983. A significant factor in the decline of African-American childless families has been the pattern of early childbearing among African American women. In 1983, 50% of all African-American women between the ages of eighteen and twenty-four had given birth to at least one child. The data also indicate that by age twenty-seven, most African-American women have completed their childbearing experience. The consequence of this early childbearing pattern and the decline in the sex ratio is that the proportion of female-headed African-American families with children has increased. The proportion of African-American single-parent families increased from 44% in 1960 to 72% in 1983, and the proportion of African-American children living with both parents has declined from 80% in 1960 to 42% in 1987.

The ability of these single-parent units to provide adequate care and sustenance for their children is taxed severely, given the changing value system in the African-American community. In this context, the eroding economic well-being of the African-American family is of great concern. The United States has long begun a transition from an industrial-and manufacturing-based economy to one based on providing services and processing information. This shift increases the probability of the continued erosion of the economic viability of the African-

American family. Already some of the gains made by African-Americans in acquiring skilled and semiskilled occupations, blue-collar jobs, have been lost as a result of structural changes in the prime manufacturing sector of the economy, steel, automobile, rubber, etc. As the American economy retools its technology to increase productivity and maintain a competitive edge in world markets, new technological and scientific advances will continue to be introduced into the workplace. As this process unfolds, African-American workers will be disproportionately displaced because each service and information-producing economy require a different pool of skilled workers; e.g., computer programmers, analysts, media specialists, etc. Generally, African-American workers do not have these skills now and are not being trained for them in sufficient numbers.

The displacement of the African-American worker was most evident in the period from 1972 to 1982, when the unemployment rate of the African-American population increased by 140%. Although as of 1987 the unemployment rate of African-Americans had declined to 18.0% from 18.9% in 1982, it was still intolerably high.[21] A significant factor that is often overlooked in considering the unemployment rate is the withdrawal of the African-American male from the workforce. The work force participation rate of African-American males declined from 83% in 1960 to 70% in 1982. Among African-American females the opposite trend occurred, with the work force participation rate increasing from 48% in 1960 to 54% in 1982.

The participation of the African-American woman in the workforce has allowed the African-American family to maintain some semblance of economic solvency and even to approximate, in many cases, middle class living. This point needs to be stressed. In the mid-1970s, 48% of African-American women were in the workforce as compared to 35% of white women. The comparative data prior to this period are very similar to these, suggesting that, historically, African-American women participated in the work force alongside African-American men before it was fashionable as an expression of self-actualization or sex equity. This is also a fairly strong indicator of racism as a contextual variable in African-American reality. Because of racism and economic exploitation the solvency of the African-American family has almost always depended upon two wage earners. Given the changing family structure and the withdrawal of the African-American male from the workforce, it is unsound to suggest that the future African-American family is likely to have only one worker—and that worker will be a woman.

The current pattern of employment makes it unlikely that African-American females will be able to provide for their children in the way they would desire. African-American female employment has traditionally been concentrated in the lower echelons of the economic system; e.g., service and white collar occupations such as teachers, counselors, health technologists, nurses, secretaries, food service workers, custodians, etc. These occupations are characterized by low pay, high turnover rates, greater incidence of unemployment, and limited opportunities for occupational mobility. Predictably, the African-American single-parent family has and will continue to have a difficult time economically. The median income of African-American single-parent families was only $7,501 in 1981, down from the 1971 figure of $8,185 to which it still had not rebounded in 1987, when it was $7,981.[22] More than half of African-American single-parent families are living below the poverty level, and in 1987, 45.1% of all African American children lived in poverty.[23] The implication of this state of affairs is that the next generation of African American adults is likely to be less economically capable than their parents, marking a troublesome retrogression in the economic progress of the African American population.

Given the preceding observations and the analytical distinctions between public and private sector initiatives, the question of public policy capability to address the needs of African-American families becomes even more critical. However, before one can evaluate public policy's impact on African-American family functioning, one must understand what constitutes authentic African-American family functioning, as distinct from praxis problems in the African-American family system.

In order to understand what constitutes authentic African-American family functioning and, thereby, appreciate fully the intrinsic integrity of African-American family life, close attention must be paid to culture. Asa Hilliard[24] has observed that family systems cannot exist in the absence of a cultural base. Yet, a good deal of orthodox scholarship on the African American family has accepted the notions that: (1) African culture and the retention of

cultural residuals from Africa were radically destroyed and eliminated during the slave trade and America's period of slavery; and
(2) the American experience ultimately determined and shaped
the reality of African-American family life. In accepting these two
notions, those who subscribe to the orthodox examination and
understanding of African-American family life have erroneously
bound themselves to an analysis of the existential development of
African-American families in American society.

The common themes which run through most analyses of
the African-American family are that: (1) the original African cultural and philosophical heritage of African American people was
destroyed or modified qualitatively; (2) African-American families are products of the American experience; (3) American society is homogenous (a melting pot); and (4) to differ from the
standard; i.e., white, American family is an indicator of deviancy.
The African-American family has been depicted as a disorganized
and pathological form of social organization and functioning. In
stating that this perception is wrong, one does not wish to imply
that African-American family life is without problems. The family life of African-American people is marked by a range of adver-
sities, which emerge from its relationship with a racist and
oppressive social structure. To recognize this is not inconsistent
while simultaneously calling into question the character of the
scientific paradigm which misdirects analyses and overwhelmingly defines African-American family life as negativistic, problem-
laden and pathological. It is, in fact, necessary in order to explain
the difference between problems in the African-American family
and problems in the study of the African-American family.

Culture is important. In fact, many students of liberation
struggles[25] have noted that culture serves as a weapon in a people's struggle because the suppression or denial of their culture is
a part of their enslavement. Culture is the process that gives people a general design for living and patterns for interpreting their
reality.[26] It provides a people with their indigenous definition and
with the meaning of human processes. Because each culture has
its own vision or conception of the human experience, each will
also have its own intrinsic conception of how to function as a
family. Through its implicit philosophy of family, each culture
asks what the family is, what the family's purpose should be, and
how individuals and society as a whole should behave in

response to the family. Culture also defines the criteria for providing answers to these critical questions. Unfortunately, in most instances, members of a given society or culture ask and answer these questions without being conscious of the process.

It is because of the importance of public policy that one must detail and explicate African and African-American peoples' cultural vision regarding family. The cultural vision or world view of any group of people functions like a special set of lenses that when focusing upon a given slice of objective reality, perceives and is aware of those situations which are meaningful and excludes those which are not. It is primarily through this special set of lenses that the myriad of sensory impressions received by an individual is filtered, organized and transformed into mental impressions and behavioral dispositions and responses. In a very real sense, culture provides a code or set of instructions, which organizes the reception of sensory data. It occasions the rejection of what is perceived to be inappropriate information, and the acceptance of whatever is deemed appropriate. It taps the reservoir of past associations, ideas and knowledge in defining problems and constructing their solutions.

The African-American culture in the United States is the result of a special mixture of continued African orientation operating within another cultural milieu, which is defined primarily by the philosophical assumptions and underpinnings of the Anglo-American community.[27] It is the African perspective that is at the base of the African-American cultural milieu. And so, it is the continuation of that African vision which is at the root of the special features in African-American family lifestyles. This continuation of the African orientation to define the "general design for living and the patterns for interpreting reality" is characteristic of, African-American people. In order to demonstrate this contention, a brief discussion of traditional African belief systems, particularly as they relate to family, is necessary.

When considering the African-American family, it is important to understand the African philosophical, ontological and cosmological conception of the universe. The implicit African cosmological and ontological conceptions, along with the particular definitions of time and space within these cosmological and ontological constructs, suggest that the family constitutes the center of one's being or existence. Individual consciousness is such

that the family constitutes the reference point wherein one's existence is perceived as being interconnected to the existence of all
else. On this point, John Mbiti[28] observes that for Africans, the
individual owes his very existence to all the members, living, dead
and yet unborn, of the family, tribe or clan. Mbiti further notes
that the individual does not and cannot exist alone. The individual is an integral part of the collective unity, i.e., the family.

Ontologically, the African belief system understands that
the nature of all things in the universe is "force" or "spirit."[29] It
is logical, or at least consistent, that in believing that all things,
including man, are endowed with the same supreme force,
Africans would also believe that all things are "essentially" one.
This notion is referred to as the ontological principle of consubstantiation.

For the African, a natural feature of the universe is the
multiplicity of forms and moments. What characterizes African
peoples' understanding of the universe is, consequently, a simul-
taneousness respect for the concrete detail in the multiplicity of
forms and the rejection of the possibility of an absence or vacuum of forms. The African conception of the world and all of the
phenomena within it amounts to a set of syntheses and contradictions linked to a particular classification of beings as differential quantifications of force. Combined, these connective and
antagonistic participatory sets form the whole of universal relations, and, thereby, family relations.

The notion of self is based on one's individual consciousness, taking as its reference point the family, wherein one's existence is perceived as being interconnected to the existence of all
else. More specifically, one can note that the traditional philosophical notion of oneness of being requires that man conceptualize his own existence as an awareness of his universal connect-
edness, that is, man is an indispensable, integrated and interdependent part of the universe. The notions of interdependence and
oneness of being allow for a conception of self, which transcends,
throughout the historical consciousness of one's people, the
finiteness of the physical body, space and time. The notion of self,
or more specifically, the awareness of self within African peoples,
is, therefore, not limited to just the cognitive awareness of one's
own uniqueness, individuality and historical finiteness. The most
compelling property of the traditional notion of self is the process

of cosmologically grounding oneself in the collective, social and spiritual sense of the history of one's people or family.

Across African family systems the clan is believed to be a sort of total entity of which its members—like the elemental structure of the universe—are integral and interconnected parts. The family, which includes the living, the dead and the yet unborn[30], is thought to be the center or focal point, wherein the essence of the community or peoplehood is kept alive. The family is based on the unity and diversity of people and processes. It is at the very heart of one's existence, and serves as the center of the universe. In recognition of this kind of self-awareness, one can note that the traditional African view of self and the view of most contemporary African descendants is contingent upon the existence of family.

Organizational Purpose

When one examines intrinsic African-American family functions as distinct from examples of structural breakdown, the retention of the cultural vision articulated above is quite evident. It is in terms of the family organization. In effect, organizational purpose selects and determines what is of importance to a given family system. A number of African-American family researchers[31] have suggested that the functional integrity of African-American family systems remains influenced by African cultural perceptions. Thus, authentic, intrinsic family functioning has to be examined in its own right. For instance, organizational purpose refers to the primary purpose of the existence of the family organization. Organizational purpose selects and determines what is of importance to a given family system. As such, the organizational purpose of African-American families is best described as child-centered. By this is meant that the purpose of the African-American family focuses on, even if it does not require, the presence of children. The family system exists for the affirmation of life. It literally exists for the growth and development of children, rather than for the self-actualization of the adult members of the unit.

Social Organization

Social organization pertains to the organized pattern of functions and relations within the family organization. In a general sense, the social organization reflects the ethos or set of guiding principles by which the family organization operates and by which its members must abide. The social organizational quality of the African-American family reveals a close network of relationships within and between families. This family networking in the African-American community, though being seriously eroded by the vicissitudes and imperatives of urban life, has served as an unrecognized cohesive force in the community and has been the basis of many services; e.g., child care, financial aid, counseling, which are otherwise not readily available to African-American people. The special aspect of this family networking worth highlighting is the elastic nature of the family structurally. The African-American family stretches to accommodate new members; i.e., non-blood relatives, into the network. The importance of these social relatives or "para-kin" is almost indistinguishable from that of biological or legal relatives. The close intrafamily relations as well as the cohesive interfamily network serve both pragmatic and psychological functions.[32]

Many African-American families comprise several individual households, with the family definition and lines of authority and decision-making transcending any one household unit in the "family."[33] In terms of interpersonal relationships, one of the most striking qualities of African-American family life is the presence of "multiple parentage." Historically, parents in African-American families have invariably received help in rearing their children from other members of the clan or community. In a similar way, older siblings perform significant child rearing or parenting functions in the African-American family. In addition, it is not unusual for African-American children to be allowed to visit other relatives for long periods of time as members of their relatives' immediate households. These temporary and periodic "interfamilial consensual adoptions" must have a real and profound effect on the child's development.

Role Relations

Children in African-American families are also exposed to several kinds of roles, both in and out of their immediate households. Role relations within the African-American family are flexible and interchangeable. In terms of intentional or specific roles, however, African-American parents make a clear distinction between role definition and role performance. Role definitions are sex-linked while roles are performed regardless of sex. African-American parents generally feel it to be very important for their male children, for example, to learn what it means to be masculine and possess "manly" qualities, while for their female children, the emphasis is on understanding and acquiring "feminine" qualities. This pattern of socialization, though, is in relation to definition and not performance. Research data on role performance attest overwhelmingly to the belief of African-American parents that their children, regardless of sex, should be equipped with the pragmatic skills and psychological attitudes to support themselves and their families. Finally, as is true in African families, in African-American families the elderly play a crucial role in the affairs of family life. They serve the critical function of instilling in the young a sense of family, and they provide an important source of psychological support in easing the traumas of family transitions or crises.

The African-American family clearly represents a complex human phenomenon with recognizable strengths and weaknesses both intrinsically and in terms of its relationship with the external forces. It is in fact this complexity that must be captured and considered in the development of public policy.

Public Policy and African-American Family Life

Public policy ultimately must address itself to both the intrinsic functional integrity of African-American family systems and the external structural relation between the African-American family and the wider sociopolitical reality. This is especially important in the context of the observation of William Darity and Samuel Myers that private and public sector forces are in open competition for the control of American society.[34] The private sector forces represent the business establishment and its vested interests while the public sector forces represent the governmental establishment and its interests. Each of these forces, in turn, utilizes its intelligentsia in articulating and defending its interests. However, when it comes to the interests of the African-American family, the distinction between the vested interests of the private and public sectors seem to fade. The distinction, in fact, disappears when one examines the philosophical foundation and conceptual universe upon which each is built. Parenthetically, it probably should be noted that the distinction in actuality does not exist, and it is only upon applying the public/private dichotomy to the area of African-American family life that the illusory nature of the distinction is revealed.

In science the conceptual universe takes the form of paradigms which, technically speaking, serve as formalized frameworks that guide descriptions, explanations and evaluations of the empirical world. A paradigm is an instrument for knowing. At the center of the conceptual universe lies a core set of ideas which gives the conceptual universe, which in turn not only determines the people's perception of human capabilities, but also guides the development of new human inventions.[35] How a people define and classify both regular and irregular patterns of social interactions, behavior and development is determined and guided by its conceptual universe. It defines and determines the meaning and purpose of human relationships and experiences. In the United States, both public and private sector interests are filtered through a single conceptual universe that is grounded in the same philosophical and cultural traditions. Hence, in the determination of public policy, the public and private sectors approach the issue of understanding societal problems and clarifying, justifying and defending solutions from a common conceptual universe. This is illustrated well in the area of the intellectual or scholarly treatment of the African-American family.

The core idea at the center of the conceptual universe of American society regarding African-American people is the notion of inferiority and annihilation.[36] The paradigms for understanding African-American reality, especially African-American family life, have been governed by this particular conceptual universe. Syed Khatib[37] notes that from this perspective scientific examination of African-American people takes as its interpretative framework that of non-African-American people. The overemphasis on the study of negativity in African-American family research is thus under-standable as a methodological and epistemological artifact when one reflects upon the centrality of race in American social relation-ships. In further recognition of the social and racial grounding of knowledge concerning the African-American family, Robert Staples[38] observes the imposition of white values on the analysis of African-American family. Several African-American scholars[39] have in fact concluded that the major reason why African-American family life studies yield negative conclusions lies not with the intrinsic family functioning, but rather with the inappro-priateness and inapplicability of the conceptual universe utilized by the intelligentsia to guide the studies. A conceptual universe, which accepts as basic tenet the innate inferiority of African peo-ples, has real limitations for explicating the true problems associ-ated with African-American family life.

The private and public sectors draw equally from the same intellectual source. Thus, their definitions of problems and solutions in relation to African-American family life do not differ. Only the techniques and agents of change, or source of solution, differ. Consequently, it is not surprising that public policy thus far has directed itself at solving perceived intrinsic family function-ing problems. However, as noted previously, African-American family problems, upon closer examination, are observed to be related to the position of African-Americans in American society, and not intrinsic functioning problems.

The issue of public policy as it affects African-American families, therefore, must be viewed very carefully, since it is clouded by the complexity of public and private sector interests as well as by the intellectual tradition utilized by both to argue for or against public policy initiatives. There is a direct connec-tion between the establishment of "laws of the land" and the findings of the intelligentsia; i.e., social scientific information. The social scientist provides the facts and the truths upon which policies are based. Obviously, to the extent that these policies are based on incorrect or inaccurate facts, national policy is likely to become more of a problem than an aid to the people. Since the social scientific community historically has viewed the African-American family as deviant, pathological and weak organization-ally, it follows both conceptually and empirically that public poli-cies have been based on these perceptions.

Metropolitan population growth, for instance, is a basic feature of the social and economic transformation of American society. The growth and dispersion of the metropolitan population have created new and intensified old problems of social organization, and have affected several social institutions. In the case of African-Americans, the process of urbanization occurred at a dramatic pace. In 1900, the vast majority of the African-American population (77%) lived in rural areas, and only 23% lived in the urban areas. Within the short span of eighty years, the figures were completely reversed. Now, 75% of African-Americans live in urban/metropolitan areas, and only 25% live in rural areas. Several public policy programs and laws have been introduced to alleviate or solve some of the crucial problems facing urban areas. Since 1937, for example, the U.S. Congress has passed eighty-three housing laws. In 1949, public policy in the form of a housing act was passed, the purpose of which was to provide "a decent home and a suitable living environment for every American family".[40] That this program and subsequent housing laws did not solve the housing problem is evidenced by the fact that in 1974, another housing and community development act was passed. The purpose of that new act was "the development of viable urban communities, by providing decent housing and a suitable living environment and expanding economic opportunities, principally for persons of low and moderate income."[41]

In the field of employment, public policy resulted in the Employment Act of 1946. The purpose of this law was "to promote maximum employment, production, and purchasing power."[42] However, in 1964 more legislation, the Economic Opportunity Act, was still needed to "eliminate the paradox of poverty in the midst of plenty."[43] In the same year, the Civil Rights Act of 1964 was enacted in order to "eliminate discrimination and provide equal employment opportunities for all."[44] In 1965, public policy in the form of the Elementary and Secondary Education Act was established "to strengthen and improve educational opportunities in the Nation's elementary and secondary schools."[45] Eight years later the Comprehensive Employment and Training act was passed "to provide job training and employment opportunities...and enhance self-sufficiency by establishing a flexible and decentralized system of Federal, State, and local programs."[46]

An examination of public policy thus calls out the importance of the theoretical framework guiding the intellectual study of the African-American family. A review of the literature completed in the early 1980s revealed, for instance, that the "victimization orientation" prevailed in African-American family analyses in the 1940s.[47] This occurred at a time of massive migrations of African-American people to urban areas in the North, with the consequent dislocation and disruption of their family structure. Public policy initiatives emphasizing housing and urban life predictability rose in this period. Similarly, in the 1960s when the policy emphasis was on housing and urban development, African-American family research was characterized by the orientation which suggested that the internal dynamics of the African-American family was guided by the "poverty-acculturation" orientation, which emphasized economic conditions as the primary causal factor for the observed features of the purportedly dysfunctional African-American family. Public policy emphasized employment issues.

The clearest example of the way in which public policy based on incorrect social science research has negatively affected African-American families is seen in the Moynihan[48] and Coleman[49] reports. Both studies, based on the deficit model of African-American culture, implied that some internal features of the African-American family and community were weak and had to be corrected. Consequently, policies such as Head Start, Upward Bound, cultural enrichment, school integration, the Work Incentive Program and Operation Mainstream were all introduced with the intention of improving the quality of life for the "deficient" African-American population. However, by failing to provide an accurate representation of African-American family dynamics or African-American reality in the United States, the analyses of Moynihan and Coleman led to the emergence of public policies that were based upon misconceptions and "mistakes of meaning." These policies failed to occasion any positive and permanent transformation in the African-American community.

The well-being of a people is contingent upon the family system's ability to satisfy or accomplish a number of things: (1) a set of human imperatives which include procreation, protection, sustenance, rest and education; (2) specific cultural requirements, which include socio-cultural traditions, the family's sense of being, and rites, rituals and protocols; and (3) the relational essences which reflect the particular biological integrity, sense of efficacy, intimacy and permanence of the members of the family system.[50] As has been said earlier, the well-being of a people in society is contingent upon how effectively the family system functions internally and externally. Internally, the family process should result in a sense of personal worth, individual dignity and family unity. Externally, the family process should result in economic self-sufficiency, political efficacy and socio-cultural integrity. When the family system or process is weakened, public policy must be devised that aims at strengthening the family's internal and external capacities.

However, in the United States public policy solutions have, for the most part, been designed to remedy perceived weaknesses in the intrinsic functioning of the African-American family. With the exception of a few examples—the 1954 Brown decision and the Thirteenth, Fourteenth and Fifteenth Amendments—public policy has seldom been used as an instrument to change problems in African-American families resulting from their structural relationship with American society. In helping to satisfy the human imperatives and cultural requirements of a community, public policy mechanisms must respect the reality of African-American family life. To do so means that the framers and administrators of public policy must be sensitive in providing aid and resources in ways that neither disturb nor damage the authentic functional integrity of the family system when utilizing societal mechanisms to respond to the needs of African-American families. The challenge will be to design public policy that responds not only to the legitimate interests of public and private sector mechanisms, but also to the distinction between the intrinsic functioning of the African-American family and its structural relationship with societal institutions and forces. Recent public policy initiatives in the areas of maternity and paternity leave and benefits, childcare, equal employment and pay equity, maternal and child health care, and flexible working conditions must, therefore, be reviewed in relation to their impact on the African-American family. Similarly, the twenty recommendations which emerged from the 1980 White House Conference on Families,[51] and which may yet serve as a blueprint for future family policy decisions, must be reevaluated relative to the African-American family.

African American Families in the 21st Century

Public policy designed to meet the challenges of the twenty-first century must be broad and extensive enough to allow for the expression of the varied and different features of American families in a multicultural society. We must constantly remind ourselves that national policy, as it affects family features, historically has not allowed for the expression of that diversity. For example, most health care legislation works against the process of elasticity in African-American family structures, such as inter-familial consensual adoptions, in that these intrinsic cultural behaviors are not recognized by law. Similarly, the organizational purpose of African-American families which centers on the procreation and development of children is devalued by the wider society. This is evidenced by the heavy emphasis on family planning, the use of fertility as an index and the stigma attached to recipients of Aid to Families with Dependent Children; all of these things depress the quality of life. Assuming that only one form of family structure is normal, and then viewing all differences from this conceptual model as deviations, impels one to ignore the cultural diversity of American society. Public policy, based on the implicit definition of a single homogenous family type, results in the underdevelopment and oppression of families belonging to different ethnic and racial groups in the society.

Future public policy will have the dual responsibility of preserving the cultural integrity of the African-American family, while protecting it from the harmful consequences of social structures built upon sociopolitical exploitation and racial and cultural dehumanization. Public policy formation presupposes certain economic, political and social constraints, proceeding from these to develop methods and mechanisms which make resource distribution and service delivery systems more efficient, effective and, hopefully, equitable. However, when the American political process is viewed as a zero-sum game and power as absolute, Marguerite Ross Barnett correctly notes that African-American people historically have been "external" to the American creed and left out of the rewards of the American dream.[52] Accordingly, the only type of public policy, which will in fact assist African-Americans, is one, which necessitates them to confront and define for themselves their unique position in American society.

Public policy concerning African-American families must be filtered through their own self-definition. As long as public policy initiatives are not openly responsive to the cultural integrity and objective conditions of African-American people, the goals and objectives of the initiatives will fail and the conditions of African-American family life will continue to worsen. African-Americans will then truly become a permanent and irreversible underclass in American society.

[1988]

Psychometrics and African-American Reality: A Question of Cultural Antimony

The problem of psychological assessment has been the historical arena where controversy and criticism has surfaced as the cutting edge issue relative to the African-American community. From the use of the MMPI to evaluate Black men and women in this country's prisons to the use of I.Q. tests to place Black children in EMR classes to the use of various aptitude tests as "gate keepers" to future access and opportunity, psychometry has been an area of fundamental concern. The overarching issue of what is mental functioning and how it is assessed is, in fact, problematic. Grossman[1] has stated in this regard that the factors, which determine mental retardation, are developmental lags in intellectual functioning, personal independence, and social responsibility. As such, mental retardation is defined as "the condition which exists when there is significantly sub-average general intellectual functioning concurrent with deficits in adaptive behavior." Adaptive behavior, in turn, is defined as "the effectiveness, in degree, with which the individual meets the standards of personal independence and social responsibility expected of one's age and cultural group." Retarded mental functioning would, therefore, be a condition where one possesses sub-average intelligence and fails to meet the cultural expectations of one's group.

Psychometrically, the determination of mental retardation would be to measure both one's intelligence and attainment of cultural expectations. However, how does one measure the attainment of cultural expectations? The failure to do the latter, fairly and objectively, is the major point of confrontation between the discipline of Black Psychology and Western Psychology. The essential point of contention[2] in this confrontation was the recog-

nition and/or denial (depending on which group one finds oneself) that intelligence testing was culture bound and could not in
its natural content and form adequately assess the intelligence of
African-American people. The problem, of course, is that psychometry itself is culture bound. The field of mental measurement was in part developed and propagated by people committed
to a particular social world-view and cultural orientation.
Psychometry is not the objective and systematic assessment of
various mental dispositions and/or attitudes. Psychometry is a
"mega-business complex" bringing together the interest of racist
science and capitalist commercial interests. The problem with
psychometry is actually found in both its historical development
and its contemporary practice.

Psychometry and Western Consciousness

The assault on African people by the misuse of tools of
psychometry and racist scientific theories is long standing. As
early as the turn of the century, White psychologists and educators were amassing their psychometric armaments to justify the
continued oppression of African-American people.
The prevailing intellectual atmosphere was and is shaped
by racist thinking and assumptions. In 1956 the prestigious literary magazine, *Putnam's Monthly*, published the common thinking of the time wherein an anonymous author noted that:

> "The most minute and the most careful researchers have as
> yet, failed to discover a history or any knowledge of ancient times
> among the Negro races. They have invented no writing; not even
> the crude picture-writing of the lowest tribes; they have no gods
> and no heroes; no epic poems and no legend, not even simple tra-
> ditions. There never existed among them an organized govern-
> ment; they never ruled a hierarchy or an established church."

This unidentified author goes on to conclude in his argument that the few evidences of African splendor or civilization
were borrowed from Europe; and, where there is an African religion or creed or knowledge, customs and progress, they, too,
came from outside of Africa. The African, in effect, has no history and makes no history. Three decades later, Harvard

University's William McDougall indicated from his Ivy League citadel, that "a policy of segregation of the colored people of the United States is the only sound one."

The establishment of the inferiority of African and African-American peoples via psychometry assessment immediately replaced the shallow pseudo-religious theories of pre-destiny and Divine curse. The most interesting case of this psychometric propaganda occurred shortly after the 1954 *Brown v. Board of Education* decision. In 1958, Professor Audrey M. Shuey at Randolph-Macon College in Virginia published *The Testing of Negro Intelligence*[3] wherein she reviewed over three hundred original investigations of Negro intelligence conducted during the previous five decades. Professor Shuey's intention or purpose as noted by Chase[4] was to interpret the prevailing psychometric wisdom so as to substantiate her belief (offered as a conclusion) that those mental test scores "all taken together, inevitably point to the presence of native differences between Negro and white citizens as determined by intelligence tests." Parenthetically, the White Citizens Council in addition to distributing dozens of so-called scientific pamphlets and bulletins on race and racial problems, particularly Henry E. Garretts' *Race and Psychology; Heredity: The Cause of Racial Differences in Intelligence and The Relative Intelligence of Whites and Negroes*, the Council also distributed Shuey's work for the cost of $1.00.

Dr. Henry Garrett was the Chairman of the Department of Psychology at Columbia University and served consecutive terms as the president of The Psychometric Society, the Eastern Psychological Association and The American Psychological Association. Garrett waged his psychometric war on African-American people from the halls of the American Psychological Association to the shores of the Patrick Henry Press. Through this latter publication, Garrett's psychometric propaganda was printed in enormous quantities, 200,000 copies of a 26 page printing, and purposely distributed to newspaper editors and columnists, teachers, preachers, politicians and influential citizens in all of the fifty Carleton Putnam's, *Race and Reason*, which again documented the low I.Q. scores of Blacks as well as our low income and high crime rates.

The Louisiana State Board of Education purchased 5,000 copies of *Race and Reason* for use in the schools of Louisiana and a self-appointed group for the distribution of the writings, teachings and open letters of Carleton Putnam about the race problem.

It should be noted that the Society for the Psychological Study of Social Issues (SPSSI) openly opposed this type of scientific racism and psychometric warfare. In addition to its 1961 resolution attacking such scholarship, it also sponsored APA member books with a counter perspective on the problems of race, education and society. One of the most important volumes of this effort was the text, *Social Class, Race and Psychological Development* edited by Martin Deutsch, Irwin Katz and Arthur Jensen, wherein basic scientific data was offered to support the notion that socio-economic and/or environmental causes were the antecedent to differential learning capacity of the poor and non-poor, Black children and white children. Eight years later, however, one of the above mentioned scholars, Arthur Jensen, openly recanted the "error of his ways" and published in the prestigious *Harvard Education Review* his new found born-again belief or conviction that at least 80% of the intellectual development of human beings is controlled by the genes they inherit from their parents and that as a unitary trait, intelligence can be measured accurately with I.Q. tests. This born-again psychometric warrior further noted that not only is intelligence at least 80% genetic, but also that the different races differ in their racial intelligence quotients.

In this regard, he notes in his book, *Educability and Group Differences* that the possibility of a biochemical connection between skin pigmentation and intelligence is not unlikely in view of the biological relation between melanin and some of the neurotransmitter substances in the brain. In effect, Black skin is related to Black brains, which have been psychometrically proven to be inferior to white brains. In addition to Jensen, two other highly placed "generals" of the psychometric wars have emerged and gained national prominence and attention: Harvard University Professor, Richard Hornstein and Stanford University Physics Professor, William Shockley.

The evidence for an undeclared psychometric war on African-Americans is rather clearly explained in Allan Chase's *The Legacy of Malthus*. It is not, however, our task to review this record. The psychological war against African-Americans has been fairly well documented.[5] The ultimate question is why?

Why in relation to African people does science become racist and its tools, its psychometric weapons? The answer, it seems, is found in the historical clash of cultures. If one examines, for instance, the historical contact between Africa and the West, the one outstanding sign having special meaning was the invention of the Negro. It is extremely important to recognize the concept and meaning of the image and meaning of the African, which proceeded its (the concept of the Negro) inclusion into European consciousness. There is no stretching of the point to note that literally from the beginning of human consciousness to the advent of the Negro, the relationship between the African and the European had been the opposite of what it is now. The contact between cultures began long before the events of the 15th and 16th century, which set into motion ultimate domination and control of Africa. With the exception of a few minor interruptions, Black people or the Africans were feared and respected by whites or European people. The meaning of the Africans in the white historical consciousness was associated with high culture, superior civilizations and sophisticated human systems of organization, law, commerce, and family.

From the time of the Ionian philosophers, to the Roman Ascension, to the Moorish conquest of the Iberian peninsula, evidence abounds that the Europeans viewed the Blacks with awe and respect. The terms Ethiop, Blackamoor, Nubian and African all represented in the minds of the European a culture and people who were superior, dominant and their antagonists. The psychological requisite for European domination was, therefore, the destruction of African civilization and the re-definition of the African. These two conditions are the necessary and sufficient condition for European world domination. The European, in effect, had to re-define the African so that we differed in mentality, attitude, function (behavior), and belief from that which allowed us to rule the known world and shape the process of human development.

Enter here on the stage of human history the necessity for inventing the concept of "Negro" and the permanent installation of Judeo-Christian Greco-Roman ideological bases of Western civilization. With the establishment of philosophical doctrines of domination and exploitation like the Imperium Christianum, Regnum Europae or Societas Christianum, Europe emerged from the Dark Ages committed to a new interpretation of history and human consciousness steeped thoroughly and inextricably in Eurocentrism. The requisite condition for the legitimacy of this Eurocentrism was the destruction of the Afro-centric world and the establishment of the human construct known as "The Negro." Having invented "The Negro," European ascension required that it, The Negro, have a definition and meaning that proved European superiority. Hence, the adoption of the belief in the inferiority of African people as the guiding perspective of all Western scholarships as pertaining to the African, now reclassi- fied as the Negro. The ultimate proof of European superiority was, of course, not subjective opinion or personal desire but sci- entific fact. It is at this point, as mentioned above, that the queen discipline of human understanding—psychology—becomes racist and its tools of mental measurement—psychometry—as instru- ments of falsification, domination and exploitation.

Psychometrics, Paradigms and Paradox: The Question of Cultural Antimony

It is indeed unfortunate that the advent of the disciplines devoted to the study of human development, psychology, anthro- pology, etc., paralleled the establishment of Eurocentricism as a world order. As a consequence of this co-terminal development, the question of what is authentic culture and how do we under- stand and assess the human experience of other people has undergone continuous confusion, debate and criticism.

The way in which a people view the world or universe is critical, if not, fundamental to all the life-space activities they engage in. A people's conceptual universe not only determines their human capacities; it also guides the development of any new human inventions, interaction, behavior, and development. The understanding and management of all human endeavor is consequently determined and guided by our conceptual uni- verse. In fact, one could go so far as to say that the meaning of human relationships is both defined and determined by one's conceptual universe.

In terms of science the conceptual universe takes the form of a paradigm. Technically, this paradigm serves as a formalized frame work with the notion of a conceptual universe having implied in it a more central set of ideas. The centricity of the conceptual universe gives it a particular focus and/or orientation, Eurocentrism.

Given the necessities of European world domination, it is appropriate to call attention to the fact that the central set of ideas in the Eurocentric conceptual universe is the "wished for" and "imagined" inferiority of African people. Accordingly, when the Eurocentric conceptual universe takes the form of a scientific paradigm and serves thereby as an instrument for knowing there is a fundamental flaw in its allegiance to the requirement of scientific objectivity as pertaining to non-European people. Parenthetically, it should also be noted that as paradigms are replaced, or more accurately, as the centrality of a particular conceptual universe shifts to a different or new set of ideas, how we define and classify patterns of social interaction and human development, including mental measurement, also change.

In the history of the natural sciences one can best find examples of shifts on the central set of ideas, which support a particular conceptual universe. For instance, the change from Ptolemaic to Copernican celestial science really represented a paradigmatic shift in conceptualization. Likewise, the reconceptualization of mechanical rebounding to electrostatic repulsion is a similar shift in the way of knowing. These changes in paradigm, accordingly, represent a change in the way one conceives/perceives his universe.

What should be apparent here is that in the universe of people, our contemporary world has been viewed as Euro-centered. By that, it is simply meant that the core set of ideas viewed as legitimately representing the human condition were based on a European view of the universe. This Euro-centrism thus served as the paradigm for knowing. Since the 15th century, the Eurocentric paradigm, accordingly, has been used to define and classify social interaction and human development. Hence, most, if not all, standards of human behavior and understanding are shaped by this Euro-centric paradigm.

The paradigm indeed influences and shapes all aspects of the scientific enterprise, including its conceptualizations, methodology and techniques. The more general category of cross-cultural research techniques, for example, utilizes various methods and techniques to test hypotheses about human behavior among various peoples throughout the world. The application of cross-cultural methods is supposedly to ensure that one's findings relate to human behavior in general and not just to behavior of a single culture. In effect, the intent of cross-cultural research is to discover the universality of human behavior. When one examines the application of racial and comparative research as examples of cross-cultural research, an interesting phenomenon occurs. For the most part, racial and comparative research, especially, psychometric comparisons, with African-American populations do not explore the universality of behavior. Instead, there is the assumption of the innate inferiority of African people. In fact, one can argue that the racial and comparative method in psychometry rather than test the theory of Black intellectual inferiority, actually defends and protects the theory from refutation.

The problems associated with cross-cultural research are found in the notion of the equivalence of culture which in turn raise questions regarding the equivalence of meaning, for the variables, subject status, conceptualization, measurements, sampling, analyses and interpretation. If the meaning and experience of intelligence differ between two cultures, then the results of the psychometric assessment of intelligence would in fact be meaningless.

According to the anthropologist, Whiting, the acquisition of meaningful information in cross-cultural research depends on the researcher's ability to maximize cultural homogeneity within one's definition of study case. He argues in this regard that to ensure that the local community units are reasonably equivalent with respect to homogeneity, they should ideally have features which serve to reduce the variability of both individual behavior and the cultural beliefs, values and techniques held by the community members. Accordingly, he suggests that comparative units should have the following factors: (1) members have frequent face-to-face contact with one another; (2) they speak the same dialect; (3) they have some degree of sovereignty; and (4) they have a group name.

There are of course two problems with Whiting's criterion for cross-cultural research. The primary and most important flaw is that this strategy is designed so as to minimize cultural differences. The explication of cultural differences for the purpose of establishing universals is really the only valid reason for doing cross-cultural research. Unless of course one is doing mono-cultural research with the intent of demonstrating how deviant one culture is from another culture. This is not cross-cultural between cultural homogeneity. It does not address the problem to identify a culturally homogeneous Black and white group utilizing Whiting's criteria. One would still have remaining, the problem of "stimuli relevance," "comparability of response" and "differential meanings."

Consistent with Whiting's notion, in psychometric assessment the task is, therefore, to maximize cultural homogeneity by minimizing the importance and integrity of race. This occurs most often by classifying race as a "status variable" whose importance in the research process is that status variables need to be controlled, randomized or held constant so that their effects are neutralized, cancelled out or equated for all conditions.

The essential crises of psychometry is found in the difficulty it has in appropriately defining human intelligence or mental attitudes which are consistent with the cultural meanings of both human communities. Therefore, it is within the realm of culture that the crises and critical flaw of racial and comparative research, particularly psychometric assessment, is found.

The goal of science is to understand and not singularly to predict and control phenomena. The task of scientific inquiry is to ultimately establish general laws about human phenomena, which, in turn, serve as instruments for systematic explanation, and provide the basis for dependable prediction. Scientific inquiry and method are, nevertheless, idiosyncratic to a people's cultural deep structure.

The program in psychometrics is not to establish the universality of mental functioning between Black and white people. In denying the cultural integrity of Black people it fails to explicate the binding cultural laws within each group. These binding cultural laws are the basis of human mental functioning and may serve as the key to understanding the universality of human mentalities.

Racial and comparative methods, as currently utilized, are idiosyncratic to the laws and assumptions of primarily Euro-American culture. Hence, if we are to elevate the assessment of Black mental functioning to more than a tinted reflection of white mental functioning, we must start with a theoretical and empirical framework which is capable of reducing the elements of Black reality into intellectually manageable properties without compromising the historical truths and cultural principles of African and African-American people.

A paradox is a statement or tenet, which is discordant with what is held to be established belief. Scientific paradox would be those conceptualizations, data and findings that are contrary to established opinion and belief, especially, when the beliefs or opinions are unstated. Antinomy is a contradiction in a law or a contradiction between two binding laws. Culture, as the process which gives a people a general design for living and patterns for interpreting their reality, implies that there are cultural laws (guiding principles) which are consistent with the requirements of the people's cultural deep structure. Accordingly, the cultural laws of different groups can and often are in contradistinction. When the cultural substance or deep structure between two or more cultures stands in contradistinction of each other, it can result in contradiction in their respective meanings of reality. This contradiction of meaning results in a state of "cultural antinomy."

In effect, the Eurocentric cultural paradigm or the Eurocentric formalized framework which guides the assessment and evaluation of reality stands in contradistinction of the cultural laws which are consistent with the cultural deep structure of African people. The specific cultural antinomy is in the assumed white superiority. Keep in mind that up until the 15th century, the cultural law, embedded in the historical consciousness of European people, was the acceptance of African grandeur and superiority. The advent of the construct Negro with all its connotations of inferiority, savagery, unholy and uncivilized represents in fact and deed a contradiction in the European historical consciousness.

The Euro-American belief, now presented as objective scientific findings, about African and African-American inferiority stands in contradistinction with the belief about African superiority which is found in European historical consciousness. The fact that the European community set about to develop scientific theories about Black inferiority and methods—psychometry— to defend those theories from repetition does not change the state of antinomy.

The technical criticism of psychometry has ranged from issues and concerns involving: (1) the misuse (or more properly, the political use) of testing; (2) the technical weakness associated with test reliability, objectivity, validity and standardization; (3) the guiding assumption of test construction models (deficit vs. difference, heterogeneity vs. homogeneity); and (4) the educational, legal and economic implications/applications of test data. Each and every one of these concerns points to serious problems in psychometry. The source of these problems exists in or can be traced to the perceived necessity to verify the falsification of the historical presence and position of African people in relation to Europeans. Cultural antinomy complicates the comprehension of the problem. With the continued uncritical use of psychometric methods and theories one can make the phenomena equal to what the test is capable of measuring about the phenomena. By this is meant that without knowing the meaning given to mental functioning that is consistent with the cultural laws of African and African-American reality, one can mistakenly settle for or accept a meaning of African-American mental functioning that is taped or measured by the existing psychometric instrumentation and/or techniques. Hence, the tools of psychometrics can become the ultimate instrument for delimiting the meaning and definition of African and African-American mental functioning.

It will be critical for the field of mental measurement that as African-American scholars as well as the better trained Euro-American scholars engage in the continued debate surrounding psychometry and African-American reality that we understand that the real source of the problem is to be found in the historical clash of minds and confrontation between African and European cultures. If psychometry is to become a tool of mental measurement that assesses the universality of mental functioning, then the field of psychometry must free itself from the legacy of the subtle and sublime as well as the overt and intentional European obsession with justifying its own superiority, which given the centrality of culture in determining human meaning may be an impossibility.

[1988]

Mass Communications and Mythic Consciousness: The Role of Language and Culture in International Development

The role of language and culture in international development is so critical that almost every shift in developed societies as well as the major changes occurring in the developing world are deemed successful to the extent that they have effectively absorbed the question of language and culture. It is, in fact, through the processes of language and culture that one can analyze and understand both the issues of human oppression and liberation. Nowhere is this point more clearly illustrated than in the colonialization of Africa and the enslavement and oppression of African peoples. For instance, in forcing the African to adopt European languages, the European was able to instill in the African not only a particular vocabulary and grammar as well as a peculiar phonology, syntax and morphology, they were also able to simultaneously instill in the African a universe of concepts and meanings which reinforced the transformation of the African.

One only needs to note that, with the exception of several periods of high Black consciousness, many Africans on the continent, in the West Indies and throughout the Americas viewed their ability to speak "proper" like the European as a sign of personal accomplishment if not Divine Redemption. As evidence of the importance of language as a tool of oppression and human transformation one can also note the crucial role English literature (Shakespeare, Byron, Chaucer, etc.) and the Bible have played in the education of the African and New World African intelligentsia and through them the absorption and assimilation

of the "Imperial Culture." In this regard, Julius Nyerere[1] noted
that to call an African a Black European was, at one time, viewed
as a compliment.

The issue of international development and language is
made more complicated by the confusion around the distinction
between taking pride in a language and taking pride in one's own
command of a language. In the latter, one's pride is in the acquisition of an additional skill, while in the former one's pride is
found in what the language represents; i.e., the attitudes, beliefs
and values implicit in the language. In taking pride in the language many Africans and New World Africans have unknowingly accepted and adopted a culture which is not only alien to
them, but whose basic tenets are implicitly anti-Black and pathologically destructive to normal human development. This point
(language as representing a people's culture and philosophy)
alone is the crux of the problem with Third World development.
In part, the remaining discussion in this paper will attempt to
clarify this point.

Cultural Substance and Linguistic Manifestations

In order to fully understand the role of culture and language in the process of international development, a model of
culture, which explicates the interrelationship between features
of a people's cultural substance and their linguistic manifestation
is necessary.

The cornerstone in the understanding of human reality is
found in the notion of meaning. In fact, the meaning of phenomena has been the illusive mistress of all social science. More than
two decades ago, Robert Merton[2] recognized that the capacity to
understand was associated with one's ability to become "fully
aware of a group's symbolisms, feelings and values which are
critical to understanding the unwritten grammar of conduct and
the nuances of their cultural idiom." It is equally true that the
developmental question is bound in the meanings of a particular
group's cultural idiom. Unfortunately, the role of culture in the
understanding of human reality has been made inapplicable or, at
worse, irrelevant. The inapplicability of culture in understanding

human reality is due, in part, to the relegation of culture to a construct/concept which only represents the learned stylistic peculiarities of a people. Hence, as regulated and/or learned behavior, culture takes a secondary position in explaining significant aspects of human reality—particularly human and international development. That is, its use is in explaining observable peculiarities; and it is seldom used to explain or understand how people give or associate particular meanings to their condition or circumstance. The problem, of course, is in the definition. Once culture is viewed in its broadest sense as a construct representing the vast structural processes of language, behavior, customs, knowledge, symbols, ideas and values which provide people with a general design for living and patterns for interpreting reality,[3] then its utility or role in understanding the unwritten grammar of human conduct becomes evident. The concept itself becomes a valuable scientific tool comparable to mathematical statistical precision. In order for this to happen and to reveal culture's role in giving human behavior meaning, a reconceptualization of culture must be utilized.

A Reconceptualization of Culture

The reconceptualization of the culture,[4] which we have adopted, places the varied factors, aspects and manifestations of culture in functional order and suggests that culture be thought of as having a deep structure or cultural substance and a surface layer or cultural manifestations with the overall model comprised conceptually as having three levels.

The deep structure of culture or cultural substance is comprised of the factors and aspects of culture. The factors of culture are those elements or features which address a people's resolute understanding about the structure and origin of the universe — cosmology, the nature of being—ontology, and the natural character of universal relationships—axiology. Thus, cultural factors obviously influence a people's general design for living and patterns for interpreting reality. What emerges from these factors of culture are a people's codification of their implicitly cultural design. The deep structural codes which we have defined as the secondary and intermediary levels of culture are called cultural

aspects. Cultural aspects are represented by a people's most comprehensive ideas about order which some have defined as a people's worldview, their set or sets of guiding principles or ethos
and their template for clarifying and giving perspective to their
perceived social reality or ideology.

Unfortunately, what is most often understood as culture
is the surface layer of culture or the manifestations or expressions of culture. These are the things like behavior, ideas, values, rituals, customs, language, etc., which mark a people's
experience. The manifestations of culture should be viewed as
the overt expressions of the aspects and factors of a people's
cultural idiom.

Hence, a complete understanding of a people's reality
must occur by first understanding its factors, cosmology, ontology
and axiology; secondly, its emergent aspects, ethos, ideology and
worldview and; thirdly, its manifestations, customs, beliefs,
behavior, language, etc. It is both implicitly and explicitly suggested that the culture of a people and the values, attitudes and
behaviors consistent with it, help to define, select, create and
recreate what is considered good, valuable, appropriate, or desirable and conversely what is bad, dangerous, inappropriate or
undesirable in their social milieu. Just as nothing human can be
found outside of culture, so too, the meaning of everything
human can be found only within one's culture. In the larger context, the meaning of a people's reality and the experiences within it are, in part, determined by the specific interplay between the
cultural deep structure, surface level manifestations, and the concrete historical conditions in which the people find themselves.

Given the above-stated model of culture, one must next
clarify the role of consciousness in determining how people
define their concrete reality and their resolute position within that
reality. In noting that the original definition of consciousness
meant "to be with knowledge"—"con" = with and "scious" from
the latin "scire" = to know. It is of interest to point out that within Western psychology the issue of consciousness has been historically conceptualized as either personal[5] or collective[6] with a
great many spin-offs attempting to explicate the structure of one
or the other; e.g. unconscious, subconscious, etc. Though poorly
handled in Western psychology, the concept of consciousness
nevertheless remains an important component in the understand-

ing of development. In fact, like culture, the concept of consciousness must be further explicated if one is to fully appreciate its role in international development.

Dimensions of Consciousness

Consciousness, it is suggested, serves as a screen through which a people's knowledge about their condition and culture is filtered. As such, the process of being with knowledge influences the ideas which people accept which influence their behavior, including linguistic behavior. The screen of consciousness we suggest has several dimensions which separately and collectively influence one's awareness. Language can only symbolically communicate that to which the screen of consciousness gives us access. The dimensions of consciousness are: (1) mythic, (2) historical, (3) popular, (4) personal, and (5) self. Mythic conscience, to be with mythic knowledge, represents a dimension of human awareness whereby one's knowing is influenced by the ancient archetypes and primitive ideals found in one's indigenous mythology.

Myth is important because its analysis allows us to identify the prototypical, original, archaic and primitive examples of human conduct. Accordingly, myth is to be taken seriously because it reveals significant though unverifiable truths about human nature. From the explication of prototypical human conduct, one is able to trace the implication of such for modern day human behavior. An analysis of mythic perceptions provides us with a base relief or prototype of the potential and probable human conduct of the people whose myth is being analyzed.

Historical consciousness, to be with historical knowledge, represents a dimension of human awareness whereby one's knowing is influenced by critical historical experience shared in common by the identified group of people. Popular consciousness—to be with knowledge based on contemporary ideas—represents a dimension of human awareness whereby one's knowing is influenced at any given time and place by the popular ideas which have currency at that time. Personal consciousness represents the dimension of human awareness that is shaped by those personal and subjective events experienced uniquely by the individual. Self consciousness, to be with unique knowledge, represents a dimension of human awareness whereby one's knowing is influenced by the accumulative effect of the combined dimensions of consciousness; i.e. to be aware that one is aware.

In order to fully explicate the framework for the following discussion, a brief remark regarding the concept of concrete condition must also be made. In general, most thinkers understand the concept of concrete condition to represent the material reality which a people must negotiate and/or manipulate. As such the nature of one's concrete condition influences the kinds of human inventions possible. Nkrumah[7], in this regard, felt that mind or consciousness develops from the basic material or physical reality and that mind is essentially the upshot of matter. Consistent with this perception is the recognition that the material condition influences and/or necessitates particular cultural inventions. For example, the varied utilization of snow and even the many different words (descriptors) for snow were directly influenced by the physical reality of the frigid climatic (material condition) zone.

As an extension of the materialist perception, many thinkers conceptualized as features of one's concrete condition socio-political, economic, and class conditions. Hence, the ideas one holds represent, for instance, one's class interests. Few scholars who adhere to the materialist paradigm are, however, willing to recognize that physiological Blackness is not only a material condition, but also a primary condition. Hence, the uniqueness of African culture and its value orientations may very well be the upshot of our melanin content.[8] The purpose of this discussion, however, would be violated by imposing a detailed analysis of melanin as a primary material condition. It will be enough simply to note that the logic of the materialist analysis is not violated by postulating primary (physiology) and secondary (socio-political-economic) levels of the concrete reality.

With the acceptance of the notion of concrete condition the paradigmatic framework for our analysis of language and culture in international development is complete. Essentially, this framework suggests that a people's concrete condition in interacting with their cultural substance filters through the dimensions of their consciousness to influence and shape their ideas which, in turn, serve as the basis of their behavior.

A similar discussion about the relationship between English and European culture, although not as complete, was suggested. It was noted that the English language evolved out of the Anglo-European culture. It was also noted that the English language evolved out of the Anglo-European cultural pattern and that even the expected sequence of thought in English is, essentially, a Platonic-Aristotelian sequence descending from Ancient Greek culture. In accepting this fact, it suggests that Black language is based on ideas which are shaped by the cultural substance and concrete conditions as filtered through the dimensions of Black people's consciousness. Analysis of the mythic perception clearly demonstrates this position.

African Mythic Consciousness

In relation to mythic consciousness, for instance, the Memphite mythology informs us that the ancient Africans reduced the multiplicity of the Divine to a truly monotheistic conceptualization and spiritualized the concept of creation. In its simplest form, creation was conceived as birth; and it is represented as a primeval couple who are the parents of all that exists. Essentially, the mythology surrounding the ancient African city of Memphis noted that the primate of the Gods, Ptah, conceived in his heart everything that exists and by his utterance (in the beginning was the Word) created all things. In effect, the primeval chaos which was characterized by will and intention, willed itself to Be and, as a Supreme Being, manifested itself as complementary male-female Gods who, in turn, served as the substance of human beings. The mythic ideal which can be interpreted from this mythology is that human conduct is governed by the transformational and transcendental attributes of Divine Spirit and reflects the complementary (male-female) features of creation.

Hence, Black language, as an example of human conduct, should reflect this prototypical archetype. It is, in fact, not accidental that in relation to perceiving things, for instance, the English typically say, "I see it"; while the Eskimo would say, "It appears to me"; and the African-American is often heard to say, "It is outta sight." The English "I see it" is, in fact, reflective of prototypical human conduct which requires a position of domination and control over the event (I see it = 1 determine/control the event). The Eskimo's "It appears to me" is likewise reflective of prototypical human conduct which accepts a position of receiving/experiencing the event (It appears to me = the event happens to me). The African-American's "It is outta sight" is reflective of prototypical human conduct which recognizes the capability to transcend the event. It is outta sight = it has reached the height of perfection and has gone beyond itself. In essence, each statement serves as a base relief or prototype of the probable and potential human conduct predictable from the mythic ideals of the communicator.

    Understanding the role of language and culture in international development is further complicated by a good deal of conceptual confusion if not conceptual incarceration.[9] There is, for instance, some real confusion between the notion of language (the ability to speak) and communication (the ability to transmit information). This fundamental distinction is further complicated by scholars who also confuse language with intelligence, and, even worse, language with English. In the latter instance, some of the thinking in the field reflect an implicit acceptance that the English language is the only real language. In a vein no less erroneous than the abovementioned confusion, the issue of standardized English emerges as the ultimate example of confusion. In this example, it must be noted that the dawn of the industrial revolution and the rise of a mercantile class necessitated the "standardization" of the various barbaric English vernaculars[10] into a common mother tongue. The reason for this should be obvious. Standard English became, by definition, "the English used by those who carry on the affairs of the English speaking people." Hence, standard English is related more to politico-economic necessity than to formality and accuracy. Standard in this regard is not equivalent to correct; it is equivalent to common.

    Many assume that language is, by definition, an abstract system of symbols and sounds representing human cognitive structures. However, given the above-stated discussion of culture, consciousness and condition, a more thorough statement would be that language is an abstract system of symbols and sounds representing a human community's cultural deep structure's synthesis with their concrete condition and filtered through their screen of consciousness.

As explicated by the Nobles' reconceptualization model of culture, language is a cultural manifestation. Hence, before one can proceed to the issue of language and international development, the role of language and its analysis—particularly the analysis of Black language—must be explicated.

The Politics of Language

In the United States there has been a consistent and constant resistance to the recognition of Black language. If one bothers to ask the question, "Why so much resistance?" the real underlying importance of language becomes transparent. There is a direct relationship between a people having a language and the legitimacy of their peoplehood. For African-Americans to claim language status—Ebonics—is to simultaneously claim one of the indicators of peoplehood (land and self-governance would be others).

In order to oppress a people, no matter how benevolent or sophisticated, one must remove the people in question from the process of creating history.[11] This is accomplished by destroying their culture. However, as Cabral[12] has noted, one can not destroy a people's culture without actually destroying the people. Since, in most instances, imperialism stops short of genocide, the alternative to cultural destruction was cultural transformation. Hence, political, economic and social oppression are secured by the forced adoption of the alien culture. The adoption and assimilation of an alien culture is accomplished directly by the adoption of the language. The real issue is about identity and peoplehood. If one can control a people's identity and the sense of peoplehood, one controls the people.

As noted earlier, when Africans and New World Africans began to view their relationship to language as their ability to speak standard English and that ability as evidence of their human worth, then, we have unknowingly absorbed a culture whose basic tenets are anti-Black and pathologically destructive. The length of this paper will not allow for a complete discussion of the relationship between culture, condition, consciousness, racism, and racial oppression in the European community. Nevertheless, it is necessary to provide some insight into their mythic consciousness, ideas about the innate inferiority of the African and their co-determination of contemporary perspectives on Black language.

European Mythic Consciousness

In Greek mythology, for example, one finds evidence for the roots of European racist, exploitative and domineering relations to peoples of color. For instance, in the Orphic Mysteries, the prototype of European conduct is established. In one Greek myth, for instance, we are informed that Zeus had a baby son by his own daughter, Persephone (an ancient recording of incest). This son was named Zagreus and Zeus wanted him to become lord of all creation. However, the wicked Titans killed and devoured the baby Zagreus. In an act of rage Zeus struck the Titans with lightning and thunderbolts and reduced them to ashes. From these ashes, so the mythology goes, arose the race of man. Another accounting of the Orphic Mysteries tells that Dionysus was killed by the evil Titans and Zeus saved Dionysus' heart and killed the Titans. Zeus created man from the evil Titan ashes and the pure heart of Dionysus. Hence, man's nature is dual. It is both evil and good.

Beyond pointing out that within the Orphic Mysteries, the human possibilities of incest and uncontrollable emotionalism were established, a further, more critical observation needs to be made. The character of the gods, as represented by the actions of Zeus, revealed the ultimate contradiction or duality that man had as his source; i.e., the duality of the gods both creative and destructive. The pantheon, which was the source of all power, authority, value and meaning, and represented divine order, had not created a perfect cosmic order in which all its creatures and/or phenomena would always do its will.

In essence, the gods covered up their own inadequacies or character flaws by punishing their creatures for not being perfect and not doing the will of God. In actuality the imperfection of the creatures was due to the defect in the character of the creator; i.e., the gods. Man, as conceived, was seen as having both a dual nature both good and evil and an inability to obtain perfection because the creative absolute was imperfect.

The pantheon was rejected and replaced by Christianity, which similarly views God as all knowing and all powerful. The mythology of Christianity, as well as the other major Western religions did very little, however, to undo the error of the Orphic understanding of human nature. Essentially, modern Western religion is no more than ancient Western mythology reformulated as universal theories of human behavior and development. In Western religion God's omnipotence is tempered with Adam's fall from grace and expulsion from the Garden of Eden. Accordingly, God punished Adam for providing evidence of the relativity of God's omnipotence.[13] Man's desire to be godlike was, ultimately, an act of demonstrating one's innate imperfection.

In brief, the creator of all things (Zeus) brought man into being. However, it made man imperfect. It built virtue and vice into his character and punished him when man behaved according to or in response to the qualities or characteristics which made up his nature. Thus, human nature was complicated by elements of good from Zagreus/Dionysus and wickedness from the Titans. Man was further endowed with "free will," a Roman addition, and thereby, having the ability to choose to be good or bad.

This view of man as inevitably imperfect resulted in defining man in devaluing terms and/or as an object of contempt. The adding of free will, the ability to choose to be good or evil, to man's nature and/or the Roman belief in the existence of numen, mystical power the gods selectively gave to some and withheld from others, did very little in changing this conception of the nature of man. In effect, all that free will and innate good and evil have done was to produce a bias for viewing man as divided into the righteous and the evil either by choice or divine selection.

The prototype of human conduct explicated in this myth is essentially that life is characterized by uncertainty and is, at best, a struggle and a contest of wills (man versus the Divine). As noted, mythic consciousness pertains to human awareness as it is influenced by the mythic ideals; as such, the mythic perceptions provide us with the prototypical archetypes of human possibilities. The parameters of the European possibilities, as signified by this myth, are characterized by: (1) conflict with the Divine, (2) domination and control and (3) duality in opposition. Hence, the implication the mythic ideals have for modern day human behavior is that man is potentially good and evil and in perpetual conflict or competition with others. Given this perception, modern European man should be found to be a highly competitive individual who is singularly oriented toward his/her own selfish preservation.

These insights alone are not enough to explain the unfounded acceptance of the idea of African innate inferiority or the complete opposition to Black language. However, historical consciousness pertains to the awareness of reality that is influenced by critical and significant experiences that a people share in common. In fact that most of the history of the European existence was confronted with the presence and splendor of Black Africa's world dominance with several long periods of direct African governance and rule. From about 2,000 BC, the birth of Abraham, the founding patriarch of Judaism, to about 300 AD, the meeting of Bishops at Nicene, most of the physical images and representations of the Divine were Black. Therefore, one could speculate that a mythic ideal which pits man's will against Divine will combine and control Black people who represent the God figure in the mythic consciousness of White people.

Language and Legitimacy

If the issue at hand is the dominance and control of Blackness, then in order for whites to be comfortable with any aspect of things Black, they must fit it into a matrix of inferiority and deviancy. In application, this need becomes a mythic belief in the innate inferiority of African peoples. Parenthetically, one can see with very little effort that this assumption has been the building block of almost if not all social scientific investigations of African reality. Why?

Given the mythic consciousness of White folks, all phenomena are implicitly defined as linear polarities in opposition, for example:

Good	-	Evil
Advanced	-	Primitive
Developed	-	Undeveloped
Civilized	-	Savage
Genius	-	Idiot
Superior	-	Inferior
High	-	Low
White	-	Black

Of course these polarities are no more than the epistemological expressions of conflict, opposition, duality. The intellectual response to Black language is equally affected by the mythic consciousness. In this regard one notes that the linguistic literature classifies Black language as the implicit deviant form of "those who carry on the affairs of the English speaking people"; i.e., standard English. The following is only illustrative, not exhaustive of the categorizations found in the literature:

White People's Speech	Black People's Speech
Standard English	Non-standard English
Creole English	Pidgin English
Elaborated Code	Restricted Code
National Language	Indigenous Tongue
Regional differences	Dialect
Language Enriched	Language Deprivation
Proper English	Improper Talk
Vernacular	Ghetto dialect (Ghettoese)
Folk Language	Broken English

Clearly by defining the Black people's ability to transmit information as the polar opposite of good or correct, the dominance of African people is partially secured. Psychologically, if one identifies with another, one places that other in an automatic position of superiority or supremacy. By instilling in African people the idea that our indigenous language is bad, incorrect, and unsophisticated, the tangential effect is that we began to see ourselves as inferior. Remember, language is an abstract system of symbols and sounds representing a human community's cultural substance's synthesis with their concrete condition as filtered through their screen of consciousness. Once you define a people's language as inferior, you in effect are saying that their notions of what it means to be human and their human responses to the world are also inadequate. Hence, by attacking our language, the European was simultaneously attacking our Divine right to be.

The denial of Black language is, in fact, only one aspect of a larger necessity to dehumanize Black people. Once African people unknowingly buy into this psychological delusion, we find Africans being alienated from our own sense of self[14] and trying in all we do, including how we speak, "to be white."

Mass Communication and International Development

Language obviously is critical to our liberation and/or our continued oppression. Language is also critical to international development. However, it is not enough to note that when one adopts an alien language, one also adopts the human possibilities which are represented by that cultural manifestation. The adoption of an alien language essentially creates the possibility for one to internalize the cultural substance and mythic ideals of another people. Given the pre-eminence and dominance of English in the fields of science and technology, it is clearly not enough to simply say that African peoples must be fearful of the transformative implication of the language of development. It is important to note that in the process of development one understands the relationship between language and legitimacy and that through language one assumes the authority to define reality and allow and/or deny access.

Literacy campaigns and mass communication programs cannot be viewed as simply technical steps in the staircase of international development. Mass communication clearly is facilitated by a common tongue. However, the recognition that standard English and/or the elimination of indigenous first languages of African peoples calls for one to question that position. If the affairs of the English speaking people are shaped by the pathological necessity to dehumanize African peoples, and if the English language is a manifestation of that cultural substance, how then can we implement mass communication programs and literacy campaigns via the English language without simultaneously participating in our own underdevelopment?

The answer, in part, lies in the indigenous African style of responding to and manipulating reality. Psychologically, the techniques associated with our cultural disposition are improvisation, transcendence and transformation. These techniques are all governed by the human possibilities defined by our indigenous cultural substance and mythic consciousness. The technique of improvisation is a process of spontaneously creating, inventing or arranging a known experience, situation or event such that the known experience is extended into the unknown quality, state or ability. The technique of transcendance is to exceed, go beyond or rise above the limits of an experience, condition or situation. The technique of transformation is the predisposition to recognize that the condition, quality or nature of an experience or element has the potential to change into a different experience or element.

The presence of our own cultural substance and mythic consciousness has influenced our cultural manifestations, including our style of manipulating language in general and the invention of Ebonics in particular. For example, what some people may judge as the inconsistency of Black language, different and constant changing of vocabulary, can be seen as an example of the technique of improvisation. Many have noted for instance that when white people adopt/steal our words or speech style we immediately select another term. For example, Black folks used the word "hip" to represent that a thing or person was appropriate and most often was the best of its kind. However, when white folks started to use the word "hip" we began to use the word "together"; and when they picked it up, we replaced it with "cold" or "mean" and when they started to use those words we went to "raw." In each instance our response to language was to rearrange the known experience; i.e., the thing which is appropriate and excellent. The known experience (together = appropriate and excellent) is extended into the unknown (raw = appropriate and excellent), and results in the use of another word. The continuous adoption of new words is the result of the technique of improvisation.

The use of triple and quadruple negatives is an example of the technique of transcendence. For instance, the statement, "Don't nobody pay no attention to no N... that ain't crazy," is more than the Ebonics translation of "if you are a crazy N..., you will get attention." The Ebonics version goes beyond or rises above the limits of the technical structure of proper English.[15]

The metaphorical and symbolic character of Ebonics is directly related to the technique of transformation; i.e., the experience, phenomena can change into a different experience or event. For example, the word "bad" meaning "good," in Ebonics is technically an example of a linguistic reversal—negative term changing so as to have a positive meaning. The use of the term "hat up" meaning to leave and "lame" referring to someone who is odd or strange are additional examples of the transformational quality of Black language.

The popular use of the phrase "The Blacker the berry the sweeter the juice" is especially instructive. This one phrase not only reflects the transformational quality of Black language, changing a negative by White standards into a positive, but it simultaneously reflects the transcendental quality, rising above the limits of white racism, and the improvisational technique of taking a known experience—blackberries are sweet—and extending it into an unknown experience—Black people are superior and changes it into a new experience—pride in being Black.

Communication Disorders and International Development

Communication is essentially the process by which information is transmitted from one source to another. Technically, this requires the encoding and transmission of information or messages and their decoding and reception. In theories of communication, it is also noted that an important component of the communication chain is technical noise. Technical noise is anything or any medium through which the message passes, and which serves as a barrier capable of distorting the meaning of the original encoding. Since the meaning of social phenomena is determined by the cultural substance, dimensions of consciousness and concrete conditions of a people, these same features must also act as technical noise in communications between different cultures. In cross-cultural communication, different meanings given to the same message are, in this regard, the result of technical noise.

The technical noise can and does therefore result in communication disorders. In a very real sense, the different rhythms, speech rates, intonations and stress patterns (prosody) found in one culture become the technical noise for another culture. This type of cross-cultural communication problem could be labeled mild communication disorders. The source of technical noise in cross-cultural communication can also be traced to the differences between the cultural substance, dimensions of consciousness and concrete conditions of various groups. Given that these features of technical noise are capable of actually influencing the perception of reality, they can result in what is tantamount to acute cross-cultural communication disorders. In a manner similar to "auditory agnosia," the inability or failure to disseminate or identify auditory stimuli, the differences in cultural substance, dimensions of consciousness, and concrete conditions can result in failures to discern and/or discriminate another group's "symbolisms, feelings and values which are critical to understanding the unwritten grammar of cultural conduct and behavioral nuances. In effect, "cultural agnosia" is an acute cross-cultural communication disorder whose effect can directly influence international development.

If the technical noise of the communication chain is influenced by the mythic consciousness of Europeans (conflict, domination and control, duality in opposition), when the issues of international development for the "developing world" are encoded and transmitted through this technical noise, cultural agnosia occurs. In terms of international development, the belief that there should be open access to modern development and technological advancement by Third World communities is influenced by our cultural prosodics. The belief is also informed by our cultural deep structure or primacy of life, dimensions of consciousness and concrete conditions. Hence, African and other Third World communities have in their political pronouncements encoded messages about development which essentially reflect our vested self-interests. However, when these messages are filtered through the culture, consciousness and condition of imperialist countries, the message is drastically distorted and harmonious international development is hindered if not rendered impossible. What, in effect, happens is that the filtering of questions and/or positions around international development results in the developing world and the developed world responding to totally different perceptions of the question of international development. Development in the Third World is openly, maliciously and sometimes unconsciously and unknowingly resisted because the developed world sees development of the developing world as a threat to its own position of security since it sees everything in terms of domination and control. For example, when the country of Grenada transmitted the message that its developmental plans included the building of a modern international airport, the United States decoded that message as the establishment of a base for further Communist encroachment in the Western hemisphere. When the Black American community asserted that the revitalization of the urban areas was congruent with the development of the Black American, white America decoded this message as an opportunity to create free enterprise zones that would reduce safety and economic regulations. This would allow them to take further advantage of the underclass in the form of lower wages. Similarly when Black Africans in Rhodesia recognized the relationship between majority rule and their development, the white ruling government decoded the meaning of that message as a call for planned transition. As technical noise, the issues of consciousness, culture and condition can retard and/or accelerate international development.

As we enter into the world of the 21st century. We are rapidly approaching a global society. The control and management of this global society will be influenced by information and transportation. It seems relatively clear that the world of the 21st century will witness a highly mobile commuter-oriented world population as well as an information producing and dependent society. In such a society national geographical boundaries will be meaningless. The immediate impact of this situation is that political and social kinships will be based on philosophy and not geography. Similarly, population's loyalties will not be tied to a land base and most people's livelihoods will be related to the production of ideas and information. As such, world governance will depend on whose culture, consciousness and condition will serve as the bases of the ideas for human conduct and development. It would seem that if five out of six people are non-White, then the value base upon which human conduct and international development should proceed would be one having kinship to the culture, consciousness and condition of peoples of color.

In the 21st century it will be clear. He who controls the information will control.

[1989]

BEGINNING

UNLOCKING THE SAKHU AND STEPPING INTO THE LIGHT

Ejiogbe

I	I
I	I
I	I
I	I

> Let us not engage the world hurriedly. Let us not grasp at the rope of wealth impatiently that which should be treated with mature judgment. Let us not deal within a state of uncontrolled passion. We arrive at a cool place, let us rest fully. Let us give continuous attention to the future. Let us give deep consideration to the consequences of things. And this because of our eventual passing

The sketches in Section IV, Beginning, speak to the fundamental path that this thirty year walk has traversed. The thoughts reflected in these presentations all speak to the issue of illuminating African consciousness.

Sketch 16 addresses the issues of consciousness. This chapter differentiates itself from the others in the section because it dives into the realm of the soul and gives it a living backbone in order for the soul and its properties to be understood. Giving a clear and concise definition of Sakhu, Sketch 17 calls for the urgency of being aware and conscious of both the invisible and the visible. With such a dichotomy, staying in the physical, or the visible, can lead to believing all that is seen, even when it comes from others who attempt to misguide. This importance is crucial for balance between spirituality in the invisible, and at the same time, all that is apparent, in the visible.

Sketch 18 returns to the psyche, or the spirit. Being a spiritual people, Africans must follow the psychic nature, which is, in actuality, re-ascribing to the rules and roles that governed the ancients. By doing this, one is able to maintain Afrocentric ideas in a racist, oppressive society, which, in turn, allows for the maximization of productive forces and the minimization of the destructive. Using the seeding process, people must take from the former, more divinely driven ways, in order to perfect later accomplishments, for this will find and unlock the Sakhu.

The discussion in Sketch 19, "To Be African or Not To Be: The Question of Identity or Authenticity—Some Preliminary Thoughts," represents my attempt to defend the fact that African peoples' psychology is fundamentally derived from the nature of the African spirit and determined by the African spirit's manifestation as a unique historical and cultural experience. This natural and instinctual psycho-behavioral imperative is coupled with a revolutionary drive to achieve physical, mental and spiritual liberation. I further note that Eurocentric Psychology and the mental health industrial establishment created by it as well as the African Psychologist who knowingly or unknowingly participates in it cannot provide adequate explanations, rationales, theories and therapeutic practices.

The position taken in this discussion is that what is needed is a theoretical and therapeutic practice that is centered in our own African essence and integrity. If we, as African Psychologists, are to be obedient to the imperative of respecting and reflecting the human essence of our people, then our work must be guided by a discourse that is radically different from those whose intent is to verify the invalidation of our humanity.

In calling for the recognition of a different quality of thought and practice and in acknowledging the responsibility for creating one's own criteria for authenticating the reality of African human processes, an African/Black Psychology, ergo the Sakhu, must represent a radical epistemological shift and paradigmatic change wherein new questions are raised and new practices are established.

The concluding sketch, Sketch 20, "Breaking the Code of Spirit(ness) and Consciousness," is an exposition or challenge to break the code of spirit(ness). It is clear to me that the epistemological dilemma we face is bound in our inability to truly understand the invisible world (spiritual) with models and concepts derived from our comprehension of the visible (physical) world. To say, as I have, that we need to understand the DNA of spirit, is to again limit or tie our comprehension of the unknown (spirit realm) to that of the known (material reality). There is, I believe, a "Rosetta Stone" for the African spirit and consciousness and one charge for African/Black psychologists is to make explicit our spirit code and apply its rules and/or requirements to our deeper understanding of what it means to be a human being and what requirements spirit(ness) dictates for addressing issues of malfunctioning; i.e., human illness and dis-at-ease.

The ideas offered in both these sketches are simply thoughts designed to suggest that our "theoretical" understanding of what it means to be African/Black in a non-African (White supremacist) society requires "deep thought" about the psychology of African people. It is in the tradition of "thinking deeply," ergo, speaking and doing, about what it means "to be African" that I propose we discover the real understanding of African/Black Psychology or more accurately, "performing the sakhu as it should be done." It is only when we first think deeply about what it means to be a human being and subsequently, therein, how that meaning shapes our responses and reactions to living, will we learn or know anything of value and therein be able to do African/Black Psychology as it should be done. In so doing we, as African psychologists, will "Step into the Light."

Sakhu: Secret Keys in the Development of African Confidence, Competence and Consciousness
(A Lecture)

I would like to begin by saying out loud that in the presence of my elders and with their permission, I ask to be allowed to assume a position and a posture of reverence and respect while I give praise and credit to the source of all knowledge. And I do that by noting and saying out loud that the Almighty who is sometimes called Amun and is sometimes called Ptah and is sometimes called Jehovah and is sometimes called Obatala and is sometimes called the Christ and is sometimes called Shango; and is sometimes called Allah and is sometimes called Olodumare; and is sometimes called Atum and that Almighty God, Amun, Ptah, Ra, although hidden, is the source of all knowledge, all truth, and all wisdom. And I pray that in what I say Amum will be satisfied.

It is important, as we struggle to transform ourselves and to understand the transformation, the retransformation of African people, that we begin to put into practice the theories that we are struggling to clarify. In that context I hope to talk on a path of which we can all practice walking.

At the First Annual Melanin Conference in 1987, we suggested and called forth the challenge that all our knowledge about melanin means absolutely nothing if we cannot as a race, as a people, as the authors of human civilization, produce a single product. And that single product should be a competent, confident, conscious Black child. If we can't do that, then as Richard King and I were talking about recently, all of this becomes a form of masturbation. You do all know that masturbation in some context is pleasurable, but in the outcome it is a waste. We want to make sure that we don't participate in mental masturbation.

I have tried very hard in my work as a Black psychologist, or rather an African psychologist, to free myself from the influences of alien psychological thought and have, essentially, over the last twenty years never read a great deal of what the aliens were saying about human functioning. That has helped me; even though I have limited ability to converse with even my fellow Black psychologists because they want to talk about what "they" have said and I don't know what "they" have said so I can't talk with them. But I do want to make one point here, which is that I need to give you a starting point to put in the context. The only thing that you'll hear me say about, or quote, from an alien will be that which has great significance to us. There is one who I would like to make note of in this discussion . . . and that is Plato. I want to quote Plato because he spent some sixteen or seventeen years sitting in our ancestors' presence. I think I have culled from Plato what he learned in sitting in the presence of Ancient African Wisdom. Plato states, "We, Greeks" . . . and I want to quote him so I will give it verbatim. This is a first in twenty years I'm quoting a white person. Plato says:

> We, Greeks, are, in reality, children
> compared to these people with traditions ten times older
> than ours. And as nothing but precious remembrance of
> the past would long survive in our country [Greece],
> Egypt has recorded and kept eternal the wisdom of the
> old times. The walls of temples are covered with
> inscriptions and the priests have always under their eyes
> the divine heritage, that generations continue to transmit
> to successive generations those sacred things unchanged.

Now look for yourself. "Those sacred things unchanged." Song, dance, rhythm, rituals, music, painting all coming from a time immemorial when Gods governed the Earth in the dawn of human civilization. Plato, Plato. I guess I have to humbly say, if you still have an allegiance to wanting it to be right because white folks said it, then please take Plato with you. Please take Plato with you because if the white folks said it must be right. Plato said that at the dawn of civilization the African presence was so great that we must have been Gods. This was at a time immemorial and we are the continuation of that time.

My task is to talk about a concept that Na'im Akbar and myself have been toying with as a way of redefining, reclaiming a basis of African Psychology and that concept is called "Sakhu." Sakhu is an ancient term from Ancient Kemet, which means understanding, illumination, the eye/the soul of being. We feel in our work in Black Psychology, in African Psychology if you will, that because of the failure of the first affirmative action program where we allowed the Greeks to come into our systems and essentially lowered our standards that they went away not quite comprehending the fullness of what we had to teach. So, instead of seeing psychology as the study of the illumination of the human spirit, which is what our ancestors defined, they came away with psychology being the study of human behavior, trying to understand what behavior can be conditioned at .05 seconds after you give the lollipop and then call that psychology. We, unfortunately, figured out that we didn't want to give lollipops so maybe we could give something else.

Ideas are the substance of behavior and, unfortunately, they've given us an idea that the physical world is the world of reinforcement and therefore all they have to do to control the African Spirit is to define that thing which is the physical stimulus for our reinforcement. Right now they've decided that it has to be crack cocaine, and it is working. As long as we, as African people, find ourselves on the realm of the physical, we will always be subject to the rule of those people who are unable to go beyond the physical. We have to understand with whom we are dealing.

Sakhu is the study of the illumination of the human spirit. We taught the world what it means to be family. It was an African experience that stood up at the beginning of human time and taught the world what it was to be human. We define humanity as composed of a mortal element and an immortal element. We conceptualize reality to understand that there was a visible aspect and an invisible aspect. It's important to see that our ancestors understood that the visible and the invisible were one and the same, but at the same time the invisible was far greater than the visible. As long as we live and exist on the visible plane, we will never comprehend the fullness of who we are as African people that is in the invisible and the hidden. In fact, our ancestors always made that complementarity. I'm choosing that term purposely. It wasn't a dichotomy of the invisible and the visible. It was the complementarity of the visible and the invisible. It seems to me that that's the key for us to understand the fullness of this melanin potential.

We have talked about melanin in a context of its biological aspects and we know a great deal about melanin in its biological aspects. Richard King, Hunter Adams, Neferkare Stewart, Frances Cress-Welsing, Malachi Andrews and a whole host of other folk have taught us and told us about melanin in terms of what is its capacity. We have in fact celebrated them in song. At one level we were surprised by it, one level knew it all along and another level saw that as another weapon to defend ourselves against the history that talked about our basic biological nature as being the indicator of our inferiority. So, our brothers and sisters armed us with a physical weapon to fight against the atrocities that have perpetrated against African people based upon our biology. They've helped us to see that melanin is everywhere.

I sit with Richard and the folk and I get amazed. They tell me it's in the retina of my eye; they tell me it's in my inner ear, they tell me it's in the skin tissue, they tell me it's in my genitals —I say whoops! They tell me it's in my bloodstream; they tell me it is in all the vital organs—my heart, my liver, my kidneys, my brain. I just walk around saying that this melanin is everywhere and I understand and do believe that it is everywhere. They also tell us that . . . some interesting little side bits with which Richard King have literally entertained me, little side bits about the pineal gland. White people, especially, European white women, have the interesting phenomena of their pineal calcifying at the third and fourth decade. When they get to be 30 and 40 years of age, their pineal calcifies. Richard and I have talked about this. I said, "Well, that must mean that that's the first example, the first indicator of what they used to call the 'bonehead'." In fact, when their pineal turns to bone that means they are what? . . . Ignorant. They have an inability to comprehend the fullness of the information that is provided for them. But they make us believe that we're the boneheads and our pineal glands do not calcify. They, in fact, are walking on their heads and have us walking right behind them; looking just like them.

Richard King has helped us; Neferkare Stewart and Malachi Andrews have helped us understand that melanin on the

epidermal level actually sheds. For a long time what our ancestors were doing was preventing, in terms of Black folks, getting
"ashy". . . and "'Oh, Lord' you don't send your child to school all
ashy." You make sure you what? . . . You grease them up. We
grease them up. But think about it, use the vehicle here. Don't
just make this the sort of peculiarity of a unique people. We were
polishing our children because in our ancient, our typical mind,
to be human is to be resplendent, to shine. It is not a physical
phenomenon; understand, it is not a physical phenomenon. The
visible is a manifestation of the invisible and invisible is always
greater than the visible. So, our parents in an instinctual way
understood that as the melanin shed, there was a momentary sit-
uational phenomenon and that the real nature of African people
is to glow. That glowing is, in fact, an aspect of our spirits.

Our melanin scholars help us—and I say this because I
don't consider myself a melanin scholar, right. I like to mess with
them because this is their stuff; they've got to deal with it. But I
do know and I'm sharing with them and using my role as an insti-
gator to suggest that this is greater than we ever imagined. That
it is not just physical stuff and everyone is now talking about that
it's not just physical stuff. Melanin helps to heal wounds. That,
in fact, it is central to the phenomena of spiritual insight. All of
the things that we've been talking about in psychology as para-
psychological phenomena and the powers of the mind and fore-
thought and astral travel are probably critical and connected to
this melanic capacity.

I suggested some ten years ago that we may need to redefine our understanding of human understanding and psychology.
For a long time we've centered around this notion of the central
nervous system and the brain as the critical components in
human beingness that were related to awareness, consciousness
and understanding. I suggested that the problem that we had in
psychology is that we localized human thought in the mind and
localized the mind in the brain. When Descartes came along and
said the mind and the body were separate, we had these heads
walking around and these bodies walking around, separate from
each other. With the racist kinds of interpretations, the mind
being seen as the more elegant, more important aspect—white
folks got the mind and Black folks got the body—and so we were
physical people, they were mental people. We still have our chil-

dren being nurtured on that same kind of alien conceptualization. Understanding that you can be a Dr. J because that's physical and not understanding that the visible, our physical superiority, is a manifestation of the invisible, our spiritual superiority. So, I suggested that we may need to reconceptualize in terms of a theory of differential self-realization.

This reconceptualization is possible in the evolution of the species, in what some people call the "Autogenetic Evolution of Human Kind." In the evolution of the species, the human family separated in a sense that one branch of the family stopped its evolutionary path and simply depended upon the central nervous system as the total machinery for understanding reality. Whereas, the root of the family continued its path, and not only evolved a central nervous system but developed what I called, at that time, an "essential melanic system." I went so far as to try to develop a little formula and suggested that $CNS + EMS = HB$. That is, CNS (Central Nervous System) + EMS (Essential Melanic System) = HB (Human Being). That the central nervous system combined with the essential melanic system is what makes you human. That, in fact, to be human is to be Black. As you begin to look at the development of humankind, the problem for us is that we have followed others' Gods, not our own. We have followed alien thought that talked about humanity as being separate from God, that talked about humans being the creatures of God, and not conceptualizing the reality as our ancestors did, which is "that although hidden it is the source of all things," that although hidden it is in me. That, in fact, the melanin that we see as a physical phenomenon is, I suggest to you, the manifestation of that which makes us one with God.

Melanin is the physical manifestation of that which makes us divine. On the inside, regardless of the distinctions and we're playing as researchers, we're looking at neuro-melanin and epidermal melanin and the relationship to pigmentation. Regardless of all that physical reality, it is on the inside, in the underworld, in the innerworld that is total blackness. That is, in fact, the womb that those dreams burst through that Richard King talks about and gives us signs that we do not understand because we're using the archetypes and symbols of an alien people. Therefore we are blocked from fully appreciating our own way.

It seems to me the ancestors, in their divinity, knew all this and simply decided that their children were going to be lost and as good parents they left signs and a path for us to follow. It was so profound. They said, "Well, I understand that some of our children are going to play tricks on the others and therefore we better put this in stone so they can't be erased because we don't want anyone to come along, erase the signs and put them on papyrus and say, 'Hey! This is our stuff.'" You know they go to Egypt and take it and come back to Greece and put it down, write their names on it and footnote themselves and make us believe that it's theirs; when, in fact, our ancestors said, "Just come home, sit at the kitchen table and you will see the truth."

But it is in the doing of that that is difficult. I just want to say grab hold to Dr. Ben's coattail and go to Egypt and you'll see it, because it is difficult. It is a totally different way of comprehending reality that is required in order to fully appreciate the ancient ways. But the ancestors gave us signs and I want to suggest to you that that is a methodology. There's methodology there that we can utilize for developing this challenge, for meeting this challenge of developing a competent, confident, conscious Black child. The ancestors helped us. They said that the origin of African excellence, the origin of Black excellence, is found in that time when African people stood up and taught the world that we were conscious, we were aware and in our awareness, in our consciousness we were aware that we were divine.

The first "Know Thyself" lesson for African people is that we are divine. If you know that, there is nothing else you cannot know. But if you don't know that, we will always struggle, struggle to know anything. They helped us to understand that at the dawn of human consciousness, human behavior, and human beingness, is governed by principle. That you just don't do anything and everything and say, "Wee, the devil got into me" or "I was conditioned to do that" or "My environment influenced me to do that" or "Because I'm unemployed I had to do that." Our African ancestors understood that wherever we find ourselves, in whatever situation we find ourselves in, our behavior is governed by law, by principle. And that principle that was first established was the principle of MAAT. This first principle tried to explicate some rules and regulations that helped us to try and see there is a blueprint.

We know that every single process ends in a product. I tell my students that every single process ends in a product except for European psycho-analytic therapy. Because psycho-analysis is designed to be just, to be what . . . a process. You don't get healed; you just stay there, forever being sick. So, that's the only process that I can think of that doesn't end in a product. That every single human process (and this may have been the problem with Sigmund Freud and some of his cocaine experiences; that he forgot about what the law says), at least according to the Natural Law, says that every single process ends in a product. The process of germination and fertilization ends in a product that is ushered in by birth. Everything . . . that's a Natural Law is a divine law. So, we have to begin to look at our ancient teachings and understand what we have to take and utilize in our challenge to develop a competent, confident, conscious Black child.

Our ancestors helped us to see that there was an attitude about learning and education; it wasn't just facts and figures. It wasn't just enough for me to memorize that George Washington cut down a cherry tree. It wasn't facts and figures; it was an attitude about education. And that attitude about education was found in the goal of education itself. The goal of education as a human phenomena was to bring about and to guarantee harmony, not hostility. The purpose of education was to bring about understanding and ultimately the purpose of education was to bring about enlightenment.

Even though the time is very precious, I need to make a quick footnote that the ancients understood that there were, in fact, two tendencies in humanity. They developed a lot of analogy and a lot of tales to reveal this to us. Those two tendencies were an ascendant tendency and a descendant tendency. Some even call those natures, but I want to be careful with that because I think it is just a tendency. In that ascendant tendency . . . the tendency to ascend in humanity was to move instinctually towards the enlightenment, to move towards understanding for the illumination toward knowledge. The descending tendency was to move toward ignorance and that ignorance was sometimes talked about symbolically as the darkness. The intelligence, or the illumination, was sometimes talked about as the enlightenment. Our poor students, the Greeks, who we allowed to come into the universities, took that notion of the ascending/descending tendencies—and every Black person should understand this—and defined reality as a linear polarity, with superior and inferior positions. The enlightenment became the light and the darkness became the dark and then placed over that, the physical reality of white and Black. So, as long as we are stuck in the physical, we will see and believe in their dichotomy that the light or white is good, the dark or Black is bad.

Our ancestors were simply saying there are some tendencies in nature and that there are laws that govern nature. One of the laws that we have to understand in terms of the Mysteries is that there are some laws that will stimulate us to move to the higher levels and there are laws that will stimulate us to move to the lower levels. We must understand our nature so that we can, in fact, benefit from the tendencies that our ancestors have laid down for us and not get trapped. We must remember the goal of education: harmony, understanding and enlightenment. The university systems that we set up were devised in terms of understanding the heavens, in terms of the same principles of Natural Law, like understanding the lands, the depths, the secret world, or even the laws of communication.

Our ancestors provided us with instructions for how to do that, a methodology that I am still struggling with personally, in terms of trying to understand. They suggest to us that there were four senses of instruction. And as we develop, as I struggle now in front of you and think through how do we develop a competent, confident, conscious Black child, my ancestors have told me that there are centers of instruction that we need to focus on.

The first center of instruction was how do you describe the indescribable. How do you describe the indescribable? Well, our Aristotelian logic says, "Well, if it is indescribable, therefore I must conclude that it cannot be described. So, why would you ask me how to describe the indescribable?" Our ancestors say the invisible is greater than the visible.

We have to go deeper.
The second center of instruction was how do you show the unshowable.
The third center of instruction was how do you express the unutterable.
The fourth center of instruction was how do you seize the ungraspable instant.

Now think about what our ancestors were saying. How do you describe the indescribable? How do you show the unshowable? How do you express the unutterable? How do you seize the ungraspable instant? I suggest, and I could be wrong, that our ancestors were pointing us to the fact that it is in the hidden domain where all knowledge lies. And when you describe the indescribable you have gone into the realm of Wsir (Osiris). You have, in fact, begun to struggle with a quest for understanding and that's the key to the melanin issue. Melanin is the physical; it is the describable; it is the showable; it is the expressible.

Malachi Andrews gives us the best example of melanin as the expressible. It is in the movement. It is expressed and we can seize the ungraspable instant that we, in fact, know there were African people who had the melanin and who mastered the indescribable, the unshowable, the unutterable, by doing it in a physical way. I can give you the roll call: Imhotep, Akhenaton . . . and, if you will allow me to give you just males because I've been working with young boys and, so, these lists are designed for them in terms of that metaphysical plane of human reality called the male principle, Imhotep, Akhenaton, Tutankhamun, Ramses, Hannibal (all with the glow), Shaka Zulu, Toussaint L'Ouverture, Nat Turner, Joseph Cinque, Denmark Vesey, Elijah McCoy, Benjamin Banneker, Louis Lattimer, Granville Woods, David Walker, Garrett Morgan, Wilmot Blyden, George Washington Carver, Martin Delany, Marcus Garvey, Crispus Attucks, Father Divine, Elijah Muhammad, Carter Woodson, Jack Johnson, Joe Louis (all with the glow), all able to grab the indescribable, to meet the moment (the instant), Joe Louis, Jackie Robinson, Sweet Daddy Grace, Dorie Miller, Muhammad Ali, Malcolm X, Ronald McNair (brother who was blowing saxophone and doing physics problems at the same time). Understanding at the physical level that it is based upon the invisible, the glow, the spirit. Benjamin Davis, Adam Clayton Powell, Louis Farrakhan, Jesse Jackson, Douglas Williams. Douglas Williams, who stood up and was hurt and went beyond the boundary; that's the complementarity between the visible and the invisible.

We have to see that and understand that in the context and in the relationship to our melanic capacity. It is not enough to talk about it in terms of our pigmentation. It is not enough to even talk about it in terms of its role in those critical organs that make us human. It is important that we stretch our notions of melanin to the point of understanding what the ancients have given us, they laid it down for us. Richard King just gave you the best example of it there; he laid it down for us. They had a method of teaching character. We had a method of teaching commitment. We had a method of teaching consciousness. We did it in ways, understanding that each of us comes to the path of illumination at different levels, but we didn't lower our standards.

We understood that you give the information and as I evolve and as I ascend then I will comprehend the greater message. But because I have not evolved, or I have not ascended, doesn't mean I should be tracked in special classes. It doesn't mean I should be given vocational education. It simply means that the task of master is to continue to place the information at a level that in my natural evolution I will attain. Our ancestors did it in such an elegant way and so there is something called "exoteric instruction," overt and intentional. At some levels you give overt and intentional instruction. You train the human sense and the mind by applying the Laws of MAAT and in doing that you bring about the goal of understanding. It is done in specific ways our ancestors told us. You do that by helping the student, the initiate, to understand the conformity of the name of each thing with its true nature.

Why have African peoples, who were brought to the New World, spent so much time struggling with a name? We were Black Anglo-Saxons; we were dark-skinned Europeans; we were colored people; we were Negroes; we were Blacks; we were Nubians; we were Bilalians; we were Afros; we were Afriques; we were Afro-Americans; we were Africans—not even debating the question of whether or not—many of those names are the best application for us as a people. But the process itself tells us something. The visible and invisible. The visible says bloods were struggling with trying to know what name to call themselves. The invisible says that in our esoteric instruction it is important to bring conformity with the name of each thing with its own nature. So we were acting African, even though we didn't say we were Africans. We were attempting, in the historical process, to define a name that brought us into conformity with our nature.

The second thing the ancients told us in terms of esoteric instruction is that you must help the student, the initiate, to

understand the conformity of the appearance given to manufactured things. You must understand the conformity of the appearance given to manufactured things. Take note, the ancients said,
of the shape, the color, the dislocation (I interpret that as out of
rhythm) of the thing with its purpose and function. If we simply
apply that rule to those folk who Leonard Jeffries calls the
"People of the Ice," we would be far, far ahead in terms of understanding. Understanding that conformity of the appearance given
to manufactured things with their purpose and function. It is their
purpose and function to keep us at a physical level so that we will
never reclaim our divinity. It is upon us claiming our divinity that
their children will say once again as Plato said that Black people
ruled the world in a time when Gods walked the Earth.

The third esoteric center of instruction that our ancestors
gave us is to recognize and appreciate the conformity of a building's measurements and proportion with the law. It was meant to
teach that even in building a building our ancestors said there is
a law based upon the proportions of it. There is a law that is
needed to be taught. Here I will give a quick footnote.

Why did our ancestors always center our instructions in a
circle? Infinity line. In a circle, with the elders in the middle and
going out by gradations of age to the parameter. The laws we
must understand are in relationship to measurement and proportion and why the Europeans invented high tables, rows and
columns. All that is mathematics that has a visible and an invisible meaning that maybe we need to, as we reclaim the responsibility for world rulership and governance, begin to not only talk
about poor teachers in our schools messing with our children, but
also the architectural design of the physical environment that
then stimulates the physical melanin to excite the invisible spirituality. Our ancestors also helped us to understand that the exoteric is just one-half of the problem, one-half of the equation; that
there is also esoteric instruction. In that esoteric instruction you
teach by stimulating the symbolic in the subliminal. You train the
initiate's senses and mind to interpret the signs and symbols of
reality. We are a sign symbol people. You all know and I know
you know about the Mason's Square, but we never looked at the
fact that we do signs and symbols with our bodies. When an
African-American male doesn't do right and comes late, or comes
out of pocket, Sister will always put her hand on her hip. If you

will allow me, she will put her hand on her hip and her left foot forward. We don't understand the symbolism. The symbolism of her hand on her hip is not that Sister got big hips (even though Sisters do have big hips); but the symbolism is that she is establishing a sign of righteousness and when we have done wrong she gives us a sign of righteousness. The left foot forward — in fact, you can go to Egypt today and you cannot buy a statue — you cannot even have one made with a human being having the right foot forward. That's out of balance. The left foot was a sign that represented the ability to stamp out disharmony. Understand, in the sense of beingness, in her physical melanin, in her beingness, she is establishing a message that is an encyclopedia of ancient African wisdom of proper conduct. We need to understand the invisible. Brothers do the same thing.

It wasn't accidental that, as we were tracked into those arenas that we call athletics, we could get great success there. That when Brothers and the aliens would do the same thing, the alien would go down to the basketball court and shoot it up and then look up and see mathematically that there was a number that shifted and he'd say, "did good." That's true in their context of reality.

When the Brother went down the same way, we would go beyond, we would describe in our movement the indescribable. And when the brother did what ever it was, the "sky hook," the "hook shot", the floating in the air . . . it didn't matter. When we play for each other, we would look at each other and go higher. Now they saw it as a high sign, that was a sign of Ka . . .Ka . . .Ka. We have to understand fundamentally that we do it instinctually, even though intellectually we are bound and caught on a physical plain. Our natural behavior always reveals that the invisible is greater than the visible and we have to begin to understand the signs. The ancients said through symbolic, through subliminal, we can teach the lessons of Djuhuty—Thoth. We can teach the lessons of Shesat. We can teach the letters of writing. We can teach about geometric patterns and shapes.

Think about it. There's a guide there. The ancients are saying have your child not watch Dr. J., not to see basketball, but to understand mathematics and physics, to understand the Laws of Nature, to understand how you show the unshowable. Do you understand? There's something here that we need to understand in a systematic way as we reclaim in the esoteric instructions of the ancients. They taught us the symbolic configuration and signatures of nature. That nature signs itself, that it creates a configuration that is important for us to understand because everything on Earth reveals its own character and its own property. They developed a particular methodology that was important of which we were to struggle. A methodology is based upon accentuation, based upon association, based upon attribution, based upon analogy, not analysis. Analogy is that accentuation of the characteristics of some species helps us to learn from them. If you accentuate the nature of the bear then when you fight him as Muhammad Ali did, you will be successful. If you accentuate the nature of bumblebee, you will modify your own behavior in that context.

We can look at that one example of the melanin being visible and invisible through Muhammad Ali and see that every single opponent that he fought he utilized the ancient African Law of Accentuation in order to defeat them. He said, "You're the Bear. You're the Gorilla in Manila. You're the Hare." All those things he did were tools through Natural Law. Now, could we take those in 1988 currency in Harlem and utilize those to do the same kinds of things that our ancestors did from the very beginning of time?

They said that through association, that within association there's a science of certain plants and animals, which live in symbiosis. If you study that symbiotic relationship in nature, you can reestablish the symbiotic relationship in society. How do we do that? Attribution, giving to each being and each object a name which reveals itself and is composed in such a way that every thing that lives on Earth respects that.

I have to tell you that it's sort of embarrassing for me, until I get a little more comfortable with it, that in Biblical text, remember: attribution, giving each being and each object a name which reveals its characteristic, that when those people who kept messing with The Bible finally got down to talking about what our destiny was, our purpose was, they said in it Psalms 68:31:

And the nobles shall come forth out of ancient Egypt, and Ethiopia shall soon set forth her hand [her Ka] unto the world.

Now I, embarrassingly, teach my children this, but I want to share with you that the Nobles were not the name of this folk who left slavery and said we're going to be "Nobles" from now on. But nobility was an attribute on which they were commenting. An attribute that represents those people of high character, excellence of thought; quality will soon set forth their Ka until the world. That is the path of attribution, to give each thing its name and in its name you understand its destiny.

Using analogies through puns, the difficulty in terms of mastering it in the Medu Netcher, hieroglyphs, is not trying to memorize all those signs, but what matters is that we use a system of language that was based on homonyms and puns to create greater meaning, the visible and the invisible. The visible was the words upon the double meanings, but the invisible was the greater meaning. So, we have to understand our way of teaching. How does one do this? Knowledge is taught to many in ritual, in Rites of Passage. There are many experiments going on now with Rites of Passage. I just want to share with you a system that we've developed in California working with young Black ninth-grade boys who are identified by their school systems as the boys who are identified by their school systems as the incorrigible, the future criminals. We developed a program for them that was supposedly designed to do teen-age pregnancy prevention. But as a psychologist approaching the needs of society from an African perspective, we understood and appreciated that the visible, the high incidence of teen-age pregnancy, is not the issue. It is the invisible that is critical. So, if you want to solve the visible problem of teen-age pregnancy, you do that by developing a solution based upon the invisible, not the visible. The visible solution would be to tell Blood to keep his stuff in his pants, tell Sister to keep her panties up; that doesn't work. Because we know once you touch it you've got to go back. So, it's not a question about the physical level. So, we developed something trying to utilize our own teachings as we understood the ancient ways and we developed something called the HAWK Project for Young Black ninth grade males. The HAWK Project was based upon one ancient understanding and one contemporary one. HAWK stood for High Achievement, Wisdom and Knowledge based upon our original understanding of education. High Achievement Wisdom and Knowledge. We developed for these young brothers something called the "Book of the Way," that's a secret text that these young Brothers in San Francisco and Sacramento know and believe that they're not going to let nobody see this, because this is our secret that they keep and it bonds them together.

We chose the term HAWK also because the hawk was the symbol of Heru (Horus), the Black Man, who was the prototype, the archetype, and it is, in fact, what all human beings speak to when they say this person is a hero. We also help them to see that more in terms of their contemporary definition, that there is a Brother on television now named Hawk, who is some kind of Brother, he might be criminal but the Brother has competence, confidence and consciousness. It is probably a mistake on television, but if you study this Brother on "Spencer for Hire," here is a Brother that reveals in himself principled conduct in what he says and does. He has competence, confidence, consciousness. So, we have these young Brothers memorizing because the mind is what we utilize in the development. They, in fact, are called her-bak, the face of Heru (Horus), the face of the Falcon. They refer to each other as her-bak as a way of talking about how the name represents our nature. We know for instance that in righteousness, on the visible level the concept of righteousness means you stand upright. When man stands upright all his critical organs fall in their proper position. So I stand upright. My genitalia are here, a critical organ, my stomach is here, a critical organ, my heart is here, a critical organ, my mind (the crown) is here. So, when I stand upright, I take what ?... the position of righteousness.

So, we're teaching young Black boys the old time stuff; it is nothing new, nothing invented. But when you see the presence of Black womanhood, it is your responsibility to take the position of righteousness. You don't slouch in front of a black woman. You literally stand up and take the position of righteousness. That's a little minor insignificant thing we could say, "You got blood standing up because a sister comes in the room." But we understand that the invisible is greater than the visible. So, the little things you see as the visible is based upon something far greater than that. And at the ninth grade level what we want to do is to provide them with the rituals that they can comprehend and attain at their level. Later we will talk to them about, as they grow in manhood, the fuller responsibilities of African manhood. But we have them learn and memorize—they have to memorize — and quote from memory the Seven ancient African Cardinal Virtues of MAAT. They have to know Truth, Justice, Righteousness, Propriety, Harmony, Balance and Order. We even develop rules of conduct for those in the context of that. And I will just share with you those rules:

> We say to the HAWKS: The rule of Truth and they say to us: We believe in Truth. I will always seek to know what is correct and I will not lie or speak falsely.

> We say to them: The rule of Justice
> And they say to us: We believe in Justice. I will always be fair in what I do. And I will not cheat myself, my race or my family.

> We say to them: The rule of Righteousness
> And they say to us: We believe in righteousness. I will always be correct in what I do and I will not allow others to influence me to do wrong.

> We say to them: The rule of Propriety
> And they say: We believe in Propriety. I will always strive to do the proper thing at the right time and I will not bring shame to my family, myself or my race.

> We say to them: The rule of Harmony
> And they say: We believe in Harmony. I will always be in rhythm with what is good and I will never be in opposition to what is good for me, my race or my family.

> We say to them: The rule of Balance
> And they say to us: We believe in Balance. I will strive to understand and respect the need to be complementary and I will not be in conflict with myself, my family or my race.

> We say to them: The Rule of Order
> And they say to us: We believe in Order. I will respect the Natural Order of the divinely governed universe and I will not separate myself from that which gives order to the world.

Now we are having young Brothers begin to at least memorize these concepts of the Ancient African Cardinal Virtues. The next step, obviously, is to develop song. Song that reflects our way, to develop dance that rewards us in our humanity and our Africanity. To develop a whole host of rituals and ceremonies and practices that reinforce our principles; the ten principles of initiatory mastery that we need to pull and reclaim from the ancient ways and to utilize as a way of understanding the visible and the invisible.

Ten Principles

The principle of controlling one's thought. Mastery of one's thought. Mastery of one's behavior. Devotion to a higher purpose. Faith in the ability of one's teachers (meaning one's parents) to teach the truth. Faith that one can know the truth. Faith that one can use the truth. Faith that one can be free from resentment when one is punished. Faith that one will be free from resentment when one is wrong. Cultivating in one the ability to tell right from wrong. And ultimately cultivating in our children the ability to tell the difference between what is real and what is unreal. The ability to describe the indescribable, the ability to show the unshowable.

Our task, as we struggle as melanin scholars and scholars of all disciplines is that we need to begin to go to the greater issue. The greater issue was set for us by our ancestors and it is inscribed in every single cell of our bodies. It is our task to show the unshowable, to glow.

In the beginning of time, at the dawn of human civilization, our ancestors who stood at the foot of the Mountain of the Moon called Kilimanjaro stood up and in their glow said to the world:

I am the eternal spirit; I am the sun that rose from the primeval waters. My soul my spirit, my melanin is God. I am the Creator of the word. Evil is my abomination. I see it not. I am the Creator of the order wherein I live. I am the word which will never be annihilated and this my name of soul.

In the quiet night of the African mind, the African-American woman, Mary McCleod Bethune, stood up and said to us:

I leave you love, I leave you hope, I leave you thirst for education. I leave you faith. I leave you racial dignity. I leave you a desire to live harmoniously with your fellow man. And I ultimately leave you with the final responsibility for our young people.

Ptah hotep.

[1988]

Liberating the African Consciousness

(A Lecture)

I have a strange and glorious reaction of always coming to this place and I mentioned to a sister as we were sitting and chatting, that African scholarship is really different from other scholarship. I don't want to spend a lot of time talking about other folk because that's really a waste of intellectual ability. However, what I want to point out is that we grow our scholars as we grow collard greens. In growing scholars it is the interaction between the community and the scholar that shapes the thought, just as it is the interaction between the seed, soil and the farmer that results in the collard greens. It is not that we are off in the Eiffel tower or away in some room by ourselves and have magical and creative ideas and then return to laudatory praise by our community. There is a dialectic between us and the community that clarifies the information. It is through this clarification process that grounded scholarship is nurtured. The community nurtures the scholars, and yet at times the community has to prune the scholar as well. Sometimes we get too far out, and the community has to cut off a branch here or there and pull us back into shape, because that too is part of the process.

It is in coming here to this place that I see another part of that process. In an interesting way a brother named Bill Jones just commands me to think about things. He'll call me late at night and it's especially late here because it's a different time zone and I wonder why is Bill up at this time of night calling me. But he'll call and say, "Have you thought about this?" or "Have you thought about that?" and I'll say, "No, I haven't thought about it." And he'll say, "Well think about it." And it is as if I want to say, "Brother, I got other things to do besides to do these assignments." But we have this relationship that when he says, "think about it," I actually start thinking about it. It is in the process of "thinking about it" that mistakes are made but out of it comes clarity and I appreciate and really benefit from that process, even though I may be dragging my feet sometimes. Brother Bill can hear the long pauses of silence on the telephone when I don't know what to say or do. He gave me the assignment to talk about liberating our African consciousness.

As commanded, I've given some thought to the topic and I want to share with you some ideas that have emerged as a consequence of the question, "How does one liberate the African consciousness?" It is really a very good and important question because we are in the midst of the heightening of this issue of things African. We were debating about whether it's "Afrocentric," "Africentric," or "African centered." There is a lot of discussion, as well as activity where people are running around overnight changing that which was once considered Negro, and Black, and Colored, and instead putting "African centered" on it. But now we're asking, "What is African centered?" People are creating Afrocentric ice cream to Afrocentric shoe polish. Sure, this shows there is a fervor going around about such African issues yet at the same time we have confusion in our community. We fail to see that part of the confusion results from the opposition, the white power elite, trying to paint a particular image of the African centered movement that frightens and divides our community. This is done to get the Black community to say that we don't want any part of that. As a scientist, looking at this, I can say that we have an opportunity to study a very interesting and complex phenomenon. On the other hand, as a practitioner, it is very difficult to do things that are productive for our community with all this confusion. So it is good that we have an opportunity to talk about the issue of the African consciousness.

I want to entitle my thinking for the moment with the single word character, as a way of bridging into a dialogue about the question of liberating the African consciousness. However, first, let me speak to the issue of oppression. Now I've mentioned in other contexts that the major dilemma for the African community is how to minimize the destructive impact of racist oppression. The clearest statement of that racist oppression is clearly white supremacy.

White Supremacy has to do with the need to force people of color, particularly people with the most color, African folk, to serve the interest, obey the will, and satisfy the needs of white

people. It happens over and over again and it happens in terms
of defining Black people, African people, in terms of our value
being associated with the extent to which we provide pleasure or
profit to white folks. That is, as an African being you have no
value in a white supremacist society unless you can demonstrate
your ability to provide pleasure and profit to white folks. We
engage in that all the time. Sometimes we slip into it and we don't
realize it and before we know it we're doing the song and dance
that is designed to benefit white people. It's often done because
we know there is some reward, sometimes it's just our lives. For
example, when a police officer has an African person against the
wall with a gun pointed to his head, he could talk about the rich-
ness of his heritage saying, "I'm a descendant of Imhotep," but
that doesn't work. Then this becomes a pleasure and profit rou-
tine that moves one to the next block, and that's probably the
only time when it's okay to do it. Because if you don't "be," it
don't matter. So, at some point you've got to deal with just being.

      The other issue that needs to be discussed is that while
we are trying to minimize the destructive forces of white
supremacy, we also have to make efforts to maximize the utilization of our cultural systems for human development. These seem
to be the twin pillars associated with this question of how to liberate the African consciousness in terms of everything we do.
IIow do we minimize the destructive forces and at the same time,
maximize the productive forces in terms of our own culture?
In the political realm, it is important to note that the question of
White supremacy has translated in terms of the African world
wide community to a system of colonization. As I look at the system, the political system of colonization, it is clear that colonialism means, in its simplest forms, organization and arrangement.
The clarification, or definition, is the technical scientific notion of
colonization, as opposed to the political perspective that is normally given. It should be made clear that the singular goal of colonization is to rearrange an area. When colonization takes place
there are outside forces that enter and rearrange that area, along
with all its resources, to something different than its natural state.
European contact with Africa has always been driven by the
desire to transform, or rearrange, things African into fundamental European constructs. This idea needs to be looked at very
carefully and very slowly. We must know that every single thing

we deal with in terms of that intercultural relationship with Europe is driven by the desire to transform aspects which are African into European. At some point Black psychologists have to look at this as a specialty, the psychiatric problem of white supremacy. We have so many problems that need to be fixed within ourselves because of white supremacy that it is not possible to address each concern directly at this time.

There are three methods of colonial reorganization that will help to better clarify this issue in terms of understanding the minimization of the impact of White supremacy. The first is that colonial reorganization always has to deal with the domination of the physical space. Most often, we talk about that as the domination and destruction of the land. Many political scientists will express peoples' relationship to the land and how they are being affected because of the destruction by colonization. The domination of the physical space is really the ability of the colonizer to acquire, distribute, and exploit resources. And so, if you look at Harlem, in terms of the domination of the land, this is a colonial state just as any other area because there are alien folk who determine the acquiring, distributing, and contributing to the exploitation of the resources that make up the Harlem community just as it is done in many so called underdeveloped nations.

The second method which colonial reorganization requires is the managing of the indigenous modes of production. This has been a major problem for Africa as a continent. Managing indigenous modes of production means that the alien integrates his own modes of production into the traditional natural modes of production. Whereas, Africa was in a path of development that had lain out certain notions of political, social, and family organization. What was infused into that was the European notions of political, social, family organization. As a consequence we don't see the development of an African economic system. What we do see is Africans grabbing Marx or any other dead white person and using them to try to figure out how to deal with their distribution of resources, not realizing that integration of those alien ideas is an act of colonization.

The third method, which I think is the most important aspect of colonization, has to do with the reformation, or the reforming, of the African mind. Once the other two methods have been employed, the ultimate task is to replace the African mind with a European mind, which is done by replacing African indigenous education, religious, and psychological systems. It is not accidental that for the first time people have come out against Black folk with a vengeance and viciousness based upon some Black folk saying we want African centered education. When we were talking about integrated education, it was integration into their ideas, beliefs, and actions. Many acted as if they didn't want Black people, but they really did want us in there. That was a trick. We thought they were keeping us out. So they kept telling us we got some good items here and although we wanted them, we couldn't have it. We ran trying to get it and what they understood was that the more we give African people European education the less we have to worry about them.

And so the moment Africans begin to say there is something about the educational system, which must reflect the image and the interest of African people there will be debate and discussion against it. The *New York Times* brought out one of their oldest employees who happened to be the premiere historian, Arthur Schlesinger. He started talking about the dis-uniting of America, as if the United States was ever united in the first place. But then we run around here figuring out that we must be the bad guys now because we're doing something against America, not realizing that they're giving us a sign. We should realize that this whole question of African centered things, particularly African centered education, particularly African centered religion, particularly African centered psychology, indicates we're on the right path. We're on the right path just based upon what the enemy is doing. When they are disappointed or disagree about something that we're doing, then we know (highly likely) that we're completely on the right path.

Now from my vantage point, I would argue that the colonial regime that sees as its mandate the reformation of the African mind is the place where we should begin to seek deeper understanding. Keeping in mind that exploitation always is centered around the exploitation of land, labor, and life. Control over these three results in being completely controlled. It is as simple as that. But the land and the labor, I think even at the cost of being wrong, are secondary. This is the reason why we haven't been totally victimized.

It is because they never really have wiped out our minds that we were able to maintain our sense of Africanness. Every now and then we get a crazy epic. We might get one or two Black folk who are somewhat mentally out of touch with reality but for the most part the African community in the New World has never given up this African mind. We know it is so because it can be seen in our little anecdotes. For example, if we were to send our kids to these integrated experiences, called "higher education," the elders would say, "Yeah, it's cute you are going to school. That's nice. But, son don't go up there and come back no educated fool." Now, why would they say that? You know when the fact of the matter is that all of the glory, all of the grandeur, all of the best of life is there at the Yales and there at the Stanfords. Why would your mother tell you to "be cool here for a minute. Don't just go get everything." It's because she had not lost her mind. If she had lost her mind she would be saying, "Go there and get everything. Eat it up; swallow it; take it all because it's yours." But she knew better and she only wanted some piece of sanity for her children.

The fact of the matter is that we are losing our minds. And we are losing our minds because the system of colonialism requires the reformation of the African mind. It is the same reformation that raises for me the question of the importance of character. I want to use that term as a way of thinking with you out loud. Diop is considered an important intellectual in the African centered movement. And most folk give reference to Diop[1] in terms of his seminal work. Diop suggests some important things and he raises some questions that he does not answer. It is important for us to see and appreciate that because sometimes we make gods and play-things out of intellectuals. Then we begin to believe it, so that we justify almost anything by saying, "Well, Diop said it." Be careful because Diop was an intellectual and as such he had insight, but, more often than not, he has unanswered questions. And it is our task to try to answer those questions as we move the process of revitalizing our community.

Diop suggests in his thinking, particularly in Civilization or Barbarism[2], that individual identity or individual psychology is a function of cultural psychology, the cultural identity of your people. In effect, he's saying there's no separation between your individual psychological well-being and the psychological well-being of your cultural community. We cannot separate individual psychology from our cultural psychology. In this analysis, Diop argues that there are three factors that can contribute to the cultural identity of a people. He pointed to the historical factor, the linguistic factor, and the psychological factor.

First, he argues that the perfect cultural identity corresponds to the full simultaneous presence of these three factors. He's arguing that we have to take control and mastery of the historical factor, the linguistic factor, and the psychological factor in order to have psychological wealth to begin the liberation of the African consciousness. And he seems to say that there are specific combinations of these three factors at which we need to look. Then, Diop says, which I think it is important for you all to recognize, "This analysis is brief." In so stating, Diop says the historical factor is the cultural cement which unifies the separate elements of a people to make them whole. I asked a question, "What is meant by and why is it important to have a feeling of historical continuity?" I argue that because our history has been so maligned through the systems of colonialism, or white supremacy, that sometimes we believe that what Diop means by the historical factor is that we simply need to add up and tell the truth about our historical events. We think we need to tell the story from the time before Kemet until now. That's not reality. It simply isn't enough to just lay out all the history of a people.

In fact, the obvious thing that our youth challenges us with is our lack of continuity in historical experiences and events. When they see a string of historical events which have somehow come to an end, they begin to wonder why it is that the experiences or events stopped. And we can only sit in silence because these historical events stopped and we haven't done the analysis to understand what caused the historical greatness in terms of achievement to stop? And that's the question, why is it that since the beginning of recorded time African men and women have accomplished greatness beyond measure and, then, it stopped.

The answer to this question has to do with something being more than the presence of that historical moment than historical achievement. Diop says that the historical consciousness provides the people with a feeling of cohesion. We who are Afrocentrists argue that we have to get this history correct because that's what gives us the cohesion. We know, obviously, that a major problem impacting the Black community is the lack of unity. And so if history deals with the cohesion then maybe history is an important part of the equation that needs restoration and correction in order to heal and preserve the African-American community.

I raise the question because in dialoguing with Diop, I asked, "How does the historical consciousness result in the feeling of cohesion? How does knowing that Imhotep existed and Imhotep is like me; how does knowing that Hatshesput existed and Hatshesput is like sister; how does knowing these historical things result in a feeling of cohesion?"

The answer is not in Civilization or Barbarism. The answer is ours to discover. Diop says the historical consciousness constitutes the safest and the most solid shield of cultural security. Well, if my beginning premise said that we have to minimize the destructive racism and maximize our cultural integrity, then it seems to me that this historical consciousness has something important for us.

The next question that comes to mind is, "What is cultural security?" Is cultural security riding on the trains in Philadelphia and New York and becoming aware that people are looking and pointing because of one's African attire? White folks want to ask if one is from another country. This too is part of cultural security. The real question is what does it mean? Diop says the essential thing is to rediscover the thread that connects us to our remote ancestral past. What is the thread of which Diop speaks? Is the thread giving an account by account list of one's history? He says the most efficient cultural weapon is the feeling of historical continuity. And I think Diop does a good job of arguing for the importance of history but in one sense it misleads us because the simplistic interpretation is that historical continuity is the laying out of the historical moments.

And so you have a catalogue, or chronology, if you will, of all the things that African folk have done. Diop leaves that unattended and the dialogue somewhat moves to the linguistic factor. Diop is trying to critique elder scholarship, and it is an act of humility, especially since Diop is bound by his own training at the Sorbonne. He argues that the linguistic factor is the constant element of cultured personality, or in other words, that the linguistic factor constitutes one's cultural personality.

If that statement were true, then I can no longer ascribe to being a member of an African cultural community. But, in the tradition of Europe, at the time Diop was a student, there was this elegant and elaborate family of languages that made up the European community, and it was babble and confusion in the African community. They could make the argument that it is their linguistic system that constitutes our cultural system because, for them this was true. But for the African community, it was not just a question of language. In defense of Diop, he argues that we need to conduct authentic African linguistic research that brings our people to experience their linguistic unity. Given the many languages that African people speak and the many ways in which we mispronounce other languages, how do we attain this notion of linguistic unity.

That is a question that in this audience people need to stand up and think about and take as their challenge. What does African linguistic unity mean and how is it experienced? Does it mean that we have to become bi-lingual and each of us learn an African language and some other language, or does it mean that there is something that is more fundamental than the spoken word that gives us the unity? And there is evidence of that based upon the fact that every African community is forced to speak a European language to the point that sometimes Europeans don't understand their own language. And so there is a key here that we need to look at that might be the linguistic unifier.

And finally Diop goes into the question of psychological factor which bridges us into the question of liberating the African consciousness. In first, and even a couple of times, reading Diop, I missed the point he was trying to make in relation to psychological factor. Diop says that the historical and the linguistic factors constitute a quasi-absolute reference point in relationship to the permanent flux of psychic changes in the African community. What does that mean? Diop is arguing in this one sentence that the historical factor and the linguistic factor serve as barometers to measure the psychic change in African people. It is the psychic that is fundamental, not the historical, not the linguistic stuff. What is fundamental is the psyche, the spirit of African people. In that spirituality you can see the changes in our essence based upon shifts in historical and linguistic factors.

So, we begin to look at these, it gives us a running record or a key to raise the question about what is meant by consciousness? Consciousness is not simply an awareness of all of our achievements or accomplishments. Neither is consciousness just an awareness of the fact that I can speak three African languages, thinking that my ability to do such makes me more African than someone else. That's not what this consciousness is all about. The consciousness is the psyche. The consciousness is the spirit, and we need to look at it as a barometer for measuring the shifts in that psychic fabric.

Diop continues by saying that in the light of African people becoming more individualistic, the question arises of how to explain the feeling of cultural identity throughout time as a permanent being, a permanent domination of European people? He's saying there is a cultural identity that exists in African people that has been throughout time, even though we see indicators that we are becoming more individualistic. And in a sense he argues that there is a cultural invariant. Something that doesn't change in African people even though there are manifested level changes in our language system. We speak English but seemingly poorly, depending upon which schools we attended. We don't speak traditional African languages but we see and have a relationship to the historical events that have characterized our people.

Diop thinks that the psychological factor was traditionally grasped in a qualitative way through literature, particularly poetry. Whereas, the other two factors, history and linguistics, were more susceptible to rigorous scientific investigation. I critique Diop by noting that he was probably looking more at the negritude poets who attempted to talk about the psychological personality of African folk through both literature and through poetry. What is not clear in Diop is the recognition that while history and language are often submitted to hard rigorous scientific investigation, the Negritude poets were not the best source of understanding the psyche of African people. It is only because he was dealing with the negritude folk and not dealing with African centered Psychologists that he played down the psychic factor.

As a key to uncovering the psychic factor, in the early 1970s I tried to argue for a notion of Africanity as an attribute of our African myths, and that Africanity could be disrupted based upon our integration and acculturation with and by other worldviews and philosophies. I later went back to that concept of Africanity and tried to demonstrate that there were disruptions in our time and space co-ordinates in terms of how we understand ourselves. In addition, I suggested that there were seven events that influence the African psyche regardless of whether we are in the Diaspora or on the continent of Africa.

We do know that the reformation of the African mind results in some people saying, "Well, I am more African because I was born in Africa and you were born in Harlem." You can try to be African, but it is who I am. I do not have to make superficial attempts. Changing that attitude will result in the reformation of the African mind. The fact of the matter is that this moment in time right now, in a crowd at the University of Ghana, there may be an African psychologist who probably will be wearing an English tweed suit, which is actually a strange kind of thing that Africans do, but because of his choice of attire he is no less African than I am. And that is what we have to begin to look at if this question of psyche or the spirit is to be answered.

For instance, if someone asked me, "What is my nationality?" I have to say I am an American because that is where I have citizenship. Nationality pertains to membership in a nation state. If somebody asks, "What kind of human being are you?" I have to say African. Not Afro-American, not Afri-American, not Bilalian, not Colored, not Negro, not all those things that we claim because the fundamental concept is that our nature, our spirit is tied to being African beings, not tied to geography. If someone asks, "Where do you live?" I have to say Oakland. I do not live in Botswana, so I cannot say that is where I live. We have to be clear on understanding these kinds of distinctions. Part of that confusion comes about, I think, from the disruption of our time space realities.

I argued that six events influenced, or rather, disrupted the African consciousness for both Africans in the Diaspora and in Africa. The first experience or event that caused disruption was religious conversion. After such, Africans on the continent experienced five events: colonialism, de-colonialism, neo-colonialism, industrialization, and nationalism. For the Diasporic Africans in the New World their experiences were almost exactly paralleled, starting with religious conversion, which was soon followed by slavery, paralleling colonialism; emancipation, which paralleled de-colonialism; reconstruction, which paralleled neo-colonialism; urbanization, which paralleled industrialization; and finally Black consciousness, which paralleled nationalism.

In terms of traditional African philosophy, I've mentioned that sometimes reality is being both visible and invisible. This is so, even though the invisible is far greater than the visible. So, we can see the "visible me" but not the "invisible me" until I am seen through African glasses. Because the two are put together and they make "we." But at an individual basis we see "me." The reason there is such a problem seeing the invisible is because we are thinking as the Europeans, in terms of the individual rather than the collective group, or invisible "we." It is that relationship between me and we that parallels the African visible and invisible nature of reality.

In the African tradition the essence was always captured in the spiritual, material, conceptual, social, affective, and quantitative realms. Now, those things were much like a kaleidoscope, a spiritual understanding and a material understanding, along with all the other realms, were all connected. Whereas, we think in European ways of linear polarities and we begin to separate these realms and look at them as individual entities, which ultimately reduces their power, rather than as a collective unit. And we have, these linear polarities and independent parts, points of a continuum.

That is how we must begin to conceptualize these notions. A good analogy would be to say that we are all like the individual ingredients in a gumbo recipe. Although each ingredient can be eaten separately, the taste, or true essence of gumbo is not achieved until all are blended as one recipe. It has always been the most historical phenomenon, like the religious conversions, that forced us to see the spiritual as distinct from other things. This kind of thinking distorted our perceptions and once this is done, a people are no longer able to make the same perceptions. We do not realize the effect that distorted perceptions truly have on us. We think business is being taken care of because on Sunday at 11:00 a.m., we attend church service. That is a perceptual distortion.

Once there is distortion of the material essence of a people, their expression in terms of the physical realm becomes confused and distorted as well. This is evident with the discussion of color. The material realm says that the material is a manifestation of the spirit. What is real, is the spirit. Once that was distorted through these time space disruptions of our Africanity, we no longer focused on the material as a manifestation of the spiritual, but rather the material representing physicality. "I'm better than you because I'm lighter," or "I'm better than you because I have straight hair," or "I'm better than you because I have money and bought myself some green eyes." It should be clear that the problem here is that we are focusing on the physical and fail to see that there has been a disruption in our thinking and perceiving process.

The conceptual essence of a people's psyche is distorted when we begin to think in a cognitive way based upon other people's schema. Rather than see ourselves in terms of the African tradition of the ontological principle of consubstantiation that says we are made equally, we begin to think that which makes us who we are, are those achieved attributes and characteristics. We think that because we have gained material wealth and status that we have also attained some higher level of being that requires that we separate ourselves from the common folk. For example, many can be heard to say, "I don't have to live in Harlem anymore because I have money, therefore, I am better than the rest of them." All the while, not realizing that I am thinking in a way that is different from the kaleidoscope and gumbo of an African epistemological worldview.

Industrialization and urbanization also affected the relation between our essence and our expression. The essence includes the affective, and the feeling domain, with both expressed, in part, as emotionality. Now we are contemplating foolish questions like whether or not men should be emotional, as if that is the real issue that needs to be discussed. We want to think that the problem is simply that Black men are just so cool that they won't express their emotions and if the black women could only get them to talk more then the relationship would be all right. We cannot continue along this path, seeking answers to such ridiculous questions. We have a value system, and we need to follow it or suffer the consequences of being led to a place where we should not be.

There is no denying that the Black community has some problems between males and females, but it should be expected because we are not being true to our spirituality. Simply stated, we're following others' gods. In reference to the male/female issue, it is not a matter of the male being unemotional, the real question lies in what is considered the masculine essence and what is the appropriate expression of that masculine essence. Just as the issue for a woman is not a matter of her over sensitivity but rather what is her feminine essence and what is the appropriate expression of that feminine essence. It has nothing to do with me watching a movie and crying in the theatre.

Everything that is done should be viewed with its context to the disruption of our beingness. The problem is that we no longer view ourselves as Black and this also can be attributed to the disruptions. That's the point I'm really making, because if Diop is correct, it is the psychic factor that we have to get clarity on and this has not been done because we have inherited the notion of psychology from the West and it speaks of these little things called egos and ids that are fighting inside of us, waiting for some super ego to come along and tell them to act right, in order for us to be well.

That idea of psychology is not what our psychology has been or should be. We have to begin to get away from that. And those of us who are psychologists or psychology majors hear me very cautiously because we are still in the context of a colonial system. And consequently there is struggle to get licensure, there is struggle to get degrees, understand that the task here is the reformation of your mind. Then, there is belief in all that psychological madness and it sends us away thinking that we are going to heal the African-American community simply by carrying through these psychoanalytic theories of development and crisis. All that this results in is driving Black folk crazy. And so we have to be able to look at these differences in order for our work to benefit the African-American community.

And the final ingredient to the whole is that this continuum of continental Africans dealing with the question of nationalism and Diasporic Africans dealing with the question of Black consciousness disrupted our natural relationship between the essence of doing. Connotive means how you do something, as expressed in the political realm. And what we see is that we don't do what is consistent with the African tradition. That, in fact, what we see in Africa today is a perpetual process of coup d'etats that occur not because we understand the natural process of African development of leadership and governance, but because we borrowed someone else's notion of the political system and used their notions to take ourselves into our present state.

These notions are also accepted by Blacks in the United States. It is most evident when an African-American is elected to a political office. It is usually the Black community that waits until the person is at the point where he/she is directed some-place else and then starts to complain and make noise about what the person has not done, finalizing it by saying that the politician sold out. The question is not whether or not they have sold out. The question is how to cure a community of people who are sick in order to stop those who are just as sick as us, if not worse, from taking a political office. We are too quick to see the faults in others without taking the time to figure out the reasons why people are the way they are. In fact, what we have to do is look at or talk about the human process.

In looking at the human process, we can see how our perceptions could be changed. When we carefully analyze the situation, perhaps the difference between us; and, our Black politicians is that they have less interaction with us and therefore, they have less accountability. Less dialogue means that less responsibility on their parts because they don't have to constantly hear from us what is needed or wanted. They are actually getting feedback or direction from some other community telling them what to do. We fail to see this. We simply see them in office and assume that they have all the power that the office is supposed to have. When we don't quite know what is going on we make that group of people or individual person our enemy because it is easier to deal with and understand. And then the game is won. Because when Black folk fight each other, there is no one watching the system of colonialism, which continues to advance without any interference from our community.

Diop argued that there are some cultural, or psychological invariants; some things that don't change. Furthermore, we need to look at these if we are going to deal with the psychic variable. And I'm in agreement with him on this day that these historical and linguistic aspects are barometers, measures, if you will, of the shifts in the psychic changes. But, what are these psychological and cultural invariants that he suggests? I think they are connected. That's why the African-centered scientists are correct that we must rescue and reclaim Kemet as our foundation. Not just because it is the earliest documented expression of what Africans were doing way before we decided to drive down the Nile in our BMW's and buy condos, calling them pyramids. That's not the point. The point is that we left a lot of records there. And what we left was an understanding of African beingness that I think is tied to the liberation of African consciousness, and is tied to an understanding of the psychic factor that Diop talks about.

Beingness and becoming are inscribed in what some ethnographers call divine law. Africans believed that the behavior, the essence, and the expressions of the universe were governed by divine law. Divine law is written about in many different, complicated and elegant ways. An analysis of African philosophy says from the very beginning that up until today that divine law in the African tradition is simply that we "be." Think about it. If there is no sense of being, there is nothing. So, when you dissect all the elegant and elaborate entities about the concepts of being and becoming and expressions and subactualizations, the bottom line is that nothing can take place unless we "be."

African philosophy says that in being we must recognize that for every divine law there is a moral mandate. There is a mandate that compels us to fulfill as a question of morality. I want to make it clear that I am not referring to religion. Morality ultimately has to do with relationship. In the African tradition, the ultimate relationship is that between humans and God. Understanding that the God that we speak of is in other humans. So the relationship is between me and the God force in another. To the extent that I can acknowledge and recognize that, we have a harmonious relationship. The moment I redefine you as not human but as animal is the point that we have no link in our relationship other than cause and effect, other than an artificial relationship. Our ancestors said that the divine law of being is coupled or married to a moral mandate that says if you "be," then the quest of life is to become, and that we are to continually become.

This marriage between the two is important because our continuation in becoming is important. The way we maximize becoming is by building on the essence of our spiritual past. We have to, according to our grandmothers, "Become mo better."

This is the key. We have to always strive to be better in all that we do. It is why we constantly prepare our children for going into a world where they will be confronted with White supremacy and racism. Grandmothers, fathers, and mothers would tell them, "You got to be twice as good to get half as much in a racist society." That's a "more better" philosophy. Our parents would tell us "I don't care what you do, sweep floors. Drive buses. Be a university professor. I don't care what it is. You be the best." That's "mo better" philosophy.

So, we must look and see that we have carried a retention that had to do with not the historical moment or the linguistic expression but with the psychic factor. The psychic factor was tied to the philosophy related to the alchemic process of transformation to perfectibility. Our ancestors said that the human condition is one that is characterized by teachability and perfectibility. When there are distorted perceptions, how can there be a teaching of what is right? When there is normality, there's a great possibility of being on a path of perfection. That's important for psychologists. We run around thinking that we have to put people in some deep psycho-analytic trance to get them well. Our ancestors some how knew, four thousand years ago, that sometime, in the future, we might get off track and when that happens, we should simply seek remediation through "teaching" someone what it is to be natural and normal.

It is more than necessary to stress the importance of teaching and how we can build a new community out of the old ways. We must teach because when the unlearned are in there, when they're not off track, when not aberrant or abnormal, when they're not distorted in their normal condition, that is when it is possible to engage in the process of perfectibility of the human being. And so our development was one of teachability and perfectibility. The interesting thing that I want to point out is that it is not accidental that during every epic in ancient Kemet, especially when things had gone to ruin, we would rebuild our physical, material monuments by first taking a stone from the ruin and seed the new building. Seeding just like when we used to make bread, we would take some of the old dough and use it to start the process of the new. It is that seeding process that we do when making bread because we know that the taste of the old bread that we used to eat was so good that we can guarantee that the new bread will be just as palatable if we take some of the old as a starter for the new.

There's a lesson to be learned there. The lesson to be learned is not that the discussion of history is important because we want to play the dozens and say my mother did something more than anybody else's mother, but rather because it is in the history that we can find the seeds to build into the future. History is not the past. History is about the future. It is about understanding the psyche of which we have to deal. The names of the Neters were found after we shuffled through the debris and found retrieved pieces of the material that had inscribed on it symbols that represented the active principle by which we wanted the new civilization to be characterized. It wasn't just that we found a couple of bricks and wanted to add significance to them. That would be a falsification of history, a distortion, something that we are still trying to correct because of the amount of forgery and lies that have been presented by others. So why would we be part of such nonsense?

The intentions of our ancestors were not to mislead anyone by making it appear as if they were merely playing around and that nothing they did was of any historical significance or value to their descendants. They were doing something that we need to look at as formula and as keys for how we can revitalize our own community from the spirit. It was the relevance of the principle that one wanted to teach that determined which brick one would take to seed the new building. If we don't know what the principles are, any brick will do. If we don't know what the principles are, anybody's educational system will serve us. We have to know what the principles are so we can logically and intelligently select the proper tools, or brick, to build the new building because this will be the same brick used to build the new community.

That's why we need to look at the fact that it is not that Western education has not served us well. The fact of the matter is that Western education has done an excellent job of what it is designed to do. If we don't understand what our beingness is, then we don't have the criteria to say that this education is not doing good for us. The fact of the matter is that they know what they're doing. We are the ones who are confused, thinking that any brick will do. Any brick won't do. We have to begin to see what are the principles on the brick that we want to use to build our community. And when we look at ancient Kemet, we see why it's so valuable. We see the names of the Neters…And you all know that the Neters were the attributes or the qualities of God, the natures of God. The names of the Neters: Asar, Osiris, Amun, Ptah, Amunyah, were all modified in order to specify a particular character of the active function signifying the epic into which we wanted to enter. So at one point in Memphis the names of the Neters had to do with Ptah, and Octah, and Octave, and the creative principle was unification. And so the new epic was going to be driven by unification, and we developed a brick that could make it happen.

In Heliopolis the creative principle was self-generation. We begin to talk about acknowledgement and service to Nun, and to Atum, and to Geb, and to Nut, because they were the Neters that represented the active principle that characterized the character that we wanted to have. In Hermopholis, on the other hand, the creative principle was expressed that the nature of nature was unity of balance. There is a balance of the male principle and the female principle that characterizes reality. Reach it and we begin to talk about the four couples and the Octad and then become, just Atum. But the four couples male, female principles that came together emerged to become man and woman. So that you can see that these notions of philosophy are tied to the epic and the kind of the social society we want to have.

Ultimately, in Thebes the creative principle was one of being and becoming. In being and in becoming we are everything. That became the epic that we wanted to characterize the character of the time. It is that invisible, visible expression, essence, notion that we need to look at and see that from the beginning of time in North Africa, ancient Africa, Memphis, Hermopolis, Heliopolis, Thebes, they all talked about being in terms of the expression "being Ptah," "being Tehuti," "being Ra," "being Amun," the essence being the voice of God, the life of God, the thought of God, the power of God. The essence is always characterized by some expression of our psyche. There's the psyche that was the fundamental notion of our Africanness. When looking at the southern countries of Africa, in the Bantu civilization one can see expression as Muntu, the being and the essence was Kunto. When you analyze those with the Bantu philosophy, it is clear that it is talking about the visible and the invisible. When we go to central Africa, we see the Dogon civilization. We see that being is a term called "Gozo"; the body and the essence is Nyame—the vital force. We go to the Akan civilization in West Africa and we see that the being is Kra, and the modality is Honhom, the divine breath.

When it comes to those "strange" African people called the B.U.S.A. people, Blacks in the United States of America, what you see is that they conceptualize their place as the hood. In that, their expression is called character, in that their essence is called soul. We have some distinct parallels from the beginning of time with Ancient Egypt, all the way up to today in Harlem. We, as African people, have a lot of similarities because we conceptualize the world the same way. The problem is that we haven't had the dialogue with the intelligentsia because our intelligentsia has been too busy trying to get the white folks' light to shine upon them as the most important Black Studies professor at Harvard University, so much so, that we have not made the time to think about these issues.

We see the parallel between experience (place), expression, and essence from the beginning of time because these three factors are found in our communities. What is ironic is that even though we might at times disrespect ourselves, we still have these factors within some part of the community, as African people or as members in the African family. We use words that seem less important and talk about Hantu, and Muntu, and Huntu. When you talk about Heliopolis and Ra and the thought of God, sounds good, but it is no different, they're just words. When you talk about the hood, Black folk (B.U.S.A.) have an understanding and an appreciation and an attachment to what it means. That's the stuff that Diop was talking about in terms of the historical and the linguistic being measures of the psychic shift. When you can no longer feel good about the hood, then you've made the psychic shift. When you can no longer think that there is something called character in Black folk. In our neighborhood, we take people for their character not their list of degrees. They judge by what a person is doing because it is a reflection, or rather, an indicator of one's character. To say that Black folk don't have soul is what is meant by the psychic shift.

At one point there were great debates about whether others could have soul because we thought it belonged to us. This was true. When we got "a reformation of the mind," we started saying, "It makes sense. There is blue-eyed soul." That's a contradiction in terms. But we didn't do that because we reformed our minds. They reformed our minds, as a result we moved off of one of the critical elements that makes up our psychic foundation. Now we don't have a relationship to the community, our time and space that is the hood. We don't have a relationship to the fundamental qualities of our nature that has to do with character. And we don't have a relationship with the fundamental element which is the essence of our expression that has to do with soul. We need to begin to redefine ourselves from understanding these African notions in terms of the question of character.

In terms of African psychology, I argued and tried to point out that our psychic structure was very elaborate. It wasn't a miniscule trinity of things. It was very elaborate; we talked about the psychic nature of our beingness. It is not the historical moment; it is our beingness that makes us African. That is, only when we are true to our African beingness are we able to achieve things in the real world. The African and our conceptualization argue that our psychic nature or the spiritual constitution of Egyptian thought talked about seven divisions. Seven seems to always run around in our cosmological notion. The Ka represented the principle body of the first division of our psychic nature. It argued that the formal structure of everything is ultimately disintegrated and will return to its former form, if one seeds it right.

Essentially, we look at the Ka as Africanness. We don't know how to look at or utilize these concepts because we again have gone through this mental, mind reformation. So, when we talk about the Ka, and the Ba, and the Khaba, and all those aspects of the soul, or the spirit, we don't really know what to do with them. We think we are merely having a good dream or a nightmare. We can't even differentiate between a dream and a nightmare anymore. But, the Ba talks about the soul of breath. That is why in a lot of the Kemetic mythology, we'll talk about life coming forth by spitting. In the Yoruba tradition spitting is a divine epistemological statement; it is not a vulgar act. The shaman and the priest will begin the ritual by spitting. We need to look at that because the spitting may be an icon or a symbol of this soul or breath.

So, now that we have a little information, it is possible to talk about the access to the Ba, the second division of our psychic nature. When we make visible that invisible source of our electricity, our power, it comes through the word. We have to begin to look at these things in a different way to try to build on them as a way of saving our psychic nature. With this it is also important to point out the Khaba, the third division of the psychic nature. The Ancients of Kemet talk about the fact that there is a luminous intangible covering over the vital principles of our life. There's an illumination; it shines.

Let us look at this idea of illumination as seen in the African-American church. What happens when the minister starts going really well in church. He starts talking to the choir and asks them to sing his favorite song. The energy continues to rise as the minister calls for the Lord to "come into the house." And when he personally invites the Lord in the house, he begins to shine; go to church Sunday and it can be seen. We think he's just hot and sweating, but it is more than that. We think he's just been doing this "jamming" sermon and he starts sweating, but it is the luminous covering of the intangible that is given expression there. The effects of that luminous energy cannot be stopped. It begins to radiate out towards the other members of that congregation. Simply put, when the Lord comes into the house and the church is really jamming, the whole congregation starts shining. Everybody's polished and glowing because the illumination of the vital principle is made manifest.

This can even be seen in instances outside of the church. The first day that we send our children to school is an example of the glow or illumination. And we're traditional. We made sure that our children were clean, neat, and ready to go, but it was not complete until we would polish them. We would literally take Vaseline and polish their faces. And those who weren't as fortunate would dip into the lard can to secure their children's shine. Even though we didn't have the intelligence or the intellect to analyze what we had done, we understood that the luminous spirit was a way of stimulating the essence of the vital principle. We sent our children out glowing, believing that there was nothing they could not master. Why is it that Black people get upset when they hear, "You are ashy!" If anything, we all know that the reason why we get ashy is because we have just bathed and the water has taken the oil out of our skin. So, it is safe to say that ashiness is a sign of cleanliness. This clearly shows that it is not because we were anti-clean. It was because we understood on our psychic level that the Khaba could only function as the luminous intangible covering of the vital principle if we glowed; and we do glow.

We can begin to see these consistent patterns over and over again if we begin to start looking at ourselves as Africanized and not other "folks-ized." If it is consistent, it is not accidental. It is not that every now and then some Black person decides to grease themselves and everybody starts saying, "I'll do that too." No, it doesn't happen. You can talk to African people throughout the Diaspora who have never seen each other. In Brazil, Jamaica, Trinidad, Alabama, Mississippi, and Harlem, you can hear people talking about how their mothers and fathers had similar rituals and practices, and they do it with no cross-cultural education. It has to do with the vital principle that operates the psychic nature of our people.

The fourth division of the psychic nature that our ancestors argued for is the Akhu. The ancients argued that the whole mystery of the human mind was stimulated by stimulating the Akhu. Sometimes, I think that if we could ever understand our complexities and why we do what we do, we could find that maybe it is by trying to stimulate that division of the psychic nature that holds the whole mystery. According to this theology, of comprehending the human mind, we'll be able to have the foundation for creating solutions to the new. It's not just about knowing what we do, it's about meeting the moment, the new, that we've never experienced. Doing what is right at the right time is stimulating the Akhu.

Some people argue, as Richard King and I have discussed, that there is a possibility that the pineal may be a psychical realm of this kind of capacity. And it is not accidental that when Black folk get confused or have a difficult problem we scratch our heads. In doing this we may be stimulating the pineal and thusly artificially or psychically stimulating the Akhu. In fact, other folk, especially whites, would take that physical behavior and characterize it and make it a sign of ignorance. Instead of seeing our stimulating the collective realm of mysteries of the entire human mind, they say our action reflects a sign of dumb behavior. We even go so far as to buy books that white people have written and read them seeking to find solutions to our problems. It does not make sense.

We fail to realize that our tradition had inscribed in it a certain kind of mental perception, a certain kind of intelligence. Intelligence wasn't based on a particular score on an I.Q. test. It was traditional African intelligence and in terms of our consciousness, it was to have the attributes of will and intent. That is an operational definition of intelligence. Anytime one engages in behavior that is consciously designed and intended for one's will to be done, you are intelligent. In other words, an act of intention that places a person at the end result is an act of intelligence. What is ironic is that people do not speak of this as intelligence. Many talk about the fact that we have a structure, not understanding that it allows us to see the world and our resolute position in that world.

The fifth dimension of the psychic nature is defined and named by the ancients as the Seb. The evidence of the presence of the Seb was the power of the human being to generate its own kind. Every time we allow our children to be educated and they end up believing that evidence of their education is that they have walked like, talked like, looked like, felt like other people, we have violated the Seb principle. We have violated a fundamental aspect of our psychic nature. In argumentation, we as a community should rightfully begin to say to those powers, including ourselves, who are responsible for the education of our children that the only acceptable definition of education is that which is a process that allows a people to reproduce and refine the best of itself. If one cannot demonstrate that their curricula, content, intent, process, teachers' training strategies, and learning material are all designed to reproduce and refine the best of African people, they should not be given to African children.

It is best to get back to the issue refining our psychic nature. We can do nothing in time or space if we are unaligned with our center. Surely we have talked about this notion of being off our center and Afro-centered but we have never gone so far as to define and give substance to it. What Afrocentric means is that one is obedient to one's psychic nature. It is not just about continually expressing the good and great achievements of Black people. That is the historical issue of which Diop spoke. It's not just dealing with and analyzing our linguistic unities. That also was discussed by Diop. It is that as African people we are obedient or centered in our beingness, centered in our psychic nature.

As defined by the ancients, the Putah is the sixth division of the psychic nature. This division shows how the Putah represents the first intellectual father, which simply suggests that Putah is associated with mental maturity of the individual. The story of conception said that we did not start with all seven divisions at birth but rather acquired them through development. And as evidence of one's maturity, one has evidence of the Putah. The Putah establishes the fact that the person from the moment of its manifestation or attainment is believed to be governed by will and intent. The expression of both will and intent is a demonstration of maturity. That is why mothers and fathers tell children that it is better to be seen and not heard because children are still developing their will and intent in the presence of adults.

The dynamics of child and adult relations are not like adult peer relations. There are definite unspoken boundaries that are not to be crossed in these types of relationships, and knowing when and when not to speak sets up one of those boundaries. Adults do not usually talk to children about what they want to do. There is no conversation that takes place that guarantees that the child is going to have his or her way or say. It is the responsibility of adulthood to direct the development of youth by recognizing that the eldership is the intellectual parent of youth. If intellect is will and intent, then eldership is the intellectual parent of youth because it is our responsibility through our intention for our will to be done in the behavior of the children. Now in some sense our community is a community of children because we have become unaligned, off center, off our psychic foundation. So, we end up thinking that individuality is evidence of our maturity, but in actuality it is the realization of my position in the presence of eldership, regardless of my age, that is evidence of my maturity. It is also evidence of the fact that with all the possessions and professions that I have, when I sit in front of my Uncle Charlie, who has a third grade education, and worked for the railroad, and is now an alcoholic, when he speaks, I listen, because the question of eldership and maturity is realizing where I must position myself in relation to him.

And finally there is the seventh division of the soul, the Atmu. It is the soul that enwraps each of us and it is not violated by time or by space. The Atmu is the eternal soul. It is what I call the ontological principle of consubstantiation. It is that we are of the same spirit, of the same essence. Because that soul or spirit existed before there was time, it will be there after time as well. That is the stuff that empowers us, and we need to begin to look at that in terms of what makes us act the way we act. It isn't just that Black folk have this unique style, and we are sort of exotic and cute and we can all laugh about how we do what we do. It isn't that at all. It is that we do what we do because we are driven by the psychic nature. The psychic nature empowers us more and that is the liberation of the consciousness when we begin to see this kaleidoscope, to see this sort of gumbo mix, and to engage knowingly in its reinforcement and its nurturance.

It is this Afrocentric movement that is possible as we look at the epics of the recurrence of seeding from Thebes to Heliopolis to Hermopolis to Memphis. We see that seeding each generation. I think that we are now in a moment where we are in contemporary times witnessing the reseeding of the African psyche. It is the reseeding of the African psyche because we spent generations rumbling through ruins of Black history and accomplishments. Our scholars and all the old scholars were scrapping through and struggling with information, trying to demonstrate African presence in The Bible, and trying to demonstrate an African presence throughout history, and trying to demonstrate the relationship of Egypt to Greece and Rome. All those old scholars, by whom we are nurtured, are the bricks that we are now taking and putting into the point and conceptualizing as an Afrocentric notion. We are all tied to those three areas where it was important for us to make sure we didn't allow the reformation of the African mind in the areas of religion, education, and, especially, in psychology. So, it is not accidental that African centered materials and ideas reemerge around the question of curriculum. Keeping in mind that we do not separate anything, thinking that education equals curricula. It must be clear that education does not equal curricula, even though there have been many great debates which have led many into traps. There were complaints from Whites about having a more African focused curriculum. The debate is not whether or not there should be African historical reference points infused into the curriculum. What we are talking about is an educational process that creates the character that built the pyramids. That's what we're talking about, and one cannot do that without ever mentioning the fact that Black people built the pyramids. So, we have to begin to strategize about what battles we want to fight in public and what battles we want to understand as a part of our family's private business. If we don't take a stand and pick our battles, we end up letting them define the agenda and our pointless fighting could also lead us to believe that we do not need an Afrocentric curricula.

It is important that we focus on an African centered educational process that creates character. One that creates the character that allows us from the beginning of time to face the world and reality, a process to make sure that our images and our interests will be present long after we are gone. That's why we need to begin to look at that. Character is not just some word that needs to be overused and exploited. We as Black people know that whenever a word is heard, someone will pick it up as theirs and use it as a new weapon.

Character is something very precise; yet, we struggle with the preliminary definition of the word. I argue that character is the preliminary mark of a people, which signifies their distinctive qualities. All that is still very general because we don't know what distinction means and we don't know what quality means. One's character is the complexity of mental and spiritual traits which mark a people and is a detectable expression as evidence of their ability to transmit their own hereditary information. If we're not passing to the next generation of African children the essence of what it is to be African, we have no character. The fundamental evidence of our having character is that we pass, in very precise ways, what it means to be normal.

The idea of passing traits and practices to the next generation should not stop with character. We need to pass what it means to be healthy. We need to pass on what it means to be an African man. What are the differences between African manhood and African womanhood? We can't allow all the debate that has surrounded us about sex relations such as sexual harassment to prevent us from finding out who we are as man and woman. What exactly is sexual harassment in the work place? We can't marry someone else's definition of that for people who believe that their sexuality is an indicator of their abnormality. It appears that any time one brings attention to another's sex that is considered sexual harassment. For people who celebrate in their sexuality, the fact that I say, "Girl, you sure do look good" is a compliment. The moment we take on someone else's definition of the male essence or the female essence, we get all confused. And we begin to do the same destructive and vulgar things that we learn from our teachers.

We must begin to understand that such issues are fundamental to our survival. It is about our fundamental existence in the world. If we don't clarify this, we will be as Diop says, "a population and not a people." That is too much to lose. Jacob Carruthers provides a service by casting and arguing that the Afrocentricism is not just an education question, not just a curriculum question, but Afrocentricism, the African centered issue, is a movement. It is a movement that just as Ramses II tries to reclaim his position in the world and defines the social society in which he lived based upon the truths of the ancient time that were endurable and enviable. That is what we are seeking. We're going after the endurable, nothing related to the transitional and destructible. It is not about wearing Kente and garb and African clothes or African shields. It is about reaching and seeding our future with the bricks of the past that have the right signs on them, those that represent the principles and the character we want to carry forward in the future.

Carruthers argues that the three attributes or objectives of the African centered movement are that it ascribes to a belief that there are distinctive universal worldviews. It does not matter where or of whom, if one peels the veil of individuality in the distinctiveness, what will be seen behind African people is a common singular worldview that marries each of us to each other. Regardless of our country of residence, there is a distinctive universal worldview. He further argues, and I agree, that that distinctive universal worldview must be the foundation for all African spiritual, psychological, intellectual, social, political, economic and artistic development.

This notion simply suggests that we perform with our intentions, African centered, or more specifically, centered on the distinctive African worldview. Even if painting graffiti on the wall, and one is African, one must do that from a foundation that is consistent and obedient with an African worldview. If driving a bus on the streets of Harlem, one must do that from a consistent and obedient perspective with an African worldview. If one is a Black psychologist, take no action unless the prescription, or the analysis is built on a foundation based upon a distinctive African worldview. Everything we do must prescribe to that. Now, understand that we are not suggesting that we all should be automated robots that have no ability to be individuals. The notion of a distinctive African worldview says that that's a foundation upon which we should build the creative moment. And just as the roots of a tree are the foundation, the branches have the license and the luxury of going in whatever direction they wish and they are viable as long as they are connected to the roots. The moment the branch is disconnected it dies. It is the same way for us.

So, you can be an individual branch; but your vitality and viability are tied to your being grounded in that universal African worldview, or the roots, that is, according to Africanness, what is being called the person, as opposed to being the individual. In one's personality there is the license to express oneself. But in individuality, one is on the course of becoming insane. This is done because there has been a separation from everyone else.

The second principle that Carruthers argued is that the African centered movement advocates for the restoration of the historical truths of African reality. Obviously I argue that it should advocate for the restoration of the African character, which is the precondition for the achievement of those historical truths. We can't just talk about restoring our historical truths and putting all of our events on the wall. That is not enough. We have to create the character that caused those events to come forward. So the African centered movement must advocate for the restoring of the African character and its related historical truths as the priority in the guiding force for African scholarship and practice. Now, as scholars we have the power to do many deeds, but the priority and the grounding, or the guiding force for that work must be the restoration of the African character and its historical truths. So, you can do whatever you want to do but your priority must be in restoring the African character.

The third and final principle for an African centered movement is that it must acknowledge that there is a precondition for the liberation of the African mind and thereby African liberation and mentality. We argued that colonialism reformed the African mind and that this reformation is one of our problems. But the precondition for the freedom of the African mind, thereby the liberation of African mentality, is the development of a massive African centered education and reeducation throughout the world. Not just in Harlem, not just in Philadelphia, not just in Oakland. We seriously need to begin the process of developing projects and developing strategies, so that we can engage in massive reeducation and education from an African centered foundation. Now that's a major undertaking and we have begun the process. The only problem is we sometimes think haphazardly, thinking anything is acceptable and taking it without more thought.

If we are going to take this seriously, we need to do some behind-closed-doors family talk about how to strategically take over the educational, the psychological, and the spiritual development of African people. That is our goal. And we who are out there on the "frontline" must continue to support, respect and use each other's thinking in our work. We have to be very careful as we begin to move further and further into places where no man has gone before. We must be like the spaceship Enterprise. When we get to those places never gone to before, we need to be careful because everyone wants to be the captain. Our communities raise and nurture us not to be idolized but to maintain our historical moments. We must show everyone at every level the importance of historical moments and the African centered worldview.

In higher levels of education, namely graduate school, naturally the topics of discussion become more complex and diversified. There begins to be talk of ways to manage the psychic nature, not just how to record and recite the events of African people. And so, depending upon whether in kindergarten or whether in graduate school, one's lesson should serve well. You see we have to begin to work through those things and recognize from the beginning of recorded history in dynastic Kemet from the First Dynasties through the Seventeenth Dynasty, through the Eighteenth Dynasty, through the conquest of the Iberian peninsula, through the creation and development, and even in the resurgence of the great kings of Ghana, Mali, the Congo; to the point in history of establishing the Tuskeegee Institute, Hampton, Howard, Morehouse, Florida A & M, Spelman, Clark College; to the point of three or more folk in Harlem deciding to have a First World speaker's series, we have consistently explored the question of liberating African consciousness. What we must understand is what made these historical moments happen was that the epic experience of the time was characterized by the African character and consciousness. This quest will continue until the African community realizes and reveals its character and once it reveals its character then we will begin to be liberated.

The African character is the complex of mental and ethical traits that mark a people. It is the mental and ethical traits that are centered in, what I think is, the sort of philosophical and epistemological substance that talks about the two realms of being. We get confused and think the two realms are what Europeans talk about regarding linear polarity and opposite points. In fact, it is not such, but rather the two realms of being are a spiritual realm and a material realm. The Europeans define the material realm as superior and inferior, man and woman, old and young. They took one aspect of reality and polarized it. From this we develop theories and conceptions of how to understand Black behavior based upon their materialistic linear polarities of superior and inferior positions.

The negative aspects of such polarized thinking are picked up by Black people and we begin to think in the same distorted ways. We think that lighter skin is better. We will go to the extreme in hopes of attaining what is desired, and, in doing so, we do not realize that it is all in vain. We will never be satisfied because we think ourselves a modification of white people. The only way to break out of the foolishness of color consciousness in the African community is to reclaim and rescue our two realms of reality. We must also recognize that the spiritual realm, the subjective realm, and the formless matter in times of space that Africans called the chaos, that the ancients talked about was the foundation that emerged out of the material realm.

Our being emerges out of the spirit. Our matter emerges out of the spirit. What is real is the spirit. I'm talking about physics. I'm talking about the laws of nature, the laws of the universe that determine how things operate in relationship to each other. So, ringing those bells and burning candles will not make you spiritual. Understanding that the divine law that says Jupiter will never run into, never be in opposition with the Earth is the law that one needs to understand. There is a divine law in the universe that says things operate in harmony and balance. And it also says that the sun and the moon are related to each other and that their relationship is not based on the sun's dominance or the moon's oppression. Similarly, the relationship between man and woman is spiritual, not of dominance and oppression, but one of harmony and balance.

The liberation of African consciousness is re-ascribing to the rules that govern the universe that our ancestors laid. The same rules that we find in ancient Kemet, we find in the Yoruba tradition. The notion of the world of the living and the other world. In Kemet we find the world and the Neter world. There are these two realms of being as a model of what we need to look at and discuss. We need to talk about what chaos meant in the African tradition. We need to understand what the metaphors of our position really spoke to, particularly the Osiris drama, which has been so distorted and so misunderstood that we have to reclaim it and talk about the fact that the battle between Osiris and his brother Seth was not a battle of good and evil. It was a battle of harmony and disharmony and that the struggle in all of us is that harmony ascends in our presence, as when Seth kills and dismembers his brother and scatters his body throughout the world in all these symbolically relevant numbers. It was the sisterhood who came together and recollected up the dismembered parts of the body and put them together in an ordered and specific manner.

This is divine law in action. We need to understand divine law in terms of practices of men and women in places where we find ourselves. Auset (Isis), and her sisters reconstituted Osiris' body by first putting the skeleton in order, purifying the flesh, then reuniting the separate members of the body, reviving the corpse, then finally recalling his soul. Let me go back through those steps because they are very informative. Putting the skeleton together should be seen as the task of giving a community structure. Purifying the flesh is the task of reviving the essence, the psychic nature of the community. A community that does not know its own essence is a population. It is not a community. It is not a people. Reuniting the separate members of the body is explicating what was and is the proper function. When there is a reunion of the members of the body, we know what a particular part like the hand can do. But, when there are no tendons the hand does not reveal its function. So, we have to understand that reuniting the separate members of the body was the symbolic icon, for it is our responsibility to explicate the proper function for men and women in a community.

As the process continues, there is more information that is crucial for building our African communities. It is with a kiss that one of the women revives Osiris' corpse while he was lying on his back. It is in the kiss that some religious thinking talks about as artificial insemination. It is in the kiss that a woman determines and instills in the body the life force, determining its destiny. As Marcus Garvey argued years ago, we must understand that we have one mind, one God, and one destiny. It is in understanding destiny that we have the kiss, or we have, as I talked about earlier, the spit, the power of psychic nature.

And then, finally, let us discuss the recalling of the soul. Recalling the soul is a metaphor for the task of identifying the history and purpose of a people. History and purpose go hand in hand. There is no sense in studying history if the analysis of such is not used to identify one's future purpose in life. It is in this metaphor of the Osiris drama that we realize that the struggle between Osiris and Seth was a struggle between chaos and order. Chaos was not confusion. That is why it is so important to really work with the Kemetic teaching. Chaos was a manifestation of the spirit which is evidenced by the harmonious relationship between individual components in the universe. And so the struggle is not between good and evil, between God and the devil. The struggle is between each of us to bring out of us that which contributes to the harmony of our community. That is the Osiris; that is the domestic metaphor.

And in that domestic metaphor, if I can go back and finish on this point, what is seen is that some rules or some lessons can be used as strategies for liberating the African consciousness. One rule, or one formula, is that the centrality of the feminine principle is that there is a relationship to the harmonious development of community. This can be said because of the metaphor of the Neters reconstituting of the brother.

The second rule or formula is the complementarity between the male and the female principle. The African consciousness will never exist until we have a complementary relationship, a balance, a unity between the masculine and the feminine principle.

The third key is that the masculine principle represents causality and not domination. There is a difference. I always point out that among African folk, that children, kindergarten age children, if you will, are taught that the man is the head of the house. Don't go over to New York and start talking about women's liberation; women are equal to men. The man is the head of the house and that is what we need to understand. And the woman is the neck that turns the head. There is a balanced relationship.

Many argue over the significance of being considered a neck as opposed to the head. Some would say, "A neck is not important, it is the head." What the African is saying is that our direction, our ability to go anywhere is based upon the complementarity between the head and the neck. One cannot be normal, natural, and alive as a head without a neck. One cannot be normal, natural, and alive with a neck and no head. Simply stated, our humanity is tied in the complementarity between the male principle and the female principle.

Some theologians and some philosophers talk about paralleling a masculine principle and a feminine principle with the idea that the feminine principle is the form and the masculine principle is the force. We think form is just a shell and force is what is most desired. But, don't get confused with that. That is not what our ancestors were talking about. They were showing that for every force there is a form that gives a force its form and its reality. The form that gives us evidence and power in reality is the feminine principle which is more than just a protector of the force or masculine principle.

And it makes sense. There is no one who can deny that they came forth through a female. This principle gives us the expression to the force, which comes forth in biological terms of a girl or a boy. This shows that there is a link between the divine law and the natural order.

It is character, I would argue, that we must reconsider as a rule for the liberation of our consciousness. It is this same character that began back in 6000 B.C. when it was said, "I'm going to reunite Southern and Northern Kemet and make it one unified force that will live forever in the mouths and minds of people." That was character, not a political conquest. It was character that caused Martin Luther King to dig deep in his psychic nature to pull out the metaphor that says, "Judge my people by the content of their character and not the color of their skin." King did not know what he was digging into when he spoke those words. He did not know where he was going, he thought he was being poetic. In actuality, he was digging into ancient knowledge. It was Blyden who argued for the importance of character when he stated:

> If the African educated on European lines is unable or unwilling to teach the outside world something of the institutions and the (the psychic nature) inner feelings of his own people; If for some reason or other he can show nothing of his real self to those anxious to learn and to assist him; if he cannot make his friends feel the force of his racial character and sympathize with his racial aspirations then it is evident that his education has been defective. That his training by aliens has done little for him.

It makes us wonder how much one's training by aliens helped. The question becomes one of character. We have to begin to look at this question of character and ask ourselves to redefine religion, economics, governance, and education. If we are able to take responsibility for the implementation of religion, economics, governance, and education, in our community, through our character then we will solve this dilemma. If we don't, our religion, our economics, our governance, and our education, will be alien to us, and we can answer the question that Blyden asks: It has not served us well.

It is in the quest for character and consciousness that the African community must find and filter our great achievements. We built the pyramids as an expression of character and consciousness. We built historical Black colleges as a response to our character and consciousness. We even manipulated and shuffled and fooled white folk into thinking that we were Uncle Tom's when we perceived that our very lives were on the line as a strategy of character and consciousness.

The question of character and consciousness says that we give license and legitimacy to every Black person to be Black. That's our job. It is not to challenge. It is not to degrade them. It is to prune them now and then when their weeds get real crazy. We have to prune them every now and then but we can never say you are no longer part of the African family. The African family says that our character is based upon the psychic factor, the psychic nature, and that psychic nature is inalienable. It is irrefutable and it began before there was a concept such as time. And it will be there after the existence of time.

In regard to the African character, the God, Amun, says, "Fear, knowledge is in our heart." Shu, the word, the spit is on our lips. Our Ka is everything that exists. Our spirit is everything that exists by virtue of our tongue. The spitting metaphor again, by virtue of our tongue, our Ba is soul, it is Shu. Our soul is the air. Our heart is Tefnut. Our heart is the fire. We are the Horus of the double horizon who is in the sky. Our right eye is the day. Our left eye is the night. We are everyone's guide in all directions. Think about that. Everybody imitates Black people. We are everyone's guide in all directions. Our body is Nun. We give birth to everything that is and cause all in existence to exist. And the Book of Knowing, the modes of existence of Ra, the overthrowing of the serpent Ipothy, thus spoke the Lord of all, "Keperi, Keper, Keperu, Kepper Ku, in Keperu, the becoming became. I have become in becoming."

In conclusion, it is with the symbolism of the ancient Kemetic heart and tongue that I say to you that I have spoken with you with my heart and through my tongue. It is my prayer that Ptah is satisfied.

[1989]

African Consciousness and Unlocking the African Soul

(A Lecture)

"On the Origins of Things."

Look around you Black Child
Your creation is everywhere
Though tainted, distorted
Given meanings
They bare your priest, just the same
So sharpen your eyes, tune your ear
So you know what you see
Understand what you hear
You are the first to write
The first to read
Humanity sprang from your Black seed
So one hundred and ten thousand years
You were here alone
And though the Caucasian man is born
Behind the ice inside the cold
A chill set in this new man's soul
Other minds have been credited with the things they learned from you
Newton, Pythagoreus, Kepler, and Galileo, too
Sharpen your eyes, tune your ear
So you know what you see
Understand what you hear
You made the serpent the symbol of the healing arts
And African trust us was God is Maat
She weighed herself against the African soul
Truth and justice blind fold
The George Washington monument is yours, too
A copy of the African technu
The symbol of the Black man's power of creation
The Black man's penis and divine procreation
The king of southern Egypt wore the White crown
Keep listening and you will catch your mouth
When you learn that the central government in Egypt

Was known as the "White House"
Sharpen your eyes, tune your ear
So you will know what you see, understand what you hear
Your God Osiris was restored to life
Long before Buddha, long before Christ
And today what you call the Madonna and child
Is but the first Black family worshipped along the Nile
And when you feel the spirit the Holy Ghost
You should know it started at Abydos
Where God, Osiris' body was laid
The holy land where Africans prayed
Minute by minute, hour by hour
As you lose your history
You lose your power
So sharpen your eyes, tune your ear
So you know what you see
Understand what you hear

—Lestervelt Middleton

My task is to talk about African consciousness and the unlocking of the African soul. I want to talk about two things. The key issues are consciousness and soul. Oftentimes we really have a difficult time understanding these issues because people who trained us really were not trained well and they left a legacy of definitions about these two critical concepts, consciousness and soul, that have confused us. They relegated the soul to somewhere in the after life and somewhere in the spirit world. And we relegated the consciousness to something that is hidden, that is deep and dark and unknowable that required some psychologist or psychotherapist to help us struggle through to understand what that consciousness was and is all about.

I want to say promptly that that is foolishness and that we should put those beliefs aside because consciousness and soul had nothing to do with what the ancestors of Sigmund Freud ultimately wrote them up to be. We are confused because we run after Freud and Jung and Adler and all these great White fathers of psychology and think that we are intelligent and intellectual because we either know their theories or, even better, we have gone through psychotherapy and somehow or another through this process we have gained firsthand knowledge.

We have Black psychologists who are taking pride in the fact that they are trained as psychotherapists, and unfortunately they do not like for me to mention the fact that they are really confused. The best advice is to stay away from them. Until we develop an African theory and an African therapy, our utilization and participation with European theory and therapy will continue to aid in turning African people away from being African. Ironically, it is in the not being African that we call being well.

Here is a model of consciousness that I have been working with in trying to develop an understanding that says there are dimensions in consciousness as we try to understand why we do what we do and how we do what we do. Ultimately as psychologists we have to explain the why's of human functioning. In order to explain the why of human functioning we have to have some model or guidelines that help us see the importance of critical thesis.

A part of the explanation is found and inscribed in Ancient Kemet. It is important that African psychologists are now looking at and struggling with interpretations of the sacred keys that were lain down by our ancestors. In seeking models of consciousness I think that what is important is that we should recognize that our teachings, the teachings of African people, were really very simple. It was in the simplicity of everything that we were able to understand the fundamental yet highly complicated and complex aspects of human functioning. It is the simplification on which we should focus. Ultimately, consciousness means to be with awareness. In this case, an awareness which will lead us to a particular understanding of the subject.

In the ancient ways there was always the notion of being with, or being in, or being of, a thing. Consciousness simply means to be with awareness, to see awareness as part of one structure, one fundamental beingness. In taking that notion into mind, we began to look at (by we, I mean some folk who are thinking along with me as African psychologists) the dimensions of awareness that are important for our understanding. One of the most important dimensions is found in understanding the "why" of human behavior.

I have suggested that there are several dimensions in the model of which we are playing. Sometimes I have to caution myself because, when you say that I'm "playing" with this model, people think that there is no serious involvement in the work being done. But, the fact of the matter is that if you think about it as a metaphor, playing is really what is done before the task has been completely sufficiently. Right now, in terms of African psychology, we are somewhat playing because we do not really know yet. But, when we get it right we can work 'em. So, as I've said, I'm playing with a model of consciousness that consists of levels of consciousness whose dimensions or aspects are important in order to see how they influence the "why" of human functioning.

There are five dimensions of consciousness that aid in this understanding of human functioning. They are mythic, historical, popular, personal, and self. Mythic consciousness is simply the recognition that the ancient, archaic mythology of a people is critical to understanding their sense of awareness. There are icons and archetypes in the original mythology of a people that are essential and that influence our formulation of our sense of awareness and understanding of the world. This is understood clearly, when one examines the ideas and information that the Western world has embraced, especially when relating to the issues of good and evil, man and woman, black and white.

When, in fact, one further examines Western mythology, one sees that the mythology of the Judeo-Christian ethic, and the mythology of the Greco-Roman culture are really translated into notions of good and evil, right and wrong, etc, that become the basis of the drama of programs like "Dallas," and "Dynasty," "Days of our Lives," and "Happy Days." In fact, all the information and entertainment that one received in this society are really just dramatizations and representations of the principles that were locked in ancient Western mythology.

African people must, therefore, in order to get a clear understanding of the "why" of our behavior, understand the principles that are locked into our mythology. By studying ancient Kemetic-Nubian mythology, one begins to unlock principles that are dramatized by the story of mythic consciousness. There is an aspect of African awareness that comes about or is influenced by the retention or the residuals of ancient archaic African mythology. It is in us, and I would suggest that at some point we will find out that it may be encoded in the psycho-physiological domain in the arena that we are now playing around with called melanin. We simply have not unlocked that key yet. Once that is done, African psychologists will discover that our culture and philosophy are inscribed in our psycho-physical nature. It is here where caution is recommended because sometimes we as Africans get confused and say, "Oh! It's a physical thing." Therefore, it means that if I'm darker than someone else, it is erroneous to interpret that I have more of the key than another person and in doing so I fail to look at the pigmentation piece as a light/energy phenomenon. Melanin is a real big heavy issue that is fixed in the place where the physical and spiritual realms become one and because of this in-between state, it becomes hard to differentiate the physical being and the spiritual being. But, we don't even have knowledge of claiming that as of yet.

The second important dimension of consciousness, particularly because it influences our central awareness, is what we call historical consciousness. Historical consciousness pertains to the fact that there are events in time that are so significant and so critical that they influence how our people see themselves in their position in the world. All historians like to tell us that slavery was one of those influential events for Black folk. It is true that slavery was influential because it shaped us and on that same note, that is why we are the way we are and that is why our communities are the way they are because slavery took out of us any sense of integrity, any sense of our being. Consequently, because of this significant event we are a destroyed people.

What they failed to look at in that analogy is that there are significant events that far preceded our minor period of time of being captive in this country. There are major significant events that were experiences of African people that were encoded in our historical consciousness. We simply do not have the ability or understanding of how to stimulate that historical memory so that it brings that consciousness to the forefront so that we are able to utilize it, to not only explain the "why" of behavior but, also to predict what behaviors are appropriate in what contexts.

Consequently, the building of the great civilizations of Ancient Kemet and all of those civilizations of African culture are inscribed in our historical consciousness. We simply have to stimulate and reawaken that knowledge in terms of understanding and making use of it.

The third dimension of consciousness is popular consciousness which helps us to recognize in this space and time that, wherever one finds oneself, there are events that influence how the world is perceived. So, this is stuff that is in the past and in the great past. The events and experiences that happen to me today are the ideas that people perpetuate about me today that, in turn, become popular notions of African people. We all know all those things that are thought to be true about Black folk. Some people actually believe that Black folk have long fangs and are oversexed and that Black women are hot and are unnaturally procreative. Others believe if you just look at Black women, they will get pregnant. Among the stereotypes about Black people, it is believed that we cannot think in intellectual and abstract forms. We are thought to be real physical people who are only capable of using our hands and not our minds. As we began to internalize the ideas embedded in the popular consciousness of the wider society, these ideas began to influence how we see ourselves now.

So, young Black children, young African children growing up are bombarded with images about what African manhood is and they interpret the popular consciousness of the time. So, it's important to see how these dynamics influence our understanding of the why. The popular ideas that television portrays and the popular ideas that the African community itself perpetuates about African men and women are unhealthy. Yet we simply tolerate them and do not take strong positions against them. There is a whole plethora of ideas that are going through the Black community as part of the popular consciousness. The notion that I am allowed to say, "Niggas ain't..." (one can figure out the rest) and that it is a popular idea that we perpetuate in our community. We internalize it as part of the why of what we do and, looking at these things is a part of a sense of being with awareness.

Every single idea that is in the community touches a Black person. If we are not really careful about ideas we allow to have life in our community, the popular consciousness can literally overshadow the mythic and historical consciousness and all the other dimensions that come into play to make us who we are.

Personal Consciousness is the fourth notion of consciousness and is connected to the idea of who we are. Personal consciousness, the fourth dimension, simply recognizes that we are one and we are guided by a principle of consubstantiation. Even though we as African people are one, there are personal occurrences that a particular Black man experiences in and of itself that other Black men may not experience. There are some personal circumstances and experiences. There are many things that we do separately and those become part of our sense of awareness.

Now to the extent that I am a representation, a symbolic representation of African manhood, the personal circumstances that I experience get laid on as that of African men. And so if I had the first experience of growing up in an integrated community, white folks would believe that I was different from those other Black people because I could talk and chew bubble gum at the same time, and they would keep putting in me that I was different from other Black people. Consequently, I would grow up thinking that I was something separate and special, i.e. better than other Black folk. Unfortunately, we are seeing too much of that in our communities. You grow up believing you are not representative of all African people, you stand out as a problem for African people because your personal experience was such that it did not re-enforce the oneness of African people. Instead it re-enforced that which made me special and distinct. For example, people were favored for having light colored eyes and, now, ten or twenty years later white or Korean entrepreneurs figured it out. It made sense, so they started making colored contact lens. And now Black folks run and buy contacts so they can have light eyes because that further differentiates them from other Black people.

One can see in that example where a personal experience gets played out as a collective experience and these beliefs of collective experiences are the problems from which all African people suffer. So we have to be extremely careful and conscious about understanding how my personal experiences are and should be considered individual, even though they are not looked at this way. I mean we have a responsibility to every single Black person, every single African we see in the streets. We can not contribute to the division. We have a responsibility of planting in that person a consciousness, with a readiness that re-enforces the collective Africanity. Because I'm African, I wear this or look this way or do like this. I cannot look down on those Africans who are lost and don't understand or believe that their salvation is buying into corporate America, or who believe that their salvation is moving into an integrated community. Because I reject him as an African man, I only push them further and further away from their own sense of Africanity. So, we have our own responsibility for taking care of the issue of personal consciousness. Each of us has a personal consciousness.

Finally, there is the dimension called self-consciousness or the self-conscious. This is when one is conscious of one's consciousness. It is at this point that I'm going to move to discuss the issue of soul. I'm thinking through these ideas and the next time I may have it better; or, I may have changed my thinking because as you learn more, if you are smart, you refine your work and correct your errors. And, if this is a mistake here, I'm going to correct it later. But, today here is my current thinking. Self-consciousness has to do with this thing called soul. We have defined soul the stuff that gives Black people rhythm, or that which makes us sort of cool, that which causes us to lean a certain way, and that's what soul is. All of that is true but I want you to understand it on a deeper rather than stylistic level. Style is the least important part of the soul.

Soul has to do with being aware of one's own awareness. Being aware of the rhythm and the energy that motivates our beingness. We have to begin to think in a different way. In order to understand, we have to delve into the difficulties that have to do with Kemetic symbolism. By doing that we are being trained to look at symbolism as the object or symbol that stands for something else which was not what the ancestors meant by symbolism at all. It is because we have been trained as scholars, but we have been trained fundamentally as Western scholars and thinking in a particular way. Now we are to bridge or try to understand a mentality that is authentically African, which cannot be understood utilizing a Western mentality. This is a confession. I only know that I have not been able to demonstrate this in my work, but you cannot fully comprehend the African mind as long as you think as a Westerner or as a White person. And all that we can do is say that. It is important that I stated that reality.

That kind of statement always gets applause, but the problem is that all we can do is say it. We have not been able to get beyond attempting to think as an African to spell this out in any detailed way. In trying to do this there is frustration. It is because we know there is something there that is greater than what we even think it to be, but we have not gotten into it yet. We have not jumped into it yet. We are just sort of wiggling with our toes saying, "Is the water cool?... What should we do with this stuff?"

There are two concepts of this notion of beingness I am working through now in psychology in ancient ways that I think are critical which have to do with those things called "being" and "becoming." In studying being and becoming it is necessary to understand the relationship between being and becoming. We should take each step separately. In the ancient Kemetic law the ancestors understood that being meant to be comprised of both a mortal element, which is visible, and an immortal element which is invisible. To see me here, that's the mortal part of my being. That was called the "Kha" or the Body.

On the other hand, the invisible or immortal element had three subsets or three different levels beyond that, three complexities if you will. The immortal element was comprised of the spirit, which was called the "Akh." The "Ba," the second dimension or level of the immortal state, is the soul. Third, the "Kah" is the psyche. The point that I really wanted to discuss in pointing out these levels of immortality is that Western psychology took the issue and talked about the "Kah" as the shadow and what Jung took and tried to develop as some archetype. The problem is that Western psychology had no idea what the stages of immortality were or their functions. They just did not know what they were doing. We were even more confused because we learned these ideas very well and have no idea that what we are learning is inaccurate in the first place.

Now the visible and the invisible elements become important to understand because the invisible is greater than the visible even though they are one in the same. That sounds like a contradiction but when we put Aristotle into the game, we start talking about logical consistencies, meaning that something can not be one in the same or equal and one be greater than the other at the same time. But in the African mind it is very clear that the invisible is far greater than the visible. Even though the two can be separate while at the same time coexist. My body, my physical being is a manifestation of my spirit even though my spirit is far greater than my body. I should not even call it my spirit because it is not mine, it is ours. It belongs to the whole African beingness.

Some folks say, "Now you use psychology and you're studying all that ol' ancient Egyptian stuff or all that witch stuff, and just fantasizing because all that stuff is not important because we know that the moon people came down and built the pyramids."

We have to begin to think about these issues in a different way. Kemetic symbolism becomes really important to understand. This attitude shows that people do not want to know the truth and that there are all kinds of theories for why we did what we did. Because it is so great when you think about it, it becomes sort of an interesting proposition. The things that we did in ancient times were so great that the folks that were nearest to us in time, the ancestors of the European community reached the ultimate conclusion that we must have been gods. They felt that we could not have been humans and did what we did. And so that ran through a whole long literature about the "god" man and the "god" people. They saw African people as gods.

On the other hand, contemporary children of the Europeans do not like this God notion so we cannot say that Black folks are God, partly because they do not want to have God. The slighter thing is that their scholarship requires them to do other kinds of atheistic notions, which say I cannot be objective and scientific and give notion to a higher force. So, Western scholarship has a healthy disregard for God. And so in making God Black, it becomes even worse because now not only is there a healthy disregard for God, but they certainly do not like us. So they make a big deal about this. They are saying we cannot have Black folk of ancient Kemet being God. Well, they say that what was developed had to be developed based upon something from outer space coming here and developing it and then going back and leaving so that the temples and intellectual centers that our ancestors built, would be known as products of space creatures. They say that those were landing sites and that they were places where we beamed to outer space to get some other stuff and it had nothing to do with Black folk.

So, the European intellectuals are about the business of writing fairy tales to take care of their sense of insecurity and in one sense, as psychologists we should understand. But in another sense there is more important business to deal with, such as understanding our own reality. Where the Kemetic symbolism becomes important is in its understanding of the meaning of symbolism and the use of symbolism in ancient Kemet because that is where we are able to properly reclaim our intellectual and developmental heritage. See, we cannot explain why we are here. If you think about it, the kind of oppression, the kind of destruction, the kind of hate, and especially the kind of hostility that African people have experienced in the New World cannot explain how we are still here even today. We should have been wiped out. We should have been eliminated from the planet. One cannot explain the African presence unless there will be an explanation about the developmental heritage that is part of the law of the psychology of African people. And that is what we are after. We are running after it like we are chasing behind something that belongs to us and it is just a little bit out of reach. But, we have to understand the developmental heritage.

I use the term "ancients" because the ancients were those people who were interesting in all times. Even in ancient times there were ancients. Through the use of symbolism and symbols, the ancients were the people who were responsible for establishing and maintaining the law; maintaining the wisdom without modification. Now we modify and retranslate and write our own way. I was talking to a brother a little while ago about just the way we use the hieroglyphs to put our names on cartouches. It has gotten so bad that there are some letters translated with little rationality and appear totally made up. Someone just decided to put it together so they can make some translations that have nothing to do with the original scripture. But the ancients did not allow that because they understood that things should not be modified so that one could maintain the magic of it. Now how does this idea of magic stuff come in? "Oh, there he go again talking about this ol' magic stuff."

But the magic issue is really something we need to understand because magic was not hocus-pocus and pulling rabbits out of hats. Magic was the foundation of medicine, of healing. It was a metaphysical process that was scientific that was understood in terms of the interaction with energy in the universe and in the world. Now we do not know how to deal with such issues because we only see magic in terms of hocus pocus and magicians with magic wands. We do not even understand all the symbolism within the magic. We should start exploring that and understand what magic really was and not see it as we do today with magicians being able to materialize and transport themselves to the top of the building here in New York. Mirrors are also considered some part of our idea of magic and that's not magic at all.

The use of symbolism becomes important because the ancients used symbols and symbolism as a way of revealing their inner vision, their intuitive vision. So symbols and symbolism became important because it allowed us to see that the phenomenon of nature, the ultimate blueprint of nature's phenomenon is the human. We are the maps. But we do not understand that. We see ourselves as being part of the whole; but, we are basically the map to understanding the universe. Everything that is in the universe is in us and all the knowledge that ever existed in time in the universe is within us. But, we walk around talking about how dumb and stupid we are and that we don't know anything and that we can't do anything. We do not realize that it is all within us and that we just don't have the key to stimulate it to bring it out.

Some of that has to and is going to be found in this new quest for unlocking the issues of melanin. But, if we do our job right, melanin is going to be key to this. We are struggling to understand these critical issues while at the same time we are also making important discoveries and that's what it's really about.

The symbolism becomes important. The phenomenon of nature was seen by the ancients as symbolic writing when relating to the tree growing, the plant growing, the river moving, or the grass blowing in the wind. All those are seen as phenomena of nature, but more importantly as symbolic writing. Because the visible and the invisible are one in the same even though the invisible is far greater. When I look at something in nature, I am seeing a script being written, and I have to get beyond just the picture of it because it is more than visible. For instance the color of it. I've been talking about green as the color of vegetation in a lot of the ancient things. And it is true. What happens then is that we begin to put color all around, thinking that we have solved our problems, but the color is not the issue. It is just the physical manifestation of something far greater. What is greater is vegetation, or the life giving force becomes far greater than the color green. It should be clear that we have to go beyond the visible to understand those things.

African symbolism is unlike the European mentality that says the symbol or the sign stands for something. For example, I can write WADE and that tells you that WADE is my name. If somebody calls the name Wade, I'm going to turn my head and look, but the fact of the matter is that Wade in the Western mind, stands for me. That is why there are signatures on checks and contracts. We don't realize when it is done that it is a joke because we are actually putting more on the paper than just some signs. That ol' bill is going to follow you forever, because you are tied up into this debt thing. But, the letters on a piece of paper stand for something; and it is something far greater than the ancient mentality that said that the sign was just a symbol. For instance, the symbols of animals in Ancient Kemet were worshipped a great deal. There are a whole lot of animal figures, but the animals themselves were not seen as the thing to be worshipped. The animals represented the vital essential function. So if there was a god that had the head of a lion or the god that had the head of an ape on his body, the ancients were telling us that there is an essential function that is represented by the sign that is far greater than the fact that someone else could belong... these Black folk were really insightful. They had human bodies and animal legs and human heads. The Europeans did not understand what the ancients were doing; they thought the ancients were just paganistic and were not able to see that there was a science going on that had to be understood in terms of this symbolism.

The greatest use of symbolism is found in the mythology because we see that the mythology guides us to understand the human possibility, probability and potentiality. In fact, I'm going to talk more about the mythology piece some other time, but I want to just share with you briefly that mythology becomes the dramatic cloak or the code for understanding the consciousness of the ancients because the mythology was in fact a dramatization of the conscious. In effect, it is a people's awareness in dramatic form—as story. All people use myths to dramatize their consciousness. It's not something unique about African folk. All people do that. That's why you can see the consciousness of the European reflected in their mythology. How does one explain the fact that the premier Roman Myth is the myth of Romulus and Remus. These two little boys get lost or thrown away by their parents. The wolf comes along and nurtures them and brings them to life. In the midst of the mythology, once they get grown, the only profound thing they could do as brothers was to turn on each other. And one killed the other and the remaining survivor founded the city of Rome.

Now there is human possibility, probability, and potentiality spelled out in the drama of the myth. What is it about the genesis myths of these people that once they mature and develop the only redeeming thing they can do is to destroy and to kill their own blood? Now we need to understand these people before we follow after them. Instead, we are chasing behind them like they are the models and yet we don't understand what they are really about. We seriously need to look at the mythology because the mythology reveals the human possibilities, probabilities and potentialities.

The mythology is the symbolic script that is capable of revealing the forces and the laws that govern the universe. It is those forces and laws that we must not only understand as ancient stuff, but must be able to apply to our condition today. How do we apply those ancient laws that the mythology gave as a measure of what is relevant and what is real? In the *Book of the Knowing of the Evolutions of Ra*, a creation myth is told to us. It is best that it is illustrated in order to pull out the human possibilities, probabilities, and potentialities of ancient Egyptian myth.

The Genesis myth in the *Book of Knowing of the Evolutions of Ra* says, "I am he who evolved himself under the Khepera, I the evolver of the evolution." Now it is best to stop right there. It is here that has the most important issues at hand. That is it. There's the key. "I, the evolver of the evolution." The brother is saying that nothing is happening here without me. Essentially he is saying that he is the main event. Basically, "I am the source, I am the cause," and we need to understand what's being said to us that was spelled out in mythology. "I, the evolver of the evolutions and the developments which come forth from my mouth," he says. From my mouth. We need to look at that. What is the symbolism of the mouth? We say, "Oh, the sister got a mean mouth on her" or "that's a mean mouth so and so" or even, "that's a big mouth so and so." We don't realize that there's symbolism in this sign of the mouth that we must understand in order to get into those laws and rules that govern the universe. "Which came forth from my mouth. No heaven existed and no earth and no terrestrial animals or reptiles had come into being. I formed them. I formed them."

The creator was saying that the principle here was that he was the cause. You hear that the African is saying, "I am the cause." I formed them out of the mass of watery matter. I found no place where upon to stand. I was alone and gods Shu and Tefnut had not come forth from me. There existed none other who worked with me. I laid the foundations of all things. I laid the foundations of all things by my will—by my will. I'm the cause in all things. I united myself to my shadow and sent forth Shu and Tefnut out of myself. Thus, from being one God I became three"—the first holy trinity.

We have to look at our mythology in terms of understanding what it has to say about essential functions about the laws that govern the universe. The essence of God is revealed in the myth as thought—will and command—intent. In fact, in one mythology it talks about divine energy or divine force or divine spirit manifesting itself as being. This then willed itself to become a being and in turn manifested itself as man and woman. In the mythology of the ancient Kemets, we always see the evolution of humanity as the complementary presence of man and woman. Go to the Genesis myth and Moses. The myth talks about God creating man and woman and gave man mastery over the world and the job of naming and defining everything in the Garden of Eden. But, he is the first creature of God and then God decides as an afterthought that Adam needs a helpmate. In the King James' version of the Bible it is spelled helpmeet. And I always remembered back in the South that old men would always say that it was "helpmeat," which meant that the man was supposed to help himself to the "meat." Now, I often say that because somehow I have to give homage to those old men even though they may have been ignorant or because you grow up with personal consciousness being imprinted with certain ideas that stay with you. Even intellectually you may see beyond those that are in you. One of the most informative experiences to have is to get a bunch of African intellectuals together at a bar and start drinking. They start acting like they are just thinking people and not intellectuals and the kinds of things that come out in that dialogue around what we do is most profound.

The real issue of God being thought of as in command becomes important because what it says is that I willed myself to be. If I willed myself to be, then I am in command of that which happens to me. But we end up allowing ourselves to be victimized because we don't understand the essentialness, the essential function that is in our nature. What is the nature of the African? In the nature of the African is the power to will things to be. We do it all the time. For example, your mother and your grandmother would start rubbing her elbow and then think about some sister or cousin half way across the country and get on the phone and call that person and one hundred percent of the time without degree of error, something out of the ordinary will have happened to someone back home somewhere. It could be anything like she hit the lottery or maybe she is on her way back to Africa or her son got arrested and he's going to jail. But, there is nothing mundane, there is no regularity, it's something out of the ordinary because Mama felt it. She felt because she understood the spirit and the energy that we often disregard because we get so busy being professionals that when we start thinking about somebody, we're so busy that we wait until later or have a secretary call the other person's secretary to figure out what is happening, not realizing that we are moving away from our own sense of Africanity by not reading the signs and symbols of the universe.

The issues of will and intent become important because they are divine attributes and divine characteristics. It is better to have divine will and intent and for one's intent to be done. We fail to see that as mastery, and we don't see ourselves as masters of the universe anymore because we don't understand the essential function that is part of our African beingness. The essence of Ptah is divine intelligence and/or intellect which is really will and intent. When one gives up that will or gives up one's intention for one's will to be done, that is not wise. Then one can be considered stupid.

But, we are running around thinking that if we could just help some kids learn these informational items on the SAT tests or learn this material of European made tasks that this would be an indicator of their intelligence. All that is indicated is that they know facts and figures which are considered important, especially since a lot of bridges are put up in front of us that keep us from going places based upon access through tasks. But, that is not a measure of intelligence or intellect; and we need to stop making the argument that it is important for our kids to know these things. Accumulated knowledge doesn't make them intelligent. Intellect is in the knowing that over the thing one has mastery and that one's own will and intent will be done. We could change our communities if we simply operated from this knowledge. We, in fact, have the highest per capita, well educated, well fed, well nurtured African people.

And our communities suffer because we have understood facts and information but we have not been intellectual concerning mastery. We just simply have not been.

[1989]

To Be African or Not to Be: The Question of Identity or Authenticity—Some Preliminary Thoughts

In earlier works[1] I attempted to understand the scientific treatment of Black Identity and more recently[2] made an attempt to briefly critique one of the dominant theories of Black Identity development. However, given the requisites of an African paradigm and episteme, I am now convinced that the utility of the construct itself should be reviewed. While I will not at this time attempt to dismiss the whole notion of Black Identity, I will note that the construct of identity seems wanting when placed against the requirements of discourse and the demand for accuracy in assessing and evaluating "African" reality.

This notion essentially relocates the debate. In calling for the recognition of a different quality of thought and practice and in acknowledging the responsibility for creating one's own criteria for authenticating the reality of African human processes, the African centered notion represents a radical epistemological shift and paradigmatic change wherein new questions may be raised. Accordingly, I would like to end my preliminary thoughts on the idea of "To Be African or not to Be: The Question of Identity or Authenticity" with a brief discussion focused on: (1) re-visiting the African meaning of human beingness; and (2) re-examining the African meaning of the person.

The ideas offered here are simply thoughts designed to suggest that our "theoretical" understanding of what it means to be African/Black in a non-African/white supremacist society requires "deep thought" about the psychology of African people. It is in the tradition of "thinking deeply" about what it means to be African that I propose that the real understanding of Black identity and our resolute response to living in an anti-African society will be attainable. It is only when we first think deeply about what it means to be a human being and subsequently, therein, how that meaning shapes our responses and reactions to living, will we learn or know anything of value. Hence, I think the notion of "human authenticity" and its expression as the "person" are the constructs that could offer a new research agenda in which to explore the frontiers of "African theory development."

Some Preliminary Thoughts

Where theory is founded on analogy between puzzling observations and familiar phenomena, it is generally only a limited aspect of such phenomena that is incorporated into the resulting model[3]

During the 1995 Pre-conference African Psychology Institute of the Association of Black Psychologists' Annual Convention, Dr. Asa Hilliard was invited to address the issue of African Psychology. In the context of his remarks, Dr. Hilliard attempted to paraphrase Shakespeare's often quoted phrase, "To be or not to be, that is the question." In restating Shakespeare, Dr. Hilliard's intention, I think, was to say, "To be African or not to be African, that is the question." However, in attempting to restate the phrase, I believe Dr. Hilliard's tongue was captured by the ancestral spirits of Africa and what came forward was a divinely fundamental and spiritually essential question. Asa Hilliard stated, "To be African or not to be, that is the question." In making that simple pronouncement, the level of discourse was fundamentally clarified and simultaneously shifted.

The ancestors, through Dr. Hilliard's genius, had directed Black psychologists to deal with "the real deal." Can we be and not be African? While this level of question frightened many of us and made most of us uncomfortable, I think it is the only place for us, as Black psychologists, to begin. Accordingly, I would like to address the question of African-American identity development from the framework of what is fundamental to our "Be"-ing.

This question "To be African or not to be?" becomes even more complex when one factors in the context of African people living in a non-African and/or anti-African society. Given such a context, I have suggested that the understanding of what it means to be African must be informed by what I have defined as the Triangular Law of Knowing, Being and Doing for Africans living in an anti-African reality. The three laws are: (1) the law of (mis)knowing; (2) the law of (non)being; and (3) the law of (un)doing. These laws note that "if you don't understand white supremacy, then everything else you think you know will simply confuse you"—law of (mis)knowing; "If you don't exist according to your cultural essence (nature/spirit), then everything that you think you are will only be a diminishment"—law of (non)being; and "the experience of one generation becomes the history of the next generation and the history of several generations will become the tradition of the people—law of (un)doing. Several scholars[4] have suggested that the psychological understanding of African people must be informed by the extent to which we understand the impact of white supremacy, the retentions, residuals, and radiance of the African nature/spirit and the reverberating power to reinvent ourselves.

In discussing the falsification of African consciousness as it relates to psychiatry and the politics of White Supremacy, Amos N. Wilson noted specifically, "In the context of a racist social system, psychological diagnosis, labeling and treatment of the behavior of politically oppressed persons are political acts performed to attain political ends. For oppression begins as a psychological fact and is in good part a psychological state. If oppression is to operate with maximum efficiency, it must become and remain a psychological condition achieving self-perpetuating motion by its own internal dynamics and by its own inertial momentum."[5] The Eurocentric mental health establishment, he rightly suggests, is a participant and beneficiary of the white domination of African peoples. Psychology and the mental health industry is a very important cog in the self-perpetuating machine of African dehumanization, mental dysfunction, and dehumanization.

The discipline of Western Psychology's reason for being is to nurture and sanction the imperialist and racist political regime which fathered it. In this regard, Wilson concludes that the explanatory systems and treatment approaches of Western Psychology ultimately must be exposed as "political ideology and oppressive political governance parading as empirically validated principles of psychological and medical science, and 'objective' psychotherapeutic and psychiatric practices."[6]   This is equally true with the act of theory development.

African peoples' psychology is fundamentally derived from the nature of the African spirit and determined by the African spirit's manifestation as a unique historical and cultural experience. This natural and instinctual psycho-behavioral imperative is coupled with a revolutionary drive to achieve physical, mental and spiritual liberation. Given this unique condition, Eurocentric psychology and the mental health industrial establishment created by it as well as the African psychologist who knowingly or unknowingly participates in it cannot provide adequate explanations, rationales, theories and therapeutic practices.

The position taken in this discussion is that what is needed is a theoretical and therapeutic practice that is centered in our own African essence and integrity. This position is in fact consistent with our raison d'être. The Association of Black Psychologists was formed in part to utilize our skills to benefit the Black community. Specifically the raison d'être of the Association was to address the significant social problems affecting the Black community and to positively impact upon the mental health of the national Black community through planning, programs, services, training and advocacy. It was clear then as it is now that the African community's mental health depended upon our ability to (1) resist and/or inoculate ourselves from the degradation and dehumanization resulting from the effects of White supremacy; and (2) to advance and/or increase our human essence and vitality resulting from the maintenance of our cultural integrity. What emerged from these two psychological imperatives is the ultimate recognition that if our practice, including theorizing, does not respect and reflect the African essence and integrity, and if we do not exist and function personally and collectively according to our own African essence/nature, then everything we do or provide (teaching, service, treatment and theorizing) will only disserve and de-humanize ourselves and our people.

Ofo   Ase: Toward   a   Different   Discourse

The quest for explanatory 'theory' is basically the quest
for unity underlying apparent diversity; for implicity underlying apparent complexity; for order underlying apparent
disorder and for regularity underlying apparent anomaly[7]

If we, as Black psychologists, are to be obedient to the
imperative of respecting and reflecting the human essence of our
people, then our work must be guided by Ofo Ase[8] or a discourse
that is radically different from those whose intent is to verify the
invalidation of our humanity. Discourse is simply a formal, honest, and intelligent discussion relative to an idea or subject. The
discourse is formal because it is systematic and rule governed via
its alignment with a particular episteme and paradigm. It is honest in that it is an accurate representation of the truth as defined
and experienced by the people who are subject to and have
agency with the lived experience of that truth. Finally, discourse
is intelligent when there is a discernible connection between
thoughts, ideas and domains of functioning; i.e., it is rational.

The criteria for discourse is further clarified when it is
placed in the context of the idea of intimacy. To be intimate is to
have a close relationship/experience with, detailed knowledge
and deep understanding of the innermost and essential nature of
a thing or another being. In terms of human beings, I would further suggest that there are at least three important realms of intimacy. First there is sexual intimacy, which at its most fundamental basis is procreation wherein humans re-invent themselves.
One could suggest that the coming together of the egg and sperm
in fertilization can only occur when they have a detailed knowledge and deep understanding of each other's innermost and
essential nature. Second, there is eating, which at its most primitive utility is nurturance, whereby humans sustain and replenish
themselves. The processes of ingestion, digestion and transformation equally require knowledge and understanding. Finally, there
is talking, which at its best expression, is discourse wherein
humans define, perfect, educate, explain and give meaning to
themselves. Not only is discourse important as a human intimacy, but also it is important, as Karenga notes[9] because through
discourse humans are able to attain authenticity, obtain historical
place, and establish engagement as human subject and agent.

What should be called for in this book is a formal, honest and intelligent discussion of "African American Identity Development." Parenthetically, it should be noted that the historical shift in conceptual classification from the so-called Negro self-concept[10] to Black Identity[11] to African-American Identity Development should mean either the identification of new phenomena or the refinement of old theory. It is not clear which of these guide the contemporary discussion. More so, in terms of this discussion, when the subject of African American identity is submitted to the requirements of: (1) epistemic and paradigmatic alignment (the condition of formal); (2) accuracy in its representation of our truth as human subject and agent (the condition of honesty); and (3) illustrating a discernible connection between thoughts, ideas and functioning (the condition of intelligence), then the demands of discourse—to define, perfect, explain and understand—require that we rethink the actual utility of the concept of identity.

While the constraints of this chapter limit a full explanation of this conclusion, I can briefly note that this position is driven, in part, by Dr. Hilliard's axiom, "To be African or not to be," and the need to utilize an African epistemology and paradigm for understanding things African. A paradigm, in this regard, is simply the formalized framework which guides the assessment and evaluation of reality. As is well known, the paradigm is, in effect, the perceptual, cognitive and affective achievement representing the organizational plan for thinking, feeling, understanding and doing. A people's *cultural essence*, the ontological, cosmological and axiological positions; worldview, the most comprehensive ideas about order; normative assumptions, a priori truths, and philosophical perspectives, frame of reference combine to form and inform the centrality or core of their paradigm. The episteme concerns itself with what is real knowledge and the study and understanding of how one knows. As such, epistemology concerns the study of: (1) what is the nature of reality; (2) how truth is defined; (3) what is the relationship between the knower (intent), knowing (process) and the known (will); (4) what can be known; and (5) what should/could be done in response to the known.

There are several features or assumptions which distinguish an African paradigm. An African paradigm assumes that (1) the universe is cosmos; (2) the ultimate nature of reality is spiritual; (3) human beings are organically related to everything in the universe; (4) knowledge comes from participation with and experience in the universe (reality); (5) human relatedness is the praxis of our humanity; and (6) that the mode of our epistemological method is that of Participation (equilibrium- balance between knowing, knower and known), Relatedness (harmony) and Unicity (balance between rationality and intuition; analyses and synthesis; known and unknown and the visible and invisible).

In earlier works[12] I attempted to understand the scientific treatment of Black Identity. More recently[13] I made an attempt to briefly critique one of the dominant theories of Black Identity development. However, given the requisites of an African paradigm and episteme, I am now convinced that the utility of the construct itself should be reviewed. While I will not at this time attempt to dismiss the whole notion of Black Identity, I will note that the construct of identity seems wanting when placed against the requirements of discourse and the demand for accuracy in assessing and evaluating African reality.

Therefore, in order to be rigorous and have scientific utility, the construct should be consistent with the abovementioned assumptions. For instance, the construct must appreciate the idea that the ultimate nature of reality is spirit. Similarly, it should illustrate the significance of participation, relatedness and unicity for the human condition and reveal the ultimate organic connection.

Ultimately the problem with Black Identity theory is that it represents only a limited, albeit damaged, aspect of what it means "to be African (or not to be)." Black Identity theory is, for the most part, founded upon an unwarranted acceptance of the Western, a.k.a. white supremacy, notions of human functioning with African people living in an anti-African reality. And like Horton's precepts on theory suggest, these puzzling observations about African-American identity range from the reactions to de-Africanization and the hegemonic domination of white esthetics/existence, to creative responses to re-Africanizing and reinventing African American culture and traditions.

In order to engage a different discourse, one has to begin with a different question. The statement, "To be African or not to be, that is the question," requires the thinker to examine the notion of human essence (the invisible) and expression (the vis-

ible). Hence, I propose that our concern should be with the
notion of authenticity rather than the idea of identity

Atunwa: Human Authenticity or Black Identity

While it is awesome to address the question of Atunwa:
Human Authenticity[14] or Human Essence, it is indeed timely,
given the contemporary thrust of African reawakening occurring
in the USA. This thrust is best represented by what in some areas
is called the African centered movement. African centeredness in
this context is not simply a call for Afrocentric curriculum in
schools or the inclusion of African contributions to world history
and civilization. African centeredness represents a concept which
categorizes a "quality of thought and practice" which is rooted in
the cultural image and interest of people of African ancestry and
which represents and reflects the life experiences, history and traditions of people of African ancestry as the center of analyses. It,
in effect, represents the intellectual and philosophical foundations upon which people of African ancestry should create their
own scientific and moral criteria for authenticating the reality of
African human processes. It represents the core and fundamental
quality of the "Belonging," "Being" and "Becoming" of people of
African ancestry. In essence, African centeredness represents the
fact, that as human beings, people of African ancestry have the
right and responsibility to center themselves in their own subjective possibilities and potentialities and through the re-centering
process reproduce and refine the best of the human essence.

This notion essentially relocates the debate. In calling for
the recognition of a different quality of thought and practice and
in acknowledging the responsibility for creating one's own criteria
for authenticating the reality of African human processes, the
African centered notion represents a radical epistemological shift
and paradigmatic change wherein new questions may be raised.
The real meaning and significance of African centeredness is that
its logical extension directs the thinker to explore the deeper
meaning of human essence and the quest for human authenticity.

The boundaries for this exploration have indeed no limitations. In fact, I would make the argument that African-American
Identity should be informed by an appreciation of our truly pan-

African definition.[15] I would further argue that a full understanding of African-American identity will only be attainable when the deeper meaning of our pan African definition or constitution is fully comprehended. In order to encourage such a conceptualization, I have suggested that African, Black people, in the United States should culturally view themselves as another African group, no less African than the Africans left behind in Africa and made victims of European colonialism and Christian and Islamic religious conversion. I have recommended, in this regard, that as Blacks in the United States of America, we call ourselves the "BUSA People." It is, in fact, the case that the "BUSA people" have ancestral rights and spiritual connections to African peoples living in the Senegambia (Bantu, Wolof, Mandingo, Malinka, Bambara, Fulani, Papel, Limba, Bola, Balante, etc.); the Sierra Leone Coast (Temne, Mende, etc.); the Liberian Coast (Vai, De, Gola, Kisa, Bassa, Crabo, etc.,); the Gold Coast (Yoruba, Nupe, Benin, Fon, Ewe, Ga, Pop, Edo-Bini, Asante-Fante, etc.);   the Niger-Delta (Efik-Ibibio, Ijan, Ibani, Igbos, etc.) and Central Africa (Bakongo, Malimbo, Bambo, Ndungo, Balimbe, Badongo, Luba, Loango, Ovimbundu, etc.) and, of course, the ancient Nile valley. The question of identity must, therefore, explore the psychological residuals, retentions, and resonances of our pan African legacy across time, space and place.

Our ancestral rights and spiritual connections were not severed or destroyed by the circumstance of enslavement, just as the ancestral rights and spiritual connections of our brothers and sisters in Africa were not destroyed or severed by colonialism. We are all African people. Those of us living in the United States remain an African people and should, therefore, be rightfully referred to as the Busa tribe or Busa people (Blacks in the United States of America).

Hence, it is correct, I believe, to seek an appreciation of the implications ancient African thought and conceptualizations have for contemporary African conduct. Can the African discourse be informed by knowing that the scene of the *Psychostasia*[16] from the ancient African Hu-Nefer Papyrus depicts the Ka, the human spirit, reciting from the PER-EM-HRU[17] *The Book of Coming Forth from Darkness to Light*, misnamed the *Book of the Dead*, and that the *Psychostasia* symbolically represented the first conceptualization of human Psychology (circa 1370-1333 BCE) as the illumination and judgment of the human spirit? Through its symbolism the *Psychostasia* perceived the central and mutual interdependent roles of intellect, emotion, spirit, conduct and judgment in the process of human functioning.

In our contemporary theorizing and discourse, what is the role of illumination and judgment? Should the illumination and judgment be criteria for guaranteeing epistemic and paradigmatic alignment? Does the absence of them call into question the accuracy of the construct's or theory's ability to represent our truth as human subject and agent. Finally, will the inclusion of illumination and judgment reveal the discernible connection between thoughts, ideas, and functioning?

In classical African, Kemetic, philosophy, the significance of the human being is found in the fact of "Being, Becoming and Belonging." The human being as well as human reality were all governed by divine law and the basic divine law was simply "to be" and in being, one was the creative cause which made humans divine. This divine law was, in turn, translated into an enduring moral mandate which stated that "to be" was permanently guaranteed by the human instinct "to become." The moral mandate of African humanity was "to become" and in becoming, humans revealed their "belongingness" to God(liness); i.e., capacity to be the creative cause.

During ancient times, the process of being and becoming was accomplished through what was later called "an alchemical process of transformation to perfectibility."[18] In classic form, all African life is characterized as "Being, Becoming and Belonging." In Being, life is characterized by three basic attributes: Desire, Thought and Action. These attributes are subject to transformation, and, thereby, are "perfectible." Hence, Desire, when "perfected" (transformed), becomes pure love. Thought, when perfected, becomes clear understanding. Action, when perfected, becomes acts of sacrifice or service to benefit the whole—all. In becoming, one's basic beingness was transformed to a more perfect being. Hence, through the experience of right living one is transformed from being a lesser material being (animal) into a greater spiritual being (Godlike).

How should the discourse, which is to define, perfect, explain, and understand, on human attributes, namely, identity, personality, esteem, etc., relate to the notion of perfectibility?

Any theoretical model of African functioning should, at a minimum: (1) illustrate and explain how African Peoples, especially in the USA, reproduce themselves as human beings in a non-African and even anti-African reality; (2) show how the sense of human authenticity is related to the satisfaction of needs and the realization of power; (3) explain and provide an understanding of the grounding for being self-conscious of one's real essence in an alienating reality; and (4) illustrate and explain the relevance of African conceptualizations of human beingness for human growth and development.

Accordingly, I would like to end my preliminary thoughts on the idea of "To Be African or Not to Be: the Question of Identity or Authenticity" with a brief discussion focused on: (1) re-visiting the African meaning of human beingness; and (2) re-examining the African meaning of the person.

Ori Ire: The Quest for Authenticity

The question of human authenticity or Ori Ire[19] takes us directly to Dr. Hilliard's dictate, "To be African or not to be." The term "authenticity" refers to the condition or quality of being "authentic" or "genuine." To be "authentic" is to possess the condition of actually being what one claims to be. It is to be real. To be "authentic" is to have an undisputed origin that is directly connected to the producer or creator. It is to be genuine, which means to be original, unchanged or not a copy, variant or distortion. The "gen" in "genuine" or "generate" means to produce, to bring into existence. Hence, the deeper meaning of "human authenticity" is to be indisputably connected to that which brought you into existence. "To be African or not to be" suggests that to be human, African people must realize their indisputable connection to their African origin and that which brought the African into existence. This is the quest for human authenticity. In this regard, the search for human meaning is the search for the authentic core which gives one a sense of essence and drives the proper response to the demands of experiencing life.

An analysis of classical and traditional African beliefs about the authentic core will reveal the importance of the construct, human authenticity. The African authentic core is found in the African belief about the meaning of human beingness and the concept of the person.

The African Meaning of Human Beingness

The birth of a child is perceived by the Bantu-Kongo people as the rising of a living sun into the upper world.[20] Therefore, to be human is to be a being who is a living sun possessing a knowing and knowable spirit, energy, through which one has an enduring relationship with the total perceptible and ponderable universe. The person as energy, spirit or power is a phenomenon of perpetual veneration. The person is both the container and instrument of Divine energy and relationships. The human being is a power, a phenomena of *perpetual veneration*. Given this sense of human beingness, the observation regarding the spirituality of African people is somewhat of a misnomer. Spirituality pertains to having the quality of being spiritual. African people have more than the quality of being spiritual. In fact, for the African to be human is to be a spirit. Spirit is the energy, force or power that is both the inner essence and the outer envelope of human beingness. Spiritness, rather than spirituality, pertains to the condition of being a spirit. This spiritness is often misconceived as spiritual or a religious quality. As energy, spirit becomes spiritness, and, therein, serves to ignite and enliven the human state of being. Human beings experience their spiritness simultaneously as a metaphysical state and an ethereal extension or connection into and between the supra world of the deities, the inter world of other beings and the inner world of the self.

At this point, I want to explain my use of traditional African languages to represent the scientific concepts that emerge from the recommended African paradigm and episteme. Not only is this consistent with the dictates of the proposed new discourse, it is appropriate as an act of authenticity or authority. The use of African language terminology is critical to the reclaiming of African centered discourse. In this regard, Vera L. Nobles[21] points out that "concepts can be misconstrued or not fully understood or developed when they are defined, interpreted or constructed using a language not specific to the particular culture." Concepts reflect and/or represent phenomena within a particular culture. Every language reflects and represents some particular peoples' culture. Given African peoples sensitivity to the power of the word (Nommo), we more so than most people, recognize that words have psychological transformative power in that they are capable of legitimizing the material manifestation of phenomena. Concepts, represented by words, can and do have the ability to reinforce or reject the cultural moorings or foundations of a cultural community. Therefore African-American theorists should be especially sensitive to the words used in constructing their theory.

When one uses a language that is hostile or irrelevant to the cultural system under examination, then the concepts, via the language, will severely limit the understanding of the phenomena within that culture.[22] I suspect that when the African theorists utilize non-African concepts, such as, Latin, Greek, Roman, Anglo-Saxon, to represent the social phenomena of African life, they unknowingly incorporate the psychological energy, via subliminal meanings, associated with these concepts, and, thereby, create false positives in the discoveries of African-American conduct. Whenever possible, the African researcher should use African concepts to describe and give meaning to African phenomena.

Accordingly, for the Sonay people of Mali, the word for "black" is *bibi*. [23] "Bibi" is actually a concept used to refer to the essential goodness of things. It is never used to refer to anything negative or inferior. The full significance of this concept is found in the expression, *wayne bibi* (black sun). Dr. Hassimi Maiga[24] notes that the Gao people of Mali use the term "wayne bibi" to refer to the hottest part of the day when the sun is at its fullest. In effect, *wayne bibi* refers to the fullest expression of the sun. It is when the sun is the brightest, the most dazzling and the most radiant. The black sun (wayne bibi) symbolizes luminosity, the state of being unlimited and the condition when a thing achieves its total expression. Similarly, the Sonay people use the term, *Ay moo hari bibi*(Give me black water) to signify water that is from the deepest part of the river and the most clear and clean. Bibi in this context represents the depth or essence, clarity and purity of a thing. Hence, the term, *bibi*, especially *wayne bibi* connotes a state wherein a thing is pure, clean, clear, limitless luminous, radiant and exuding its totality or fullest expression.

I am suggesting that the Sonay term "wayne bibi" be used to represent the notion of spiritness in human beings. In the state of being a spirit and in recognition of the idea that the birth of a human being symbolizes the rising of a living sun in the upper world, the spiritness or wayne bibi, black sun, of our being represents the unlimited radiance, luminosity, dazzle, and total expression of being human.

I believe that when the person and/or community experience congruity between the supra, inter, and inner realms of the wayne bibi, then the sense of human integrity is achieved. This is a critical formulation because I believe that for African people, particularly those who were colonized and enslaved, it is only when one has a sense of the wayne bibi that one has the instinct to resist dehumanization or oppression as well as the capability to even contemplate human liberation and potential. It is also the awakening of the wayne bibi that allows us to contemplate and believe in the certainty of victory and human possibility.

At the metaphysical level, the wayne bibi is the unlimited and total expression of energy and power that represents human possibility, probability and potential. At the physical level, the wayne bibi is experienced as a drive or human condition. Wayne bibi is experienced as an urge and desire for what is excellent, good and right. As the fullest expression of goodness, it eventuates in the ever-expanding love and feeling of good will for all life. It is the wayne bibi that makes for ethical character and proper conduct. Being the black sun, a person has an ever-present urge to kindness, goodwill and fellowship. This is often experienced as the "felt need" to love and be loved for no particular reason at all. The wayne bibi gives the person the desire for order and the beautiful; i.e., that which is essential, pure, clean, clear, radiant. It is the wayne bibi that serves as the impetus for concern beyond self to other and the emotional sense of the Divine agency and relationship in human affairs; i.e., the compelling need to understand the nature of the Divine and, thereby, life itself and our meaning and purpose in life. The human being as a living sun expresses one's humanity as the magnetic pull away from mere animal/physical existence and toward that which is higher, nobler, better and more excellent (The Godness/Goodness). It is the wayne bibi, the Black Sun, the unlimited luminosity, the radiance, the totality or fullest expression of Divine energy that gives one the sense of inner power and dignity and makes one human.

The notion of being a power, a wayne bibi, of perpetual veneration suggests precise meanings for the concepts of being, becoming, and belonging found in the African centered discourse. Being is the state of wayne bibi; i.e., having the quality of a living sun. It is to have an essence or substance that is an attribute of the Divine and is absolutely invariant and indestructible. Becoming is to fulfill one's destiny. It is the continuous and constant movement toward achievement or realization of potential to reach higher levels of actuality. Belonging is the condition wherein one is conscious of the state of being one with that which is whole. It is a condition wherein one is integrally and essentially infused or blended with that which is greater.

The African Meaning of the Person

Kemetic beliefs about the person are well documented and upon review, one can see that the Kemetic meaning of the person is similar to the meaning of the person reflected throughout the major cultures of Africa. In the *Book of Knowing the Evolutions of Ra*, the creator God, Neb-er-tcher, states:

I am he who evolved himself under the form of the God Khepera. I, the evolver of the evolutions, evolved myself after many evolutions and developments which came forth from my mouth. No heavens existed, and no earth, and no terrestrial animals or reptiles had come into being. I formed them out of the inert mass of watery matter, I found no place whereupon to stand. I was alone. There existed none other who worked with me. I laid the foundations of all things by my will, and all things evolved themselves therefrom. I sent forth Shu and Tefnut out from myself. Shu and Tefnut gave birth to Nut and Seb, and Nut gave birth to Osiris, Horus-Khent-an-maa, Sut, Isis and Nephtys. At one birth, one after the other, and their many children multiply upon this earth.[25]

These Ancient Africans believed that the Neb-er-tcher evolved himself from the primordial substance and facilitated the evolution of forms into phenomena. The creative principle emerged out of the primordial substance, Nu, and all phenomena were, in fact, extensions of Nu. The Kemites believed in the consubstantiality of all phenomena.

The key to understanding Ancient Kemetic Philosophy, is the belief about the meaning of the person. Because the person was a manifestation or expression of Nu, the primordial substance, the ancients regarded the form of the human being as destined to live forever. Hence, institutions were developed to enable the person to evolve in response to the challenges of nature. The human person, like other forms, has an unchanging value and evolves in response to the demands of that value. Since the ancients regarded the primordial substance, Nu, as infinite. The infinity operated according to its law, which was its will. As a manifestation of Nu, the person represents a manifestation of the Law.

Ancient Kemetic mythology suggests that Nu manifested itself as a person, so that it could appear in glory on earth. As the antecedent form, Nu produced variant words for the person that signify a common African meaning of the person. To recognize this, one can note that different African peoples developed variant forms of Nu in their creation of words representing the person; e.g., Du, Nho, Ntu, Nwo, Tu, Di, Ni, Ntfu, etc.. For instance, the Hausa word for person is *Mutum*. The Ibo word is *Nmadu*. The Yoruba call the person, "Eniya" while the Xosha say *Umntu*. The Zulu and the Swazi use *Umuntu* and *Muntfu* respectfully.[26]

The ancient Kemetic definition of the human being emphasized, at minimum, the consubstantiality of the primordial substance and phenomenal expressions; the primacy of the person; perpetual evolution (perfectibility) and eternal life. The character of the person was continually challenged in response to the challenge of one's destiny. For the Kemites the challenge was, through perfecting, to live throughout the millennia, to be forever noble," to be "the princes of eternity."

As mentioned above, the Bantu-Kongo people believe that the person is an energy, spirit or power. And as a spirit, the person is a phenomenon of perpetual veneration. The person is both the container and instrument of Divine energy and relationships. Consistent with the Mali notion wayne bibi, to be human, is the Bantu-Kongo concept, to be a person who is a living Black sun, possessing a knowing and knowable spirit through which one has an enduring relationship with the total perceptible and ponderable universe.

The Zulu speaking people of South Africa, like almost all African people, have an ancient text, the *Izaga*, in which they define the meaning of what it is to be a person.[27] The text of wise sayings contain the Zulu interpretation of the teachings of the Sudic philosophy. Within these teachings the Zulu say *Umuntu Ngumuntu*, meaning, "the person is human." In this same regard, Dr. Marimba Ani teaches that the Bantu belief about the concept of the person is crystallized in the saying, *Umuntu Ngu Muntu Nga Bantu*, which means "A person is a person because there are people." In believing that the primordial substance was infinite, the Zulu believe that all phenomena was made of the primordial substance. The person was one such phenomenon. The ancient Zulu philosophers taught, in this regard, that through the *Umuntu Ngumuntu*, the human person was unique in that the person defined oneself and is essentially knowledgeable of ones own intrinsic value. For the Zulu to be human is to be able to say what and who one is and to be able to define oneself as a value.

Ngubane[28] argues that the African understanding of the person is a "protein" evaluation of the human being which flowed into Nile Valley high culture of the Ancient Kemites and subsequently created clusters of similar conceptions all over Africa. What, in fact, is recognized as African culture and civilization is the combined social conventions and inventions emerging from a common African meaning of the person.

Like the Kemites, the Zulu believed that all phenomena, *Uluthu*, had their origins in a living consciousness,[29] which they called Uqobu. The person evolved from the *Uqobu* in response to Umthetho weMvelo (the law of appearing); the demands of Isimu (One's nature) and Ukuma Njalu (perpetual evolution). According to Ngubane[30] the central teachings of the Bantu is that all things originated from *Uqobu* and evolve in response to the challenge of their nature. The person, according to the Zulu, is a self-defining value and that life's purpose for the person is perpetual evolution.

The Zulu ideal emphasized the primacy of the person and the creation of a society which equipped, enabled and ensured that the person would realize the promise of being or becoming human, Ukuba Ngumuntu. As a person, the components of realizing the promise of being human are: (a) the person by law is human (*Umuntu Ngumuntu*); (b) the person has to evolve over

the distance of being human (*Amabanga Okuba Ngumuntu*); and
(c) human compassion dictates that the person cannot be thrown
away (*Ukuba Ngumuntu*).

The Akan conception of the nature of being human also
informs the concept of the person. The Akan people consider a
human being to be comprised of three elements. The first element
is the *Okra* which constitutes the innermost self, the essence of
the person.[31] The *Okra* is considered the living soul of the person and is sometimes referred to as the *Okrateasafo*. As the living soul, the *Okra* is identical with life. It is also the embodiment
and transmitter of the individual's Nkrabea (destiny). As the life
force, the *Okra* is linked to *Honhom* (breath). The Honam (the
body), however, is the tangible and recognizable manifestation of
the presence of the *Okra*.

The second element of the person is the *Sunsum*. The
term *Sunsum* is used to refer to all unperceivable, mystical beings
and forces. It is the activating principle in the person. The
Sunsum is what molds the child's personality and disposition. It
is that which determines the character. The *Okra*, in turn, manifests itself in the world of experience through the *Sunsum*.

The final component is simply the Honam (the body),
which is made up of Ntoro and Mogya. While the *Okra* and the
Sunsum come from Onyame (God), the *Ntoro* and the *Mogya* are
derived from other humans; i.e., one's parents. In their conception of the nature of the person, the Akan believe that the *Ntoro*
is derived from the father's sperm and the *Mogya* is derived from
the mother's blood. The *Okra* and the *Sunsum* constitute a spiritual unity. Hence, the person is made up of two principal components, the immaterial/spiritual (*Okra* and *Sunsum*) and the mate-
rial/physical (*Honam*). In terms of the relation between the soul
and the body, Akan thinkers contend that not only does the body
influence the soul, the soul also influences the body. The Akan
believe that the relation between the soul (*Okra* and *Sunsum*)
and the body (*Honam*) is so close that they comprise an indissol-
uble and indivisible unity. Hence, the person is a homogeneous
entity or value.

Similarly, The Yoruba believe that the person is made up
of a spirit and a body.[32] The body or *Ara* is formed by the divinity, *Orisha-nla*. It is through the *Ara* that man responds to his
environment. It is the part of the person which can be touched

and felt. It can be damaged and disintegrates after death. The spirit component of the person is the *Emi* (spirit). The *Emi* gives life to the person. The *Emi* is the divine element of the person and links the person directly to God. Upon the death of the person, the *Emi* returns to *Elemi*, the owner of the spirit, God, and continues to live. As a person, one also possesses an inner head or *Ori Inu*. The *Ori Inu* is given directly by *Olodumare*. It is the person's personal spirit. The *Ori Inu* is the guardian of the self and the carrier of one's destiny. It also influences the personality of the person. In addition to the *Emi* and the *Ori Inu*, the person has an *Okan*. The word *Okan* means heart, but as a constituent component of the person, it represents the immaterial element that is the seat of intelligence, thought and action. Hence, it is sometimes referred to as the "heart-soul" of the person. The *Okan* is believed to exist even before the person's birth. It is the *Okan* of the ancestors which is reincarnated in the newborn child. To be a person, the Yoruba also believe that one must have *Ori* and *Eje*. The *Ori* rules, controls and guides the person's life and actually activates the person. The *Ori* is the bearer of one's destiny and helps the person to fulfill what they came to earth to do. The *Ori* is simultaneously the essence of the person and the person's guardian and protector. The *Ori* is closely associated with the *Emi*. The *Eje* is the blood. It is the physical expression of an electro-chemical/magnetic energy that is the force which binds and animates life. The Yoruba also believe that the *Iye* is a component of the person. The *Iye* is the immaterial element that is sometimes referred to as the mind.[33] The person also has *Ojiji* (shadow). The *Ojiji* is a constant companion throughout one's life and ceases to exist when the *Ara* (body) dies.

According to the Mende, the person is made up of the *Ngafa* (the spirit) and the *Nduwai* (the flesh). The *Ngafa* is immaterial and is provided by the mother. It leaves the body at death and goes into the land of the spirits. The *Ngafa* is the psychic constituent of the person. The *Nduwai* is the physical part of the person and is provided by the father. The *Nduwai* is contained in the seminal fluid. The shadow (*Nenei*) is also part of the person[34] and is believed to report the death of the body to God. The Mende believe that a healthy spirit (*Ngatha*) produces a state of *Guhun* (total well-being). The person's name is closely associated with his *Ngafa*. The significance of the name is that the Mende believe that a person's *Ngafa* can travel from the person during sleep or other state of unconsciousness. However, a person can be revived or awakened when one's name is called repeatedly. The Mende, therefore, believe that the person's name may be the component that wakes up the Ngafa or the human spirit.

In their discussion of African elements of human being-ness, Grills and Rowe[35] note that the Lebou people of Senegal believe that the person is, first and foremost, comprised of the *Fit* (vital energy or life force) which is what makes them human. *Fit* is referred to as the spiritual heart of the person. The part of the person that gives one physical life is called *Roo*. This is the breath of life which leaves the body at death. The Lebou believe that each of us has a spiritual shadow that is always present and pro-tects the person. This shadow is called the *Takondeer*. Additionally to be a person, one must possess and cultivate the qualities of *Yel* (intelligence) and *Sago* (reason). Finally, to be a person is to have a *Raab*. *Raabs* are constellations of spiritual forces, like the Yoruba Orishas, that possess, guide and protect the person. They are, in fact, ancestral spirits that influence and shape the personality and behavior of the person.

With this review, it appears that the African authentic core is comprised of the belief that the person is human because there is an indisputable connection between the person and God. In fact, the person is really seen as an undeniable expression or manifestation of God. Included in the authentic core is also the belief that: (1) the complexity (immaterial and material) of the person gives one an intrinsic human value; and (2) that the per-son is, in fact, a "process" characterized by the divinely governed laws of appearing, perfecting and compassion which are revealed within or through one's destiny. The final common belief in the African authentic core is that harmony and balance between/within the supra, inter and intra worlds of the person are key to human beingness.

If one of the responsibilities of theory is to engage in the quest for understanding the (1) unity underlying apparent diver-sity; (2) implicity underlying apparent complexity; (3) order underlying apparent disorder; and (4) regularity underlying apparent anomaly, then given these preliminary thoughts, it seems that the notion of authenticity is a better concept to repre-sent the unity that underlies the diversity of African people. With the idea of human essence or originality justified by an indis-putable connection to one's origin, it makes explicit the implicit underlying the complexity of contemporary African life. The sense of "authenticity," in the final analyses, gives the person, whether theorist or subject, a sense of order where disorder seems to reign, while simultaneously preventing the person, as well as the research, from experiencing the sense of alienation and anomaly.

Although they are preliminary, my thoughts on this mat-ter should not in any way be construed to mean that I believe that racial identity, for people living in a racist and oppressive socie-ty, is irrelevant. In fact, it is just the opposite. African-American identity development is a critical concern for defining self and determining one's meaning and value. This ability is essential to African-American well-being, especially for those Africans living in a society characterized by racism and other forms of human alienation and exploitation.

Sakhu Sheti: Deep Thought and Theory— Some Closing Suggestions

The ideas offered here are simply thoughts designed to suggest that our theoretical understanding or Sakhu Sheti[36] of what it means to be African, Black, in a non-African, white, soci-ety requires deep thought about the psychology of African peo-ple.[37] We cannot, as Carruthers points out, spend a lifetime of scholarship and realize what E. Franklin Frazier[38] identified as the "failure of the Negro intellectual." Frazier, after a lifetime career as the premier Black scholar, recognized that the Black intellectual had failed to study the problems of "Negro" life in America in a manner which would place the fate of the "Negro" in the broad framework of man's experience in this world.[39] The "Negro Scholar" (sic) he concludes was virtually useless, in terms of pro-viding theoretical guidance in overcoming white supremacy. Frazier believed that the sterility and irrelevance of Black intellec-tual activity was due to the fact that the work of the Black intel-lectual demonstrated that Black intellectuals had not reflected upon the fundamental problems of human knowledge and the meaning of human existence.

While this may have been the state of our intellectual tradition thirty years ago, it is not our reality now. There exist a whole
army of Africa[40] and African American[41] intellectuals who are
thinking deeply about the question of African humanity, philosophy, science, traditions and culture. It is in the tradition of thinking
deeply about what it means to be African that I propose that the
real understanding of Black identity and our resolute response to
living in an anti-African society will be attainable. It is only when
we first think deeply about what it means to be a human being
and, subsequently, how that meaning shapes our responses and
reactions to living, will we learn or know anything of value. Hence,
I think the notion of human authenticity and its expression as the
person are the constructs that could offer a new research agenda in
which to explore the frontiers of African theory development.

In thinking deeply about that small but significant
moment in the history of ABPsi, when Dr. Hilliard stated, "To be
African or not to be: that is the question," I believe the discourse
has been forever clarified. With an African episteme and paradigm, there are new questions to be asked. For instance, given the
notion of wayne bibi, one could ask, "In what ways are the various African peoples both those on the African continent,
Ghanaian, Yoruba, Senegalese, Bantu, Ethiopian, Sonay, South
African, etc. and those in the diaspora, Cuban, Mexican,
Brazilian, West Indian, European, Asian, North and South
American, etc., organically related? How does the *wayne bibi*
function and/or express itself in different geo-political, socio-economic environments? Is full consciousness of the wayne bibi
necessary for a complete sense of personhood? How does it relate
to the meaning of gender and sex-related performance? What are
the physical, social, and psychological manifestations of the
wayne bibi? How does the *wayne bibi* affect the sense of efficacy and human dignity?"

In the context of participation, are there experiences or
conditions that accelerate or retard one's awareness of the *wayne
bibi*? Are different levels of racial concentration relevant to the
awareness or expression of the *wayne bibi*? How does an activated *wayne bibi* versus an inactive or dormant *wayne bibi* relate to
various types of human conduct—intelligence, emotion, creativity, etc.? What is the role of the *wayne bibi* in determining
responses to different types of relationships—egalitarian, oppres-

sive, dominating, just, harmonious, etc.? Can one's wayne bibi be intentionally, via the mind, activated or diffused? What are the features of those lived experiences where African "beingness" is in a state of unlimited totality or at its fullest expression and what import does that condition have for the question of racial identity? How is *wayne bibi* associated with tolerance or acceptance of discrimination and dehumanization? At what point and/or under what conditions in an anti-African environment does *wayne bibi* cause the African to contemplate orthogonal possibilities and/or the certainty of self value and collective victory?

In all of these questions, one could and should ask the additional question, how does it affect the racial identity of African populations; equally interesting would be how does an activated wayne bibi affect the racial identity of non-African peoples?. Engaging in a different discourse with a different paradigm obviously creates unlimited new questions and new puzzles to address. For this reason alone, it is worth considering.

It may be that the living spirit of the Ancestors commands it and that the requirements of our own authenticity dictate that we do so. Ultimately, it may be that our recognition that to be a person is to be human and that as humans who are being, becoming, and belonging, we have a direct and indisputable connection to our African origin and that our subsequent sacred responsibility to our Ancestors and our profound sense of human authenticity demands that we do no less.

[1997]

Breaking the Code of Spirit(ness) and Consciousness

I have come to realize that to describe Black psychology as a perspective in psychology is to indeed betray that which is authentic and human in African or Black psychology. The question that has been constantly spoken from the epistemological shadows is, how do you know? What is our proof of this African psychology? If the essential challenge of inadequacy of Western psychology is warranted, then the notions of proof, which are relevant or valid in Western psychology, are probably not sufficient for this area as well. Nevertheless, the question of proof is one which must be addressed if the place called African psychology is to be found.

For Black psychology—and the many other social science areas that are attempting to explain contemporary African peoples—the epistemological question centers in some ways around the notion of tenacity. More specifically, it centers on how one proves that a particular element, construct, artifact or psychological disposition has been retained. In other words, how can one prove that the existence or expression of some phenomenon is due to the retention of African substances and/or form?

The differences in position or opinion around this question are clearly defined. In one historical camp one finds the "Frazierites" claiming that most of what one could call African in Black America has been totally lost or destroyed. In the other camp, the "Herskovitians" who claim that a great deal has been retained. Again, the question becomes one of proof. Who is right? It would be expedient or, to say the least, diplomatic to say that the truth lies somewhere in between. However, I do not believe necessarily in the truth-in-moderation notion. Truth can be on the extreme. Thus, I believe that the truth lies, in this case, in the camp of African retention. But how does one prove it? It has been stated elsewhere that one must note the orientation of most African scholars, whose incidental whiteness colored much of what they have to say. Hence, one must be very critical of the so-called "objective" treatment of Africans currently available. In the main, that treatment has been an emphasis on differences and negation. The intention, it is believed, was to separate or disallow the common definition of African peoples wherever they are. The ultimate goal was to divide and conquer.

Although the question of the proof of the tenacity of elements, particularly as they relate to African consciousness as a critical component of African/Black Psychology, is the concern of these remarks, the discussion will flow as if the concern was with the question of proving tenacity of African elements in general. Melville Herskovits[1] has suggested that one can understand or discover the tenacity of cultural elements—what he calls Africanisms—by New World Negroes through the utilization of several anthropological notions: (1) cultural conservatism, (2) syncretism, (3) reinterpretation, (4) cultural focus, and (5) cultural imponderables. Each of these is discussed very clearly by Herskovits. However, I would like to briefly elaborate on how I see their function in relation to the tenacity of Africanism. Cultural conservatism assumes that cultures are: (1) learned, and (2) constantly changing. It also assumes there to be a high degree of stability in every culture. The latter statement is in fact assured by individual members of the culture learning its customs, beliefs, and institutions and transmitting these to the next generation. Syncretism is simply the recognition that rewards are received and punishments avoided only when appropriate responses are made to new forms; and, whenever available, the tendency is to identify those elements in the new situation, such as, Catholic saints, who are similar to elements in the old situation or specifically to African deities, and then, to make the appropriate substitutions. The remaining three notions can be combined. Reinterpretation is important because it is a methodological tool. However, cultural focus and cultural imponderables are the most important because they set the foundation or parameters to the reinterpretation process.

Cultural focus is the priority or weight a people give to certain aspects of their everyday world. Cultural imponderables are the unconscious, culturally-defined dispositions which determine much of the behavior of a particular people. These dispositions define the types of motor habits, value systems, and codes of etiquette the people adhere to. As such, cultural focus and cultural imponderables are both directly related to the consciousness and philosophical orientation of the people in question and are unquestionably the most resistant to alien inculturation.

Like Herskovits, Lorenzo Turner believes that Africans transplanted in the New World did not lose their African cultural heritage. He, in fact, states that "the study of the influence of African culture upon the Western hemisphere reveals that the slaves on reaching the New World did not wholly abandon their native culture, but retained much of it with surprisingly little change." Clearly Herskovits and Turner feel that they see enough evidence in the New World to suggest that African traditional culture is being maintained in the Western Hemisphere. Again, the question comes back to how can one prove it?

In addressing that question, one must ask, "If these things were maintained, what was the maintenance process; how were they maintained; and what were the mechanisms that allowed them to be maintained?" The abovementioned notions of Herskovits' are helpful here and I would further like to propose that cultural elements are maintained when they are (1) isolated and/or insulated from alien cultural interaction, and (2) do not openly conflict with the cultural elements of the "host" or dominant society. Given my two conditions, one could assume that it is highly probable that the African elements were retained by New World Blacks if the conditions of Africans transplanted to the New World met one or both of the stated conditions.

The accessibility of the enslaved to Western indoctrination is related to the degree of the retention of African elements. Often, it is proposed, a condition which facilitated the retention of African cultural elements was the physical features of the particular regions. Such conditions were in fact the actual case. The highly enforced separation and/or blocking of the admittance of Blacks into white society allowed for the New World Africans to retain their heritage. Hence, the tendency of the oppressor to isolate the oppressed from normal interaction was advantageous for the retention process. It is contended that the oppressive system assisted indirectly in the retention of, rather than the destruction of the African cultural elements or, more precisely, African consciousness.

The New World conditions tended to reflect a concentration of large numbers of Africans living in a given area. Turner notes that wherever Negroes were in the majority, African consciousness, and, thereby, cultural elements had a better chance of surviving. In the United States the policy of racial segregation must have often aided in keeping alive the African sense of being African. It seems that a comparative analysis between the ecological and geographical constitution of areas, such as Brazil, Jamaica, Dutch Guyana, the South Carolina coastal islands, etc. and the proximity and accessibility of interaction with Westerners of these same regions will reveal a strikingly direct correlation with the retention of an African consciousness and the maintenance of Africanisms.

On the Question of Parsimony

I must respond to the part of our conversation which centered on parsimony and the ability to explain existing behavior and retained cultural elements solely in the context of the New World experience. The law of parsimony as a decision-making rule is acceptable only as a description of one aspect of the scientific method "as is," and it is not my intention to betray science. Parsimony may not be appropriate as we delve and explore deeper and deeper into the area. We must recognize that this area of study reflects a paradox in itself. On the one hand, one is studying those circumstances in which so-called cultural changes are instituted; yet we ascribe to the notion that those very circumstances allowed for the retention of conventions which make for successful resistance to change. It may just be possible that complex phenomena do in fact require complex explanations. The question of consciousness and spiritness are such complex phenomena.

The only other position I would like to state is that, if one is able to explain the behavior of Africans living in the New World solely in the context of that experience and one could also show valid or probable cause for the same behavior being a retention of basic African definitions, I would not accept the conclusion that the former disproves the latter. The thought that also rings loudest in my mind is that the former has too often been the explanation offered by those whose vested interest was to maintain their privileged positions.

Consciousness

In regards to the notion of consciousness, it is fairly well documented that Africa conceives of reality and all that is within reality as a mental expression of the Divine. In ancient Nile Valley metaphysics, for instance, Djehuti, whom the Greeks call Hermes, is considered the mind and will of the creative Demiurge. From this personified Divine mind emerges the "word" that brings all things into being. Similarly, Dogon metaphysics states that the universe is the thought in the mind of Amma, the creator. In terms of consciousness, the philosophical thinking of the Akan makes a distinction between "realms of knowing" as thought—Adwen; that which cannot be perceived—Nea Wonhu; that which transcends thought—Nea etra Adwen. Furthermore the Akan thinking perceives "levels of awareness" as being conscious—Anidho; awareness of self-Anidahoso; and perception beyond the ordinary —Oben. The Bantu-Kongo believe that humans are surrounded by diverse forces and waves of energy which govern life. This fire-force called *Kalunga*, is complete in and of itself. It was merged within the emptiness or nothingness and became the source of life on Earth. This *Kalunga* as force in motion can be considered consciousness. The Bantu-Kongo believe that the heated force of Kalunga blew up and down as a huge storm of projectiles, *Kimbwandende*, producing a huge mass in fusion. In the process of cooling the mass in fusion, solidification occurs giving birth to the Earth.[2] In a very real way, the world as a physical reality, floating in Kalunga, emerges as an act of consciousness.

Consciousness is a construct that represents the ability of human beings to know, perceive, understand and be aware of self in relation to self and all else. All that is consciousness is, in fact, revealed in and determined by relationships (energy in motion). At the most fundamental level, consciousness is found in the pulse that gives us life. A heart cell, for example, is unique in that it produces a strong electromagnetic signal that radiates out beyond itself. The electromagnetic field produced by the heart radiates outward some twelve to fifteen feet beyond our bodies. In effect, we are in constant contact or relationship with other human beings and energy-vibrating life forms at all times. One, in fact, can take two live heart cells, keep them apart and when they begin to die, as evidenced by fibrillation, bring them into close proximity to each other and they will resume their regular life producing pulsation. Not only is cellular relationship indicated here, but also the awareness and understanding of each cell to each other is evidenced and critical to life. What is most important to understand is that the electromagnetic energy of the cells carries information or awareness.

What the ancient Africans of the Nile Valley, the Kemites, called the "Intelligence of the Heart" was, in fact, an intricate dialog between the electromagnetic fields generated by the knowing cells in our hearts, minds and bodies and the electromagnetic energy fields in the world at large and selected energy fields found in our particular time, place and spatial experiences.

The African is distinguished by a particular consciousness, which is reflected in a special capacity for having intelligence of the mind and heart. Every knowable and perceivable object in the natural universe is a hieroglyph of Divine consciousness; i.e., comprehension and imagination. The Divine consciousness is more than thinking, feeling and awareness. It is potentiality contained in itself. As potentiality contained in itself, the entire universe, as a never-ending totality of possibilities, is consciousness. Consciousness is, in effect, the intelligent energy of the Divine. The spectrum of consciousness includes numerous levels, which differ in degree of frequency and density. In fact, the configuration of matter is determined by the level of consciousness. Level is indicated by vibration. Consciousness is inscribed in and determines the nature of every organism. Each animal, each species of plant, each mineral and each of their respective components are conscious energy vibrating at different speeds. In terms of human beings, one vibratory level becomes heart. Another vibration level becomes liver, another will become lung, another the synergetic being known as human. The variety of so-called races of humanity, which are biologically organized in essentially the same way, are also made distinct by the degree of differential organic vibration.

At the human level, consciousness is always a collective experience and passes from one collective generation to the next. Like the energy or vibration indicative of it, consciousness is never destroyed. In fact, it is the reincarnation of consciousness, as psyche, that constitutes the reincarnation of a person. A reincarnated person is a new person only in the carnal sense. The collective consciousness or what some call racial consciousness is constantly renewed in each succeeding generation. The reincarnated are different from the preceding generation only to the extent that the consciousness of the "next" generation vibrates at a new or different speed. African people, as a particular vibratory phenomena, reincarnate consciousness from one generation to the next irrespective of geographical location. Many of the great deep thinkers throughout the African world have spoken through this sense of consciousness, this force in motion. A consciousness that is in-born. "We are Africans not because we are born in Africa, but because Africa is born in us."[3] The Africa born in us is that in-born sense of consciousness, that vibratory fire force in motion that is complete in and of itself yet continually emerging to become the source and the consequence of living.

Consciousness is the essence, energy, expression and experience of Black spirit in the form of awareness, knowing, comprehension and existing/being. It is that which allows African people to reflect, respond, project and create from before and beyond the time of one's experience. Consciousness is intricately merged with spirit. It is the "knowing" of what a knowing and knowable spirit knows. The hermeneutics of consciousness, in a sense, determines or allows African people to conceive of and understand themselves as fundamentally spirit. Having an awareness of oneself as spirit, in turn, allows one to access realms of knowing that are not limited to just cognition or perception. It connects knowing and awareness to both the perceivable (visible) and the unperceivable (invisible). Hence, consciousness as an eternal living spirit is not bound by time, space or place. It connects knowing, awareness, and comprehension to the universal and the Divine. Consciousness is, therefore, that which gives congruity between the supra-inter-and inner-realms of being. It allows for the retention of ancestral sensibilities that interpret and give meaning to contemporary experiences. It is consciousness, as awareness, knowing and comprehension, and its subsequent meaning that gives particular content, context and contour to Black character and style. The desire to always function at a higher level (the sense of excellence) is characteristic of the consciousness of African people from time immemorial.

Consciousness functions as both retentive and residual knowing and awareness. As retentive energy, consciousness allows for the remembering or retention of all previous information, experience and ideas. As residual energy, consciousness provides a conduit or circuit for tapping into the residue of human knowing and awareness, thereby, and creates new knowing and awareness.

The vibratory spiraling of African consciousness towards ascension is best understood as self-generating energy. In the ancient Nile Valley, it is this sense of consciousness that is reflected in the *Book of Knowing the Evolutions of Ra* where the God Neb-er-tcher records the creation and birth of the Gods in noting, "I am he who evolved himself under the form of the God Khepera. I, the evolver of the evolutions and developments, which came forth from my mouth... I laid the foundations of all things by my will and all things evolved themselves there from." The same consciousness, the sense of essence, energy and experience is further symbolized in the ancient Nile valley text which states, "Kheper-i, Kheper Kheperu, Kheper-kuy, M Keperu, (When I Became, The Becoming Became, I have Become in Becoming). This consciousness of evolving the evolutions, of vibrating knowable and knowing energy, and of the pulse that gives us life is continually reincarnated in Black awareness or consciousness. It is found in the logos of "advancement" in the framing and motivation for establishing the National Association for the ADVANCEMENT of Colored People or in the "improvement" of the Universal Negro IMPROVEMENT Association or in the "Lift Every Voice and Sing" of the Negro National Anthem. Finally, the consciousness of W. E. B. DuBois speaks directly to the complexity of the vibratory radiance. He immortalized it as the "double consciousness," the "two unreconciled strivings; two warring ideals in one dark body, whose dogged strength alone keeps it from being torn asunder." Consciousness, as defined, allowed and still allows Black people to draw upon a meaning of being that is antithetical to the socially constructed objectifications of negation, nullification and dehumanization. However, without understanding the vibratory energy that configured itself into being, becoming and belonging to African people, one is incapable, for instance, of fully comprehending why DuBois, Garvey, Truth, and other Black leaders and lay people alike react to and determine reality in a unique and special way.

An African centered understanding of consciousness requires one to meet the challenge of awareness, knowing, comprehension, and existing through the realms of knowing and levels of awareness that are the very same aspects of being that one is attempting to define. Consciousness is the knowing and knowable vibratory fire force that is the never ending totality of possibilities emerging from itself.

Spiritness

Included in the African notion of essentialism or spiritness is the belief that the complexity (immaterial and material) of being a person gives one an intrinsic human value and that the person is, in fact, a process characterized by the divinely governed laws of essence, appearing, perfecting and compassion.[4] The concept of "spirit" or "essence" as defined by African thought[5] further suggests that the examination of African-American psychology should be guided by strategies of knowing that allow for the examination of the continuation and refinement, across time, space and place, of the African conceptualization of human beingness.

Ngubane[6] argues that the African understanding of the person is a "protein" evaluation of the human being, which flowed into Nile Valley high culture of the Ancient Kemites and subsequently created clusters of similar conceptions all over Africa. What is recognized as African culture and civilization is the combined social conventions and inventions emerging from a common African meaning of the person.

Constructs designed to understand the meaning and functioning of energy could prove helpful in understanding African and African-American metaphysics and psychology. Notions may prove helpful like: "retentions," the act or power of remembering or retaining an aspect, feature or part of something or idea; "residuals," the act or power that constitute the residue or remaining value after repeated usage of an original form or process; "resonance," the state of a system in which a vibration or energy field is produced in response to an external stimulus; resonance, occurrences in one object when the characteristics or qualities of an external or neighboring system or subject is the same as nearly the same as the qualities or features of the target system; and, "reverberations," the persistence of a phenomenon or act, like sound after its source has stopped, caused by multiple reflections of the thing in a closed space. These notions may serve to aid in unfolding our understanding of African/Black psychology.

How do we explain and/or understand those practices, products and/or protocols that are retained and/or those inventions that are shaped or stimulated by the retentive idea or energy found in African-American music (gospel, jazz, rhthym and blues. hip-hop); in the method of religious ceremonies; the protocols of eldership; dietary habits/cooking attitude and style; and language structure and use like Ebonics? If we posit that there are attitudes, beliefs, values and practices that remain from or are carried over from original African prototypes; e.g., hands-up in church, high five sign in sports, the Almighty look, child-rearing practices, the African-American aesthetic, the use of signs and symbols. What impact do they have for our sense of psychological well-being? Similarly, the state of being—thinking, feeling or doing - produced, as resonating forms in response to unknown stimuli whose characteristics or qualities are the same or nearly the same as the original African form are found in behavioral practices like the stance of the left foot forward; the use of "Yo," thought or will which takes form and comes from itself; the use of "Heka"; improvisation in most performances such as music and sports; the African-American aesthetic; Black women's neck motion and hands on her hips. How do we explain their seemingly spontaneous appearance in time and space?

It is clear to me that the epistemological dilemma faced by Black Psychology is bound up in the inability of our Black psychologists to truly understand the invisible world of spirit with models and concepts derived from our comprehension of the visible/physical world. Our charge, or at least the charge I have given myself, is to break the code of African spirit(ness) and consciousness on African terms. It seems to me that a full and complete development or re-ascension of African psychology will require a language and logic driven by an explication of spirit and consciousness. It is in the translation of the "Rosetta Stone" of African Spirit and consciousness and the utilization of our spirit(ness) as the medium of human comprehension and understanding that I accept as the challenge for my future work.

[2000]

Post Narrative:
My Father, Dr. Wade W. Nobles

Halima B. Nobles

Background and Early Education

My father, Wade W. Nobles, was born to Annie Mae Cotton and John Nobles on June 6, 1945, the youngest of six children. A native of Boston, Massachusetts he attended several primary schools in the area including Sarah J. Baker Elementary, Patrick T. Campbell Jr. High School, and Boston Latin for three months and Boston English schools through eleventh grade. He finished high school at Oakland High School in Oakland, California. It was at this period in his life when he experienced his first racial experience. In the third grade there was one particular white boy with whom my father was appointed to the prestigious job of student crossing guard. This was a position of authority and power. According to my father, he could make adults stop their cars and direct other children to move at his command. He remembers the incident that prompted his first racial experience:

> The white boy didn't take his job very seriously and he kept playing around. He would start playing tag, hit me, and then run out of retaliatory reach. As a result of his playing and teasing me all the while claiming friendship, I "saluted" him as I had with my other friends and called him a "n...". No sooner than the word came out of my mouth, the white boy stopped in his tracks, turned on his heals, looked coldly in my eyes and corrected me. He matter-of-factly told me that I was the "n...," not him.

It was at that instant that my father realized that "n..." was a derogatory term reserved by white people to use on Black people in order to make themselves feel superior and powerful.

My father also likes to tell the story that my grandmother began working at the Boston State Hospital for the Mentally Ill in Mattapan, Massachusetts the year he was born and in this pre-television age she nurtured my Uncle Henry and my father with stories of "crazy" Black people, white doctors and the confusion she witnessed in the treatment and mistreatment of the mentally ill. Because of these stories my father says he began his Black Psychology training from birth.

As a young child he became so enthralled by watching people that he appeared to be in trance. Many people even advised my grandmother to take him to see a specialist because something was obviously wrong with him. In many ways, my father believes, that his early childhood experiences both good and bad are indicators that he was bred to search for an understanding of the human condition of Black people. His path from childhood has been seeking an understanding of the human spirit and in so doing assist in the re-ascension of African Psychology.

Adolescence and Early Adult Experience

As a young boy my father had older family members who were involved in gangs. He never actually joined, but he hung around a lot with his cousins in the gang circle. This was a good affiliation for my father because the gangs did not bother him or try to recruit him. The association provided him with a deeper understanding of his surroundings. It also taught him about everyday psychological influences, pressures, loyalties, and courage.

All of my father's schooling in Boston had been at gender-segregated schools. Imagine his awkwardness when he moved 3000 miles away to Oakland, California as a teenager. His social skills were not very great in Oakland High School. Instead of talking and interacting with the girls in school, his shyness led him to the library. He spent most of his time reading and studying, improving his grade point average and college eligibility. When college became an option, he had a meeting with his high school counselor and told him he wanted to become a psychologist. Instead of providing him with the proper course sequence in readiness for college, his counselor advised him that Black people did not become psychologists and programmed him into Woodshop. This would have devastated most high school students, but my father did not let that counselor's advice break him or his dreams and he went to college.

While attending Merritt College in Oakland, he met Huey P. Newton and Bobby Seals, founders of the Black Panther Party, attended school with him.

My father recalls reading one thing about Black people during his primary education, which was that Black people were slaves, and that Abraham Lincoln freed them. Instinctively, he knew that Black people were more than that and aspired to find out about Black greatness. Toward the end of high school he read about Greeks, Romans, and Persians, but nothing more about Black people. Now he realizes that many of the stories he read about Greeks, Romans, and Persians were actually about Black people even though those stories did not make that fact obvious.

Graduate Studies

Soon enough my father's professional dreams seemed closer to reality when his professor at Merritt College, Dr. Sylvia Obradovitch asked him to work as a teaching assistant for her course dealing with psychology and people of color. After completing his Associate Degree in Behavioral and Social Sciences, he went on to pursue his Bachelor's degree from San Francisco State University where he participated in the student strike that closed the university down. At a time when the Black population on campus was minimal, the Black leadership stepped forward in support of the students, such as Dr. Carlton Goodlett, editor of the *Sun Reporter*. My father clearly remembers the words of advice received from Dr. Goodlett. He told him that instead of making bombs, he should pursue his doctoral degree because he would be more powerful teaching Black people than by blowing up buildings.

There were other encouraging people to come in contact with my father. One in particular, William Thornton, encouraged his psychological studies, but advised him to study Physics and Statistics, as well. After years of being told he was not smart enough, my father was frightened by the ideas of Physics and Statistics. As a side note, Physics was the most exciting and interesting subject he has studied.

At San Francisco State University there were only two Black students in his Psychology classes. My father realized that hardly anything he was taught applied to him or to his community. He affiliated himself with the Black Psychologists on campus. Two of them, Dr. Joseph White and Dr. Gerald West, took him under their wings. It was Dr. White who gave him the opportunity to first teach a fledgling new course called "Black Psychology, (circa 1966-67). White guided and advised the Black student Psychology Club and suggested he attend a psychologists' convention in San Francisco. It was at that APA convention where my father first met Black psychologists, Bob Williams, Anna Jackson, Charles Thomas, Bob Green, and Henry Tomes.

There were others who had a profound influence on him while he was studying at San Francisco State. They included Amiri Baraka, Sonia Sanchez, and Dr. Nathan Hare, all hired on as lecturers after the student strike. Dr. Hare once told my father that being a Black scholar meant that you also have to be a fighter. My father has held onto those words ever since that time.

After receiving his Bachelor's degree from San Francisco State, my father went on to apply to Stanford University in Palo Alto, California for Graduate school. Stanford was a different kind of school. The faculty instilled in the students that they were the best and the brightest because Stanford had accepted them. My father remembers that Stanford's Psychology Department hosted "Sherry Hours" once a week for the students to interact with the faculty to discuss how smart the students were and how great the faculty was. Before my father entered the program there was only one Black student in the Graduate program. However, the year my father was accepted into the program, there were a total of four students in the program, the most in the history of Stanford at that time. There was a number of good white faculty members in the Psychology Department. Two Black faculty were also added in the department at that time, Cedric Clark (later to become Syed Katib) and Philip McGee. My father would get together with these two men. As friends and intelligent scholars they would discuss various ideas about Black Psychology. After Na'im Akbar joined their union,

Society for the Study of African Sciences (SSAS), was formed. The intent of this union was to branch away from Westernized thinking and re-establish the field of African science. As more Black faculty and students came to Stanford, my father recalls that they would go to the home of Cedric Clark to eat fried chicken and drink wine. This was a support mechanism between the Black people, faculty and students, at Stanford. They would meet socially as well as academically, by critiquing each other's work.

The other influence at Stanford included Dr. St Clair Drake. He advised my father to write a grant and do research in Africa. Dr. Drake presented my father with an opportunity to travel to Ghana, West Africa in 1971 to study psychological trance states with Traditional Priests and Priestesses.

Professional Life and Career

After completing his doctoral degree in 1972, my father applied for two post-doctoral programs, one at the University of California, Berkeley in the Anthropology Department and the other at the Langley Porter Psychological Institute. My father spent one year at UC Berkeley as an independent scholar attached to the Anthropology Department. It was at this time that he began to study more in depth into the areas of African philosophy and traditional religious systems.

He began his working career at Westside Community Mental Health Center in San Francisco. At Westside, he was responsible for writing grants and conducting research on Black family life. In this position, my father united with Bill Hayes, Thomas Hilliard, Asa Hilliard, and Patricia Butler to form a consultant company called The Urban Institute. The research at Westside was limited to mental health and my father wanted to do more beyond conventional mental health notions and explore the liberation of the African mind and the worldwide development of African people. Later he established the Institute for the Advanced Study of Black Family Life and Culture, Inc. with the collaboration and inspiration of his two life-long colleagues, Lawford Goddard and William Cavil. The Institute has served as the incubator for his best and most creative thinking, programmatic ideas and intellectual development.

He returned as a professor to San Francisco State University. My father's career has come full circle. It was at San Francisco State where he first attended the American Psychological Convention meeting with Bob Williams, Anna Jackson, Charles Thomas, Bob Greene, Henry Tomes and many more great individuals. It was at that chance meeting that inevitably produced the need for an independent, autonomous organization of Black psychologists. Other associations and involvements; i.e., regularly presenting his theories and analyses at First World in Harlem, ASCAC, NCBS and educational systems and Black professional organizations throughout the US, Great Britain, Japan, the West Indies and Africa, have continued to shape my father's professional growth and development.

Presidency of ABPsi

Bob Williams asked my father to run for President of ABPsi. Dr. Williams pointed out to my father the significance of the moment. At that time, my father was the only founding member of the Association who had not served as its president and if he accepted the honor of running for the presidency his administration would symbolize the ending of the founding era of ABPsi. My father accepted Dr. Williams' persuasion and served as ABPsi's 27th President.

As ABPsi's President my father established an international agenda: "The Maafa, Media and the Mind: Keys to Illuminating the African Spirit" for the association. My father encouraged his fellow Black psychologists to use their professional skills and expertise to reawaken the African essence, force and power that is African beingness in order to support and respond to an agenda. The agenda directed the association to engage in serious and on-going discussions and analyses designed to understand the forces that debilitate and destroy African people mentally, physically and spiritually. My father's leadership of ABPsi attempted to focus on the responsibility of Black Psychologists to clarify and claim the authority for defining the meaning of African human being ness and the process of healing the whole race.

He specifically challenged his colleagues to recognize how important and critical it was for Black psychologists to continue to accept the challenge of dedicating their abilities, skills and resources to the higher purpose of liberating the African mind, empowering the African character and illuminating and living the African spirit. And by so doing, he argued, "We, Black psychologists, will provide the scientific and therapeutic analyses of the systematic and systemic physical, mental and spiritual destruction and devastation experienced by the African community as a consequence of living in the United States and, simultaneously, explicate the resonant power of the spirit resulting from being, becoming and belonging to Africa."

As the President of ABPsi, my father reminded Black Psychologists that, regardless of sub-specialty, they were "the healers" and as such must have an African centered vision and praxis. In introducing Marimba Ani's concept of the Maafa, he also introduced to the Association the notions of *Funda dia Tambukusa*, a genetic package, that as African people gives us healing power, (*Lendo Kiandiakina*), which Black psychologists, must strive to understand and master.

In 1995, my father accepted the invitation to formally participate in the establishment of a collaborative venture between ABPsi and Ghana National Association of Traditional Healers (GNATH) and offered for review, discussion and adoption an "African Healers Association Covenant" that was designed to guide mutual commitment to the promotion and advancement of traditional African healing sciences and the mutual exchange of skills, techniques and experiences relative to the healing of Africans in Ghana and the United States. Upon deeper reflection, my father says that while still unfulfilled, he believes that the African Healers Association Covenant will be more significant than initially imagined because it represents the coming together of African healers in Ghana (GNATH) and the United States (ABPsi). My father says, "through the union we may stimulate the *Ngolo Zandiakina* (self healing potential) which resides in the power and everlasting integrity of the African spirit and in so doing, reproduce and refine the best of African science and healing techniques."

Distinguised Psychologist

My father was inducted into a special community of ABPsi's Distinguished Psychologists because of a long history of critical and essential work in the field of Black Psychology and Mental Health.

In addition to being acknowledged as a Distinguished Black Psychologist by the ABPsi, my father was also the first recipient of the ABPsi Annual Award in "recognition of Outstanding Scholarly Research," the "Award for Excellence, Scholarship, and Dedication in the Study of African Peoples," given by the Black Student Psychological Association (1977); the "Award for Recognition and Outstanding Scholarly Research on the Black Family" given by the Bay Area National Hampton Alumni Association (1982) and the recipient of the "Congressional Award for Outstanding Contribution to the Community, the State and the Nation," by the 99th Session of United States Congress (1985).

Role Models and Heroes: The Three Johns

When asked about the role models in his life, my father said that he has three "heroes" named John that he considers his significant role models.

The First John: My father's first "hero" was John Cotton, my paternal great grandfather and his grandfather. He proudly says that John Cotton who was born in 1898 shared his same birthday, June 6th. My father says that he grew up hearing stories about how John Cotton protected his family and took no mess from anybody. One story that my father likes to tell is one his mother told all of her children about her father. The family story is that John Cotton and his wife, Seth Lee Baston, lived in Macon, Georgia, and had 8 children (six boys and 2 girls). My father says that one day one of his mother's brothers, his uncle, was accused of disrespecting a white person. My father remembers the story being that while in town his uncle looked too long at a white woman or showed some other sign of not keeping in his place so the local branch of the KKK decided to go out to the Cotton's place and teach "that boy" a lesson. My father relates:

That night they rode onto my great granddaddy's land and proceeded to terrorize the family by drinking, firing their weapons into the sky, and shouting all sorts of threats and obscenities. My grandfather was, however, ready. He had all of his family "loaded and cocked" and at his pre-arranged signal, they were to start firing at the terrorists. Granddaddy left out of the back door, crawled under the house and out into the midst of drunken white invaders. While hollering and getting more and more drunk as a prelude to their "teaching them n_ _ _ _ _ _ a lesson" by killing one or more of the Cotton clan, the white Klu Kluckers, as my mother called them, didn't notice Granddaddy crawling beneath their horses' legs and slitting the hind tendon of each horse whose whinnying went unnoticed. Then, Granddaddy gave the signal and all of the Cottons down to the youngest one big enough to point a gun commenced to shooting. Big Mama, my granddaddy's mother, Rachel Hayward, who was, we were told a full blooded Indian started to "hatcheting" everyone who fell from a horse. Those who weren't killed or wounded fled the property in total fear.

From that night on, my father was told that no one messed with John Cotton or his family. Around those parts, John Cotton was considered a "crazy N... and even the babies could shoot." My father said that what he learned from the stories about his grandfather and from watching John Cotton relate to all kinds of people was that one of the most important qualities of a black man was courage and intelligence and that the first and foremost responsibility of being a man was to love, defend, and protect your family. Nothing was more important than family.

The Second John: My father claims his own father, John Nobles, as his hero and role model. John Nobles was a big man, around 6'4" tall and weighed over 300 pounds. While a big man, John Nobles was soft spoken, loving and especially wise and caring. My father remembers how men in the community would always come by their house in Roxbury, the black inner district of Boston, on the weekends or on holidays simply to pay their respects to Big John whom they called "Tiny." My father, says he later learned that his father belonged to a Masonic Order and had some distant connection to Marcus Garvey's UNIA movement and that, he didn't know if these "respect visitors" were members of his father's lodge, the UNIA or just black men living in the community and giving respect.

While John Nobles passed when my father had just turned 13, my father remembers how important a presence his father was in life and even after his transition. He recalls with some joy his father's special brand of childrearing. He recalls how his father would give him and his brother, Henry, some household chore to do and say, "I'm going out, and when I get back this house better be clean or you better not be here and you better not be gone." Later with some maturity, my father says he figured out that his father understood the most important psychological key to good parenting, which is not to kill the spirit of children but to give them structure that allows them to grow and develop. Through his parental instructions, my grandfather respected his children as human beings, not just as children, and always gave them choice. According to my father, one always has choice and to deny one's ability to choose is to deny them freewill and by definition they are oppressed. John Nobles' particular instruction set up a problematic that guaranteed his children the power to choose. But more than simply choosing, the structure of his directive; i.e., do your chores or you better not be here and you better not be gone required that the only real choice they had was to do what was right. In his opinion this was pure parental genius.

He told of how if he or one of his siblings did something wrong they all got punished. There were many occurrences when he and his brother would be lack in their chores and did not take out the trash or clean the ashes from the stove; then, his father would whip everyone. Once, my father told me, his older sister, my Aunt Victoria, who was married, went out one night and returned home very late. John Nobles gave this "grown married woman" a "whoopin" and, when her new young husband tried to object and make the point that her daddy "can't give his wife no spanking," John Nobles proceeded to whip them both. My father lovingly recalled seeing his sister and her husband crying themselves to sleep with their infant baby nestled safely in between them.

My father said that what he has learned from being John Nobles' son is that "We have only one destiny. The failures and successes of each one of us belong to all of us. That as a family and as black people, we are completely and totally responsible for each other."

The Third John: My father's third hero and role model was Professor John Henrik Clarke. Professor Clarke has been a master teacher, friend, senior colleague, role model and intellectual father for my father. He recalls that, when he introduced the concept of "Jegna" into the discourse of Black Psychology and Africana studies, John Henrik Clarke was one of a small handful of Black scholar-activists who filled the criteria. John Clarke, as a "Jegna," was one of those special people who had been tested in struggle or battle; had demonstrated extraordinary and unusual fearlessness; had shown courage, diligence and dedication in protecting his people, land and culture; had always produced exceptionally high quality work and finally had dedicated his life to the protection, defense, nurturance and development of African people by advancing African people, place and culture.

While not realizing it at the time, my father believes that John Henrik Clarke passed the torch of "African Redemption" onto him while visiting the Elmina Slave Dungeon in Ghana. Professor Clarke was leading a group of African American people through the dungeon and teaching the truth of our experience in history. In the beginning of the tour, Professor Clarke singled out my father and asked him to read aloud the statement of the paramount chief of Elmina to the King of Portugal admonishing the foreigners to leave Africa in peace. My father says that at the time he thought about that moment as just a reading assignment. He now knows that in "the request" Professor Clarke was conferring upon him a life long assignment to join the ranks of African redemptionists, protectors and defenders. My father recalls visiting Professor Clarke's home in Harlem on several different occasions and during each visit being more amazed at Professor Clarke's personal library and how sharing he was of his knowledge and information. Professor Clarke knew his books like one knows an old friend. On one visit to Professor Clarke's home his visit was interrupted by a phone call from someone in charge of the production of the Budweiser African Kings poster series. My father marveled at the detail and precision in which Professor Clarke made corrections to the imaging of our African heritage.

My father says that Professor Clarke would often say to him, usually after he had presented at First World or ASCAC, "Man, when you going to write a big book." The question continually haunts my father as an unfinished assignment or incomplete grade given by his favorite and most important teacher. It was a source of pride and humility to have an intellectual giant like John Henrik Clarke believe that his scholarship was worthy and valuable continues to fortify my father's commitment to the work of African liberation and development.

My father recalls how he and his comrade-in-arms, Dr. Na'im Akbar would sit in the audience of lectures by Dr. Ben Jochanan and Professor Clarke like two scholars-in-training and critique their different styles, information, methods and impact. My father says he would always tell Dr. Akbar that when they grew up, he was going to be like Professor Clarke and Na'im was going to be like Dr. Ben.

My father says that what he learned from John Henrik Clarke was that scholarship is a long, careful, precise and deliberate process guided by a profound and deep "love" of one's people. John Henrik Clarke told my father that the one defining, binding and indispensable attribute of a Black scholar/teacher is "humility." Only in humility, Professor Clarke told my father, can the scholar or intellectual keep in balance the willingness to be a servant of his/her people and the clarity of vision to honestly speak and seek the truth regarding one's people.

My father had several other role models throughout his life like Marcus Garvey because he understood the psyche of Black people and he organized the largest independent movement of Black people. Malcolm X because he wanted to serve Black people without fulfilling his own personal needs. Frantz Fanon because he used Psychology to liberate the minds of Black people and he had the courage and knowledge to critique white people's insanity. My father also respects Kwame Nkrumah because he went home to Africa and tried to build an independent free African nation. My father holds Sojourner Truth in high regard because she said that Black people should be dead rather than be slaves and because she selflessly put her own life in jeopardy to try to help Black people.

AFTERWORD

Cheryl Tawede Grills

Despite the calls for the development of psychology as an international discipline, the amount of attention devoted to African psychology has been minimal though. Even in publications highlighting indigenous psychological perspective, Africa remains underrepresented. In formal psychological terms, Africa, north and south of Sahara, continues to be the dark and forgotten continent.[1]

In this work, *Seeking the Sakhu*, Mwalimu Nobles frames thirty years of his quest to explain "what is Black Psychology?" Dr. Nobles has consistently insisted and instructed us to "think deeply" about matters related to the psychology, culture, history, circumstance, and future of African people and that our work be "governed by a deep, profound and penetrating search, study and mastery of the processes of 'illuminating' the human spirit or essence, ergo, the Sakhu Sheti.[2] One of my fondest and most unnerving memories of Dr. Nobles in this regard was a simple question posed to me and Dr. Daryl Rowe at our paper presentation at the 1992 Council of Black Studies Conference held in Accra, Ghana. As we concluded the description of a model of African youth development called the Kusudi Saba based in part on the Nguzo Saba and current thinking on Black culture and psychology, Dr. Nobles simply asked "Where did you get the model from?" The point of his question had to do with the conceptual basis of model and theory development in Black and African Psychology. This earnest, simple, yet profoundly important question led to what for me became a fourteen year sojourn into the cultural reality of African traditional culture, philosophy, family life, medicine, and religion. The sojourn has been fruitful, but is far from over. Now, if Mwalimu should ask that question of any component of my work I have clear, definitive, answers grounded in an African worldview. *Me da wo ase* (Thank You), Nana.

Dr. Nobles' work has without question inspired and cultivated the "reascension of African Psychology". Each "sketch" in this compilation offers a vista into the heart and soul of African Psychology. Furthermore, it challenges us to stretch beyond the confines of our cerebral training in the Western tradition of knowledge production.

Cerebral intelligence needs opposition in order to function: we and the object, man and woman, yes and no, night and day...every living organism constituted; a ceaseless oscillation between birth and death, increase and decrease. It is "impossible for cerebral intelligence to conceive an abstraction without defining it by a concrete image...be aware of distinguishing moments of cerebral intelligence from moments of intelligence-of-the-heart...origin of the universe, one single source of energy, ...innumerable possibilities emerge."[3]

Dr. Nobles' work encourages intelligence and foresight of the heart if we are to recapture African Psychology. His work is consistent with many of the teachings as yet revealed in Kemetic teachings. For example, Kemetic thought instructs that intelligence-of-the-heart is purely a function of experienced innate consciousness and that the awakening of the consciousness will become "heart." We see a similar train of thought implied in Dr. Nobles' more recent discussions on consciousness.

Ancient Kemetic thought teaches us that the first four senses (vision, touch, smell, and taste) pass through the brain. The fifth sense, hearing, passes through the "heart" without speaking directly to the brain. It is the spiritual sense and the door to intelligence-of-the-heart. How do we come to an understanding of the deeper meaning of this teaching, and how do we use it to further our understanding of African world view and science? These are the queries that the trajectory of Dr. Nobles' work would lead us. From the tradition of our ancestors, one could argue that function does not create the organ and thought does not create consciousness. Again, mirroring the rich tradition of science and knowledge of our ancestors, Dr. Nobles' own work would argue that we must do more than simply cogitate and apply the principles of Aristotelian logic to the job of defining the essence, expression, and function of consciousness.

Seeking the Sakhu: Foundational Writings for an African Psychology represents both Dr. Nobles' commitment to the reclamation, reformation, and restoration of the African mind and his charge to the community of African-minded scholars to critique, extend, and apply this work to the liberation of the African mind, spirit, soul and condition. This necessitates reconstruction of an African worldview from which to pursue the generation of theory, conduct of research, and application of interventions aimed at liberation.

While very familiar with, influenced by, and conversant in Dr. Nobles' scholarship, I did not recognize until I read this anthology, that my own path in search of the rubric and character of African psychology was in fact a road well-traveled, and, obvious to me now, a necessary route to a conscious understanding and articulation of African Psychology. Ahead of their time and a little beyond some of our scholarly comfort zones, Dr. Nobles and other jegnoch cleared a path and led the way. This path, this necessary route includes:

●Deconstructing Western psychology by piercing its hegemonic veil of universalism, objectivity, and relevance;

• Recognizing that Black psychology is something more than a testament of the negative effects of racism on Black life in White America or the psychology of underprivileged peoples or the darker dimension of Western psychology;

• Engaging in critical thought and analyses of the historical and contextual factors that comprise Western and African socio-political realities;

• Immersing in and absorbing the critical thought, enquiry, and perspective of African philosophy, religion, medicine, and cultural studies;

• Pursuing with an unquenchable thirst the source and foundation of African psychology contained in ancient Kemetic thought and traditional African culture, thought, and practice—the last 600 years of traditional African medicine and religion;

• Identifying, exploring, and defining the nucleus of African Psychology—consciousness;

- Recognizing the relationship between consciousness and core human functions such as identity (To Be African or Not to Be) and sense of self; and

- Balancing theory and scholarship in answer to the ever-present call to address the practical needs of social justice, community and community development.

The experiential communality implied in this path reflects an African stream of consciousness that I believe is available to be shared by those who are willing to remove the blinders of Western imperialistic thought and science. To the extent we heed the call by Dr. Nobles to think deeply we will be capable of taking his work to the next level of African epistemology, theory development, and praxis. To heed the call, however, requires us to exercise the principle of courage mandated in the Association of Black Psychologists' Code of Ethics. To heed the call requires us to free our thinking of the shackles of Western thought and engage in this reclamation and restoration work as a process of experiential communality. In other words, we do the work within the community of our professional organizations, collegial partnerships, student-teacher collaborations, and community-professional collaborations. Just as Dr. Nobles instructs that experiential communality is "important in determining society's fundamental principles—its beliefs about the nature of man and what kind of society man should create for himself" it has equal importance in determining what emerges in the reclamation, reformation and restoration of African Psychology and the African mind.

I encourage us to be mindful of what we have in the work of Dr. Nobles and other trailblazing African scholars in our midst— "Learn with the left hand while you still have the right one." Dr. Nobles has taught us much about African Psychology and African Centered thought, yet there is much left for him to teach us and for us to learn from him. The impact of his work on my own research and practice in clinical and community psychology is evident in all of its spheres, namely, substance abuse prevention and treatment models, theories, research and interventions; consciousness research, theory development on African Psychology; community psychology research and program development.

His impact on the field of Black and African Psychology and Africana Studies is without question well beyond the scope of this discussion to itemize. The impact of his work on the future of African Psychology can be summed up in the following. Responding to the moral mandate of divine law as ascribed to him, Dr. Nobles lived his own process of being and becoming and consequently sealed his belonging to the family of African people as he leaves with us a legacy of scholarship central to the liberation of the African spirit. His legacy is our moral mandate to think deeply, feel with the atenka and rhythm of African ways of knowing, and see with eyes African. If we can rise to the occasion, then we would have achieved "divine law in action".

Dr. Nobles' work transcends the artificial boundaries of Western academics and instructs us to integrate multiple areas of scholarship including psychology, philosophy, anthropology, religious studies, medicine, physics, biology, mythology, literature, art, political science, public health, economics, and history. It will be important to future developments in African Psychology that we continue in this vein. Among the critical contributions of Jegna Nobles is the moral call to African psychologists to consider their role in the perpetuation and consequences of racism, colonialism, imperialism and the Western hegemonic control of information and knowledge. At a minimum, Dr. Nobles' work challenges and broadens traditional Black Psychology's approach to the study and treatment of African people. But more, it stimulates new thought about the premises of Black Psychology and the rudiments of African Psychology. For example, we say "God" and do not know what this means; we say "spirit" and do not understand this abstraction; we say "energy" and know nothing whatsoever of its nature. We see effects and attribute to them a cause which is sometimes God, sometimes Spirit-Word, and sometimes energy.[4] These are the queries required of the serious student of Dr. Nobles' work.

He has given us much. He has more yet to give. It is incumbent upon us to take this work to the next level of deep and penetrating thought, reflection, and action. I believe the ancestors are saying to Jegna Nobles of his life's quest: "You have done well. You are indeed an elder and one day when your work is done, you will surely be welcomed into the realm of ancestorhood."

END NOTES

Foreword

i. Nobles, Wade. "Psychometrics and African-American Reality: a Question of Cultural Antimony." In Asa G. Hilliard III, (ed.) *Testing African American Students*. Chicago: Third World Press pp 15-25, 1995.

ii. Nobles, Wade. "The Infusion of African and African American Content: a question of content and intent." Hilliard, Asa G.; Payton-Stewart, Lucretia; and Williams, Larry Obadele (1994) *The Infusion of African and African American Content in School Curriculum.* Chicago: Third World Press pp 5-26, 1994.

iii. Guthrie, Robert V. *Even the Rat was White: A Historical View of Psychology* (2nd ed.), Boston: Allyn and Bacon, 1998.

iv. Jones, Reginald L. *Black Psychology: Fourth Edition.* Hampton, Va.: Cobb and Henry, 2004.

v. Burlew, Kathleen A.; Banks, Curtis W.; McAdoo, Harriette Pipes; & ya Azibo, Daudi Ajani (Eds.). *African American Psychology: Theory, Research, and Practice.* Newbury Park, CA.: SAGE publications, (992.

vi. Azibo. *African Psychology.* Red Sea Press, 1996.

vii. Kambon, Kobi K. *Misorientation.* Tallahassee: Nubian Nations Publications, 2003.

viii. Guthrie, Robert V. *Even the Rat was White: A Historical View of Psychology* (2nd ed.), Boston: Allyn and Bacon, 1998.

ix. Grills, Cheryl Tawede. in "African Psychology," In Reginald L. Jones *Black Psychology: Fourth Edition.* Hampton, Va.: Cobb and Henry, 2004.

x. Akbar, Na'im. *Breaking the Chains of Psychological Slavery.* Tallahassee: Mind Productions and Associates, 1996.

xi. King, Lewis (Ed.). *African Philosophy: Assumptions and Paradigms for Research on Black Persons.* Los Angeles: Fanon Research and Development Center, 1976.

xii. Schmidt, Jeff. *Disciplined Minds: A Critical Look at Salaried Professionals and the Soul-Battering Systems that Shapes their Lives.* New York: Rowman and Littlefield, 2002.

xiii. Kuhn, Thomas. *The Structure of Scientific Revolutions.* Chicago: University of Chicago Press, 1970.

xiv. Smith, Linda T. *Decolonizing Methodologies: Research and Indigenous Peoples.* New York: Zed Borders Ltd and the University of Otago Press. Dunedin, New Zealand, 1999.

Sketch One

1. Like most words that refer to things African, the English usage of the word "tribe" has mixed connotations. In addition, one must recognize that the defining characteristic for a tribe was completely alien and arbitrary. As British and American anthropologists changed their definitions of what constituted a tribe, so changed the physical size of the tribe's membership. Although Africa can be considered a cultural entity, most African Americans came from West Africa. While there is diversity, the author assumes that there are unifying cultural themes. For a rather different point, however, see R. A. Lavine, Personality and Change in J.N. Padden and E.W. Soja, The African Experience, Vol. 1. (Evanston, Il.: Northwestern University Press, 1970). For present purposes, West Africa is seen as extending from Senegal to Angola.

2. J.S. Mbiti. *African Religions and Philosophies.* Anchor Books, Doubleday. Garden City, New York, 1970; M.J. Herskovits. *The Myth of the Negro Past.* Beacon Press, Boston, MA 1958.

3. Note that African philosophy is for the most part unwritten and has no conceptual terms as we know them. Therefore, the understanding of African philosophy is accomplished by analyzing the traditional structures reflected in tales, proverbs, myths, and such. It is these, which in turn reflect the structural concepts of the philosophy.

4. J.S. Mbiti. *African Religions and Philosophies.* Anchor Books, Doubleday. Garden City, New York, 1970.

5. J.S. Mbiti. *African Religions and Philosophies.* Anchor Books, Doubleday. Garden City, New York, 1970.

6. D. Forde. *African Worlds.* London: Oxford University Press, 1954.

7. D. Forde. *African Worlds.* London: Oxford University Press, 1954.

8. D. Forde. *African Worlds.* London: Oxford University Press, 1954.

9. D. Forde. *African Worlds.* London: Oxford University Press, 1954.

10. J.S. Mbiti. *African Religions and Philosophies.* Anchor Books, Doubleday. Garden City, New York, 1970.

11. J.S. Mbiti. *African Religions and Philosophies.* Anchor Books, Doubleday. Garden City, New York, 1970.

12. D. Forde. *African Worlds.* London: Oxford University Press, 1954.

13. Africa is a very large continent and there are some differences in the concept of time in different areas. For example, hunters have a different conception of time than those in farming communities. In the present paper, the author is making certain simplifying assumptions for purposes of exposition.

14. J.S. Mbiti. *African Religions and Philosophies.* Anchor Books, Doubleday. Garden City, New York, 1970.

15. J.S. Mbiti. *African Religions and Philosophies.* Anchor Books, Doubleday. Garden City, New York, 1970.

16. J.S. Mbiti. *African Religions and Philosophies.* Anchor Books, Doubleday. Garden City, New York, 1970.

17. J.S. Mbiti. *African Religions and Philosophies.* Anchor Books, Doubleday. Garden City, New York, 1970.

18. J.S. Mbiti. *African Religions and Philosophies.* Anchor Books, Doubleday. Garden City, New York, 1970.

19. D. Forde. *African Worlds.* London: Oxford University Press, 1954.

20. D. Forde. *African Worlds.* London: Oxford University Press, 1954.

21. J.S. Mbiti. *African Religions and Philosophies.* Anchor Books, Doubleday. Garden City, New York, 1970.

22. J.S. Mbiti. *African Religions and Philosophies.* Anchor Books, Doubleday. Garden City, New York, 1970.

23. J.S. Mbiti. *African Religions and Philosophies.* Anchor Books, Doubleday. Garden City, New York, 1970.

24. J.S. Mbiti. *African Religions and Philosophies.* Anchor Books, Doubleday. Garden City, New York, 1970.

25. J.S. Mbiti. *African Religions and Philosophies.* Anchor Books, Doubleday. Garden City, New York, 1970.

26. Primitive is used here in the original sense (without negative connotations)—that is, primary, first, early.

27. P. Bohannan. *Africa and Africans.* New York: American Museum of Science Books, 1964.

28. A. Werner. *Structure and Relationship of African Languages.* London: Kegan Paul, 1925.

29. P. Bohannan. *Africa and Africans.* New York: American Museum of Science Books, 1964.

30. P. Bohannan. *Africa and Africans.* New York: American Museum of Science Books, 1964.

31. In this case, behavioral tools—that is, languages.

32. M. Bloch. *The Historians Craft.* Translated by Peter Putnam. New York: Knopf, 1953.

33. Lorenzo Turner. "African Survivals in the New World with Special Emphasis on the Arts." *Africa Seen by American Negroes.* Paris: Presence Africaine, 1958.

34. Joseph White. "Guidelines for Black Psychologists." *The Black Scholar*, 1970, Vol.1, 52-57.

35. Melville Jean Herskovits. *The New World Negro*, Melville J. Herskovits; ed. by Frances S. Herskovits. Bloomington; London: Indiana Univ. Press, 1966.

36. D. Forde. *African Worlds*. London: Oxford University Press, 1954.

Sketch Two

1. R.A. de Lubicz Schwaller. *Symbol and the Symbolic: Ancient Egypt, Science and the Evolution of Consciousness*, Inner Traditions International, New York, 1978.

2. R.A. de Lubicz Schwaller. *Symbol and the Symbolic: Ancient Egypt, Science and the Evolution of Consciousness*, Inner Traditions International, New York, 1978.

3. R.A. de Lubicz Schwaller. *Symbol and the Symbolic: Ancient Egypt, Science and the Evolution of Consciousness*, Inner Traditions International, New York, 1978.

4. Paul Macleans. In Carl Sagans, *The Dragon of Eden*, 1977.

5. Cheikh Anta Diop. *The Afrikan Origin of Civilization: Myth or Reality*, Westport, Lawrence Hill & company, 1967.

6. Jacob Carruthers."Orientation and Problems in Redemption of Ancient Egypt," *Journal of Black Studies*, San Francisco State University, Black Studies Department, Vol. 1, 2, 1983.

7. R.T. Clark, *Myth and Symbol in Ancient Egypt*, London: Thames and Hudson, 1959.

8. Chancelor Williams. *The Destruction of Black Civilization: Great Issues of Race from 4500 BC to 2000 AD*. Third World Press, Chicago, 1976.

9. H. Frankfurt, et al. *The Intellectual Adventure of Ancient Man*. University of Chicago Press, Chicago, 1946.

10. George James. *Stolen Legacy*. Julian Richardson Associates Publishers, San Francisco, California, 1976.

11. H. Frankfurt, et al. *The Intellectual Adventure of Ancient Man.* University of Chicago Press, Chicago, 1946.

12. Wallis E.A. Budge. *The Egyptian Book of the Dead: The Papyrus of Ani.* Diver Publications, Inc. New York, 1967.

13. H. Frankfurt, et al. *The Intellectual Adventure of Ancient Man.* University of Chicago Press, Chicago, 1946.

14. Wade W. Nobles. "Standing in the River, Transformed and Transforming: The Reascension of Black Psychology" submitted for publication, Race Relations Abstracts, 1984.

15. Wade W. Nobles. "African Philosophy: Foundations for Black Psychology" in Reginald Jones (ed) *Black Psychology*, submitted for publication, Race Relations Abstract, 1984.

16. Na'im Akbar. "Mental Disorders Among African-Americans" *Black Books Bulletin*, Vol. 7.2, pp. 18-25. 1981.

17. Cedric X. *Voodoo or I.Q.: An Introduction to African Psychology*, Institute of Positive Education, Chicago, IL. 1976.

18. Na'im Akbar, 1975; J. A. Baldwin. "Afrikan (Black) Psychology: Issues and Synthesis." Unpublished Paper, Florida A&M, 1980; G. Jackson. "The Origin and Development of Black Psychology: Implications for Black Studies and Human Behavior." *Studies Africaine*, Volume 1.3, pp. 271-292. 1976; Wade W. Nobles. "Afrikan Philosophy: Foundations for Black Psychology," in Reginald Jones (ed), *Black Psychology*, Harper and Row: New York, NY. Pp. 18-32, 1972; L. Semaj. "Meaningful Male/Female Relationships in the State of Declining Sex-Ratio," *Black Books Bulletin*, Vol. 6.4, pp. 4-10, 1980.

19. Basil Matthews, "Black Perspectives, Black Family and Black Community," paper presented to the Annual Philosophy Conference, Baltimore, MD, 1972.

20. Cedric X. *Voodoo or I.Q.: An Introduction to African Psychology*, Institute of Positive Education, Chicago, IL. 1976.

21. P. Temples, "Bantu Philosophy" *Presence Africaine*, 1959.

22. L. V. Thomas, A Senegalese Philosophical System: The Cosmology of the Joloh People. *Presence Africaine*, Vol. 4-5, 1961.

23. L. V. Thomas, A Senegalese Philosophical System: The Cosmology of the Joloh People. *Presence Africaine*, Vol. 4-5, 1961.

24. J. Mbiti, *African Religions and Philosophy*. Anchor Press, New York, NY, 1970; W.W Nobles, "Psychological Research and the Black Self Concept: A Critical Review." Journal of Social Issues, Vol. 29, 1, pp. 11-31, 1973.

25. K. Busia, "the Ashanti of the of the Gold Coast." in *African Worlds* (ed) Darryl Forde, London: Oxford University Press 1954.

Sketch Four

1. D. Phillip McGee, 1976

Sketch Five

1. It is believed that change in the aspect of culture is extremely slow and that the factors of culture may be totally resistant to change.

2. Wade W. Nobles, "Understanding Human Transformation: The Praxis of Science and Culture." Paper delivered to the Fanon Center International Conference on Human Development Models in Action: Praxis and History, Somalia, East Africa, June 1979.

3. Boxhill, 1979

4. M. Karenga, *Essays on Struggle: Position an Analysis*. San Diego: Kawaida Publications, 1978.

5. Amilcar Cabral, *Return to the Source: Selected Speeches of Amilcar Cabral*. New York: Monthly Review Press, 1973.

6. J.H. Howard, "Toward a Social Psychology of Colonialism." *Black Psychology* 1st Ed.
Ed. Reginald Jones. New York: Harper & Row Publishers, 1972.

7. Von Lue, 1975

8. M. Karenga, *Essays on Struggle: Position an Analysis.* San Diego: Kawaida Publications, 1978.

9. R. Rothschild. "Laws of Symbolic Mediation in the Dynamics of Self and Personality." *Annals of the New York Academic of Science,* Vol. 96, pp. 774-783, 1962.

10. R. Rothschild. "Laws of Symbolic Mediation in the Dynamics of Self and Personality." *Annals of the New York Academic of Science,* Vol. 96, pp. 778, 1962.

11. P. Ehrlich & R. Holm, *The Process of Evolution.* New York: McGraw Hill, 1963.

12. T. Dobzhansky, *Evolution, Genetics and Man.* John Wiley & Sons, Inc., New York, 1963.

Sketch Seven

1. R. Rothschild. "Laws of Symbolic Mediation in the Dynamics of Self and Personality." *Annals of the New York Academic of Science,* Vol. 96, pp. 774-783, 1962.

2. R. Rothschild. "Laws of Symbolic Mediation in the Dynamics of Self and Personality." *Annals of the New York Academic of Science,* Vol. 96, pp. 774-783, 1962.

3. R. Rothschild. "Laws of Symbolic Mediation in the Dynamics of Self and Personality." *Annals of the New York Academic of Science,* Vol. 96, pp. 775, 1962.

4. R. Rothschild. "Laws of Symbolic Mediation in the Dynamics of Self and Personality." *Annals of the New York Academic of Science,* Vol. 96, pp. 777, 1962.

5. R. Rothschild. "Laws of Symbolic Mediation in the Dynamics of Self and Personality." *Annals of the New York Academic of Science,* Vol. 96, pp. 778, 1962.

6. P. Ehrlich & R. Holm. *The Process of Evolution.* New York: McGraw Hill, 1963.

7. T. Dobzhansky. *Evolution*, Genetics and Man. JohnWiley & Sons, Inc., New York, 1963.

8. R. Rothschild. "Laws of Symbolic Mediation in the Dynamics of Self and Personality." Annals of the New York Academic of Science, Vol. 96, pp. 779, 1962.

9. P. Ehrlich & R. Holm. *The Process of Evolution*. New York: McGraw Hill, 1963.

10. R. Rothschild. "Laws of Symbolic Mediation in the Dynamics of Self and Personality." *Annals of the New York Academic of Science*, Vol. 96, pp. 781, 1962.

11. R. Rothschild. "Laws of Symbolic Mediation in the Dynamics of Self and Personality." *Annals of the New York Academic of Science*, Vol. 96, pp. 774-783, 1962.

12. L. Senghor, *Presence* Africaine, pp. 10, 1959.

13. J. Schaffer, *Philosophy of the Mind*, 19__

Sketch Eight

1. Albert Memmi. *The Colonizer and the Colonized*. Beacon Press: Boston, 1991.

2. D. Lewis. "Anthropology and Colonialism," *Current Anthropology*, Volume 14. University of Chicago Press: Chicago, 1973.

3. J. Galtuny. "*After Camelot*," The Rise and Fall of Project Camelot. Ed. Irving Hurowitz. Cambridge MIT Press, Cambridge, 1967.

4. WW. Nobles. "Psychological Research and the Black Self-Concept: A Critical Review," *Journal of Social Issues*. Vol. 29, No. 1, 1973.

5. C. Clark. "Black Studies on the Study of Black People," *Black Psychology*, Ed. Reginald Jones. Harper & Row: New York, 1972.

6. W.W. Nobles. "African Philosophy: Foundations for Black Psychology," *Black Psychology*, Ed. Reginald Jones. Harper & Row Publishers: New York, 1972.

7. J. S. Mbiti. *African Religions and Philosophy*. Anchor Press: New York, 1970.

8. J. S. Mbiti. *African Religions and Philosophy*. Anchor Press: New York, 1970.

9. W.W. Nobles. "African Philosophy: Foundations for Black Psychology," *Black Psychology*, Ed. Reginald Jones. Harper & Row Publishers: New York, 1972

10. S.K. Brown. "Empathic Process as a Dimension of African Reality," Unpublished Doctoral Dissertation, Stanford University, 1972.

11. B. Brown. "The Assessment of Self-Concept Among Four-Year Old Negro and White Children: A Comparative Study Using the Brown – IDS Self Concept Referents Test." Institute for Developmental Studies: New York, 1967.

12. E. Muhammad. *Message to the Black Man*. United Brothers Communication Systems: New Port News, Virginia, 1965.

13. WEB DuBois. *The Souls of Black Folks*, Essays and Sketches. Chicago Press, Chicago, 1973.

Sketch Nine

1. Andrew Billingsley. *Black Families in White America*. Prentice-Hall: Englewood Cliffs, NJ, 1968.

2. Talcott Parsons & Robert Bales. *Family, Socialization and Interaction Process*. The Free Press: New York, 1955

3. Andrew Billingsley. *Black Families in White America*. Prentice-Hall: Englewood Cliffs, NJ, 1968.

4. John S. Mbiti. *African Religions and Philosophies*. Anchor Press: New York, 1970.

5. Wade W. Nobles. "African Philosophy: Foundations for Black Psychology," *Black Psychology*, Ed. Reginald Jones. Harper & Row: New York, 1972.

6. John S. Mbiti. *African Religions and Philosophies.* Anchor Press: New York, 1970.

7. Melville J. Herskovits. *The Myth of the Negro* Past. Beacon Press: Boston, 1958

8. John S. Mbiti. *African Religions and Philosophies.* Anchor Press: New York, 1970.

9. John S. Mbiti. *African Religions and Philosophies.* Anchor Press: New York, 1970.

10. G.K. Osei. *The African Philosophy of Life.* The African Publication Society: London, 1970.

11. Franklin E. Frazier. Negro Youth at the Crossways: *Their Personality Development in the Middle States.* Prepared for the American Youth Commission, American Council on Education. Schocken Books: New York, 1940

12. Charles S. Johnson. *Growing Up Black in the Black Belt.* Washington, DC, 1941.

13. Allison Davis & J. Dollard. *Children of Bondage.* Washington, DC, 1940.

14. Melville J. Herskovits. *The Myth of the Negro Past.* Beacon Press: Boston, 1958

15. Cheikh A. Diop. "The Cultural Unity of Negro America: The Domains of Patriarchy and of Matriarchy in Classical Antiquity." *Presence Africaine.* Paris, France. 1959.

16. G.K. Osei. *The African Philosophy of Life.* The African Publication Society: London, 1970.

17. John W. Blassingame. *The Slave Community: Plantation Life in the Antebellum South.* Oxford University Press: New York, 1979.

18. David B. Davis. *The Problem of Slavery in Western Culture.* Cornell University Press: Ithaca, New York, 1966

19. Lorenzo J. Greene. *The Negro in Colonial New England.* Antheneum Press: New York, 1969.

20. Charles H. Cooley. *Human Nature and Social Order.* Scribners: New York, 1902.

Sketch Ten

1. J. Kennedy. Message from the President of the United States Relative to Mental Illness and Mental Retardation. 88th Congress, First Session, United States House of Representatives Document No. 58, U.S. Government Printing Office, 1963.

2. B. Bloom. *Community Mental Health: A Historical and Critical Analysis.* Morristown, New Jersey: General Learning Press, 1973.

3. Alfred Memmi. *The Colonizer and the Colonized.* Beacon Press: Boston, MA. 1991.

4. D.P. McGee and C. Clark. "Critical Elements to Black Mental Health." *Journal of Black Mental Health Perspectives.* August/September 1974.

5. D. Forde. *African Worlds: Studies in the Cosmological Ideas and Social Values of African People.* Oxford University Press: New York, 1954.

6. P. Temples. "Bantu Philosophy." *Presence Africaine: Paris*, 1959.

7. L.V. Thomas. "A Senegalese Philosophical System: The Cosmology of the Jolah People." *Presence Africaine*, Vol. 4-5, 1969.

8. J. Mbiti. *African Religious and Philosophy.* Anchor Press: New York, 1970.

Sketch Eleven

1. C. Becker. "The Clinical Pharmacology of Alcohol." *California Medicine*, Vol. 113, pp. 37-45. 1970.

2. J.H. Mendelson. "Biological Concomitants of Alcoholism, Part I." *New England Journal of Medicine*, Vol. 283, pp. 24-32. Massachusetts Medical Society: Waltham, MA, 1970.

3. M.A. Schucket. "A Study of Alcoholism in Half Siblings." *American Journal of Psychiatry*, Vol. 128, No. 9, pp. 122-126. 1973.

4. V.E. Davis and M.J. Walsh. "Alcohol, Amines and Alkaloids: A Possible Biochemical Basis for Alcohol Addiction." *Science.* Vol. 16, pp. 1005-1007. American Association for the Advancement of Science: Washington, DC. 1970.

5. R.A. Williams. *Textbook of Black-Related Diseases.* McGraw-Hill, Inc: New York, 1975.

6. I. Gregory. "Family Data Concerning the Hypothesis of Hereditary Predispositions Toward Alcoholism." *Journal of Mental Science.* Vol. 106, pp. 1068-1072. 1960; D.W. Goodwin. "Alcoholism Hereditary?" *Archives of General Psychiatry.* Vol. 25, pp. 545-548. American Medical Association: Chicago, 1971; G.S. Omenn and A.G. Motulsky. "A Biochemical and Genetic Approach to Alcoholism." *Annals of the New York Academy of Sciences.* Vol. 197, pp. 16-23. 1972.

7. L.R. Allman, H.A. Taylor & P.E. Nathan "Group Drinking During Stress: Effects on Drinking Behavior, Affect and Psychopathology." *American Journal of Psychiatry*, Vol. 129, pp. 669-678. American Psychiatric Association: Washington, DC, 1972; R. M. Atkinson. "Importance of Alcohol and Drug abuse in Psychiatric Emergencies." *California Medicine*, Vol. 118(4): 1-4, 1973; A.F. Brunswick and C. Tarica. "Drinking and Health: A Study of Urban Black Adolescents." *Addictive Diseases* 1(1): 21-42, 1974; A. Goss and T.E. Morosko. "Relation Between A Dimension of Internal-External Control and the MMPI with an Alcoholic Population." *Journal of Counseling and Clinical Psychology* 34: 189-192, 1970; M.C. Jones. "Personality Antecedents and Correlates of Drinking Patterns in Women." *Journal of Counseling and Clinical Psychology* 36: 61-69. 1971; B.M Jones and A. Paredes. "Outcome of Offspring of Chronic Alcoholic Women." *The Lancet* 1:1076-1078 Lancet Publications: New York, 1974; F. R. Freeman. "An Electroencephalographic Study of Memory Loss During

Alcoholic Intoxication." *Disorders of the Nervous System*, Vol. 32:848-852; D.A. Rodgers. " A Psychological Interpretation of Alcoholism." *Annals of the New York Academy of Sciences*. Vol. 197: 222-225; J. A. Vanderpool. "Alcoholism and the Self-Concept." *Quarterly Journal of the Study of Alcoholism*. Vol. 30: 59-77, 1969.

8. D.W. Goodwin. "Alcohol Problems in Adoptees Raised Apart from Alcoholic Biological Parents." *Archives of General Psychiatry*, Vol. 128: 239-243, 1973; H. Barry, III and H.T. Blane. " Birth Order as a Method of Studying Environmental Influences in Alcoholism." *Annals New York Academy of Sciences*. Vol. 197, pp. 189-197, 1972; C.N. Alexander. "Consensus and Mutual Attraction in Natural Cliques: A Study of Adolescent Drinkers." *American Journal of Sociology*, Vol. 69 (4): 395-403. 1964; G. Globetti. "The Drinking Patterns of Negro and White High School Students in Two Mississippi Communities." *Journal of Negro Education*, Vol. 39 (1): 60-69. Howard University Bureau of Educational Research: Washington, DC, 1970; D.E. Harrison. "Emerging Drinking Patterns of Pre-Adolescents: A Study of the Influence of Significant Others." Dissertation Abstracts International 31, Vol. A. 1971; B.M Jones and A. Paredes. "Outcome of Offspring of Chronic Alcoholic Women." *The Lancet* 1:1076-1078 Lancet Publications: New York, 1974. R. Jessor, M.J. Collins, and S.L. Jessor. " On Becoming a Drinker: Socio-Psychological Aspects of an Adolescent Transition." *Annals of the New York Academy of Sciences*, pp. 199-213. 1975; M.L. Kammeier. "Adolescents from Families With or Without Alcohol Problems." *Quarterly Journal of the Study of Alcoholism*, Vol. 32 (2): 364-372. 1971; G.L. Maddox and B.C. McCall. *Drinking Among Teen-agers*. *Rutgers Center of Alcohol Studies:* New Brunswick, NJ. 1964.

9. M.K. Bacon. "The Dependency-Conflict Hypothesis and the Frequency of Drunkenness: Further Evidence from a Cross-Cultural Study." *Quarterly Journal of The Study of Alcoholism*, Vol. 35: 863-876. 1974; E.M. Blum and R.H. Blum. *Alcoholism*. San Francisco: Jossey-Bass, Inc. 1967; B.P. Dohrenwend. "Social Status, Stress and Psychological Symptoms." *Milbank Memorial Fund Quarterly*, Vol. 47: 137-150. 1969; M.L. Kammeier. "Adolescents from Families With or Without Alcohol Problems." *Quarterly Journal of the Study of Alcoholism*, Vol. 32 (2): 364-372. 1971; J. Rimmer, F.N. Pitts, Jr, T. Reich, & G. Winokur. "Alcoholism II. Sex, Socioeconomic Status, and Race, in Two Hospitalized Samples." *Quarterly Journal of the Study of Alcoholism*. Vol. 32 (4): pp 942-952. 1971; A. Sytinsky. "A Schema of the Etiology of Alcoholism As a Pathological Motivation: A Working Hypotheses Involving the Interplay of Sociological, Psychological and

Physiobiochemical Factors on Molecular, Cellular and Organo-Systemic Levels." *Quarterly Journal of The Study of Alcoholism.* Vol. 34, pp. 1140-1145. 1973.

10. E.D. Burk "Some Contemporary Issues in Child Development and the Children of Alcoholic Parents." *Annals New York Academy of Sciences.* Vol. 197, pp. 189-197, 1972.

11. M.M. Glatt & D.R. Hills. "Alcohol Abuse and Alcoholism in the Young." *British Journal of Addiction.* Vol. 63, pp. 183-191. 1968.

12. G.N. Braucht. "Deviant Drug Use in Adolescence: A Review of Psychosocial Correlates." *Psychological Bulletin*, Vol. 76. Washington D.C.: American Psychological Association, pp. 92-106. 1973.

13. Lisansky-Gomberg, E.S. "Etiology of Alcoholism." *Journal of Counseling and Clinical Psychology*, Vol, 32, pp. 18-20.

14. M.C. Jones. "Personality Antecedents and Correlates of Drinking Patterns in Women." *Journal of Counseling and Clinical Psychology*, Vol. 32, pp. 18-20. 1968.

15. J.D. Cone. "Locus of Control and Social Desirability." *Journal of Counseling and Clinical Psychology*, Vol. 36, pp. 4491. 1971; J. Gozalli & J. Sloane. "Control Orientation As A Personality Dimension Among Alcoholics." *Quarterly Journal of the Study of Alcoholism*, Vol. 32, pp. 159-161; W.F. Gross & F.J. Nerviano. "Note on the Control Orientation of Alcoholics." *Psychological Reprints*, Vol. 31 (2), pp. 406. 1972.

16. B. Segal. "Locus of Control and Drug and Alcohol Use in College Students." *Journal of Alcohol and Drug Education*, Vol. 19 (3): pp. 1-5. American Alcohol and Drug Information Foundation: Lansing, MI., 1974.

17. S. Eisenthal & H. Udin. "Psychological Factors Associated with Drug and Alcohol Usage Among Neighborhood Youth Corps Enrollees." *Developmental Psychology*, Vol. 7 (2): pp. 119-123. American Psychological Association: Washington, DC, 1972.

18. M.M Vitols. "Culture Patterns of Drinking in Negro and White Alcoholics." *Disorders of the Nervous System*, Vol. 29 (6): pp. 391-394, 1968.

19. M.K. Bacon & M.B. Jones. *Teenage Drinking.* Thomas Y. Crowell Company: New York, NY, 1968.

20. H. Marcuse. *One – Dimensional Man.* Beacon Press: Boston, MA.

21. J.K. Ngubane. Conflicts of Minds: Changing Power Depositions in South Africa. Book in Focus, 1979; W.W. Nobles. "Standing in the River, Transformed and Transforming: The (Re) Ascension of Black Psychology." Unpublished Paper. 1983.

22. M.J. Herskovits. The Myth of the Negro Past. Beacon Press: Boston, 1958; D.P. Forde. *African Worlds: Studies in the Cosmological Ideas and Social Values of African Peoples.* Oxford University Press: New York, NY, 1954; W.W. Nobles. " Black People in White Insanity: An Issue for Black Community Mental Health." *Journal of Afro-American Issues.* Vol.4: pp. 21-27. Winter 1976; P. Temples. "Bantu Philosophy" *Presence Africaine*: Paris, France. 1959.

Sketch Thirteen

1. Wade W. Nobles and Lawford L. Goddard, *Understanding the Black Family: A Guide for Scholarship and Research* (Oakland, CA" Black Family Institute Publications, 1984), pp. 1-10.

2. John Wanat, *Introduction to Budgeting* (Scituate, MA: Duxbury Press, 1978), pp.14-25.

3. Joel S. Kovel, *White Racism: Psychohistory* (New York: Vintage Books, 1971, © 1970). Kovel argues that racism is deeply embedded in the white psyche, an essential part of white American culture that is indistinguishable from the rest of American life. Hence, even with "business decisions," racism plays a central role.

4. Norman Bell and Ezra Vogel, eds., *A Modern Introduction to the Family*, revised ed. (New York: Free Press, 1968, © 1960), pp. 14-16. Bell and Vogel note that in every society, the family submits to the rulership of government and exchanges its loyalty to governmental constraints for greater leadership and benefits on the form of direct and indirect services and security. In regard to the specific case of African-American families, however, they note that historically the exchange principle has been violated.

5. Robert Staples, "Public Policy and the Changing Status of Black Families," in Robert Staples, ed., *The Black Family:* Essays and Studies, 2d Ed. (Belmont, CA: Wadsworth Publishing Co., 1978) pp.263-269

6. Andrew Billingsley, *Black Families in White America* (Englewood Cliffs, NJ: Prentice-Hall, 1978), pp. 177-181. Billingsley points out that when the public sector is contaminated by the philosophies of domination and control, then the control mechanism society utilizes or invents will by definition be incapable of effectively intervening on behalf of the dominated and exploited. Accordingly, he notes, in the case of African-American families, the control mechanism of this society too often serves as an additional negative force in guaranteeing their disenfranchisement.

7. Staples, op.cit. note 5, p.264.

8. Nathan and Julia Hare, *The Endangered Black Family: Coping with the Unisexualization and Coming Extinction of the Black Race* (San Francisco: Black Think Tank Publishers, 1984), pp. 7-19. The Hares discuss the sociopolitical aspects of research on the black family and note that due to political and not scientific considerations, some black and most white intellectuals adopted a theoretical approach which misdirected the analyses of black family life, drawing attention away from analyzing the conditions imposed on black families by an oppressive and racist society.

9. Benjamin Bowser, 'Community and Economic Context of Black Families: A Critical Review of the Literature, 1909-1985, " *Journal of Social Psychiatry* 6:1 (Winter 1986): 17-26.

10. U.S. Bureau of the Census, Statistical Abstract of the United States: 1989, 109th Ed. (Washington, DC: U.S. Government Printing Office, 1989), p.50.

11. "Minority Population State by State," New York Times (June 21, 1989).

12. U.S. Bureau of the Census, op. cit. note 10, p.445

13. Ibid., p. 393.

14. Ibid.

15. American Council on Education, Office of Minority Concerns, "Minorities in Higher Education, 1987), p.3. (Author's italics.)

16. Wade W. Nobles, et al., "The Mental Health Impact of Drugs and Drug Trafficking on African-American Children and Families in Oakland; Alameda County Final Report" (Oakland, CA: Black Family Institute Publications, 1987), pp. 57-89. Rather than focusing on drug use and abuse as a social, economic, legal or health problem, the Nobles team examined the impact of an emerging drug culture and value system on the mental health of African-American families and children. They concluded that if left unattended, the drug culture is capable of inflicting irreversible damage on the African-American family.

17. U.S. Bureau of the Census, op.cit., note 10, p.14.

18. Lawford L. Goddard, "The Future of the African-American Family," *Southern Christian Leadership Conference National Magazine* 15:2 (May/June 1986): 82-85. Goddard views the decline in the sex ratio between African-American males and females as the consequence of three fundamental processes specifically affecting African-American males: Inordinate loss of life in the Korean and Vietnam wars; differential patterns of institutionalization; and the effects of community-based violence.

19. U.S. Bureau of the Census, Statistical Abstract of the United States: 1988, 108th Ed. (Washington, DC: U.S. Government Printing Office, 1988), p.175.

20. U.S. Bureau of the Census, op.cit., note 10, p.168

21. Ibid., p. 393

22. Ibid., p.442

23. Ibid., p.454

24. Asa Hilliard, "The Maroon in the United States: The Lessons of Africa for Parenting and Education on African-American Children," *Journal of African-American Studies* (San Francisco State University) 1:2 (Fall/Winter 1983): 14-22. According to Hilliard, no family system can exist in the absence of a cultural base; the reclamation of their indigenous cultural base is the necessary foundation of effective African-American parenting.

25. Africa Information Service, ed., *Return to the Source: Selected Speeches [of Amilcar Cabrall]* (New York: Monthly Review Press, 1974, © 1973), pp. 75-92.

26. Wade W. Nobles, Africanity and the Black Family: The Development of a Theoretical Model (Oakland, CA: Black Family Institute Publications, 1985), p.54. The problem of imposing inappropriate ethnocentric an analysis on the black family is addressed, an act that, it is argued, results in the false depiction of the African-American family as an "illegitimate white family." In calling for a more appropriate theoretical model, the article further highlights the implications of the epistemological shift in the study of the African-American family.

27. Ibid., p. 55.

28. John S. Mbiti, *African Religions and Philosophy* (Garden City, NY: Doubleday, 1970), pp. 33-45.

29. Placide Tempels, *Bantu Philosophy* (Paris: Presence Africaine, 1959), pp.3-34.

30. Pierre Erny, *Childhood and Cosmos: The Social Psychology of the Black African Child* (Washington, D.C.: Black Orpheus Press, 1973), pp. 183-197.

31. Wade W. Nobles, "A Formulative and Empirical Study of Black Families: Final Report" (Washington, D.C.:U.S. Department of Health, Education and Welfare, Pub. No. OCD-90-C-225, 1976), pp.14-42. In this federally funded research, the operative relations and residuals of African psychocultural behavioral practices and beliefs in the contemporary African-American family were documented empirically. See also Janice Hale, "Black Children: Their Roots, Culture, and Learning Styles," *Young Children* 36: 2 (January 1981): 37-50. Professor Hale's research not only supports the recognition that cognitive styles and the way black children learn are a direct result of their culturally specific family process. The Hale findings have strong implications for any discussion of public policy, particularly the interface of public and private initiatives in education.

32. See Herbert G. Gutman, *The Black Family in Slavery and Freedom, 1750-1925* (New York: Vintage Books, 1976), especially pp. 185-229.

33. See Harriette Pipes McAdoo, "Black Kinship," *Psychology Today* 12:12 (May 1979): 67-70, 79; and Elmer P. Martin and Joanne M. Martin, *The Black Extended Family* (Chicago: University of Chicago Press, 1978), pp. 5-16.

34. William A. Darity, Jr., and Samuel L. Myers, Jr., "Public Policy and the Condition of Black Family," *The Review of Black Political Economy* 13: 1-2 (Summer/Fall 1984): 165-187

35. Wade W. Nobles, "The Reclamation of Culture and the Right to Reconciliation: An Afrocentric Perspective for Developing and Implementing Programs for the Mentally Retarded Offender," in Aminitu R. Harvey and Terry L. Carr, eds., *The African-American Mentally Retarded Offender: A Holistic Approach to Prevention and Rehabilitation* (New York: United Church of Christ, Commission for Racial Justice, 1982), pp.39-63.

36. F. Cress Welsing, *The Cress Theory of Color Confrontation and Racism (White Supremacy)* (Washington, D.C.: Frances Welsing, 1970), pp.4-5.

37. Syed Khatib (aka Cedric X. Clark), "African-American Studies and the Study of African-American People," in Reginald L. Jones, ed., *African-American Psychology*, 2d ed. (New York: Harper and Row, 1980).

38. Robert Staples, "Toward A Sociology of the Black Family: A Theoretical and Methodological Assessment," *Journal of Marriage and the Family* 33: 1(February 1971): 119-138.

39. See Robert B. Hill, ed., *The Strengths of Black Families* (New York: Emerson Hall Pub., distributed by Independent Publishers Group, 1972); Joyce A. Ladner, *Tomorrow's Tomorrow: The Black Woman* (New York: Anchor Press, 1972), pp. 1-43; Wade W. Nobles, "African Root and American Fruit: The Black Family," *Journal of Social and Behavioral Sciences* 20: 2 (Spring 1974): 52-64; and Lewis M. King, "The Assessment of Afro-American Families: Issues in Search of Theory," in Barbara Ann Bass, Gail Elizabeth Wyatt and Gloria Johnson Powell, eds., *The Afro-American Family: Assessment, Treatment, and Research Issues* (New York: Grune and Stratton, Inc., 1982), pp. 101-117.

40. Housing Act of 1949, P.L 171 (81st Congress, 1st Session), sec. 2.

41. Housing and Community Development Act of 1974, P.L., 93-383 (93d Congress, 2d Session), sec. 101(c).

42. Employment Act of 1946, P.L.304 (79th Congress, 2d Session), sec. 2.

43. Economic Opportunity Act of 1964, P.L. 88-452 (88th Congress, 2d Session), sec.2.

44. See Civil Rights Act of 1964, P.L. 88-352 (88th Congress, 2d Session), Title VII, Equal Employment Opportunity.

45. Elementary and Secondary Education Act of 1965, P.L. 89-10 (89th Congress, 1st Session), sec. 2.

46. Comprehensive Employment and Training Act of 1973, P.L. 93-203 (93d Congress, 1st Session), sec.2.

47. Wade W. Nobles, "Critical Analysis of Scholarship on Black Family Life." Final Report (New York: United Church of Christ, Commission fro Racial Justice, 1983), pp. 12-19.

48. Daniel P. Moynihan, *The Negro Family: The Case for National Action* (Washington, D.C.: U.S. Department of Labor, Office of Policy Planning and Research, March 1965).

49. James S. Coleman, Equality of Educational Opportunity (Washington, D.C.: U.S. Department of Health, Education and Welfare, Office of Education, 1966), pp. 3-9.

50. Wade W. Nobles, Km Ebit Husia: Authoritative Utterances of Exceptional Insight for the Black Family (Oakland, CA: Black Family Institute Publications, 1986), p.4.

51. White House Conference on Families, Listening to America's Families: Action for the 80's, Report to the President, Congress and Families of the Nation (Washington, D.C.: U.S. Government Printing Office, October 1980).

52. Marguerite Ross Barnett, "A Theoretical Perspective on American Racial Public Policy," in Marguerite Ross Barnett and James A. Hefner, eds., Public Policy for the Black Community: Strategies and Perspectives (Port Washington, NY: Alfred Publishing Co., Inc., 1976), pp.1-54 at 13.

Sketch Fourteen

1. H.J. Grossman, Ed. *Manual on Terminology and Classification in Mental Retardation.* 1977.

2. Bay Area Association of Black Psychologists. "Position Statement on the Use of I.Q. and Ability Tests," *Black Psychology,* Reginald Jones, Ed. Harper & Row Publishers: New York, 1976; Asa G. Hilliard III. Alternatives to I.Q. Testing: An Approach to the Identification of 'Gifted' Minority Children," Final Report. California State Department of Education, Special Education Support Unit. Eric Clearinghouse of Early Childhood Education, 146-009, 1976; Leon J. Kamin. *The Science of Politics of I.Q.* Lawrence Erlbaum Associates. Potomac, Maryland, 1979.

3. Audrey M. Shuey. *The Testing of Negro Intelligence,* 2nd Edition. Social Science Press: New York, 1966.

4. Allan Chase. *The Legacy of Malthus: The Social Cost of the New Scientific Racism.* University of Illinois Press: Chicago, 1980.

5. Robert V. Guthrie. *Even the Rat was White.* Harper & Row Publishers: New York, 1976; Asa G. Hilliard. 1982; Wade W. Nobles. 1983.

Sketch Fifteen

1. Julius Nyerere. President's Address to the Tanganyika National Assembly, Special Publications, p.21. December 10, 1962.

2. Robert K. Merton. *Social Theory and Social Structure,* Rev Ed; Glencoe, IL. 1957.

3. Wade W. Nobles. "African Science: The Consciousness of Self" in Lewis M. King, Vernon J. Dixon and Wade W. Nobles (eds). *African Philosophy: Assumption and Paradigms for Research on Black Persons.* Fanon Research and Development Center Publications, 1976.

4. Wade W. Nobles, 1981

5. William James. *The Principles of Psychology.* 1980.

6. C.G. Jung. *Man and His Symbols.* Garden City New York: Doubleday, 1964.

7. Kwame Nkrumah. *Consciencism.* Modern Reader: New York, 1964.

8. Wade W. Nobles. "African Science: The Consciousness of Self" in Lewis M. King, Vernon J. Dixon and Wade W. Nobles (eds). *African Philosophy: Assumption and Paradigms for Research on Black Persons.* Fanon Research and Development Center Publications, 1976.

9. Wade W. Nobles. "Critical Analyses of Scholarship on Black Family Life" Final Report. Black Family Life Programs, United Church of Christ, Commission for Racial Justice, February 1983.

10. Geneva Smitherman. "Language and Liberation," *The Journal of Negro Education*, 52 (1), Winter 1983.

11. J.H. Howard. "Toward a Social Psychology of Colonialism" in Reginald Jones (ed) *Black Psychology*, Harper & Row Publishers, 1972.

12. Amilcar Cabral. *Return to the Source.* African Information Service: New York, 1970.

13. Jordon K. Ngubane. *Conflict of Mind: Changing Power Dispositions in South Africa.* Books in Focus, New York, 1979.

14. Na'im Akbar. "Cultural Expressions of the African American Child," *Black Child Journal*, 2, Winter 1981.

15. Geneva Smitherman. *Talkin and Testifyin: The Language of Black America.* Houghton Mifflin: Boston, 1977.

Sketch Seventeen

1. Diop, Cheikh Anta. *The African Origin of Civilization: Myth or Reality.* Lawrence Hill & Company: Westport. 1967.

2. Diop, Cheikh Anta. *Civilization or Barbarism: An Authentic Anthropology.* Lawrence Hill Books. Brooklyn, 1991

S k e t c h   N i n e t e e n

1. Nobles, Wade W. Psychological Research and the Black Self-concept: A Critical Review. *Journal of Social Issues*. Vol 29(1) 1976b 11-21

2. Nobles, Wade W. 1989. "Psychological Nigrescence: An Afrocentric Review." The Counseling Psychologists. vol 17(2) pp 253-257

3. Horton, Robin, African Traditional Thought and Western Science, Africa, Vol. 37(1) Jan, 1967, p. 65

4. Carruthers, Jacob. 1972 *Science and Oppression*. Chicago: Northwestern Illinois University Center for inner City Studies; Nobles, Wade W. 1978. "African Consciousness and Liberation Struggles: Implications for the Development and Construction of Scientific Paradigms." *Journal of Black Studies* . San Francisco State University. San Francisco; Akbar, Na'im. 1984 "Africentric Social Science for Human liberation." *Journal of Black Studies*, vol. 14(4) pp 395-414; Banks, W.C. 1992 "The Theoretical and Methodological Crises of the Africentric Conception." *Journal of Negro Education*, vol 61(3).

5. Wilson, Amos. "The Falsification of Afrikan Consciousness: Eurocentric History, Psychiatry and the Politics of White Supremacy." The African World Infosystems: Bronx, New York, 1993

6. ibid, 1993:3

7. Horton, Robert. African Traditional Thought and Western Science. Africa. Vol. 37:1 Jan. 1967, p. 65.

8. *Ofa Ase* is a Yoruba term meaning power of the word or power of the word to evoke that which it represents. It is therefore implied that when the theories of African Psychologists are guided by an African discourse, then new and more appropriate ideas, concepts, notions, etc., will become part of the scientific enterprise.

9. Karenga, Maulana. (ed) 1990. Reconstructing Kemetic Culture: Papers, Perspectives, Projects. Los Angeles: University of Sankore Press

10. Kardiner, A. and Ovessey, L. 1951. *The Mark of Oppression*. Norton: New York; Clark, K. & Clark M. 1952 "Racial; Identification and Preference in Negro Children." In T.M. Newcomb & E.L. Hartley (eds), *Readings in Social Psychology* (rev ed) New York: Holt; Caplan, N. 1970 "The New Negro Man: A Review of Recent Empirical Studies." *Journal of Social issues*. vol 26. Pp 57-73; Banks, W. and Grambs, J. 1972. *Black Self Concept*. New York: McGraw-Hill.

11. Jackson, B., 1975 "Black Identity Development." *Journal of Educational Diversity*. vol 2. pp 19-25; Cross, W.E. 1978 "The Cross and Thomas Models of Psychological Nigrescence" *Journal of Black Psychology*, vol 5(1) pp. 13-19; Semaj, L. 1981 "The Black Self: Identity and Models for Psychological Liberation" *Western Journal of Black Studies*. vol 5(3), pp 158-171; Parham, T.A. 1989 "Cycles of Psychological Nigrescence." *The Counseling Psychologist*. vol 17(2). pp 187-226; Helms, J. 1990. *Black and White Racial Identity: Theory, Research and Practice*. New York: Greenwood Press.

12. Nobles, Wade W. 1986a. African Psychology: Toward its Reclamation, Reascension and Revitalization. Oakland. A Black Family Institute Publication; Nobles, Wade W. 1986b. Ancient Egyptian Thought and the Renaissance of African (Black) Psychology. in Kemet and the African Worldview, edited by Maulana Karenga and Jacob Carruthers. Los Angeles. University of Sankore Press.

13. Nobles, Wade W. 1989. "Psychological Nigrescence: An Afrocentric Review." *The Counseling Psychologists*. vol 17(2) pp 253-257.

14. "Atunwa" is a Yoruba term representing the idea of rebirth of character or integrity. If in psychology we are concerned with the essential and deeper meaning, then the rebirth of the essential character of African people should be the intent and the consequent of these theoretical formulations.

15. The reader is directed to *Africanisms in American Culture* edited by Joseph E. Holloway (1991) for an excellent discussion and defense of the heritage of new world Africans.

16. Myer, Isaac. II.B. 1900. *Oldest Book in the World: An Account of the Religion, Wisdom, Philosophy, Ethics, Psychology, Manners, Proverbs, Sayings, Refinements, Etc., of The Ancient Egyptians*. New York, Dayton Publishers

17. Massey, Gerald. 1970 *Ancient Egypt: The Light of the World.* Vol I & II. Reprint London: Stuart & Watkins.

18. Dawkins, Peter. 1988. Arcadia, The Ancient Egyptian Mysteries & The Arcadia and the Arcadian Academy: Studies in Ancient Wisdom. The Francis Bacon Research Trust Journal, Series I, Volume 5: London, England. Coventry Printers.

19. "Ori Ire" is a Yoruba concept representing the state when one's consciousness is properly aligned with one's destiny. In this regard it clarifies and gives deeper meaning for the quest for authenticity. It is human destiny for a people to be conscious (to find and establish) of their own sense of authenticity.

20. Fu-Kiau. 1991. *Self Healing Power and Therapy-Old Teachings from Africa.* New York. Vantage Press, p. 8.

21. Nobles, Vera L. 1995. "Emi: The Concept of Spirit in Selected Plays of August Wilson." Diss. UMI 63-69

22. ibid, 1995:7.

23. Maiga Hassimi Oumarou, 1996. *Conversational Sonay Language of Mali.* Albarka International Publishers, Inc. p. 17.

24. ibid, 1996:18.

25. Allen, George Thomas, translator: *The Book of the Dead*, prepared for publication by Elizabeth Blaisdell Hauser; Chicago University Press, Chicago, 1974 Spells 63 and 64.

26. Ngubane, Jordan K. 1979. *Conflict of Minds: Changing Power Depositions in South Africa.* Books in Focus, New York. p. 60.

27. ibid, 1979: 59.

28. ibid, 1979: 62.

29. ibid, 1979: 40.

30. ibid, 1979: 77.

31. Gyekye, Kwame. 1987. An Essay on African Philosophical Thought: The Akan Conceptual Scheme. Cambridge University Press. p. 85.

32. Opoku, Kofi Asare. 1978. *West African Traditional Religion*. FEP International Private Limited. Accra, Ghana. p. 92.

33. ibid, 1978: 93.

34. Harris, W. T & Sawyer H. *The Springs of Mende Belief and Conduct*. Sierra Leone University Press. Freetown. 1968, p.88.

35. Grills, C. and Darryl Rowe. (1996) "African Traditional Medicine: Implications for African Centered Approaches to Healing" in Reginald Jobes (Ed) *Advances in African American Psychology: Theory, Paradigms and Research*. Cobb and Henry Publishers, Hampton, VA.

36. Sakhu Sheti are two terms from the Medu Netcher (Egyptian Hieroglyphs). The word "Sahku" means "understanding, the illuminator, the eye and the soul of the being, that which inspires." "Sheti" means "to go deeply into a subject; to study profoundly; to search magical books; to penetrate deeply." Accordingly, I have suggested that the term, "Sahku Sheti" be used to represent the deep, profound and penetrating search, study, understanding and mastery of the process of illuminating the human spirit. Hence, in closing I am suggesting that the Thought and theory of African Psychologists should be governed by deep, profound and penetrating search, study, understanding and mastery of the process of "illuminating" the human spirit in its full and complete authenticity.

37. Carruthers, Jacob. *MDW NTR-Divine Speech: A Historical Reflection of African Deep Thought from the Time of the Pharaohs to the Present*. Red Sea Press 1995. p. 2.

38. Frazier, E. Franklin. 1973. "The Failure of the Negro Intellectual," in *Death of White Sociology*. Joyce Ladner (Ed) New York Vintage Books, p. 60.

39. ibid, 1973: 60.

40. Abimbola, Wande. 1976. *Ifa: An Exploration of the Ifa Literary Corpus*. Ibadan, Nigeria. Oxford University Press; Abraham, W. E. 1970. *The Mind of Africa*. Chicago: The University of Chicago Press; Adams, Hunter, III. 1979. African Observers of the Universe: The Sirius Question. *Journal of African Civilization*. Vol I(2). 1-20; Chinweizu. 1978. *The West and the Rest of Us*. Ansosi. Nok Publishers; Diop, Cheihk Anta. 1959. *The Cultural Unity of Black Africa*. Chicago: Third World Press; Diop, Cheihk Anta. 1974. *The African Origin of Civilization: Myth or reality*. Westport: Lawrence Hill & Company; Diop, Cheihk Anta.

1991. *Civilization or Barbarism: An Authentic Anthropology*. New York. Lawrence Hill Books; Nkrumah, Kwame. 1964. *Consciencism*. New York. Modern Reader; Armah, Ayi Kwei. 1973. *Two Thousand Seasons*. Nairobi: East African Publishing House; Obenga, Theophile. 1992. *Ancient Egypt and Black Africa*. London: Karnak House.

41. Ben Jochanan, Yosef 1971. *Africa: Mother of Civilization*. Baltimore MD: Black Classic Press; Ankh, Mi Ra. 1995. *Let the Ancestors Speak*. Temple Hills. Md.: Jom International Hilliard, Asa G. III. 1986. The *Wisdom of Kemetic Governance. in Kemet and the African Worldview*, Edited by Maulana Karenga and Jacob Carruthers. Los Angeles. University of Sankore Press; Hilliard, Asa G. III. 1989. Waset. The Eye of Ra and the Abode of Ma'at: The Pinnacle of Black Leadership in the Ancient World. Egypt Revisited, *Journal of African Civilizations*, Edited by Ivan Van Sertima. New Brunswick. Transaction Publishers; Hilliard, Asa G. III. 1995. *The Maroon Within Us*. Baltimore, Md. Black Classic Press; Karenga, Maulana. 1984. Selections from the Husia: Sacred Wisdom of Ancient Egypt. Los Angeles. Kawaida Publications; Kambon, Kobi Kazembe Kalongi. 1992. *The African Personality in America: An African centered Framework*. Tallahassee: Nubian Nation Publications; Asante, Molefi Kete. 1990 *Afrocentricity and Knowledge*. Trenton, N.J. African World Press; Asante, Molefi Kete and Kariamu Welsh Asante (eds) 1990. *African Culture: The Rhythms of Unity*. New Jersey. African World Press, Inc.; Myers, Linda James. 1988. *Understanding an Afrocentric Worldview*. DuBuque: Kendall/Hall; Nobles, Wade W. 1972. African Psychology: Foundations for Black Psychology. In Regional Jones (ed) *Black Psychology*. New York: Harper & Row. 18-32; Nobles, Wade W. 1976a. Extended-self: Rethinking the So-called Negro Self-concept. *Journal of Black Psychology*. Vol II(2); Nobles, Wade W. 1976b. Psychological Research and the Black Self-concept: A Critical Review. *Journal of Social Issues*. Vol 29(1) 11-21; Nobles, Wade W. 1985. Africanity and the Black Family: The Development of a Theoretical Model. Oakland. A Black Family Institute Publication; Spight, Carl. 1977. Toward a Black Science and Technology. *Black Books Bulletin*. Vol 5(3). Chicago: Institute of Positive Education; T'Shaka, Oba 1995. *Return to the African Mother Principle of Male and Female Equality*. Vol I. Oakland. Pan African Publishers and Distributors; Van Sertima, Ivan. 1985. Nile Valley Civilizations. Journal of African Civilizations. New Brunswick; Transaction Publishers; Van Sertima, Ivan. 1989. Egypt Revisited, *Journal of African Civilisations*. New Brunswick: Transaction Publishers; Ani, Marimba. (aka Donna Marimba Richards) 1994. *Let the Circle be Unbroken: The Implications of African Spirituality in the Diaspora*. Trenton, NJ. Red Sea Press.

Sketch Twenty

1. Melville Herskovits. *The Myth of Negro Past*. Beacon Press, Boston, MA 1958. pp. 56-58.

2. Fu-kiau. 1969. 1991. *Self Healing Power and Therapy-Old Teachings from Africa*. New York. Vantage Press, p. 8.

3. Higgins. Chester. *Feeling the Spirit: Searching the World for the People of Africa*. New York. Bantum Press 1994, p.233

4. Ba Amadou Hampate. 1981. *The Living Tradition. General History of Africa*. Vol I. Methodology and African Prehistory. Edited by J. Ki-Zerbo. California: UNESCO: 166-203.

5. Kamalu, Chukwunyere. 1990 *Foundations of African Thought*. London: Karnak House.

6. Ngubane, Jordan K. 1979. *Conflict of Minds: Changing Power Dispositions in South Africa*. Books in Focus, New York. p. 60.

Afterword

1. Holdstock, T.L. (2000). *Re-examining Psychology: Critical Perspectives and African Insights*. London: Routledge. P. 16. Please not the following removed from quote Holdstock references (e.g., Heelas and Lock, 1981 Kim and Berry, 1993; Roland, 1992; Rosenberger, 1992.).

2. Nobles, W. W. (1997). "To be African or not to be: African spirituality." Presentation at the semi-annual Meeting of the Association of Black Psychologists' African Psychology Institute, Raleigh-Durham, NC.

3. Schwaller de Lubicz, R.A. (1998). *The Temple of Man: Apet at the South of Luxor*. Rochester, VT: Inner Traditions International.

4. Ibid, 1998.

Publications List and Scholarly Works

drnobles@iasbclc.org

Books

AFRICAN PHILOSOPHY: ASSUMPTIONS AND PARADIGMS FOR RESEARCH ON BLACK PEOPLE. (Co-edited with Lewis King and Vernon Dixon) Fanon Center Publication. J. Alfred Cannon Research Conference Proceedings, Los Angeles, 1976

VOODOO OR IQ: AN INTRODUCTION TO AFRICAN PSYCHOLOGY. (Co-authored with Syed khatib, D. Phillip Mcgee & Na'im Akbar). A Third World Press, Chicago 1980.

UNDERSTANDING THE BLACK FAMILY: A GUIDE FOR SCHOLAR-SHIP AND RESEARCH. (Co-authored with Lawford L. Goddard). A Black Family Institute Publication, Oakland, 1984

AFRICANITY AND THE BLACK FAMILY: THE DEVELOPMENT OF A THEORETICAL MODEL. A Black Family Institute Publication, Oakland, 1984

THE KM EBIT HUSIA: AUTHORITATIVE UTTERANCE OF EXCEP-TIONAL INSIGHT FOR THE BLACK FAMILY. (Co-authored with Lawford L. Goddard and William E. Cavil III) A Black Family Institute Publication, Oakland, 1985

AFRICAN PSYCHOLOGY: TOWARD ITS RECLAMATION, REASCEN-SION AND REVITALIZATION. A Black Family Institute Publication, Oakland, 1986

AFRICAN-AMERICAN FAMILIES: ISSUES, INSIGHT, AND DIREC-TIONS (Co-authored with Lawford L. Goddard, William E. Cavil III and Pamela Y. George) A Black Family Institute Publication, Oakland, 1987.

SEEKING THE SAKHU: FOUNDATIONAL WRITINGS FOR AN AFRICAN PSYCHOLOGY Third World Press, Chicago publication date, Fall, 2005.

Chapters/Articles

African Philosophy: Foundation for Black Psychology. In R. L. Jones (ed) BLACK PSYCHOLOGY, New York: Harper & Row, 1972, pp.18-32.

Psychological Research and the Black Self-Concept: A Critical Review. JOURNAL OF SOCIAL ISSUES, 1973, Vol. 29, No. 1, pp. 11-31

African Root and American Fruit: The Black Family. JOURNAL OF SOCIAL AND BEHAVIORAL SCIENCES, Winter, 1974.

Africanity: Its Role in Black Families. THE BLACK SCHOLAR, 1974 Vol. 5, No. 9, Pp. 10-17

Voodoo or I.Q.: An Introduction to African Psychology. JOURNAL OF BLACK PSYCHOLOGY, 1975, Vol. l, No. 2, Pp. 1-20. (Co-authored with Cedric X (Clark), D. Phillip McGee, and Luther X (Weems)

African-Science and Black Research: The Consciousness of Self. In Lewis M. King, Vernon Dixon, and Wade W. Nobles (eds) AFRICAN PHILOSOPHY: ASSUMPTIONS AND PARADIGMS FOR RESEARCH ON BLACK PEOPLE. J. Alfred Cannon Resarch Conference Proceedings, April,1976. pp. 163-174

African Roots in Black Families: The Social Psychological Dynamics of the Black Family and Its Implications for Nursing Care. In Dorothy Luckraft, R.N. (ed) BLACK AWARENESS: IMPLICATIONS FOR BLACK PATIENT CARE. The American Journal of Nursing Company, New York, 1976

Extended-Self: Re-Thinking the So-Called Negro Self-Concept. JOURNAL OF BLACK PSYCHOLOGY, Vol. II, No.2, February, 1976

Black People in White Insanity: An Issue for Black Community Mental Health. JOURNAL OF AFRO-AMERICAN ISSUES, Vol. 4, No. 1 Winter, 1976, pp. 21-27.

Media Black Families: Carbon Copies of White Families. Paper presented to Symposium Workshop: Positive Presentation of Blacks in the

Media. Children's Television Fair, San Francisco, April, 1975. (Co-authored with William Cail III)

The Black Family and Its Children: The Survival of Humaneness. Paper presented at National Council for Black Child Development, BLACK BOOKS BULLETIN, VOL. 6, NO. 2, June, 1978, pp 7-12

Black Parental Involvement in Education: The African Connection. Alton Childs Series, Atlanta University School of Social Work, Atlanta, Georgia, 1976, pp. 23-26. (Co-authored with Shirley Tarver)

The Black Family Speaks: Family Research and Mental Health. INSIDE WESTSIDE, Vol. 4, No. 2. San Francisco, Ca. March/April, 1976

Rhythm, Racism and Reactions A Psycho-Cultural Analysis of Black Youth's Responses to Alienation. Paper presented to National Conference on the Black Family in America Workshop, Black Youth: Culture, Racism Alienation. March, 1976

Information Processing and Behavioral Prescriptions: The Need for Broader Telecommunications Research. Paper presented to 1976 Telecommunications Policy Research Conference. Arlie, Virginia, 1976

A Formulative and Empirical Study of Black Families: Final Report. Department of Health, Education and Welfare. Office of Child Development. Washington, D. C. 1976

Consciousness, Adaptability and Coping Strategies: Socio-Economic Characteristic and Ecological Issues in Black Families. THE WESTERN JOURNAL OF BLACK STUDIES, Vol. l, No. 2, June, 1977. pp. 105-113. (Co-authored with Lawford L. Goddard)

Historical Foundations of African Psychology and Their Philosophical Consequences. JOURNAL OF BLACK PSYCHOLOGY, Vol. 4, No. 1, August, 1977. Vol 4, No. 2, February, 1978. (Co-authored with S. M. Khatib)

The Gift and the Responsibility: Black Father's Role in the Rearing of Our Young. NEW DIMENSIONS IN HEAD START, January, 1978.

Toward an Empirical and Theoretical Framework for Defining Black Families. JOURNAL OF MARRIAGE AND FAMILY, November, 1978, pp. 679-688.

The Effectively Coping Black Family. MILITARY FAMILIES: Adaptation to Change. Edna J. Hunter and E. Stephen Nile (Eds) Praeyer Publishers, New York, 1978, pp, 57-74. (Co-authored with Robert Hayles)

African Consciousness and Liberation Struggles: Implications for the Development and Construction of Scientific Paradigms. Journal of Black Studies . San Francisco State University. San Francisco.1978.

African-American Family Life: An Instrument of Culture.   In McAdoo, H. (Ed) BLACK FAMILIES. Beverly Hills, Sage Publications, 1981

The Reclamation of Culture and the Right to Reconciliation: An Afro-Centric Perspective on Developing and Implementing Programs for the Mentally Retarded Offender. In Harvey, A. R. and T. L. Carr (Eds) THE BLACK MENTALLY RETARDED OFFENDER: A Holistic Approach, 1982

Alienation, Human Transformation and Adolescent Drug Use: Toward a Reconceptualization of the Problem. JOURNAL OF DRUG ISSUES, January, 1984.

What is the Black Family and Where is it Going. SCLC NATIONAL MAGAZINE, Vol. 13(5), Dec/Jan 1984-85

Religion, Spirituality and the Black Family. SCLC NATIONAL MAGA-ZINE, Vol 14(1), Dec/Jan 1985-86

Ancient Egyptian Thought and the Renaissance of African (Black) Psychology. In Kemet and the African Worldview, edited by Maulana Karenga and Jacob Carruthers. Los Angeles. University of Sankore Press. 1986.

Psychometrics and African-American Reality: The Question of Cultural Antimony. Accepted for Publication, JOURNAL OF NEGRO EDUCATION. 1988

Public Policy and the African-American Family: 20th Century Assessment and 21st Century Prognosis. Accepted for publication in ETHNICITY AND PUBLIC POLICY. University of Wisconsin Press, 1988

Nobles, Wade W.   1986b. Ancient Egyptian Thought and the Renaissance of African (Black) Psychology. In Kemet and the African

Worldview, edited by Maulana Karenga and Jacob Carruthers. Los Angeles. University of Sankore Press.

A National Agenda, Association of Black Psychologist Address, Psych Discourse. Washington, D.C. 1994

To Be African or Not To Be: The Question of Identity or Authenticity – Some preliminary Thoughts" in Reginald Jones (ed) African American Identity Development: Theory, Research and Intervention. Nobles, 1997

The Archeology of the African Spirit: Toward a Deeper Discourse in Black Studies Journal of Black Studies . San Francisco State University. San Francisco.1978.

From Na Ezaleli to the Jegnoch: The Force of the African Family for Black Men in Higher Education. In MAKING IT ON BROKEN PROMISES – AFRICAN AMERICAN MALE SCHOLARS CONFRONT THE CULTURE OF HIGHER EDUCATION Stylus press, Sterling Va. 2002

Reparations and Health Care for African Americans: Repairing the Damage from the legacy of Slavery in SHOULD AMERICA PAY? SLAVERY AND THE RAGING DEBATE ON REPARATIONS, Raymond Winbush, (ed) Amistad press, New York 2003

SAKHU SHETI, Reclaiming African Centered Psychology: Focus on Afro-Brazil:Theory and Practice. Accepted for publication in "AFROCENTRICI-DADE: UMA ANTOLOGIA BASICA TO SEL NEGRO EDICOES". Elisa Larkin Nascimento (ed). Summus/Selo Negro Publications, Sao Paulo, Brazil, 2004

Research Reports and Training Manuals

A Formulative and Empirical Study of Black Family Life and Culture Final Report. DHEW, Office of Child Development, Washington, D. C. 1976

Mental Health Support Systems in Black Families: Final Report. Department of Health, Education, and Welfare. ADAMHA, Center for Minority Group Mental Health Program, NIMH, Washington, D. C. 1979

Changing Childrearing Orientations and Black Child Development: Final Report. Department of Health, Education and Welfare, Administration for Children, Youth and Families, Washington, D. C. 1979

Critical Analysis of Scholarship on Black Family Life: Final Report. Black Family Life Programs, United Church of Christ Commission for Racial Justice, 1983

The Psychology of Black Girls Becoming Mothers: The Female Side of Black Teenage Pregnancy. Final Report. NIMH, Department of Health and Human Services, 1984

The Psychology of Black Boys Becoming Fathers: The Male Side of Black Teenage Pregnancy. Final Report. NIMH, Department of Health and Human Services, 1984

Resource Directory of Teen Fathers/Partners Services Report, East Bay Perinatal Council, Oakland, 1985

The Climate of Drugs and Service Delivery: The Impact of Drug Trafficking and Drug-Related Behavior on Service Delivery in County Funded Agencies, Final Report. Alameda County Health Care Services Agency. Oakland, 1987

A Clear and Present Danger: The Effects of Drugs and Drug Trafficking on the Mental Health of Black Children and Families in Oakland, Final Report. Alameda County Health Care Services Agency. Oakland, 1987

Achieving Educational Excellence and Cultural Excellence for African American Students: A New Model of Teaching and Learning, Oakland, 1998

Cultural Cornerstones - CACSEA's Professional Development Training Manual, Oakland, 1993

Cultural Cornerstones II - CACSEA's Professional Development Training Manual, Oakland, 1994

Touching the Spirit: Success for African American Students" Professional Development Institute Training Manual, Oakland, 1995

"Touching the Spirit: Success for African American Students" Professional Development Institute Training Manual, Oakland, 1996

"Touching the Spirit: Success for African American Students" Professional Development Institute Training Manual, Oakland, 1997

"Touching the Spirit: Success for African American Students" (hosted by West Contra Costa Unified School District) Professional Development Institute Training Manual, Oakland, 1998

The Nsaka Sunsum Pedagogy and Process, Oakland, 1999

Nsaka Sunsum (Touching the Spirit): Guidelines for Educational Excellence with African American Children, Oakland, 2001

The Nsaka Sunsum (Touching of the Spirit) Observation Tools: A Supplement to Classroom Observation Protocol, Oakland, 2001

The Nsaka Sunsum Class Environment - Kaleidoscoping The Classroom Process, Oakland, 2001